THE EGYPTIAN CAMPAIGNS.

VOL. I.

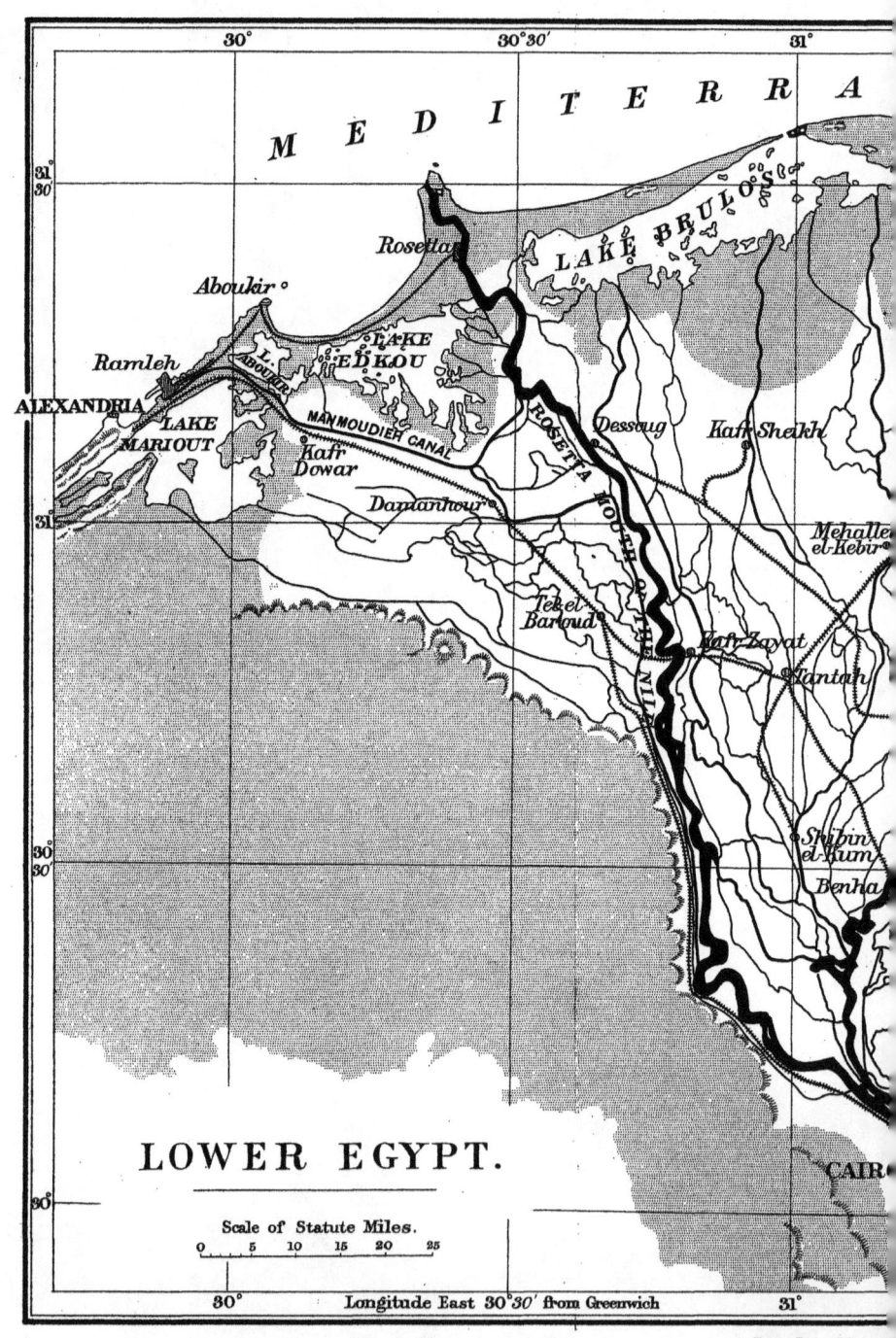

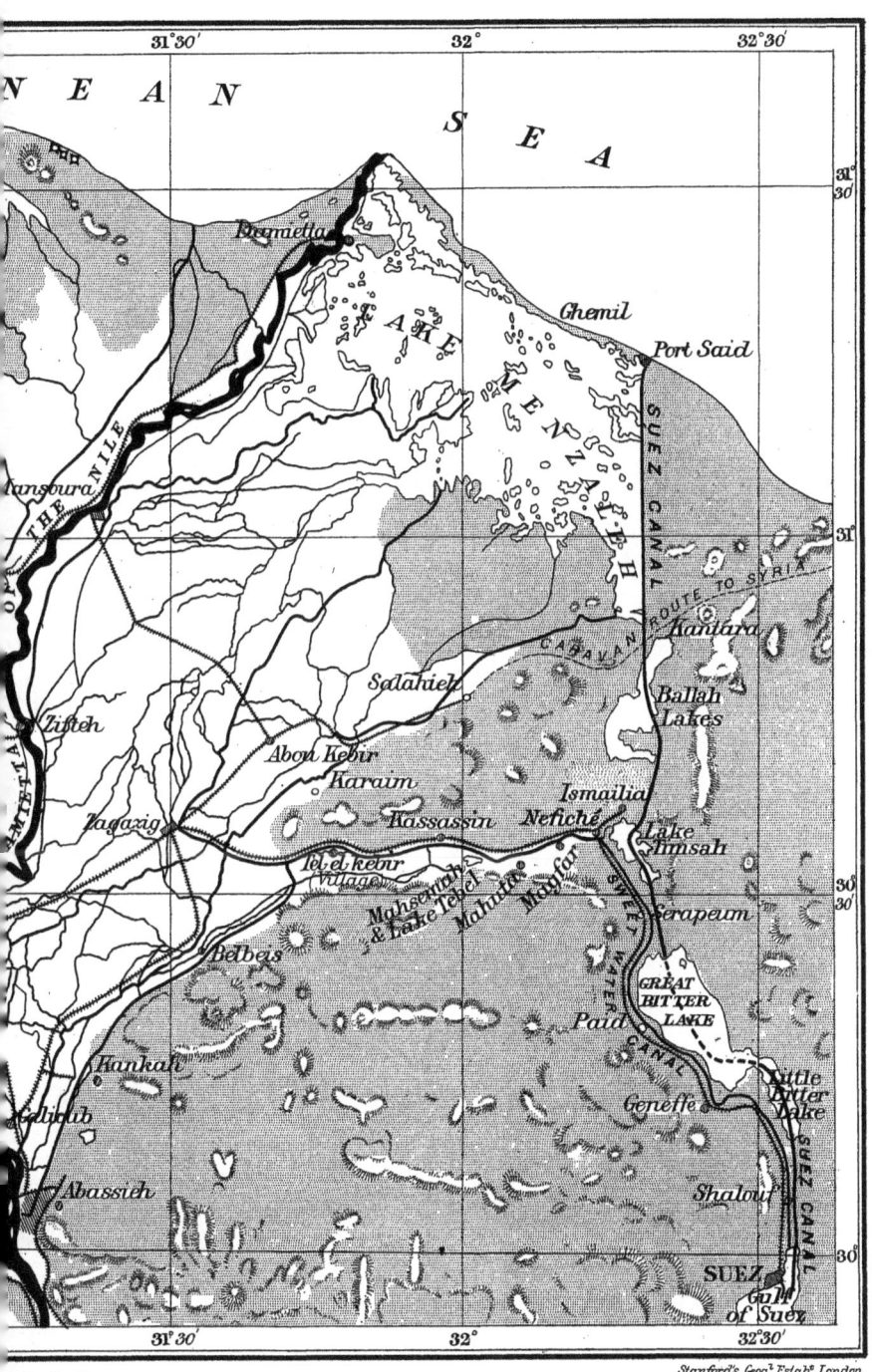

THE
EGYPTIAN CAMPAIGNS,

1882 TO 1885,

AND THE

EVENTS WHICH LED TO THEM.

BY

CHARLES ROYLE,
BARRISTER-AT-LAW.

IN TWO VOLUMES.

VOL. I.

ILLUSTRATED BY MAPS AND PLANS.

LONDON:
HURST AND BLACKETT, PUBLISHERS,
13 GREAT MARLBOROUGH STREET.
1886.

All Rights Reserved.

Printed and bound by Antony Rowe Ltd, Eastbourne

PREFACE.

In offering the present work to the Public, the author does not claim for himself any special qualification for the task he has undertaken.

He has, however, had the advantage, if such it can be called, of residing in Egypt during the last ten years, and has enjoyed, so far as the expression is applicable, opportunities for personally observing many of the events referred to.

He has also been brought in contact with several of the principal actors in the drama, or rather series of dramas, played in the 'Land of the Nile.'

Whatever pretensions to merit may be found in this work are based on its being, so far as the author has been able to make it, a fair and impartial narrative of the circumstances recorded. The author, being, happily as independent of the Egyptian as of any other Government, his opinions, if they have no other value, are at least unbiassed. Moreover, the pages which follow are written in no party spirit. England's Egyptian policy during the period comprised in this book has been directed by both Liberal and Conservative Administrations. Neither has shown itself able to look beyond the immediate present, and both have proved themselves equally incapable of understanding the Egyptian problem.

If Mr. Gladstone's Ministry has perpetrated a series of blunders, there is no reason to suppose that a Conservative Government, if in power, during the same period would have done better. English statesmen, whether Liberal or Conservative, have not of late years shown such conspicuous ability in dealing with foreign affairs as to justify much confidence in either party.

To render his work intelligible, the author has been compelled to go into a number of matters not strictly within the limits of his subject. Many of these date from a period long anterior to the actual campaigns of which a history is given, and much space has thus been occupied. For this, the additional completeness gained will, it is hoped, be some justification.

For some of the information contained in the following pages, the author is indebted to 'Egypt and the Egyptian Question,' by Mr. D. Mackenzie Wallace, to the able work known as 'Khedives and Pashas,' and to the comprehensive Report of Commander Goodrich, of the United States Navy.

The author must not omit his acknowledgments to Mr. A. V. Philip, proprietor of the *Egyptian Gazette*, and to Dr. Haicalis Bey, of the Egyptian journal *Phare d'Alexandrie*, as well as to the many officers of Her Majesty's Army and Navy, who have rendered assistance in preparing the present work.

ALEXANDRIA,
    20*th November*, 1885.

CONTENTS OF THE FIRST VOLUME.

CHAP.		PAGE
I.	INTRODUCTORY	1
II.	EGYPTIAN FINANCES	7
III.	CHANGE OF KHEDIVES	18
IV.	MILITARY MOVEMENTS	26
V.	TRIUMPH OF THE ARMY	35
VI.	SUPPORT OF ENGLAND AND FRANCE	45
VII.	TROUBLES WITH THE NOTABLES	52
VIII.	NEGOTIATIONS AND EXPLANATIONS	57
IX.	PROGRESS OF EVENTS	65
X.	CRITICAL POSITION	73
XI.	ARABI'S PREPARATIONS	83
XII.	THE MASSACRE OF JUNE 11	87
XIII.	AFTER THE MASSACRE	106
XIV.	HOSTILE PREPARATIONS	116
XV.	THE SHIPS AND FORTS	125
XVI.	BOMBARDMENT OF THE FORTS OF ALEXANDRIA	132
XVII.	EFFECTS OF THE BOMBARDMENT	146
XVIII.	OBSERVATIONS ON THE BOMBARDMENT	154
XIX.	THE DAY AFTER THE BOMBARDMENT	160
XX.	ALEXANDRIA DURING THE BOMBARDMENT	167
XXI.	THE KHEDIVE AT RAMLEH	180
XXII.	THE DESTRUCTION OF ALEXANDRIA	185
XXIII.	OCCUPATION OF ALEXANDRIA	190
XXIV.	THE SITUATION IN EGYPT	199
XXV.	OPERATIONS AT ALEXANDRIA	204

CONTENTS

CHAP.		PAGE
XXVI.	OPERATIONS AT RAMLEH	210
XXVII.	THE CONFERENCE	220
XXVIII.	THE PORTE AND THE POWERS	230
XXIX.	EVENTS AT ALEXANDRIA	237
XXX.	PORT SAÏD, SUEZ, AND ISMAILIA	241
XXXI.	M. DE LESSEPS AND THE SUEZ CANAL	247
XXXII.	SEIZURE OF THE SUEZ CANAL	258
XXXIII.	M. VICTOR DE LESSEPS' NARRATIVE OF OPERATIONS ON THE SUEZ CANAL	274
XXXIV.	TEL-EL-MAHUTA	280
XXXV.	MAHSAMEH	287
XXXVI.	KASSASSIN	292
XXXVII.	ENGAGEMENT AT KASSASSIN	303
XXXVIII.	TEL-EL-KEBIR	312
XXXIX.	CAPTURE OF CAIRO	331
XL.	SURRENDER OF KAFR DOWAR	343
XLI.	OBSERVATIONS ON THE CAMPAIGN	350
XLII.	ENGLAND AND THE PORTE	356
XLIII.	EVENTS IN CAIRO	363
XLIV.	TRIAL OF THE REBEL LEADERS	369

ILLUSTRATIONS.

MAP OF LOWER EGYPT	*(Frontispiece)*
PLAN OF THE BOMBARDMENT AT ALEXANDRIA	132
THE LINES OF TEL-EL-KEBIR	315

THE EGYPTIAN CAMPAIGNS.

CHAPTER I.

INTRODUCTORY.

Purchase of Suez Canal Shares—The Financial Decrees of 1876—Reluctance of the British Government to take any part in the Arrangements thereunder—Readiness of the French Government—International Tribunals—The Financial Situation—Mr. Vivian—Commission of Inquiry demanded by England and France—Interference for Protection of the Egyptian Bondholders.

In the year 1875, when the English Government temporarily relieved Ismail Pasha's necessities by purchasing for four millions sterling his Suez Canal shares, people who understood the situation foresaw that this was but a prelude to a more active interference in Egyptian affairs.

Mr. Cave's financial mission, undertaken about the same time, tended to strengthen this impression, notwithstanding the declaration of Lord Derby (then Foreign Secretary) that the mission in question 'must not be taken to imply any desire to interfere in the internal affairs of Egypt.'

There can be no doubt that Lord Derby was perfectly sincere.

The Egyptian policy of Lord Beaconsfield's Cabinet,

as well as of that which succeeded it, was originally one of non-intervention, and it was only modified by force of circumstances.

England's first wish was that no Power should interfere in Egypt; her second, that in case any interference should become necessary, England should not be left out in the cold.

When this is borne in mind, the policy of Her Majesty's Ministers, if the ever-varying attitude they assumed towards Egypt can be dignified by the name of a policy, becomes comparatively intelligible.

It will be seen that although the ultimate action of England on the banks of the Nile can be traced to her mixing herself up in questions of Egyptian finance, every attempt to induce her to intervene met for a long time with failure.

When Mr. Cave's Report, and later on that of Mr. Goschen, revealed the embarrassed state of the country, and led to the Decrees of May and November 1876, Her Majesty's Government steadily resisted all attempts to induce it to take any part in the financial scheme which the Decrees embodied. Her Majesty's representatives were indeed instructed to give Mr. Goschen, the representative of the British bondholders, 'an unofficial support,' but that was all; and the repeated applications made to England to nominate a Controller-General, a Commissioner of the Public Debt, and two Directors for the Railways, under the Decrees, encountered only a refusal. The French, Italian, and Austrian members of the Commission of the Public Debt, were nominated by their respective Governments as early as May 1876, whereas, up to December in the same year, their English colleague had not been appointed.

There were, nevertheless, reasons which might well have justified England in acting otherwise. Not only was she interested in seeing that the payment of the five per cent interest on the purchase money of the Suez Canal shares was secured to her, but there was also the Turkish tribute to which she had to look, to cover the interest of the Ottoman Loan guaranteed by England jointly with France.

This latter power, throughout the negotiations relative to the settlement of the Egyptian Debt, appears to have been always ready to come to the front.

On the 5th December, 1876, the Duke Decazes, the French Minister of Foreign Affairs, when asked to nominate a French Controller-General of Egyptian Finance, declared that he felt no difficulty whatever in the matter.

Lord Derby, however, with characteristic caution, declined to take the same view, and to meet his scruples it was suggested that the two Western Powers should be asked, not to 'appoint' the two Controllers, but merely to 'authorise' the persons whom the Khedive might designate, to accept the posts.

Even this failed to remove the objections of the English Foreign Office, Lord Derby observing that as by English law a British subject was free to enter the civil service of a foreign state, no such authorization, as was asked for, was necessary. Eventually the Khedive Ismail was under the necessity of himself nominating all the Englishmen required to fill the posts created by the Financial Decrees.

The hesitation of the English Government to accept even the slightest responsibility at this period formed a striking contrast to the action of the other Powers, and especially to that of our neighbours the French.

The readiness with which France adopted the Financial Scheme from the first appears to have alarmed the English Foreign Office, for the Secretary of State had, as early as March 1876, felt it necessary to express the satisfaction with which Her Majesty's Government had received the assurance that France was not disposed to take any step which could lead to an interference with the independence of Egypt, and added 'that Her Majesty's Government could not view with indifference any attempt by another Power to gain administrative control over Egypt.'

Eventually, as we know, the Financial Scheme with other administrative reforms came into operation, and for some time seemed likely to secure to Egypt and her creditors a fair share of the blessings intended.

This, however, was not destined to last. The Decree containing the final arrangement of the Public Debt was signed on the 18th November, 1876, and as early as July of the following year it became evident that the revenues assigned to meet the Coupons and Sinking Fund would not nearly suffice. In fact, the estimates given to Messrs. Goschen and Joubert, as the basis of their calculations, were fallacious. A deficit of no less than 820,000*l.* already appeared in the revenues set apart for the Unified Debt, and of 200,000*l.* in those assigned for the Privileged Debt. Moreover, there were strong reasons for supposing that considerable portions of the revenue were being diverted from their legitimate channel by authority of Ismail Pasha or his agents.

At the same time serious difficulty arose in satisfying the judgments obtained against the Egyptian Government in the International Tribunals, which had been established by treaties with the European Powers and the United States. The judgment creditors in many cases issued execution against the property of their illustrious debtor, and when this was resisted by force,

INTRODUCTORY.

they sought the aid of their respective Consuls-General.

Mr. Vivian, then British Consul-General in Cairo, a diplomatist who took a prominent part in this and the subsequent stages of Egypt's history, had, as England's representative, to remonstrate with the Khedive. The advice which Mr. Vivian gave, that the amount of these judgments should be paid, was excellent, but under the circumstances, about as easy of adoption as if he had counselled His Highness to take steps to secure an annual high Nile.

In February 1878, things were gradually going from bad to worse, when M. Waddington, who had become the French Minister of Foreign Affairs, addressed a communication to Lord Derby on the subject of the various financial questions, and made the significant observation that if England and France did not exert themselves at once, the matter would slip out of their hands.

This suggestion was not without its effect, and the English Foreign Secretary, in reply, went a little further than he had previously done, and stated that 'Her Majesty's Government would be happy to co-operate with that of France in any useful measure not inconsistent with the Khedive's independent administration of Egypt.'

This statement was backed up by the subsequent action of Mr. Vivian, who, in conformity with the views of the French Minister, pressed upon the Khedive the necessity for 'a thorough and exhaustive inquiry into the finances of the country.'

As this constituted a fresh departure in the policy of England with regard to the Egyptian question, it may be interesting to mark the manner in which the change was brought about.

Mr. Vivian, on the 23rd February, had pointed out to Her Majesty's Government that—

'Although he could well understand their disinclination and hesitation to depart from the established principle not to interfere officially for the protection of persons who had chosen to invest their capital in foreign stocks with the hope of obtaining a high rate of interest, yet he considered this sound rule did not quite apply to Egypt. Here,' he remarked, 'it was not only the bondholders and creditors whose interests were imperilled, but the whole government of the country was thrown out of gear by financial mismanagement. The want of means was pleaded as an excuse for failing to keep engagements sanctioned and protected by solemn conventions with Foreign Governments, such as the execution of the sentences of the International Tribunals. The resources of the country,' he continued, 'were becoming seriously exhausted, and its credit impaired; whilst affairs were becoming so entangled as to challenge the interference of Foreign Governments for the protection of the interests of their subjects, although such interference could hardly be viewed with indifference by Her Majesty's Government.' Mr. Vivian concluded by urging 'that the case of Egypt was so exceptional as to justify Her Majesty's Government in departing in some measure from their sound rule of non-interference in similar cases.'

After all, there is nothing like being hopelessly indebted, to induce people to take an interest in one's affairs, and it would appear that the views of their representative in Cairo found favour with Lord Derby and his colleagues, who, from this period, adopted a position which ultimately led to that complete interference in Egypt, which the Foreign Office had so much desired to avoid.

CHAPTER II.

EGYPTIAN FINANCES.

Sitting of Commission of Inquiry—Rivers Wilson—Cherif Pasha—Riaz succeeds Cherif—Deficit for May Coupon—Pressure of England and France—Report of Commission of Inquiry—Rivers Wilson and De Blignières appointed Ministers—The Khedive declares his intention to become a Constitutional Sovereign—The Khedive Ismail Pasha—Appointment of European Officials—The 'Domain' Loan—Suppression of the Control—Warning to Ismail—Nubar and Rivers Wilson mobbed by the Soldiery—Resignation of Nubar—Despatch of English and French Vessels of War to Alexandria.

EVENTS succeeded events; the Commission of Inquiry, instituted by Decree of the 30th March, 1878, assembled in Cairo, and under the Vice-Presidency of Mr. (afterwards Sir C. Rivers) Wilson,* revealed the most startling facts relating to the administration.

The Commission had no easy task before it, and it only attained its object through the dogged resolution of its Vice-President, backed by the moral support of the Powers.

At the outset, Cherif Pasha, the Khedive's Minister of Foreign Affairs and of Justice, refused point-blank to obey the Decree, and submit to be personally examined by the Commission.

As Cherif is a statesman who will be frequently referred to in the following pages, it may be opportune to briefly describe him. He is about sixty years of age, and like most of those who have held the highest posts

* M. Ferdinand de Lesseps was for some occult reason appointed President, but took no part in the labours of the Commission.

in Egypt, is of Circassian origin. He was amongst the favoured individuals who had been sent to France by Mehemet Ali to be educated. He gradually passed through nearly every post in the State with that facility which is so frequently seen in Egypt, where a man is one day a Station-master on the railway, the next a Judge in the Tribunals, and eventually a Master of Ceremonies, or a Cabinet Minister.

Cherif has pleasing manners, speaks French fluently, and is in every respect a gentleman. A Mahometan by religion, he was, from an early period in Ismail's reign, a prominent character in Egyptian history. He soon became a rival of Nubar Pasha (referred to further on), and he and Nubar alternated as the Khedive's Prime ministers for many years.

Of a naturally indolent character, Cherif always represented the 'laissez aller' side of Egyptian politics. With an excellent temper, and a supremely apathetic disposition, he was always willing to accept almost any proposition, provided it did not entail upon him any personal exertion, or interfere with his favourite pastime, a game of billiards.

Cherif's notion in refusing to appear before the Commission was probably of a two-fold character. Educated with Oriental ideas, and accustomed to regard Europeans with suspicion, it is not unlikely that he resented the appointment of the Commission as an unwarrantable intrusion on the part of the Western Powers.

'Here,' thought he, 'was a number of people coming to make disagreeable inquiries, and to ask indiscreet questions. Others might answer them; he, for his part, could not, and for two reasons: first, because he couldn't if he would; and second, because he wouldn't if he could. Was he, at his time of life, to be asked to give reasons for all he had done? It was ridiculous; all the world knew that he had no reasons.'*

Probably, also, Cherif had his own motives for not wishing to afford too much information. Though enjoying a deservedly high reputation for honesty, he belonged to what must be regarded as the 'privileged' class in the country. For years this class had benefited by certain immunities from taxation, and notably from the land-tax, the chief revenue of Egypt. These advantages the work of the Commission threatened to do away with. Further, Cherif's love of ease and comfort, and absence of energy, indisposed him to give himself unnecessary trouble about anything in particular. Be this as it may, Cherif, though expressing his readiness to reply in writing to any communications which the Commission might address to him, declined to do more.

The Decree, however, provided that every functionary of State should be bound to appear before the Commission. This might have placed a less astute minister in a dilemma. Cherif at once evaded the difficulty by resigning office, rightly calculating on again returning to power when the Commission should have become a thing of the past. Riaz Pasha, then second Vice-President of the Commission, succeeded Cherif as Minister, and the inquiry proceeded without him.

Meanwhile the English Government had allow itself to advance one stage further in its Egyptian policy. In authorising Rivers Wilson, an English public servant, to sit as first Vice-President on the Commission, and in granting him leave of absence for the

* *Khedives and Pashas*, page 172.

purpose, as well as in defraying his expenses, Lord Derby took a step, the significance of which was only partially disguised by the cautious intimation made to Mr. Vivian on the 23rd March, 1878, 'that the employé of the British Government was not to be considered as invested with any official character.'

But in April, in the same year, when it became evident that there would be a deficit of 1,200,000*l*. in the funds required to pay the May coupon of the Unified Debt, further influences had been brought to bear, and Mr. Vivian was instructed to join the French Consul-General in urging upon the Khedive the necessity of finding the necessary funds at whatever sacrifice to himself. Ismail, who could adopt any line which suited his purpose, pointed out that this result could only be accomplished by ruinous sacrifices which, he said, should, nevertheless, be made if insisted on. The Agents of England and France remained firm, and the bondholders got their money. By what means this was accomplished it is unnecessary to inquire. Rumours of frightful pressure being put on the unfortunate fellaheen, of forced loans, and other desperate expedients, were prevalent in Cairo, and were, probably, too well founded.

However, as has been stated, the coupon was paid, and not only this, but England had interfered, to quote Mr. Vivian's words, ' for the protection of persons who had chosen to invest their capital in foreign stocks with the hope of obtaining a high rate of interest.'

The responsibility incurred by this step can hardly be overstated, and the later measures adopted by Her Majesty's Government with regard to Egyptian finance followed almost as a natural consequence.

It would require too much space to give at length the details of the Report which the Commission of

Inquiry presented. Suffice it to say, that it showed confusion and irregularity everywhere. Taxes were collected in the most arbitrary and oppressive manner, and at the most unfavourable periods of the year. The land tenures were so arranged that the wealthier proprietors evaded a great portion of the land-tax, and the *corvée*, or system of forced labour, was applied in a way which was ruinous to the country.

Further than this, the Khedive and his family had amassed, at the expense of the State, colossal properties, amounting in fact to as much as one-fifth of the whole cultivable land of Egypt, and this property, the Commission declared, ought to be given up. On every side the most flagrant abuses were found to prevail.

In conclusion, it was found that the arrangements made by the Financial Decrees of 1876 could not possibly be adhered to, and that a fresh liquidation was inevitable.

Ismail Pasha, after every effort to make better terms for himself, yielded to Rivers Wilson's requisitions, and accepted the conclusions of the Commission of Inquiry. He acquiesced with as good grace as he could in making over to the State the landed property of himself and family. He went even further, and in August 1878, approved the formation of a Cabinet under the presidency of Nubar Pasha with Rivers Wilson as Minister of Finance and M. De Blignières (who had been the French Member of the Commission of the Public Debt) as Minister of Public Works.

At the same time, as if to show to Europe that he had seriously entered on the path of reform, the Khedive proclaimed his intention to renounce personal rule, and become a Constitutional Sovereign, governing only through his Council of Ministers.

Any history of Egyptian affairs at this time would be incomplete without a sketch of Ismail himself. The Khedive was then forty-six years of age, short in person, corpulent in figure; with a reddish-brown beard, and with one eye startlingly bright, and the other habitually almost closed; he gave one the idea of a man of no ordinary intelligence. Speaking French fluently, and possessed of a peculiarly fascinating manner, Ismail exercised an almost mesmeric influence on those who came in contact with him. He was, and is, perhaps, one of the best judges of men and their various peculiarities and weaknesses, that the present century has seen.

Ismail's business capabilities were unbounded; not the smallest detail, from the purchase of a cargo of coal to the sale of the whole sugar crop on the Daira Estates, was carried out, without his personal sanction.

His so-called Ministers were so many lay figures, or at best only puppets, upon whom he could, in case of need, put all the responsibility. In this he went too far. In attempting to do everything he ended in doing nothing, that is, in doing nothing well. By this system, aided by the most reckless personal extravagance, he succeeded, in fifteen years in raising the National Debt of Egypt from 3,292,800*l*., at which his predecessor Saïd Pasha had left it, to over 90,000,000*l*. To do Ismail justice it must be admitted that a large part of this money was spent in making railways, and other improvements, and beautifying Cairo, which city it was his aim to convert into a sort of Oriental Paris. Of Ismail's boundless hospitality it is unnecessary to speak. The fêtes which attended the opening, in 1869, of the Suez Canal, and which cost over 2,000,000*l*., have long since become historic.

The great defect of Ismail's character was his

insincerity. When his reckless administration had brought his country to the brink of ruin, he inaugurated the system of financial control set forth in the Decrees of 1876.

It must not be supposed that he ever for a moment meant that they should be carried into effect. At the same time he enlisted a great number of Europeans into his service, and placed them in ostensibly high positions. Did Ismail intend that these officials should exercise the functions attributed to them? Not for an instant. In this, and in his subsequent acts, all that he intended was to throw dust in the eyes of Europe. For a while he succeeded ; but it was not to last. After a time the Powers recognised that they were being played with, and from that moment the downfall of Ismail was certain.

In nominally transforming himself into a constitutional ruler, Ismail was only following out the policy which had so long actuated him. By his personal rule he had brought his country to ruin. By calling himself a constitutional sovereign, he would, he thought, be able to transfer all responsibility to his Ministers.

The appointment of Rivers Wilson as the Khedive's Minister of Finance was so unprecedented an event, that it required all the care of the Marquis of Salisbury (who had now succeeded Lord Derby at the Foreign Office), to attenuate its political importance. To save appearances it was arranged that Her Majesty's Government should do nothing more than give that consent, which the Marquis of Salisbury's predecessor had declared on a similar occasion to be unnecessary, to Rivers Wilson accepting the post.

In taking this step, the Queen's Government was probably somewhat influenced by the fact, that although the month of September (1878) had been reached, the finances of Egypt were in such a state of disorder, that the money due for the preceding February dividend of the Turkish Guaranteed Loan (for which England was responsible), had not been forthcoming.

It is significant, that in a despatch, dated the 12th October, 1878, the selection of Rivers Wilson for the Ministry of Finance is spoken of as 'an object which Her Majesty's Government are concerned in facilitating for reasons of public policy.'

This was followed by the conclusion of the Rothschild Loan of 8,500,000*l.*, on the security of the 'Domain Lands,' that is, the private property retroceded to the State by the Khedive and the members of his family, in accordance with the recommendation of the Commission of Inquiry.

One of the conditions of the Loan was, that the property to be hypothecated should be managed by three persons, one to be nominated by the English, one by the French, and the other by the Egyptian Government. The Marquis of Salisbury in October, 1878, had advanced so far ahead of the policy of his predecessor as to consent to appoint the English Agent,* and to intimate that Her Majesty's Government assumed that the agent nominated by it should not be divested of his functions without its consent.

Thanks to our co-operation, the arrangement was concluded with the Rothschilds on the 31st October, and the advance was made in time to meet the coupon of the Unified Debt falling due on the following day. Twice, therefore, had the Egyptian bondholders been indebted to the interference of the English Government for the payment of their dividends.

As a consequence of the installation of a Constitu-

---

* Mr. F. W. Rowsell, C.B., Director of Navy Contracts.

tional Government with European Ministers in the Cabinet, the English and French Controllers-General were deemed unnecessary, and the Control was declared suspended. On the adoption of the new order of things, a hint, the significance of which was shown by subsequent events, was given to the Khedive that Her Majesty's Government relied on his steady support being given to the endeavours of the new Cabinet to re-establish the financial credit of the country, and that the position of the Khedive and his dynasty might become seriously compromised in the event of a contrary course being adopted.

Ismail, who had already made great sacrifices at the bidding of the Commission of Inquiry, was much hurt when Mr. Vivian made the above communication to him. The difference in tone did not escape the notice of the Khedive, who began to realise that the grasp of England was tightening upon him. He complained that hitherto the English Government had been contented with giving him advice in a benevolent spirit, whilst now they seemed to have taken a *parti pris* against him.

With great plausibility he pointed out that he was now a Constitutional Ruler, and that all responsibility for the future rested with his Ministers, and not with himself. At the same time Ismail was far too clever not to see that the meaning of the British Government was that he was expected not to thwart the new Ministry, by availing himself of the prestige which he possessed as the ruler of an Oriental State, combined with a knowledge of Egypt greater than that of any other living person.

It would have been well for him had he taken the advice thus given. Unfortunately, Ismail was too much habituated in Eastern intrigue, and too fond of the power which he had only nominally surrendered, to bend to the new order of things.

The earliest symptom of this was the military outbreak which occurred in Cairo on the 18th February, 1879, when a party of 400 officers, who with 2000 men had been discharged from the army from motives of economy, mobbed Nubar Pasha and Rivers Wilson at the Ministry of Finance. The ostensible grievance was the non-payment of arrears of salary and the large reduction of the army. Anyhow, Nubar and Rivers Wilson were actually assaulted, and the cry of 'Death to the Christians,' was raised. The Khedive himself appeared on the scene, and as if by magic, order was at once restored.

Everything tended to show that His Highness had arranged the whole of this little comedy. However this might be, he speedily took advantage of it to inform the Consuls-General that he could no longer retain his position of responsibility without power or authority, and unless a change were made he would not be answerable for the consequences. At the same time he informed Mr. Vivian that he could on no account longer retain as President of the Ministry Nubar Pasha, on whom he threw the blame for what had occurred. A little later on, the Khedive insisted that he should be allowed his fair share in the government of the country, by being permitted either to preside in person at the Council of Ministers, or to appoint a President in whom he could have confidence.

Immediately after the disturbance, Nubar took the only course open to him and resigned his post as Premier. His example was followed by his colleague Riaz, whilst Rivers Wilson and Monsieur De Blignières awaited from their respective Governments instructions as to the course they should pursue.

These events were succeeded by the despatch of English and French vessels of war to Alexandria.

The progress made at this period in British intervention in Egypt will not fail to strike the reader. Only a little more than two years had elapsed since Lord Derby had refused to incur the responsibility of naming an Englishman to be Controller-General under the Decrees of 1876. In the interval, England had twice interfered to secure the payment of the interest of the Egyptian Debt, had nominated an English official as agent of the State Domains, had authorised another to accept the post of Egyptian Minister of Finance, and had followed this up by sending a ship of war to Alexandria.

CHAPTER III.

CHANGE OF KHEDIVES.

Ismail Pasha's Motive in bringing about the *Émeute* of the 18th February, 1879—Financial Difficulties—Decree suspending Payment of Interest of Debt—Ismail's counter Project—The Support of the Country secured—The Dismissal of the Ministry—Formation of a Native Ministry under Cherif—Increase of the Army—Remonstrances of English and French Consuls-General—Intervention of German Government—Deposition of Ismail—Ismail's Departure from Egypt.

ISMAIL's motive in bringing about the military *émeute* mentioned in the last chapter was to get back his authority, and to demonstrate, in the same way as Arabi Pasha did later, namely, on the 11th June, 1882, that he was the only real power in the country.

In doing this, Ismail, as it turned out, played a most dangerous game, and one which by laying bare his duplicity, shortly after cost him his throne. For the moment a *modus vivendi* was found in the nomination of the Khedive's son, Prince Tewfik, as President of the Council of Ministers.

The acceptance by the Western Powers of this arrangement was accompanied by another warning, namely, that any further difficulties or disturbances of the public peace would be regarded by Her Majesty's Government as the result of action on the Khedive's part, and the consequences for himself would be very serious.

The financial difficulties of the country at this period became such that a Decree suspending the payment of the April Coupon had to be signed at the end

CHANGE OF KHEDIVES. 19

of March, by the advice of the Ministers. His Highness the Khedive then suddenly turned round and announced that the measure was unnecessary, and that the country could afford to meet all its engagements. He went further, and proposed a financial scheme of his own in opposition to that of his Ministers. How Ismail could reconcile this with his repeated declarations that he was a Constitutional Ruler is not clear. But petitions in support of the counter-project of the Khedive poured in from all quarters. Meetings of the Notables and Ulemas were convened by the Sheik-el-Bakri with the object of exciting religious animosity against the European Ministers. One conspicuous member of the Cabinet, Riaz Pasha, was denounced in the mosques as a friend of the Christians. In fact, no intrigue known to the Oriental mind was wanting to produce a fresh crisis.

The arguments by which the movement was brought about were such as could not fail to influence the minds of the wealthier and more important class of natives.

There are in Egypt vast distinctions in the tenure of lands. One called 'Kharadjih' supposes the freehold to be in the sovereign, and subjects the owners to a heavy land-tax. This varied at the time from P.T. 120 to P.T. 170 per feddan (or acre) per annum. Another called 'Ouchoury' consisted of lands, which in theory had been reclaimed by the cultivators from the desert, and paid a land-tax of P.T. $83\frac{1}{2}$ per annum. The Commission of Inquiry had found out that oddly enough nearly all the 'Ouchoury' lands were owned by the wealthy inhabitants of the country, who paid consequently a comparatively small tax. It was given out with considerable truth that it was the intention of the European Minister of Finance to largely increase the taxes on the 'Ouchoury' lands. This step was calculated beyond all others to arouse the opposition of the large landowners. The Ulemas, or religious bodies, backed this up by declaring that it was the aim of the Ministers to hand over the country to the Europeans.

These reasons alone would be sufficient to account for the movement. But there was one more powerful still, namely, that it was believed to be agreeable to the Khedive.

These events were followed on the 7th April, 1879, by the dismissal of the Ministers and the formation of a purely native Ministry, of which Cherif Pasha took the lead, in place of Prince Tewfik. So secretly had the change been determined on that the former Ministers only found it out when, on going to their offices, they discovered that their places were already filled by their successors.

This veritable *coup d'état* placed the English and French representatives in a position of some difficulty. On the one hand, the right of the Khedive to change his Ministers, even under the new system of government, could not be contested. On the other, the change was of so radical a nature, and so much opposed to the new obligations which he had contracted with the Western Powers,—so like, in fact, to breaking with all previous arrangements, that it could hardly be permitted to pass. The English and French Consuls-General therefore waited on the Khedive, told him that the precipitate and causeless dismissal of Ministers whose services the Khedive had solicited the Governments of England and France to place at his disposal, constituted a grave and apparently intentional discourtesy to friendly powers, and warned him of the necessity of adopting the course which the two Governments recommended to him.

This communication does not appear to have had the effect intended, for the army was suddenly ordered to be increased to 60,000 men, sworn to defend the Khedive against all invaders. This was followed by a Decree of the 22nd April, 1879, altering the arrangements made by the Financial Decrees of 1876 in several important particulars, amongst others, reducing the interest of the Unified Debt to six per cent, and interfering with the Sinking Fund. It will not escape attention that this Decree was made by 'main strength,' as it were, without the public creditors being in any way consulted.

It was scarcely to be expected that such a measure, conceived in defiance of all Europe, should be permitted to stand. Not only had Ismail treated with gross discourtesy the Powers which had sent him two Ministers at his request, but he had also broken his solemn engagement to renounce personal rule and to govern only through his Ministry. In addition to this, he had shown his besetting failing that of absolute insincerity, and had further demonstrated his utter unfitness to govern the country.

Notwithstanding all that had occurred, it is probable that he might still have enjoyed a little longer his position of ruler of Egypt, but for another circumstance, namely, the non-payment of the judgments of the International Tribunals.

The British and French ambassadors at Constantinople were instructed to address to the Porte strong representations on the subject. They were not, however, prepared to demand Ismail's deposition. Both the Powers knew that the Sultan was but too willing to listen to any application of the kind, and by exercising his authority as 'Suzerain,' once more to assert his sovereignty. This, however, was what neither France nor England desired, and for some time neither Power would take the decisive step.

At length the hands of both were forced by a statesman who had fewer scruples, namely, Prince Bismarck. He caused it to be intimated to the French and English embassies that if they did not demand the removal of Ismail, Germany would. The Imperial Chancellor based his claim on the injuries sustained by German subjects, and on the non-fulfilment of the treaty under which the International Tribunals had been constituted. England and France, seeing that if they did not act, there was danger of the wind being taken out of their sails, at last summoned up sufficient resolution to ask the Sultan for the displacement of the man who had so long trifled with them. Even then it was a question as to the form the measure should take. England desired that it should be an abdication by Ismail in favour of his son Tewfik,—rightly judging that if the latter owed his succession to the throne to British intervention, he would be the more amenable to British influence.

On the other hand, it was not desirable to give Turkey the opportunity of interfering more than was absolutely necessary, and were a sentence of deposition actually passed, there was no knowing how far the Firman, under which Tewfik had been named Ismail's eventual successor, would be respected by the Porte. The rightful successor by Mohammedan law was Halim Pasha, the uncle of Tewfik, an utter Turk, whom it was considered most desirable to exclude.

Intrigues of every kind had been going on meanwhile at Constantinople. Ismail was sounded on the subject, and, naturally, was indisposed either to abdicate or to be deposed. Like the martyr who was given his choice of being either burned at the stake or boiled alive, he was inclined to ask if there was not some other alternative. This latter view was strengthened by the misleading information which he received from his agent, Ibrahim Pasha, at Constantinople.

The latter from time to time misled the unfortunate Khedive. When things were going from bad to worse with his master, Ibrahim repeatedly assured him that if sufficient money were only transmitted to Stamboul, all might be made right. Animated by this advice, the deluded Khedive continued to send fabulous sums to his 'Suzerain,' up to the very moment that he threw him over, as one would discard a sucked orange.

It is not, therefore, to be wondered at that Ismail, when the news of his deposition arrived, was simply thunderstruck.

On the 24th June, 1879, the Khedive received a telegram from Ibrahim that the Sultan had refused to depose him. But during the night other telegrams warned him, that in case he refused to abdicate, the nomination of Halim Pasha was imminent, and a despatch from the French Ambassador to M. Tricou, who was then French Consul-General in Cairo, requested him to warn the Khedive that his abdication was the only means of saving his dynasty.

At four in the morning of the 25th, the English and French Consuls-General sought out Cherif Pasha, and made him accompany them to the Palace. The Chief Eunuch was unwilling to awaken his master. Cherif, raising his voice, exclaimed, that when the Prime Minister, and the representatives of the Great Powers, deemed it necessary to disturb the Sovereign at such an hour, it was imperative for him to give them audience. Some minutes later Ismail was made acquainted with the despatches from Constantinople, and the Consuls-General again insisted on his abdication. He, nevertheless, refused point-blank, and referred to the telegrams he had received from Ibrahim Pasha.

Later on, he qualified his refusal by stating that he would only yield to a formal order from the Sublime Porte.

The *dénouement* was not far off. At seven in the morning Khairi Pasha, Keeper of the Seals, received a telegram addressed to 'Ismail Pasha, late Khedive of Egypt.' The despatch informed the Khedive that the Sultan, on the advice of his Ministers, had deposed Ismail, and had nominated Tewfik in his place. The stupefaction of Khairi Pasha was only equalled by the terror which he experienced. At first he dared not present the message to his master. He rushed off to Cherif Pasha, whom he induced to accompany him to his Sovereign's presence. Arrived there, the Keeper of the Seals became livid, and tried to conceal the telegram which he held in his hand. Cherif Pasha took on himself to inform Ismail that Khairi had a despatch from Constantinople to communicate. With a trembling hand the latter presented the communication. The Khedive cast his eye on its contents and turned pale. After a short silence Ismail ordered Cherif to find Tewfik and bring him to the Palace.

Tewfik had just received direct the news of his nomination to the throne. 'All Europe,' said the despatch, ' had demanded of the Sultan this change.'

The young Prince was much moved. He, nevertheless, went into the presence of his father, who received him standing. On entering, the latter invited his son to sit down, adding, ' By the will of our master, the Sultan, you are the new Khedive of Egypt. I am going. Listen, you are young, but you have a firm disposition. Hearken to your counsellors, and be happier than your father.'

Tewfik was moved to tears at this address, and the bystanders were equally unable to control their feelings.

When interviewed by the Consuls-General after his deposition Ismail showed himself most *exigeant* as to the conditions on which he would take himself away. He wished for ready money. They offered him 100,000*l*. He wished to take with him all his *entourage*. He selected Smyrna as a residence. He required that an Egyptian steamer should be placed at his disposal at the place where he was to disembark. In fact, he asked so many things that the Consuls-General were at their wits' ends to know what to do.

Their object was to get rid of him at any price, and he was in effect told that he could have nearly all he wanted if he would only be off at once.

Ismail quitted Cairo by the 11.30 train in the forenoon of the 26th with all his suite, and the same evening, accompanied by over seventy ladies of his harem, left Alexandria for Naples in the yacht *Mahroussa*, under a royal salute from the forts and vessels of war.

CHAPTER IV.

MILITARY MOVEMENTS.

Nomination of Tewfik as Khedive—Cherif's Ministry—Riaz's Cabinet—Sketch of Riaz—Commencement of the Military Movement—The Egyptian Army—The Circassian and Fellah Officers—Ali Fehmy—Osman Pasha Riffki—Abd-el-Al—Arabi Bey—Sketch of Arabi—Mahmoud Sami—Military Agitation—Arrest of the 'Three Colonels'—Military Outbreak of February 1881—Increase of the Army—Nomination of Mahmoud Sami as Minister of War.

THE Sultan's despatch announcing the deposition of Ismail Pasha and the nomination of Tewfik as his successor, mentioned ' the firm will of the Sultan to secure the progress and tranquillity of Egypt, that difficulties both internal and external to the country had necessitated the dismissal of Ismail Pasha, and that the Sultan, recognising the capacity and intelligence of Tewfik, had named him Khedive of Egypt.'

The document in no way alludes to the means by which the change was brought about, but the matter is treated as proceeding from the spontaneous will of the Sultan ; whereas, as a matter of fact, it was only by the very strong intervention of England and France that it was effected.

The first act of the new Khedive was apparently of a reactionary character, for on the 3rd July, 1879, he assembled a Ministry with Cherif Pasha at its head. On the 4th September following, the European Powers having insisted on the restoration of the Control, Major Baring and Mons. De Blignières were nominated Controllers-General by the English and French Governments.

On the 23rd September, 1879, Riaz Pasha's Ministry succeeded that of Cherif Pasha. The former was probably never intended to be more than a stop-gap till affairs settled down.

Riaz Pasha is a man who has played an important part in the recent events in Egypt, and is therefore deserving of something more than a passing notice. He is of Circassian family, and of Hebrew extraction; he is a feeble-looking man of about five feet four inches in height, and has a stooping figure and a harsh voice. Prior to Ismail's accession to the throne, Riaz occupied a very menial position in the household of his predecessor, and curious stories are told of his connexion with Said Pasha, which for the sake of both it is best to hope are unfounded.

Riaz's conception of the Creation is a divine mandate, 'Let there be Riaz and there was Riaz.' *

With all his vanity Riaz possesses considerable ability —a strong will, tenacious perseverance, and business-like habits. He is credited with more honesty than is usually to be found among Egyptian public men, and he exhibits a remarkable degree of independence. When the Control was re-established he was shrewd enough to see that England and France seriously intended to take Egyptian affairs in hand, and he accepted the situation accordingly. This led him to work cordially with the Controllers, with the happy result that during the two years of his Ministry Egypt attained an unprecedented degree of prosperity.

In April 1880, the celebrated Commission of Liquidation was appointed, and under this the public debt was subjected to various modifications, and other financial changes were made.

* *Khedives and Pashas,* page 127.

These were accompanied by the remission of taxation and other reforms. How long this pleasant state of things might have lasted it is impossible to say, had not the military movement under Arabi Bey supervened and brought about events which not even Riaz could have foreseen.

In order to understand the nature and causes of the army revolt under Arabi, it is necessary to know something of the Egyptian military organization at that time.

The army of Egypt, which had achieved such great things under Mehemet Ali, had gradually declined under his successors, and when Ismail came to the throne was represented by a total effective force of only 10,000 men. Ismail raised the number to 45,000, and remodelled the organization, tactics and drill, on French lines; subsequently this was altered, and the German army served as a pattern.

Under the Firman of Tewfik's investiture, the army, when on a peace-footing, was limited to 18,000 men. The system of recruiting was governed by the Recruiting Law of 1860. In theory every male in Egypt owes military service to the State. Exemptions could be purchased after one year's service, either by a sum down, or by an annual payment. The inhabitants of Cairo and Alexandria have, by ancient privilege, always been exempt.

The contingents were levied at irregular intervals on the requisition of the Minister of War. This official called on the Mudirs (or Governors) of the provinces to supply a certain number of men, and the Mudirs, in their turn, requisitioned the Sheiks-el-Beled (Village Chiefs) to furnish their quotas; the consequence was that those only were taken who were not rich enough to bribe the Sheiks, and the ranks of the army were

MILITARY MOVEMENTS.

filled by the poorest and lowest classes of the people. Recruits were nominally taken from men between the ages of eighteen and twenty-two, but in practice these limits were not adhered to.

The men recruited from the Soudan and from Lower Egypt were mostly compactly built, and possessed of considerable endurance; and the Soudanese had in addition certain warlike qualities; but the recruits from all the other districts, the ordinary 'fellahs,' had no taste for war. This is not to be wondered at, considering their natural character and habits.

The Egyptian 'fellah' is a type in himself. Possessed of no national pride or patriotic aspirations he cares nothing about politics. All that he asks is to be let alone to till his little plot of land on the banks of the Nile. Do not vex him too much with forced labour, or tax him beyond his strength, and he remains a peaceful, contented, law-abiding subject from his birth, until the day arrives for him to be carried out to the little cemetery whose white tombs brighten the borders of the desert.

Amongst the soldiers of the Egyptian army at the time referred to there was but little rivalry or jealousy, and a fair state of subordination prevailed. There were, however, other elements in the organization of the force from which trouble was destined to arise.

The majority of the officers up to the rank of Colonel, like the non-commissioned officers and men, were of Egyptian or 'fellah' origin, while the officers of highest rank, and holders of staff appointments were of Turkish or Circassian extraction. The latter, as belonging to the same race as the reigning monarch, naturally constituted the dominant caste; when there was a campaign in the Soudan, or any other unpleasant duty to be performed, the native officers were selected for it, but when it was a question of garrisoning Cairo or Alexandria, the Circassians were employed; naturally a good deal of jealousy and ill-feeling was thus created, but as long as Ismail was in power these were suppressed, and discipline maintained, except when it answered that ruler's purpose that it should be otherwise, as in the instance before referred to, of the demonstration against Nubar Pasha and Rivers Wilson. With the young and inexperienced Tewfik, however, things were different; a spirit of insubordination developed itself, and the two sets of officers entered upon a struggle for the mastery.

Among the prominent 'fellah' officers was Ali Fehmy, who was a favourite with the Khedive, and in command of the Guards at the Palace. In this position he was frequently called on to convey orders to Osman Pasha Riffki, the Minister of War. Osman was a Circassian, and felt hurt at receiving orders from a 'fellah' officer. By what means the change was effected is uncertain, but, eventually, Ali Fehmy fell into disfavour, and became one of a group of discontented officers belonging to the same class.

Amongst them were two other Colonels, one a gruff old soldier, Abdel-el-al, and the other Ahmed Arabi, subsequently Arabi Pasha.

These three, afterwards known as 'the Colonels,' were joined by Mahmoud Sami Pasha, a politician, and, thus associated, they formed the leaders of what began to be known as the 'National Party.'

As Arabi forms one of the chief actors in the events which followed, some details relating to him may not be out of place here.

In person Arabi is a big burly specimen of the fellah type. His features are large and prominent, and his face, though stern, has a good-natured expression. He was born about the year 1840, in the village of Heyha, in the Province of Charkieh, in Lower Egypt. His father was a fellah possessing a few acres of land, and working it himself. Arabi was one of four sons, and he got such education as could be afforded by the village school. In due time he was drafted by conscription into the army, and became an officer. At Said Pasha's death he was a Captain and one of the officers of the guard at the Palace at Cairo. He was once rather noisy under the Palace windows, and Ismail Pasha, exclaiming that he was more noisy than the big drum and less useful, ordered him to be removed and to receive punishment.

This was his first grievance against Ismail, and it induced Arabi to join a secret society of native officers, of which Ali Roubi was the leader. The objects this society proposed to itself were the abolition of the invidious favouritism shown to Circassian officers, and the deposition of Ismail, the sovereign.

War broke out between Egypt and Abyssinia; Arabi was in charge of the transports at Massowah, and a charge of corruption being made against him, he fell into disgrace. This fact strengthened his dislike to Ismail and the Circassian officers, and with time lying idle on his hands, he took to attending lectures at the religious university, known as the Mosque el Hazar, where he acquired a certain degree of eloquence superior to that of most persons in his position. After a time, Ismail, always working to increase the army, allowed him to join a regiment, and he resumed his connexion with the secret society, and soon became the head of it. One of its members informed Ali Moubarek (a member of the Cabinet), of the aims and intentions of the secret society, and he told the Khedive, upon which Ismail sent for some of the chiefs, and Arabi, Ali Roubi, and Toulba waited on him. They went as his enemies in fear and trembling, and left as his friends; seventy native officers were in one day made Lieutenant-Colonels, including Arabi and his two friends. Arabi, in addition, received the high honour of having one of the Khedivial slaves as his wife.

When the question of the deposition of Ismail came to the front, Arabi took a formal oath to defend him with his life, but forty-eight hours after went to do obeisance to Tewfik as the new Khedive of Egypt.

The latter let it be known that there was a tacit amnesty for the past, and made Arabi a full Colonel.

Of Arabi's mental gifts, it is impossible to form a high estimate. Ignorant of any language but his own, his forte seemed to be the enunciating of any number of quotations from the Koran quite regardless of their relevancy. He had, however, original ideas at times, and must be credited, at all events, with the quality of sincerity. To Europeans and European influences he was strongly opposed. On one occasion he presided at a meeting of natives assembled for the purpose of founding a free school at Zag-a-Zig. He pointed out the changes which European civilisation had wrought in Egypt, and observed that 'before the native was brought in contact with Europe, he was content to ride on a donkey, to wear a blue gown, and to drink water, whereas now he must drive in a carriage, wear a Stambouli coat, and drink champagne. Europeans,' he said, ' were ahead of us, but why? Is it because they are stronger, better, or more enduring than we? No; it is only because they are better taught. Let us then be educated, and the boasted supremacy of the Christians will disappear.' The result of this appeal was a large subscription, and the school was established.

Mahmoud Sami Pasha, unlike his associates, was not a 'fellah,' but of Turkish descent. He was a man of consummate cunning, and of great personal ambition; basing his calculations on the power of the military movement, and not believing in the disposition of the English and French to resist it, he proposed to use the simple-minded Arabi and his friends as a means of bringing himself into power.

The *dénouement* was brought about by agitators among the fellaheen officers, who objected to a proposed reduction of the army from twelve regiments to six; and petitions on the subject were presented, not only to the Minister of War, but to the Khedive himself, setting forth all their grievances, and demanding that an Egyptian should be appointed Minister of War. Osman Riffki, the actual Minister of War, could not brook this, and at a Cabinet Council, at which Mahmoud Sami was present, it was decided to put the three ringleaders, Ali Fehmy, Abdel-el-al, and Arabi under arrest. According to Arabi a steamer was in readiness to take the prisoners away, and iron boxes had been prepared in which they were to be placed and dropped into the Nile, but of this there is no proof beyond his statement.

Mahmoud Sami took care to warn 'the Colonels' of what was going to happen, and it was arranged that if they did not return from Kasr-el-Nil Barracks, to which they were summoned, the soldiers of their respective regiments should march down and liberate them.

It turned out exactly as provided for. On arriving at the Barracks on the 1st February, 1881, 'the Colonels' found themselves before a court-martial, but hardly had the proceedings begun, before a turbulent crowd of soldiery broke in, upset tables and chairs, ill-treated the members of the Court, and carried off the prisoners in triumph to the Palace. Here the three Colonels interviewed the Khedive, and demanded the substitution of Mahmoud Sami for Osman Riffki as Minister of War, an increase of the army to 18,000 men, and the establishment of a new system of promotion, which should exclude favouritism to the Circassian officers. Tewfik, having no force wherewith to resist, yielded. Mahmoud Sami was made Minister of War, and two decrees were issued, one increasing the pay of the troops, and the other directing an inquiry into the organization of the army.

CHAPTER V.

TRIUMPH OF THE ARMY.

Military Insubordination—Mahmoud Sami replaced by Daoud Pasha—
Fears of the Military Leaders—Dispersal of the Mutinous Regiments—
Military Outbreak of the 9th September, 1881—Sir Auckland Colvin—
Mr. Cookson—Demands of the Army—Apprehensions of Arabi and his
Colleagues—The Khedive Tewfik.

MATTERS progressed for some time pretty quietly after the events above referred to; but in July of the same year two incidents occurred, which were followed by important results.

An artilleryman was run over and killed in the streets of Alexandria. His comrades bore the dead body to the Palace, and forced an entrance in defiance of the orders of their officers. They were tried, and the ringleaders were condemned to severe sentences.

Next, nineteen Circassian officers brought charges against the colonel of their regiment, Abdul-el-Al, already mentioned. The charges were inquired into and found to be unfounded, whereupon the nineteen officers were removed from the active list of the army, but were restored subsequently by order of the Khedive.

This action of His Highness gave great umbrage to 'the Colonels,' who believed that the order was given with a view to encourage the insubordination of the officers towards them; and a letter was written by 'the Colonels' to the Minister of War, contrasting the leniency shown towards the nineteen officers with the severity towards the soldiers in the case of the artilleryman.

The Khedive by this time had become completely dissatisfied with his new Minister of War, and alarmed at the bearing of the Colonels. He determined to see if energetic measures would not be successful, and appointed his brother-in-law, Daoud Pasha, a Circassian, to the Ministry of War, in the place of Mahmoud Sami. Measures were at the same time taken for getting the disaffected regiments out of Cairo.

These steps were viewed with the greatest possible dissatisfaction by Arabi and his colleagues. Not only so, but they began to entertain considerable fear for their own personal safety.

A story had got abroad that the Khedive had obtained a secret 'Fetwah,' or Decree, from the Sheikh-ul-Islam, condemning them to death for high treason. There was no foundation for the story, but it was currently believed. Under these circumstances, all the chief officers signed a declaration of loyalty to the Khedive and his Government. Their next step was to organize the demonstration of the 9th September, 1881.

The chief object sought by Arabi and his party at this moment was the replacing of the Turco-Circassian Government by one which would be completely under their control. In this way they hoped to rid the country of the energetic Riaz Pasha and his friends the foreign Controllers.

The immediate origin of the disturbance was the order given by the Minister of War, in concert with Riaz, for the removal from Cairo to Alexandria of the Third Regiment of the Line, of which Arabi was the Colonel.

On the 9th September the Minister of War received a communication from Arabi, informing him that the troops in Cairo were going at 3.30 in the afternoon to the Palace of Abdin to obtain from the Khedive—

1. 'The dismissal of the Ministry which had sold the country to the English.
2. 'A Representative Chamber.
3. 'The execution of the Order raising the strength of the army to 18,000 men.'

The first news that Tewfik had of the proposed demonstration was from a farm-servant, who on the same morning came to the Palace and tremblingly told him that the troops were coming to Cairo from Abbassieh to put His Highness to death.

When the terms of Arabi's communication were laid before the Khedive none of his Ministers were present. In the absence of Sir Edward Malet, the British Consul-General (then in Europe), Tewfik consulted the British Controller, Mr. (afterwards Sir Auckland) Colvin, who with characteristic boldness invited the Khedive to take the initiative.

Two regiments were said by Riaz Pasha to be faithful. Mr. Colvin advised the Khedive to summon them to Abdin Square, with all the military police available, place himself at their head, and when Arabi arrived to arrest him. At this moment Mr. Cookson, the acting British Consul-General, arrived on the scene and expressed his concurrence in these views.

Mr. Colvin accompanied the Khedive in a separate carriage, drove to the Abdin Barracks, where the first regiment of the Guard turned out, and with the warmest protestations swore loyalty. The same thing occurred with the soldiers at the Citadel, though it was ascertained that the troops there had, previously to the Khedive's arrival, been signalling to Arabi's regiment at Abbassieh. The Khedive then announced his intention of driving to the Abbassieh Barracks, some three miles distant. It was already 3.30 p.m., and Mr. Colvin urged him to proceed at once to Abdin Square, taking with him the Citadel regiment, and when he arrived, placing himself at the head of that regiment, the regiment of the Guard, and the military police. Tewfik, however, wavered. Either he desired to assure himself of the support of more of his soldiers, or more probably he desired to put off the critical moment as long as possible. He decided to drive to Abbassieh. It was a long drive, and when he got there, he found that Arabi had marched with his regiment to Cairo. The opportunity which Mr. Colvin sought of anticipating Arabi's movements was therefore lost. The carriages were turned round, and on entering the town, took a long *détour*, and arrived at Abdin Palace by a side door. The Khedive desired to enter the Palace, but, on Mr. Colvin's entreaty, consented to come out into the square. They went together, followed at a considerable distance by Stone Pasha (an American officer in the service of the Khedive), and by half-a-dozen native and European officers. The square was entirely filled with soldiers, some 4000 in number, with thirty guns drawn up round it.

The Khedive advanced firmly into the square towards a little knot of officers and men (some of whom were mounted) in the centre. Mr. Colvin said to him, 'When Arabi presents himself, tell him to give up his sword, and follow you. Then go the round of the regiments, address each separately, and give them the " order to disperse." ' The soldiers all this time were standing in easy attitudes, chatting, laughing, rolling up cigarettes, and eating pistachio nuts, looking, in fact, as little like desperate mutineers as could well be imagined. They apparently were there in obedience only to orders, and, without being either loyal or disloyal, might almost be regarded as disinterested spectators.

Arabi approached on horseback; the Viceroy called

out to him to dismount. He did so, and came forward on foot with several others, and a guard with fixed bayonets, and saluted. As he advanced, Mr. Colvin said to the Khedive, 'Now is your moment!' He replied, 'We are between four fires. We shall be killed.' Mr. Colvin said, 'Have courage!' Tewfik again wavered, he turned for counsel to a native officer at his side, and repeated to Mr. Colvin, 'What can I do,—we are between four fires?' He then told Arabi to sheathe his sword. Arabi did so at once, his hand trembling so with nervousness that he could scarcely get the weapon back into its scabbard. The moment was lost. Instead of following Mr. Colvin's advice, and arresting Arabi on the spot, a step which would at once have put an end to the whole disturbance, the Khedive turned towards him, and commenced to parley.

He demanded what was the meaning of the demonstration. Arabi replied by enumerating the above points, adding, that the army had come there on behalf of the Egyptian people to enforce them, and would not retire until they were conceded. The Khedive addressed Mr. Colvin, and said, 'You hear what he says?' Mr. Colvin answered that it was not befitting for the Sovereign to discuss questions of this kind with Colonels, and suggested his retiring to the Palace, leaving it to Mr. Colvin to speak to the military leaders. The Khedive did so, and Mr. Colvin remained for about an hour explaining to them the gravity of the situation for themselves, and urging them to withdraw the troops whilst there was yet time.

At this moment, Mr. Cookson, General Goldsmith, Director of the Daira, and the acting Austrian Consul-General arrived, and Mr. Colvin left the continuation of the negotiations to Her Majesty's representative. The latter proved fully equal to the occasion, and pointed out to Arabi the great risk which he and those with him incurred by the menacing attitude they had assumed. He told him that if they persisted in assuming the government of the country, the army must be prepared to meet the united forces of the Sublime Porte and of the European Powers, both of whom were too much interested in the welfare and tranquillity of Egypt to allow the country to descend through a military government to anarchy. Arabi answered that the army was there to secure by arms the liberties of the Egyptian people. Mr. Cookson answered that the Khedive and Europe could not recognise a barely military revolt as the expression of the will of the Egyptian people, and added that even now if the troops were withdrawn, any representations presented in a proper manner would be attended to, and he (Mr. Cookson) would guarantee Arabi's personal safety and that of his associates.

Arabi was civil, but firmly refused the course proposed. He insisted on the adoption of the three points, viz., the dismissal of the Ministry, the convocation of the National Assembly, and the increase of the army to 18,000 men. Mr. Cookson communicated the result of the interview to the Khedive and Mr. Colvin, but found them quite unable to suggest any method of getting out of the difficulty, adding, that from expressions let fall by the crowd, he was convinced that the only concession to which the officers attached any real importance, was that of the dismissal of the Ministry. His Highness, after a short conference with Riaz Pasha, consented to this, on the understanding that the other points demanded should be in suspense until the Porte could be communicated with.

Arabi formally accepted these terms, insisting only that no member of the Khedive's family should be included in the new Cabinet, and that the Minister of War should not be a Circassian. On these conditions Arabi promised to withdraw the troops.

This, however, was not effected until after a letter had been drawn up and signed, announcing the dismissal of the Ministry, and the nomination of Cherif Pasha as the new Premier.

After this Arabi entered the Palace, and made his submission to the Khedive, and the soldiers with their bands playing, and amid loud cheers for the 'Effendina' (sovereign), retired to their barracks.

By eight o'clock all was over, and Cairo had relapsed into its ordinary tranquillity.

When the events of the day are considered, it is difficult to know which to admire most, the courage and coolness of Mr. Colvin in striving to induce the Khedive to adopt an energetic line of conduct, or the tact and good sense of Mr. Cookson in carrying out the delicate and difficult negotiation, by which the crisis was brought to a close. Both of our countrymen acted, it will be remembered, at some risk to themselves, and the subsequent decorations* which they received were never better merited.

With regard to the *émeute* itself, the third, it will be remarked, of its kind, it was on a larger scale than any previously organized, and was, as events showed, correspondingly more successful. The rebellious troops were, indeed, quieted as on former occasions, but only by concessions which went far to place the whole civil government of the country under irregular military control. One striking feature of the movement

* Mr. Colvin was created a K.C.M.G. and Mr. Cookson a C.B. for their services on this occasion.

was the odd mixture of boldness and timidity displayed by the leader of the movement, Arabi himself. There is reason to believe that in directing it he was influenced to no small extent by a continued, though unfounded, belief that he was marked down for the vengeance of the Khedive, and that the first step towards carrying this out was the dispersal of the disaffected regiments. That this was the impression of the rebel leader, appears from a letter to the Minister of War, which Arabi wrote on the day previous to the demonstration, and which was to the following effect :—

'15 *Shawal*, 1298.

'I, together with the officers and men, have ascertained that an order has been issued by your Excellency to the 3rd regiment of Infantry to proceed to Alexandria, and as such an order is intended to disperse the military power with a view to vengeance upon us, and as we cannot deliver up ourselves to death, we hereby give notice to your Excellency that all the regiments will assemble to-day at 9 o'clock Arabic time (3.30 P.M.), in the Abdin Square, for the purpose of deciding this question. We shall ourselves write to all the foreign agents what is necessary. We further inform your Excellency that no regiment will march in obedience to the orders given by your Excellency until ample security be given for the lives and interests of ourselves and our relatives.

'I therefore address you the present for your information, and in order to confirm the verbal remonstrances I made to your Excellency on your appointment to office against the intended tearing asunder of the military power. It is therefore hoped that the order given to the regiment to march may be countermanded.'

With regard to the attitude assumed by the Khedive on the occasion, considerable allowance must be made.

Tewfik in the lifetime of his father had never, or at all events until the latest period of Ismail's reign, been allowed to come to the front. He was, therefore, the less fitted for dealing with a crisis of so formidable a character as that of the 9th September. Born of one of Ismail's female slaves in the year 1853, he had always been kept in the background,

TRIUMPH OF THE ARMY. 43

Whilst Tewfik's brothers were sent to Europe to be educated he himself was kept in Cairo, and lived in quiet obscurity. Whilst they were made much of, both at home and abroad, Tewfik remained quietly cultivating his farm at Abbassieh.*

The difference in developing the character, and dispositions of the princes, was natural enough, and yet the present ruler of Egypt is in many respects in no way inferior to the other members of his family; he has at times shown himself not wanting in courage. He possesses a remarkable degree of intelligence; although a strict Mahometan, he is the husband of only one wife, and does not smoke. He is devotedly attached to his home, and manages his household on the European plan, free from ostentation and extravagance. Determined to avoid in bringing up his children the error perpetrated towards himself, he has sent his sons to Europe to be educated. In appearance he somewhat resembles his father, and like him in manner and bearing is every inch a gentleman.

Unlike Ismail, however, Tewfik has been found wanting in energy and determination.

With either Ismail, or his grandfather, Mehemet Ali, the demonstration of the 9th September would have been impossible. With Ismail, supposing such an event could have taken place, the end would not have been far off. The fate of Ismail Pasha Saddyk, known as the 'Mofettish,' sufficiently shows the means by which Arabi would have been disposed of.†

With Mehemet Ali the procedure would been yet more summary. The report of a pistol would have

---

* Tewfik went to Europe in 1870, but was recalled when he had only got as far as Vienna.

† Saddyk was taken by Ismail in his carriage to the Palace at Ghezireh, and was never after seen alive.

been heard, and Arabi would have rolled lifeless on the square of Abdin. A volley of musketry would have dispersed his followers, and the incident would have been closed. Tewfik, with his genial kindly disposition, was not the man to adopt either of the above expedients, and, as has been seen, Arabi triumphed.

CHAPTER VI.

SUPPORT OF ENGLAND AND FRANCE.

Action of the 'Chamber of Notables'—Cherif Pasha forms a Ministry with Mahmoud Sami as Minister of War—Cherif informed of the support of the English and French Governments—Submission of the Military Leaders—Proposed Intervention of the Sultan—The Turkish Envoys—Dispersal of the disaffected Regiments—Action of the Turkish Envoys—The British and French Ironclads—Withdrawal of the Envoys—Departure of the Ironclads.

GREAT difficulty was at first experienced in getting Cherif Pasha to undertake the formation of a Ministry. His idea was that it was inconsistent with a due regard for his own reputation for him to pose before the world as the accomplice of the mutinous soldiery, and at one time, after an interview with Arabi, Cherif positively declined. Meanwhile, meetings of the officers were held in which the most violent appeared to have the upper hand, and the belief that they had nothing to fear from Turkish intervention, emboldened them to reject an ultimatum of Cherif, which was that, on condition of his undertaking the government, and guaranteeing the personal safety of the leaders, they should withdraw their regiments to certain posts assigned to them. Public opinion, more particularly amongst the Europeans, became much alarmed, and the Khedive declared himself ready to yield everything in order to save public security. On the 13th September, however, things took an unexpected turn for the better. Arabi, at the suggestion of Mahmoud Sami, who hoped to render Cherif impossible, and to get himself nominated in his place, summoned to Cairo the members of the 'Chamber of Notables.' Cherif, by his action hereinbefore detailed with regard to the Commission of Inquiry, had acquired a good deal of popularity among the class to which the Notables belonged, and at their first meeting found arguments to induce them to adopt a tone hostile to Arabi and his friends, whom they told to attend to the army and mind their own business, leaving politics to those whose duty it was to look after them. The Notables went even further, and signed an address to Cherif entreating him to form a Ministry, and giving their personal guarantee that if he consented, the Army should engage to absolute submission to his orders. Arabi, it will be remembered, had professed to act on behalf of the Egyptian people, and the attitude of the Notables was a severe check to him, or rather to Mahmoud Sami, who was pulling the wires. This last individual, seeing that the Notables were playing into the hand of Cherif, at once declared himself the partizan of the latter, and of the Chamber, and as a consequence Sami was reappointed Minister of War in the Cabinet which Cherif was eventually persuaded to form. Mahmoud Sami was thus once more in a position to help his military friends as well as to guide their efforts in any direction which his own interests might require.

Notwithstanding that Cherif was the nominee of the Army, and was supported by the Chamber, he did not take office until he had, in addition, been assured of the support of the English and French Governments, who thus advanced one step further towards intervention.

The military leaders were so much struck with the attitude of the Notables that they signed a document (not the first of the kind it will be remarked) declaring their absolute submission. They insisted only on two conditions, one being the reinstatement of Mahmoud Sami, and the other the execution of the military law recommended by the Army Commission.

On the 14th September the new Ministry was gazetted, and a few days after steps were taken for the dispersal of the disaffected regiments in the provinces.

On the representation to the Sultan of the disturbance of the 9th September, and on his learning that in view of the prevailing alarm, England and France proposed despatching each an ironclad to Alexandria, His Majesty showed such an amount of readiness to exercise his sovereign rights over Egypt in restoring tranquillity, as to excite the suspicion of the Western Powers. He even offered to depose Tewfik, and expressed a strong desire to send Turkish troops to the Delta. Both measures being opposed by the English and the French Governments, they were given up, and the despatch of a Turkish Mission instead was talked of.

This met with almost equal opposition, and the idea was believed to have been abandoned, when early in October news suddenly reached Cairo that the Porte was sending two Commissioners to Egypt.

This was the more unexpected, inasmuch as a fortnight previously the Turkish Government had informed Lord Dufferin that as the Egyptian incident was at an end, there was no longer any question of sending a Mission to Egypt.

The probability that the Turkish envoys would be mixed up with intrigues with the different political parties in Egypt, did not escape the attention of the British and French Foreign Offices, and recommendations were sent to the Egyptian Government to treat the envoys with all respect, but to refuse firmly any interference on their part in the internal administration of the country. At the same time, the Porte was urged to shorten their stay in Egypt as much as possible.

The officials in question, Ali Nizami Pasha, and Ali Fuad Bey, arrived at Alexandria on the 6th October, 1881.

On the same day, Arabi and his regiment left Cairo for the military station of El Ouady. Colonel Abdel-el-Al had, it may be observed, taken his regiment of blacks off to Damietta, on the 1st October.

Before Arabi left with his three battalions, he was received by the Khedive, whom he assured of his respect and entire devotion. When one remembers how often Arabi had gone through this ceremony, one can scarcely help thinking that Tewfik must by this time have begun to get a little tired of it. Arabi, on his way to the railway station, passed through the principal thoroughfares of Cairo, being everywhere received with enthusiasm, and was finally carried from his horse to the railway carriage. Before leaving, he made speeches to the troops at Abdin, Kasr-el-Nil, the Citadel, and Abbassieh, respectively, in which he reminded them that 'they were members of a great family called the army, that every family had its duties to fulfil; that the duties of the army consisted in the general welfare of the country, and that to fulfil these duties union and concord were necessary. He exhorted them to remain always united, and to draw even more tightly if possible, those bonds of fraternity of which they had already given such striking examples. He pointed out that a new era had dawned for Egypt, and that the moment for development and prosperity had arrived. He begged his men to render homage to the excellent qualities of the new ministers, and especially of Mahmoud Sami, the Minister of War.'

Finally, after repeatedly pointing out that 'obedience

in a soldier was the first of virtues, he declared that as long as he possessed a drop of blood, or a living breath, both should belong to his beloved Sovereign.'

Notwithstanding that after the departure of the disaffected troops, Cairo appeared restored to tranquillity, the Turkish envoys were anxious that their mission should not prove altogether abortive, and Ali Nizami Pasha in his turn inspected and harangued the troops. He told them that, 'having been a soldier for forty-two years, he had never heard of an act of insubordination similar to that which had occurred.' This, considering the difference between the Turkish and Egyptian armies, was probably true enough; but the statement did not produce the effect intended, as one of the Colonels made a reply, in which he attributed the action of the army to the injustice of the late Ministry, but stated that now the soldiers were satisfied and would not again commit acts of insubordination.

With this qualified success, the envoys had to content themselves. Though treated with the greatest respect, they were closely watched and rigorously prevented from doing what they were probably sent to do, namely, interfering with the administration. Their departure from Egypt, an event which both the English and the French Governments wished to bring about as soon as possible, was accelerated by a little diplomatic *coup* characteristic of Lord Dufferin, the ambassador at Constantinople.

As already stated, the English and the French Governments, shortly after the events of the 9th September, decided that each should send an ironclad to Alexandria. Our allies, ever ready to act, had the *Alma* on the spot, only a few days after the decision was arrived at. It was not, however, till the 19th October, or nearly six weeks after the disturbance, that the English ship of war *Invincible*, could be got to Alexandria. Nevertheless, if she was late in arriving, she made up for it, as will be seen, by being early in leaving.

The Sultan, on hearing of the intended despatch of the vessels, was much perturbed, and remonstrated with Lord Dufferin, pointing out that such a demonstration was not based on any treaty rights, and was calculated to cause agitation and disturbance.

He also added, that 'information received from the Turkish emissaries, proved that perfect order existed in Egypt, and the maintenance of the *status quo* was assured.'

In making the admissions contained in the latter part of this communication, the proverbial wiliness of the Turk was for once at fault. Lord Dufferin was not slow to take advantage of the slip, and replied that 'Her Majesty's Government had learned with satisfaction His Imperial Majesty's sentiments in favour of the maintenance of the *status quo*, and his opinion that all disorder was at an end; that the situation being such as His Majesty described, the presence of his envoys appeared no longer necessary.' The ambassador added, that their withdrawal would imply the termination of the incident, and would naturally be followed by the withdrawal of the ships. The check which Abdul Hamid received in this attempt to assert his authority in Egypt, was not, as will be seen later on, sufficient to prevent his subsequently renewing it. Even this time, although worsted in diplomacy by Lord Dufferin, he was not willing to give in without a struggle, if only to save appearances, and Musurus Pasha, the Ottoman representative in London, was instructed to declare that it was impossible for the Sultan to withdraw his mission in face of the menace implied by the presence of ships of war. This was followed by a reply, that so long as the presence of the envoys in Egypt was evidence of the abnormal state of affairs, the presence of ships at Alexandria could only be regarded in the light of a proper and necessary precaution for the safety of British residents.

Eventually, the Sultan had to yield, and it was arranged that the ironclads should leave on the day that the envoys should embark. There was a difficulty in carrying out this understanding literally, owing to the delay in sending the *Invincible*, which, on arriving on the 19th, met the envoys already steaming out to sea. However, both ships of war left on the 20th.

CHAPTER VII.

TROUBLES WITH THE NOTABLES.

The Chamber of Notables—Discontent in the Country—The Control—
The Moukabeleh—European Officials—Suspicions entertained of England
and France—The Native Press—Further Military Insubordination—
Emin Bey—Sultan Pasha—Claim of the Chamber to vote the Budget
—Arabi appointed Sub-Minister of War—Amendments in the Organic
Law of the Chamber—Ministerial Crisis—Dismissal of the Ministry
demanded.

MEANWHILE the elections for the Chamber of Notables, which had been convoked by the Khedive for the 23rd December, were proceeding.

The Chamber was called together under an old law of Ismail's time made in 1866, under which the Notables had very limited functions. They were in fact simply a consultative Chamber, with power only to discuss such matters as might be brought before them by the advisers of the Government; nevertheless, to prevent any misunderstanding, Cherif Pasha, in his address to the Khedive asking for the convocation of the Notables, thought it as well to point out that the conventions and institutions created by the financial situation could not be discussed anymore than the laws and decrees which rendered them binding, and, in short, that the Chamber was only to give its advice when it was asked for.

The doctrines thus enunciated, though representing the situation correctly enough, were far from finding universal acceptance.

Apart from the military movement there was no doubt a widespread feeling of discontent in the country at this time. Ismail's merciless exactions, and the pressure of foreign money-lenders, had given rise to a desire to limit the arbitrary power of the Khedive, and, above all, to abolish the Anglo-French Control, which was considered as ruling the country simply for the benefit of the foreign bondholders. The Control was further hated by the large landowners, because the law of liquidation (with which the Controllers in the minds of the people were associated) had in a measure sacrificed their claims for compensation in respect of the cancelling of the forced loan known as the 'Moukabeleh,' and it was still more detested by the Pashas and native officials, because it interfered with the reckless squandering of public money, and the many opportunities for corruption by which they had so long benefited.

In addition to this, there was a great deal of irritation at the number of highly-paid European officials, which the reformed *régime*, inaugurated in the latter days of Ismail, involved.

The total number of these was 1325, and the aggregate amount of their salaries was 373,704*l*. E. The natives regarded these figures only, and saw in them a grievance. It never occurred to them to consider that since these functionaries had been in office many of them had saved the country the amount of their salaries twenty times over, by the economies they had effected, besides introducing order and regularity where such things were never known before. In addition to the soreness with which the native mind regarded the employment of foreigners in the government service, there was not a little suspicion, particularly among the lower classes, that what was occurring was only part of a plan for handing the country over to Europeans. The examples lately set by England, with regard to Cyprus, and by France in Tunis, were, it must be owned, but little calculated to inspire confidence in the political morality of either of these two Powers.

The prevailing irritation was kept alive by the native press, which began to indulge in the most violent abuse of Europeans.

The army, too, continued to show signs of insubordination in many ways. To add to the difficulties of the situation, the colonels of the regiments which had been expressly sent away into the provinces had acquired the habit of coming back to the capital, and joining in the many intrigues on foot. A native named Emin Bey, an adherent of the National Party, having given a fête in the Esbekieh Gardens, to celebrate the events of the 9th September, was arrested in a civil process as a fraudulent bankrupt. Arabi, hearing of this, went to the Minister of Justice, and obtained the man's release, under a threat that if it were refused he would be liberated by force.

This was followed by a demand by the Minister of War for an augmentation of the budget for war by 280,000*l*. E., in order to increase the army to 18,000 men, the maximum allowed by the Sultan's Firman. Owing to the resistance of the Controllers, an increase of only 154,000*l*. E. over the 368,000*l*. E. already allowed for 1881 was agreed to.

Under these circumstances, the Chamber of Notables assembled on the 25th December, 1881.

The President of the Chamber, Sultan Pasha, was a man of moderate views, and a large and influential landowner in Upper Egypt.*

---

* He was subsequently created a K.C.M.G. by Her Majesty's Government.

TROUBLES WITH THE NOTABLES. 55

The earliest trouble arose from the demand of the Chamber of Notables that the Organic Law, under which they were assembled, should be modified so as to give the Notables power to vote the budget so far as it related to such of the revenues as were not assigned to the public debt. This was opposed by Cherif Pasha and the Controllers, on the ground that it would deprive them of all hold upon the finances.

The claim of the Chamber, though plausible enough at first sight, was really, if granted, calculated to infringe all the international arrangements for the public debt. It was obvious that if the Chamber had the power and chose to vote an extravagant budget so far as related to the *unassigned* revenues, the administration of the country could not be carried on, national bankruptcy might ensue, and the collection of the *assigned* revenues would become impossible.

However, not only did the Chamber, which was now entirely under the influence of Mahmoud Sami, refuse to give way on the question of the budget, but it demanded that the Organic Law should be further amended by giving the Notables other privileges, namely, the right to control the acts of public functionaries, to initiate legislation, and to hold the Ministers responsible to the Chamber. By getting the Notables to make these demands, which he knew could not be accepted, Mahmoud Sami's object was to bring about a crisis which could only end in the downfall of Cherif's Cabinet. He had already persuaded Cherif to make Arabi Sub-Minister of War, under the pretext of securing him on the side of the Ministry, and so neutralising the influence which the army was exercising over the Chamber. In reality, the appointment only afforded Mahmoud Sami and Arabi increased facilities for intriguing against Cherif. The result was soon seen.

The amendments to the Organic Law, which were calculated to give the Chamber greater powers than those conferred by the most liberal of Constitutions, were inadmissible on many grounds. Were there no other objection, there was the insurmountable one that the Sultan had already refused a Constitution to other parts of his dominions, and would certainly oppose its being granted to Egypt. To put it shortly, the amendments after being submitted to the English and French Governments were declared unacceptable.

This at once brought about a crisis, and the Chamber, on the 2nd February, sent a deputation to the Khedive to require him to summon a new Ministry.

CHAPTER VIII.

NEGOTIATIONS AND EXPLANATIONS.

Military Preparations—The Joint Note—M. Gambetta—The demand of the Porte for explanation—The Reply—Mons. Freycinet—France disinclined to intervene—Circular to the Powers—Effect of the Joint Note—Sir W. Gregory and Mr. Blunt—Alarm of the Khedive—Mahmoud Sami's Ministry.

AT the period referred to at the close of the last chapter, it was reported to the English and French Governments, that increased activity was being displayed in putting all the coast fortifications in an efficient state, and that the strength of the army was being augmented under the provisions of the new war budget.

These circumstances, taken in conjunction with the political events above recorded, led the English and French Governments to conclude that if the Khedive was to be maintained in power, the time was arising for them to think about doing something in Egypt. On the 20th of January, 1882, Sir Edward Malet wrote that 'armed intervention had become necessary if the refusal to allow the Chamber to vote the budget was to be agreed to, and yet it was impossible to do otherwise, as the measure only formed part of a complete scheme of revolution.' As far back as December 1881, Mons. Gambetta, then at the head of the French Ministry, had suggested that England and France should take 'joint action in Egypt to strengthen the authority of the Khedive, and to cut short intrigues at Constantinople, as well as to make the Porte feel that any undue interference on its part would not be tolerated.'

This proposal shortly after resulted in a Joint Note communicated by the English and the French representatives to the Khedive, in Cairo, on the 8th January, 1882. The Joint Note was to the effect that the English and French Governments considered the maintenance of His Highness upon the throne in the terms laid down by the Sultan's Firmans, and officially recognised by the two Governments, as alone able to guarantee for the present and the future good order and prosperity in Egypt, in which England and France were equally interested. It continued to say that the two Governments, being closely associated in the resolve to guard by their united efforts against all cause of complication, internal or external, which might menace the order of things established in Egypt, did not doubt that the assurance publicly given of their intention in this respect would tend to avert the dangers to which the Government of the Khedive might be exposed, and which would certainly find England and France united to oppose them.

The parentage of the Joint Note is attributable to the French Government, which, up to this time, seemed bent on retaining the lead which it had from the first taken in regard to Egyptian affairs. The wording of the document had been altered more than once to suit Lord Granville, now Foreign Secretary, who appears to have been not quite sure how far he was getting out of his depth in regard to Egyptian matters.

It was under the influence of some such misgiving, that Lord Lyons was instructed on the 6th January, 1882, in communicating to the French Government England's assent to the Note, to make the reservation that she must not be considered as thereby committing herself to *any particular mode of action*, if action should be found necessary. In reply, Mons. Gambetta, by a despatch dated the following day, stated, that he observed with pleasure, 'that the only reservation of the Government of the Queen was as to the *mode of action* to be employed, and that this was a reservation in which he participated.'

When one sees how, later on, when action became necessary, the attitude of the two countries became reversed, the extreme reluctance of the English Government to move at this time seems curious enough, especially when it is contrasted with the continued readiness of France to come forward in the interval. The explanation is that Mons. Gambetta, with his clear statesmanlike intellect, foreseeing that some sort of intervention would become necessary, was determined that it should be limited to that of England and France to the exclusion of Turkey, and so long as he remained in power boldly shaped his policy with that object. The English Government, on the other hand, had throughout no real settled policy with regard to Egypt. Their first idea was to have no intervention at all ; they hoped that things would mend of themselves. When they found this was not likely to be the case, the idea of a Turkish intervention found favour. France, however, was resolutely opposed to this, and to allow the latter power to take isolated action, as indeed she appeared disposed to do if thwarted, was open to serious objections. To avoid such a catastrophe the English Government found themselves under the necessity of following, for the time being, the lead of Mons. Gambetta. However this may have been, England, by taking part in the Joint Note, assumed a definite position relative to Egypt, and, throwing off all hesitation as to 'interference with the internal affairs of the country,' pledged herself jointly with France to support the Khedive against all enemies from within or without.

The first to take offence at the Joint Note was naturally enough the Sultan, who caused Lord Granville to be informed that the Porte considered that sending the Khedive any such communication except through itself was highly improper. The Sultan added that 'To protect the immunities granted to Egypt, and to preserve the order and prosperity of that province, was the sincere wish and interest of the Porte, whose efforts had till then always been directed to that end, and that there were no circumstances in Egypt which could serve as a motive for any foreign assurances of the kind made.' Finally, the Turkish Ambassador requested that the two Powers would give an explanation of what they meant. At the same time the Sultan sent a Circular to the other Powers, protesting against the action of England and France.

Lord Granville now began to doubt whether he had not gone a little too far, and drafted an answer to the Porte of an apologetic character. The tone of the proposed reply was somewhat of the kind that a schoolboy taken to task for an act of impertinence towards his master might be expected to give. Substantially, it was that the two Powers did not mean anything at all.

The draft despatch began by disclaiming any doubt whatever as to the sovereignty of the Sultan over Egypt. It proceeded to declare that there was no change in the policy of Her Majesty's Government, which was as anxious as ever for the continuance of the sovereignty of the Porte, and for the maintenance of the liberties and administrative independence secured to Egypt by the Sultan's Firmans. Having paid the Porte the above compliments, the despatch disclaimed all ambitious views with regard to the country (of which, by the way, the Sultan had been careful never to accuse the two Powers), but said that they could never be indifferent to events which might plunge Egypt into anarchy, and that it was with a view to warding off such a catastrophe that Her Majesty's Government thought it advisable, in conjunction with the French Government, to forward a declaration showing the accord of the two in carrying out the policy described. The despatch finally pointed out that the form of the Note was not a new one, and that similar declarations had been on special occasions made to the Khedive without calling forth any remonstrance from the Porte.

Mons. Gambetta, however, viewed the matter in a different spirit. Having once gone forward he was not disposed to draw back. He had, moreover, the interests of the large body of French bondholders to protect. He at first objected that no explanation of the Joint Note at all was necessary, and that any attempt to explain it would only tend to encourage the military party. Seeing, however, that Lord Granville was determined to reply, Mons. Gambetta insisted on certain modifications in the despatch. Amongst them he suggested that the assertion of the Porte that there were no circumstances that could justify the steps taken by England and France, should be answered, and suggested that it should be pointed out, first, that the authority of the Khedive had been modified and diminished; second, that the Chamber of Notables had arrogated to itself the right of interfering with matters expressly exempted from its jurisdiction by the Khedive's Decree; and third, that the Chamber had aimed at setting aside arrangements to which Egypt was bound by international engagements with England and France.

Lord Granville once more yielded to what he had begun to recognise as the superior mind of the French statesman, and Gambetta's amendments were agreed to.

It was not until the 2nd February, however, that the reply to the Porte's remonstrance was actually sent off.

In the meantime the Gambetta Ministry had fallen, and from this moment dates a marked change in the attitude of the French Republic with regard to Egypt.

Mons. Freycinet, the successor to Gambetta, though agreeing to the amended reply to the Porte, cautiously inquired what meaning was to be attached to the reservation as to 'taking action' made by Her Majesty's Government in assenting to the original note.

Lord Granville, no longer under the influence of Mons. Gambetta, and apparently anxious to recede as far as possible from the somewhat bold position which he had been induced to adopt, answered, contrary to the plain words in which the reservation had been expressed, as well as to the meaning attributed to them by the latter, that Her Majesty's Government reserved to themselves the right to determine not merely the *particular mode of action* to be adopted in Egypt, but whether any action at all was necessary.

Mons. Freycinet, who was equally glad to back out, then plainly declared that he was disinclined to any armed intervention in Egypt, whether by France and England together, or by either separately. This announcement must have been a surprise to the British Government, which, after being led by France into sending the Joint Note, now began to discover that in the event of its becoming necessary to take any steps to carry it into effect, they could no longer count on her as an ally.

Under these circumstances, and feeling that the time when action would have to be taken might not be far off, Lord Granville addressed a Circular to the other Powers, requesting them to enter upon an exchange of views as to the best mode of dealing with the Egyptian Question.

The effect of the Joint Note upon the Porte has been stated. It only remains to consider its effect upon the Khedive and the Notables.

The Khedive received the assurances of protection given by England and France gratefully enough.

It was not so, however, with his Ministers, who, on the Joint Note being communicated on the 8th January, wanted, like the Sultan, to know what it meant.

On the 13th January Sir Edward Malet assured them that the Note was merely intended to convey to the Khedive the assurance of the friendship of the Powers, and that in point of fact it did not mean anything.

It is obvious that to produce any good effect on the Chamber and the National Party it was necessary that the Note should have been backed by the display of force, and this unfortunately was just what was wanting.

In short, England and France launched their threat without being prepared to follow it up by immediate action. It created great indignation on the part of the military leaders and in the Chamber; Arabi declared point-blank that any intervention on the part of England and France was inadmissible. Later on, when it was seen that the two Powers were not ready to act, but, on the contrary, were busy doing all they could to attenuate the step they had taken, the feeling of indignation gave way to one of contempt, very natural under the circumstances.

Amongst those who misled the chiefs of the National Party none were so conspicuous as two Englishmen, namely, Sir William Gregory, an ex-Colonial Governor, and Mr. Wilfred S. Blunt. Both these gentlemen had, whilst spending some months in Egypt, conceived a violent sympathy for the national movement. They had witnessed during their stay in the country numerous instances of misrule and oppression, and they regarded Arabi and his friends as the leaders of a genuine popular effort to secure political liberty and good government.

In addition to the assurances which they received from Sir William Gregory and Mr. Blunt, the leaders of the National Party were led to believe, and as has been seen not without reason, that England and France were not really agreed to do anything, much less to take any decisive step in the way of intervention; that the two Powers were far too jealous of each other; and that the Joint Note might be safely disregarded. The Arabists further clung to the hope that even were France and England allied, the other Powers would prevent their interference, and the protests which four of them, namely, Germany, Austria, Russia, and Italy, made at the time against any foreign interference in Egypt without their consent, certainly tended to confirm this view.

This was the condition of affairs on the 2nd February, when, as already stated, the deputation from the Chamber requested the Khedive to summon a new Ministry. Tewfik had by this time become thoroughly alarmed. The tonic effect produced by the Joint Note had gone off, and he was beginning to doubt how far he could rely on support from England and France.

He realised that by placing himself under the tutelage of the Western Powers he was injuring himself with the Porte, and he had daily proofs afforded him of his growing unpopularity with his subjects.

Under these circumstances he saw nothing for it but to yield. At the suggestion of the Chamber, Mahmoud Sami was directed to form a new Ministry, which he lost no time in doing, in conjunction with his confederate Arabi, who now filled the post of Minister of War.

CHAPTER IX.

PROGRESS OF EVENTS.

Mahmoud Sami's Ministry—The Control—Resignation of M. de Blignières—Warlike Preparations—Arabi created Pasha—Military Promotions—European Employés—Alleged Plot of Circassian Officers against Arabi—Court-martial and Sentence—Threats of Mahmoud Sami—Alarm in Cairo—Attitude of the Khedive—The Loyalty of the Bedouins—Sultan Pasha—The Ministry's offer to resign—Announcement of the expected Arrival of the Anglo-French Fleet—Submission of the Ministers—Arrival of the Fleet.

ALTHOUGH the Ministry of Mahmoud Sami was forced upon the Khedive, the position of the latter was at the time so hopeless that one must not be surprised at his endeavouring to make the best of it, and put a good face upon the matter. Accordingly, on the 4th February, 1882, Tewfik wrote to his new Premier that 'in accepting the task of forming a Cabinet he had given a fresh proof of his devotion and patriotism.' He added that 'if he had entrusted Mahmoud Sami with this mission it was because he knew the noble sentiments of which his Minister had already furnished so many proofs, and the letter ended by approving of the programme which the new Premier had drawn up.'

The programme in question referred to the arrangements for the Public Debt, including the Control, which were all spoken of as institutions which must be loyally supported by the Government. It spoke of the necessity for judicial and other reforms, and then passed on to the 'burning question' of the Chamber of Notables, and stated that the first act of the Ministry would be to obtain sanction for the Organic Law for the Chamber. This law, it was stated, would respect all rights and obligations, whether private or international, and would wisely determine the responsibility of Ministers towards the Chamber as well as the discussion of laws.

Mahmoud Sami's programme elicited from the English and French Controllers a memorandum, in which they very sensibly observed that it mattered very little whether or not the intention of attacking the Control was asserted, as by the very force of circumstances it became ineffectual when the Controllers found themselves no longer in the presence of the Khedive and of Ministers freely appointed by him, but of a Chamber and an army. It added that the Chamber under the influence of certain military chiefs did not hesitate to claim rights incompatible with the social condition of the country; it had gone so far as to compel the Khedive to change the Ministry which had his confidence, and under pressure of certain officers to impose on him the Minister of War as Prime Minister, and concluded with the significant words, — 'The Khedive's power no longer exists.'

After this it is not surprising that the Controllers resigned office. Sir Auckland Colvin was requested by the British Government to remain at his post and maintain 'an attitude of passive observation.' His French colleague was replaced by Mons. Brédif.

There is no doubt that the Controllers' view of the situation was only too just. With Arabi as Minister of War, and his co-conspirator, Mahmoud Sami, President of the Council, the country was simply under a military dictatorship.

Meanwhile the reserves of the Coast Artillery were called in and distributed amongst the coast fortifications, recruiting in the Provinces was being actively carried on, and ninety Krupp guns were ordered from Europe. Arabi had been created a Pasha by the Sultan, and the official journal, the *Moniteur Egyptien,* of the 15th March, in publishing the Decree, published another of the 9th March, by which five Colonels were promoted to the rank of General of Brigade; six Lieutenant-Colonels to that of Colonel, and sixteen 'Chefs de Bataillon' to the rank of Lieutenant-Colonel. By the end of the month 520 officers in all had been promoted.

In this way Arabi, who naturally took care to favour only those officers in whom he had implicit confidence, strengthened his hold on the army and ensured its support for his further operations.

This, however, was only part of the programme traced out by Arabi and his colleagues. The other was the replacement of foreigners in the various administrations by Egyptians, and the giving to the army many of the posts hitherto filled by civilians. The first was attempted by means of the appointment of a Commissioner of Inquiry into the 'Cadastre,' or Land Survey, and the Customs Department, both under the direction of Europeans; and the second, by the nomination of eight Colonels and Majors to various Governorships in the Provinces.

The National Party had now become complete masters of the situation. Notwithstanding this, a collision might for some little time have been averted but for an incident which occurred shortly after.

The differences between the Circassians and the native-born Egyptians in the army has been already touched upon. One peculiarity of the Arab race is their revengeful disposition. Arabi and his friends had, as already stated, met with rough usage at the hands of the Circassian party. Hence it followed that the first idea of the former on getting into power was to avenge themselves on their old enemies. This was carried out by the wholesale arrest of fifty Circassian officers, and of Osman Pasha Riffki, former Minister of War, on a charge of conspiracy to assassinate Arabi. It was also alleged that the plot comprised the deposition of the Khedive and the restoration of Ismail Pasha.

The prisoners were tried in secret by a Court-martial appointed by the military leaders, and of course found guilty. They were, it is said, subjected to torture to induce them to confess their complicity, and persons of respectability have testified that they heard at night shrieks of pain coming from the place where the prisoners were confined.

The sentence passed on forty of them, including Osman Pasha Riffki, was that of exile for life to the remotest limits of the Soudan. This was equivalent to a sentence of death as regards most of the prisoners.

It was necessary that the sentences should be confirmed by Decree of the Khedive, and he consulted Sir Edward Malet as to the course to be taken. The story of the plot was, there is reason to believe, purely imaginary. There is no doubt that there was considerable dissatisfaction amongst the Circassian officers, some 200 in number, who had been passed over in making the recent promotions, and it is a fact that a movement for petitioning the Khedive for a redress of their grievances was in progress, but that is about all. Having regard to these circumstances, and to the secrecy of the proceedings at the trial, as well as to the fact that the prisoners were undefended by counsel, the British Consul-General gave it as his opinion that the sentences should not be confirmed, but advised the Khedive to convoke the representatives of the Great Powers and be guided by their counsel. The French Consul-General, Mons. Sienkewitz, gave similar advice.

After some little hesitation, and after conferring with the other diplomatic agents of the Powers, the Khedive determined to exercise his prerogative without reference to his Ministers, and signed a decree commuting the sentences to simple banishment from Egypt, without loss of rank and honours.

This was a defiance of Mahmoud Sami, to which he was not disposed to submit. On the 10th May, the Khedive summoned the Consuls-General, and informed them that the President of the Council had insisted that this decree should be changed by condemning the prisoners to be struck off the rolls, and had threatened that his refusal would be followed by a general massacre of foreigners. The significance of this threat coming from Mahmoud Sami, the Minister who was in power when just a month later—namely, on the 11th June—the massacre of foreigners *did* take place in Alexandria, will probably be remarked.

It is, however, only fair to Mahmoud Sami to state that when waited on by the Consul-General he denied having made use of the language attributed to him, and stated that the alteration of the decree by the Khedive was a request which the latter was free to accept or reject.

The 'Chamber of Notables' had ceased to sit on the 26th March, when the session closed; but Mahmoud Sami now announced that since the Khedive and his Ministers could not agree, and as it was impossible for the Ministry to resign, they had determined themselves to convoke the Chamber, and to lay the case before it, and that he did not intend to hold any further communication with the Khedive until the difference between them had been decided by the Chamber. He added that in the meantime the Ministry would answer for the public safety. Mahmoud Sami also gave out that if the

Porte should order the sentences to be cancelled it would not be obeyed, and that if the Sultan sent Commissioners they would not be allowed to land, but would be repulsed and by force, if necessary.

The alarm in Cairo now began to be general. It was open warfare between the Khedive and his Ministry, supported by the army. The National Party made no secret of their intention to depose the Khedive as soon as the Chamber assembled.

The Notables, on arriving at the capital, proceeded as a rule, either to the house of Arabi or to the Ministry. The breach between the Sovereign and his Ministers had become so wide, that reconciliation seemed no longer possible. Arabi declared openly that when he came to power he looked upon the Khedive as an infant whom he took in his arms, and that he had resolved to support and defend him, but had tried and failed. The Minister of War added, that he did not see the necessity for the family of Mehemet Ali to be kept on the throne, and that their suppression would be an economy to the State of 300,000*l*. E. a-year.

The Khedive through all this maintained the same firm attitude which he had assumed at the beginning of the crisis, remaing quietly at his private residence in the Ismailia quarter of the town, and when driving out he was attended only by the usual escort. Large numbers of Bedouins came to Cairo, and loyally offered their services to the Khedive to enable him to rid himself of his Ministry and army together.

The Notables, when the day for assembly arrived, began to show a disinclination to support the National Party. They had commenced to realise that they had already gone further than they had intended, and also that they were being merely used as tools by Arabi and his colleagues.

At first they refused to meet at all, on the ground that they had not been convoked by the Khedive, but only by the Ministry. They were, however, induced to assemble, and on the 13th May, they met at the house of Sultan Pasha, the President of the Chamber. Here Mahmoud Sami read an indictment against the Khedive, charging him principally with not governing through his Ministers, and with compromising the liberties of Egypt in his action with the Porte. Sultan Pasha tried to smooth matters over, and to some extent succeeded. On the 14th May, the Ministers were so little sure of the support of the Notables, that Mahmoud Sami and Arabi went to the Palace, and in the names of themselves and their colleagues, offered to resign if the Khedive would guarantee public order. His Highness answered, that such a condition was a most unusual one, and that it would be the business of the new Ministry to see that public order was not troubled; he added that the only persons likely to cause trouble were Arabi and his associates. On the 15th, the English and French Consuls-General gave notice to Arabi that if there was a disturbance of public order, he would find Europe and Turkey, as well as England and France, against him, but that if, on the other hand, he remained loyal to the Khedive, his acts and person would be favourably regarded.

Arabi, in reply, stated that he would guarantee order only as long as he remained Minister, except that in the event of a fleet arriving he could not guarantee public safety.

The same day the two Consuls-General announced to the Khedive that the Anglo-French fleet was hourly expected.

This was followed by the Ministers going in a body to the Palace, and making a complete submission to the Khedive.

The reconciliation of the Khedive with his Ministers was accepted by the former only on the earnest representations of the Notables and the Consuls-General, in order that public tranquillity might not be disturbed. Another idea was to keep the Ministry in office as a temporary measure, in order that there might be some one to treat with when the fleets should arrive.

Notwithstanding the improved aspect of affairs, the alarm in Cairo continued, and crowds of people were daily leaving the city. To allay the panic, both Mahmoud Sami and Arabi declared that they would guarantee the preservation of order on the arrival of the fleets.

On the 19th May, the British gun-vessel *Bittern* arrived at Alexandria. She was followed on the 20th by the British ironclad *Invincible*, bearing the flag of Vice-Admiral Sir Beauchamp Seymour, and the gun-vessel *Falcon*.

The French squadron comprising, the ironclad *La Gallisonière*, with Admiral Conrad, and the gun-vessels *Forbin* and *Aspic*, came into harbour at the same time. The remainder of the allied squadron remained at Suda Bay, in the island of Crete.

CHAPTER X.

CRITICAL POSITION.

European Intervention—Lord Granville's Proposals—Sir Edward Malet's Despatch—Departure of Ironclads—The French Ministry—The Anglo-French Alliance—Proposed Deposition of the Khedive—The Porte requested to abstain from Interference—Instructions to the English and French Admirals—Overtures made to Arabi—The 'Dual Note'—Resignation of the Ministry—Action of the Officers and Police in Alexandria—The Reinstatement of the old Ministry—Apprehensions at Alexandria.

THE despatch of the Anglo-French fleet to Alexandria, by two Powers, each professing to be 'disinclined to armed intervention in Egypt,' was so important a step that it may be interesting to go back a little to consider the means by which it was brought about. Lord Granville, immediately after the Abdin demonstration of the 9th September, intimated to the French Government as his idea of a remedy for the military insubordination prevailing, the sending of a Turkish General to Egypt. Mons. Barthélemy St. Hilaire, Minister for Foreign Affairs, objected that this might lead to further steps, and possibly to the permanent occupation of the country by Turkish troops. The French Minister expressed himself in favour of a 'joint military control,' consisting of an English and a French General to restore discipline in the Egyptian army. Nothing was done to carry out either suggestion, although, as has been seen, the Sultan took upon himself to send the Turkish 'Envoys,' and England and France united in demanding their recall.

In March 1882, when the struggle between the Khedive and the Chamber was at its height, Lord Granville suggested that England and France should send two 'technical advisers' to assist the representatives of the two Powers in settling the details of the financial matters then pending. The proposal was so ludicrously absurd under existing circumstances, that it says much for the politeness of the French Minister, that he took the trouble to give a serious reply. He objected that the measure would give offence to the other Powers, as an attempt on the part of England and France to effect a separate settlement of Egyptian affairs, and also that it would tend to lower the Agents and Consuls-General in their own eyes and in those of the Egyptians.

Again baffled, Lord Granville, in April 1882, could think of nothing better than that the Sultan should be asked 'to send a General with full powers to restore discipline in the Egyptian army, with the understanding that he was not to exercise those powers in any way without the concurrence of an English and a French General, who would be associated with him.'

This proposal also fell through, the French Government objecting that the sending of a Turkish General at all would tend sooner or later to the sending of Turkish troops.

The despatch of a Turkish Commissioner of some kind continued to be talked about, when, on the 7th May, 1882, Sir Edward Malet wrote to the Foreign Office that the Khedive's Ministers would resist by force the arrival of any Commissioners from Turkey. After this, Lord Granville was for a time forced to abandon his favourite hobby of Turkish intervention. Sir Edward Malet's despatch contained the following significant passage :—

'I believe that some complication of an acute nature must supervene before any satisfactory solution of the Egyptian question can be attained, and that it would be wiser to hasten it than to endeavour to retard it, because the longer misgovernment lasts the more difficult it is to remedy the evils which it has caused.'

This sensible opinion had its effect, for, on the 11th May, Lord Granville was so far able to make up his mind as to say that the English Government were willing to send two ironclads to Alexandria, and a ship of war to Suez, to protect the European residents, informing other Powers in case they were disposed to do likewise. This announcement was only made after the idea had been suggested by the French Minister. Even at this period, Lord Granville could not help referring regretfully to his original idea of sending the three Generals (an expedient about as hopeful as sending three flower-pots with water to extinguish a fire), and in reply to Mons. Freycinet, his Lordship said that he could still think of nothing better.

The French Government, in agreeing to the despatch of the Anglo-French fleet, appeared resolved to abandon the cautious attitude which it had assumed on Mons. Freycinet taking office. The French Premier, on the 11th May, informed the Chamber of Deputies that in its Egyptian policy the Ministry had two objects, first, to preserve 'the preponderating influence' of France in Egypt; and, second, to maintain the independence of Egypt, as established by the Firmans; and added that the means which would be employed to carry out this policy would be an intimate alliance with England.

Mons. Freycinet, on the 12th May, informed Her Majesty's Ambassador in Paris, that as Tewfik Pasha had been acting under the advice of England and France, the French Government considered it the bounden duty of the two Powers to support his

Highness *as far as circumstances would allow*, and that France would co-operate loyally and without *arrière pensée* with England in that sense.

Mons. Freycinet, with some sense of humour, added that sending the three Generals would be inopportune.

On the 13th the English Government notified their concurrence in the views of France with regard to the Khedive, and welcomed the co-operation of the French Government. Lord Granville, at the same time, expressed the readiness of himself and his colleagues to defer to the objections raised to the mission of the three generals.

It now became known that the Notables were assembling in Cairo, and that the Ministry of Mahmoud Sami was about to propose the deposition of the Khedive and the exile of the family of Mehemet Ali. It was also reported that Mahmoud Sami proposed to declare himself 'Governor-General of Egypt by the national will.'

These alarming reports caused the preparations for the departure of the ships to be hastened, and, at the same time, with a view to keep the ground clear, the two Western Powers sent an intimation to the Porte desiring it to abstain for the moment from all intervention in Egypt. They also telegraphed to their representatives at Rome, Berlin, St. Petersburg, and Vienna, to inform the Governments to which they were accredited, of the despatch of the ships of war, and to request the respective Governments to join in inviting the Porte not to interfere.

The instructions to the British Admiral were as follows :—

'Communicate with the British Consul-General on arrival at Alexandria, and in concert with him propose to co-operate with naval forces of France to support the Khedive and protect British subjects and

Europeans, *landing a force, if required*, for latter object, such force not to leave protection of ships' guns without instructions from home.'

The French Admiral's instructions were somewhat different, and tend to show that the two Powers were not completely agreed as to the means to be employed to support Tewfik. His instructions were in these words :—

' On arrival at Alexandria communicate with the Consul-General, who will, if necessary, indicate to you what you will have to do to give a *moral* support to the Khedive. You will abstain, until you have contrary instructions, from any material act of war, unless you are attacked or have to protect the safety of Europeans.'

The English and French Consuls-General, on the arrival of the fleets, advised the Khedive to take advantage of the favourable opportunity to dismiss the existing Ministry, and to form a new Cabinet under Cherif Pasha, or any other person inspiring confidence.

Negotiations were simultaneously opened with Arabi, through the medium of Sultan Pasha, in order to induce the former to retire from the country with Mahmoud Sami, Toulba Pasha, Abd-el-Al, and Ali Fehmy, in return for which they were to be guaranteed their property, rank, and pay.

None of these plans succeeded. The Khedive recognised the futility of dismissing a Ministry that insisted on remaining in power, and the President of the Council replied that the Ministry would not retire so long as the squadrons were kept at Alexandria.

Arabi declared that he must refuse either to retire from his position or to leave the country, and a native colonel declared that the officers would hew Arabi in pieces if he deserted them.

On the 25th May the representatives of England and France handed to Mahmoud Sami, as President of the Council of Ministers, an ultimatum in the form of a Dual Note, demanding three things, viz., 1. The temporary retirement from Egypt of Arabi, with the maintenance of his rank and pay; 2. The retirement into the interior, under similar conditions, of Ali Fehmy and Abdel-el-Al; 3. The resignation of the Ministry. The note added that the two Governments would, if necessary, insist on the fulfilment of these conditions.

The Ministers, on receipt of the 'Dual Note,' waited on the Khedive to ask his opinion as to the answer that should be given, and his Highness distinctly told them that he accepted its conditions. They urged a reference to the Porte, to which the Khedive told them that it was an internal question, and that it was strange that they who had complained that he had failed to uphold the privileges of Egypt, should suggest such a course. On the 26th the Ministers resigned, alleging as a reason that the Khedive, in accepting the conditions of England and France, had acquiesced in foreign interference in Egypt, contrary to the terms of the Firmans.

The Khedive promptly accepted the resignation of the Ministry, and sent for Cherif Pasha to form a new Cabinet. Cherif refused on the ground that no Government was possible while the military chiefs remained in the country, and the Khedive had to look about for another possible Premier.

On the 27th May an event occurred in Alexandria which tended to bring matters more and more to a crisis.

The officers of the regiments and the police force in that city held a secret meeting, and telegraphed to the Khedive direct that they would not accept the resignation of Arabi, and giving the Khedive twelve hours to reply, after which the officers declared that they would not be responsible for public tranquillity.

On receipt of this message, the Khedive summoned

CRITICAL POSITION. 79

to his presence the chief personages of State, of the Chamber, and of the merchants, and the fifteen chief officers of the Cairo garrison, and placed the situation before them.

Toulba Pasha interrupted the Khedive in his speech, and stated that the army absolutely rejected the 'Dual Note,' and awaited the decision of the Porte, which was the only authority they recognised. On the same day, Arabi, at the head of about 100 officers, met the chief persons of Cairo and the Notables, at the house of Sultan Pasha, and demanded the deposition of the Khedive, threatening death to the recalcitrant. Nevertheless, almost all present, excepting the officers, persisted in supporting the Khedive. Arabi Pasha and the officers stated that they demanded of the Khedive a decree reinstating Arabi as Minister of War, and that they allowed till the 28th for its promulgation. Amongst those present, Sultan Pasha and some of the Notables warned the Khedive of what had taken place, and told him his life was not safe unless he reinstated Arabi. The Khedive consulted the English and French Consuls-General, who advised him not to comply.

In the afternoon of the same day, a deputation consisting of the Coptic Patriarch, the Chief Rabbi, the Notables, and representatives of the native schools, and of commerce, waited on the Khedive, begging him to reinstate Arabi, adding, that though he might be ready to sacrifice his own life, he ought not to sacrifice theirs, and that Arabi had threatened them all with death if they did not obtain the Khedive's assent to his re-appointment. In this perplexity, the Khedive, in order to prevent bloodshed, yielded, and issued a memorandum stating that at the repeated requests of the population, and with the desire of maintaining order and the tranquillity of the country, he had reinstated Arabi.

Although one may be disposed to blame the Khedive for his conduct on this occasion, it must be owned that his situation at the moment was a critical one. The despatch of the fleets, on which he had been led to rely, had turned out a ridiculous fiasco. Instead of ten vessels, there were only six, and these contained no troops for landing. The lamentable weakness of the demonstration had only excited the ridicule of the military party. It was beyond doubt that the guard at the Palace had been doubled, and that orders had been given to the sentries not to allow Tewfik to leave the Palace unless the deputation received a favourable reply, and to fire on him if he insisted on going out. All the issues of the Palace were carefully watched, and a mob was collected outside for the purpose of rushing into the Palace, ill-treating him, and turning him into the street if the prayer of the deputation were refused. It was also announced that there was to be a military demonstration at five in the afternoon, and that it was the intention of the army to depose the Khedive. Under these circumstances, and seeing how little material aid he had from England and France, it is not surprising that he yielded.

At 10 p.m., Tewfik was waited upon by his restored Ministers, and he inquired of Arabi whether he had cancelled an order given by the latter calling in the reserves and directing enlistments, His Highness adding that he saw no necessity for either measure. Arabi in reply contended that the measures in question were necessary, and that the matter was of great importance.

One of the first acts of Arabi on resuming office was to publish a declaration stating that now he had been reinstated, he guaranteed the security of the life and property of all the inhabitants of Egypt irrespective of nationality or religion.

This assurance was not made before it was required. For several days past a feeling of uneasiness had prevailed, especially in Alexandria.

When the military and police in that city made their demand for Arabi's reinstatement, Mr. Cookson, the British Consul and Judge, asked the Governor, Omar Pasha Loutfi, if he could answer for public order and the safety of Europeans. He replied that he had exhausted every effort to calm the officers and soldiers, but had entirely failed, and that he could not answer for their conduct, but that otherwise he saw no reason to apprehend any disturbance. Mr. Cookson asked for an interview with the Colonels of the two regiments in town, but this they refused, alleging that they were afraid of disorder among the troops if they left them, and that they were waiting for an answer to their telegram to the Khedive. On the Consul asking the Governor what were the intentions of the troops, he was answered that the Colonels had distinctly refused to disclose them.

In the prevailing state of things, Mr. Cookson thought it his duty to confer with Admiral Seymour as to the best means of protecting British subjects in case of a general attack upon Europeans, and he learned that the Admiral was not prepared to land any force, but that he would protect the embarkation of women and children and others who might seek refuge on board ships in the harbour. The Admiral sent an officer with the Consul, and a spot for embarkation was selected on the quays at the end of the broad street at right angles with the Rue des Sœurs.

The arrangement was communicated to the British residents at a meeting held at the Consulate the same day (the 28th).

The European population now became seriously

alarmed, and on the 29th a memorial was drawn up by the British residents, calling upon Her Majesty's Government to provide efficient means for the protection of their lives. It pointed out, that—

'During the twenty-four hours, from the 26th to the 27th, Alexandria was in continual danger of being stormed by the soldiery, who, it was reported, actually had cartridges served out to them to be used against Europeans.' 'There was,' it said, 'every reason to believe that the perils which had come without warning would recur again, and against them,' it continued, 'Europeans were absolutely defenceless. They had not even the means of flight, as in order to reach the ships in harbour they would have to run the gauntlet through the streets. The small squadron in port could only silence the forts, and when these forts were disabled, then would commence a period of great danger for Europeans, who would be at the mercy of soldiers exasperated by defeat, whilst the English Admiral could not risk his men ashore, as his whole available force for those operations did not exceed 300 men.' The memorial concluded by stating that 'every day's delay increased the dangerous temper of the soldiery and their growing defiance of discipline.'

Mr. Cookson at once telegraphed the contents of the memorial to the Foreign Office, where it was carefully placed amongst the archives.

CHAPTER XI.

ARABI'S PREPARATIONS.

Admiral Seymour and the Earthworks—Arabi's Refusal to discontinue warlike Preparations—Appeal to the Sultan—Application of the Khedive for the Despatch of a Turkish Commissioner—Motives of the Sultan in sending Dervish Pasha—Reception of Dervish Pasha—Action of the Commissioner—Interview with the Ministry—Apparent Submission of Arabi.

THE last chapter brought the history of events down to the 29th May, when Admiral Seymour reported that the Egyptians were raising earthworks opposite his flagship, the *Invincible*, then lying in the inner harbour at Alexandria, and requested that his squadron might be strengthened by the despatch of three of the ships of war which had been left at Suda Bay.

In a later telegram he added that when the earthworks were armed, the position of the unarmoured vessels of his squadron would be untenable, if fired on without warning. In reply, the Admiral was directed to arrange with the French Admiral to dispose the ironclads so as to silence the batteries if they opened fire.

On the 30th May, the British ironclad *Monarch*, and two gun-vessels, the *Cygnet* and the *Coquette*, as well as three French vessels of war—the *Alma*, the *Thetis* and the *Hirondelle*—were ordered from Suda Bay to Alexandria, where they arrived between the 2nd and 5th June.

The rest of the British Squadron in Crete were directed to cruise off the north coast of Egypt, and to communicate with Alexandria for orders from time to time.

Arabi, on being applied to on the subject of the earthworks, replied that repairs only were being effected, and refused to order them to be discontinued.

It was useless to remonstrate with the Khedive, whose orders that all warlike preparations should be stopped, had already been disregarded. The Sultan was therefore appealed to, and he sent an order to Tewfik to direct Arabi to desist from further armament. Arabi gave the necessary instructions, and the works, on which two guns were already mounted, were discontinued. The officers, however, boasted that they would resist by force all orders of the Sultan tending to the departure of their chiefs or the subjugation of the army.

In the meanwhile, in Cairo and in all the large towns, the adherents of Arabi circulated petitions to the Sultan, praying for the deposition of the Khedive and the substitution of Halim Pasha. The grounds alleged were that Tewfik had brought about the intervention of England and France. A great number of signatures were obtained to the petitions, under pressure of the military and police.

The Khedive, on his part, had, after obtaining the concurrence of the English and French Consuls-General, also applied to the Sultan, and requested that an Imperial Commissioner should be sent to Egypt. On the 3rd June it was known that Dervish Pasha, a Marshal of the Ottoman Empire, had left Constantinople for Alexandria as special Envoy from the Sultan, and his arrival was awaited with anxiety by both the Khedive and the Arabists.

The following observations, taken from one of the highest authorities on Egyptian matters,[*] throw a light on Dervish Pasha's mission.

---

[*] *Egypt and the Egyptian Question*, by D. Mackenzie Wallace, page 85.

ARABI'S PREPARATIONS.

'The Sultan's aim naturally was not to reinforce, but to counteract Anglo-French influence in Egypt. By accepting his intervention England and France confessed themselves worsted, and opened the door for a host of intrigues. His Majesty was not slow to take advantage of the opportunity and tried to play a complicated double game. Dervish Pasha, the First Commissioner, was instructed to support the Khedive, and if possible intimidate the leaders of the military party, while Ahmet Essad, the Second Commissioner, was instructed to conciliate Arabi and his friends, and assure them that they had in the Sultan a sure friend and ally. The Third Commissioner's duty was to act as a spy on his two colleagues, and he in his turn was closely watched by a secretary, who sent secret reports direct to Constantinople.'

On Dervish's arrival on the 7th June, he was received by the ships at Alexandria with a salute and colours hoisted. The bands played the Turkish National Anthem; a palace was prepared for him; and everything was done to mark the importance of his mission.

On Dervish's arrival in Cairo he was greeted by the acclamations of a mob of the lowest class of Arabs, who shouted before his carriage the praises of Arabi, and denounced the Christians.

'Dervish was known before his arrival to be accessible to Egyptian arguments, and there can be no doubt that they were boldly asked for and liberally given. Upon his arrival he showed marked favour to the Arabi party. Then he had a long interview with the Khedive, and then his conduct suddenly became very satisfactory to the Palace. Mahmoud Sami had arranged that the petitions from all the provinces should be brought to the Commissioner by deputation. Dervish received them graciously, placed the petitions in a pile on the divan, begged the deputation to consider all grievances settled by his arrival, and dismissed them. The Ministers came next. Mahmoud Sami entered with effusion, and introduced his colleagues severally. Dervish remained seated, continued his conversation with his secretary, Lebib Effendi, and then made a casual remark to Sami on the beautiful situation of the Palace of Ghezireh. The Ministers looked dumbfounded, but Dervish, continuing his conversation with Lebib, begged the latter to repeat to him the story of the massacre of the Mamelukes by Mehemet Ali at the Citadel,*

---

* Every reader of Egyptian history will remember that the Mamelukes, being in revolt against Mehemet Ali, were by a device induced to meet at the Citadel, where, with the exception of one who escaped by a perilous leap on horseback, they were all put to death.

which he could see from the window where he sat. When the suggestive story was completed, the Envoy, with one of his pleasantest smiles, remarked to Arabi, "The one man who escaped was a lucky dog," and with a remark on the weather dismissed them.'*

The Ministers left, feeling that there was no alternative between complete submission to the Khedive and absolute defiance of the Sultan.

Was there no third course ? Could no way be found by which Arabi might make himself indispensable, and Dervish Pasha be compelled to seek his assistance?

Before two days elapsed, events occurred at Alexandria, which demonstrated that Arabi was the only power in Egypt, and brought Dervish to his feet as a suppliant.

What those events were, will be recorded in the next chapter.

* *Khedives and Pashas*, pp. 111-2.

CHAPTER XII.

THE MASSACRE OF JUNE 11.

Demeanour of the Natives—The Cause of the Outbreak—Attack upon Mr. Cookson—Pillage of the Houses—The Conduct of the Mustaphazin—The Murders of Dr. Ribton and Messrs. Dobson and Richardson—Atrocities perpetrated—M. Mark—Intervention of the Military—Scene at the British Consulate—Proposed Landing from the Fleet—Morice Bey.

FOR some days previous to Sunday, the 11th June, 1882, the demeanour of the natives towards the European population of Alexandria had been growing more and more unfriendly; and there were indications that some disturbance, the precise nature of which no one was able to discover, was impending.

Amongst some of the incidents leading to this conclusion, were the following,—

On the 4th June, a British subject was in the Arab market buying vegetables, and had a discussion with the vendor as to the price. The dealer's clerk turned to the vendor, and said, 'Why do you talk to this fellow? At dinner-time he doesn't remember what he ate for breakfast, and he is mad like all the other Christians.' The vendor, on being remonstrated with, by his customer, added, 'We shall soon be rid of you, we shall cut you into pieces.'*

On the morning of the 6th June, a crowd of Maltese came to the British Consulate complaining that the soldiers in the 'Caracol' (police-station), near the

---

* Parliamentary Papers, Egypt, No. 16 (1882), page 5.

Place Mehemet Ali, had threatened to kill all the Christians, and had taken to their arms for that purpose. The Consul (Mr. Cookson) told them there was no cause for alarm, and ordered them to go to their houses and take no notice of threats.*

On the 8th, a number of Bedouin Arabs came to Alexandria, and were observed depositing their guns at various stores in the town, apparently to be kept there until required.†

On the 9th, a Greek subject was warned by a native at a café to 'take care, as the Arabs were going to kill the Christians either that day or the day following.'

On the 10th, natives went about the streets calling out that 'the last day for the Christians was drawing nigh.'

On the same day a European, being near a native coffee-shop, saw four natives take a bottle of wine and spill its contents on the ground, saying at that time on the following day they would shed the blood of the Christians in the same manner.

Another European, the cashier of the 'Banque Générale,' was warned on the 10th by a native, not to go into the Rue des Sœurs on Sunday, 'as there was danger;' and a clerk of another bank, an Italian, was cautioned not to go to town on the 11th.

The same day, an English resident, on quitting a native dealer of provisions, was advised by him to 'buy and eat that day, for the next the Christians would be massacred.'

Several European families were warned by their native servants not to send their children out on the

---

* Mr. Cookson at this time drew up a scheme for the defence of the European residents, and it was ready to be put into operation, but on the 11th June its disapproval by the Consuls-General was communicated to him. (Parliamentary Papers, Egypt, No. 16, 1882, page 23.)

† Parliamentary Papers, Egypt, No. 16 (1882), page 6.

THE MASSACRE OF JUNE 11.

afternoon of the 11th; and a European farmer was advised by his servant to take in his cattle, 'as there was going to be trouble.'

It subsequently transpired that the 'Wakil,' or deputy of Arabi, arrived from Cairo by the night train on the 10th June, and had an interview with Said Gandil, the Prefect of Police; also that several cartloads of 'naboots' (a species of long thick club used by the native watchmen) had been distributed amongst the lowest class of Arabs from a house near the 'Zaptieh,' or principal police-station.

The forenoon of the 11th passed without any unaccustomed incident, and the European population attended the churches and places of worship as usual.

Between two and three in the afternoon the tranquillity of the town was disturbed by the shouts and yells of some two thousand Arabs, who were suddenly seen swarming up the Rue des Sœurs, the Rue Mahmoudieh, and the adjacent streets, crying, 'Death to the Christians!' Others came soon after from the Attarin and the Ras-el-Tin quarters; and the riot, which appears to have broken out in three places almost at the same time, became general.

The crowd rushed on, striking with their 'naboots' all Europeans whom they could meet, knocking them down and trampling them under foot. Shots were fired; the soldiers and police interfered; but, in most instances, only with the object of making the butchery more complete. Many Europeans, flying for refuge to the police-stations, were there slaughtered in cold blood. Shops and houses were broken into and pillaged, and for four and a half hours, until the soldiers arrived on the scene, the usually quiet and prosperous city of Alexandria experienced a fair share of the horrors of war.

The signal that the massacre was about to take place was a feigned Arab funeral procession, in which several natives marched wearing green turbans, and which passed between 10 a.m. and noon through the main streets of Alexandria.*

The next thing which occurred was a disturbance which broke out about 1 p.m. between some Europeans and natives in the neighbourhood of a coffee-house called the 'Café Crystal,' in the Rue des Sœurs.

Of its precise origin it is difficult to speak with certainty. It has been stated that it originated in a dispute between a Maltese and a native coachman or donkey-boy, in which the Maltese, being beaten with a stick, retaliated with his knife, and, according to one account, killed his adversary. Another version is that two Arabs, named Said Salame and Billig Salame, attempted to break into the shop of a Maltese with whom they had previously quarrelled, and were violently resisted by the owner. Both accounts are involved in doubt, and the better opinion is that whatever may have been the origin of the alleged quarrel, it was only a pretext for what was to ensue. Anyhow, about the time last mentioned, Mr. Cookson, the British Consul, was summoned by the local police to assist in quelling a disturbance between some Maltese and the Arab inhabitants of the quarter of the Caracol Labban, a police-station in the Rue des Sœurs. He found there the Governor and Sub-Prefect of Police, and, after more than an hour, being under the impression that they had succeeded in calming the excitement, which did not appear to lead to anything serious, but to be owing more to the apprehensions of an impending massacre by the natives which had been present to the European population for some

* Parliamentary Papers, Egypt, No. 4, 1883, page 88.

days, Mr. Cookson returned to the Consulate. This was not, however, until he had been struck by one of the stones which were flying about.

About 3 p.m. he found a messenger, who purported to come from the Governor, waiting to summon him with all the other Consuls to a meeting at the same Caracol.

There is good reason to believe that no such request was ever made by Omar Pasha Loutfi, and that the messages sent were part of a preconceived scheme to decoy the Consuls into the streets, where they would be in the power of the mob. It is a singular thing that there were considerable intervals of time between the delivery of the messages, not warranted by the positions of the different Consulates, as if the intention was for the Consuls to arrive separately. Mr. Cookson, accompanied only by a janissary in uniform, drove immediately towards the Caracol. He found marks of recent conflict in the street, and groups of excited Arabs armed with naboots were moving about. On approaching within about ninety yards of the Caracol, at a place where four roads meet, he was assailed, first with stones, and was then struck at from behind with sticks. Without arms or other means of defence, Mr. Cookson could only stand up and look his assailants in the face. For a moment this seemed to have an effect; then a tall Arab ran behind the carriage, and uttering shouts and imprecations, felled Mr. Cookson to the ground with a blow from a naboot, and this for a moment stunned the Consul. The carriage was then overturned, and the janissary severely hurt.

When Mr. Cookson recovered consciousness, probably from the bleeding resulting from the severance of an artery in the head, he was lying in the street surrounded by a crowd, one or two of the members of which, including an Arab officer, were trying to protect him, whilst others were striking at him with sticks, and one native was brandishing a large knife or chopper.

Mr. Cookson was then with difficulty assisted to the Caracol, from which the guard did not move a step to protect him, as he staggered along streaming with blood, and pursued by howling Arabs striking at him on all sides. Fortunately, he was able to escape with his life to the Caracol, where he remained till about 4 p.m., when he was brought by a circuitous route, in the course of which he again encountered considerable danger, to the Consulate.*

Lieutenant Abdel-Hadi has stated that the inaction of the police at the different Caracols was due to the fact that the day previous all the officers and sub-officers in charge had been convoked by Youssef-el-Said, of the 5th regiment, and told that the men were to remain at their posts under any circumstances, without interfering even in the event of an outbreak or massacre happening.

Almost at the same time and place, the other members of the Consular body, as they arrived on the scene, were similarly attacked. M. Rangabé, the Greek Consul, M. Machiavelli, and M. Rozwadowski, the Italian Consul and Vice-Consul, were badly hurt, M. Svilarich, the Russian Consul, and M. Scotides, the Vice-Consul of Greece, were also severely beaten.

All this time the Governor was at the door of the Caracol, giving orders to the Mustaphazin (military police) to disperse the mob, but his orders were never executed. The Governor was in the act of assisting the Italian Consul out of his carriage, when the Arabs struck him with their naboots.

* As an acknowledgment of Mr. Cookson's services on this occasion he received by telegraph an expression of sympathy from Her Majesty's Government.

THE MASSACRE OF JUNE 11.

Whilst the fighting was going on, the Arabs, the police, and the soldiers, occupied their time in breaking open and plundering the shops and houses on the line of route, tearing down doors and shutters, and using the materials as well as the legs of tables and chairs as weapons of offence.

The rioting gradually extended up the Rue des Sœurs, towards the Place Mehemet Ali (the great square), the Europeans here and there firing at times from the terraces and balconies of the houses, and the soldiers and the mob replying with firearms and stones.

At an early period, one of the mustaphazin was killed by a shot from one of the houses, and his body being taken to an adjoining Caracol, his comrades became so exasperated, that they butchered every European who sought refuge there.

In the streets, the conduct of the mustaphazin was almost equally bad. Where they did interfere, they did so in a half-hearted, indifferent manner. In the great majority of instances, where they did not join in the killing themselves, they encouraged their countrymen to do so. They appeared, moreover, quite beyond the control of the Governor, whom they openly cursed and reviled as a traitor, when he tried to interpose on behalf of the Christians.

There is reason to believe that the mustaphazin did a large proportion of the killing, as they were armed with sword-bayonets. The Arabs, on the other hand, had in most cases only heavy sticks, with which they stunned and bruised their victims.

A considerable number of Bedouins were observed amongst the mob, which emerged from the Rue des Sœurs by the side streets leading into the adjoining quarters. The Bedouins were armed with their long guns, with which they shot down passing Europeans. One of a group of Bedouins, stationed opposite the European hospital to intercept the fugitives, was seen to shoot a European who was running past, and crouching down as he did so, in the hope of escaping observation. About 4 p.m. a second mob came down from the Attarin quarter, and a similar fight was going on in the vicinity of the Austrian Post Office, the Arabs with clubs, guns, and knives, attacking every European who came in their path. Amongst other victims, was a little boy five years old, apparently a Maltese, who was killed with a naboot in front of the Post Office. At half-past five, the portion of the Rue des Sœurs where the disturbance began, was almost deserted, the ground being strewn with *débris* of wood and glass, and the windows shattered, many of them by bullets. Opposite the Lazarist College, in the same street, but nearer the Place Mehemet Ali, the crowd from the Attarin quarter mingled with the other mob were continuing the work of destruction. They hunted down every Christian they saw; one European they fell upon and killed with sticks and pieces of wood at the very door of the College itself. All this while the mustaphazin, some thirty or forty in number, in front of the College, were seen firing off their rifles without any apparent motive. They saw the European being killed at their feet without making an effort to protect him. One mustaphazin fired off his rifle in the direction of the European, but no one interfered to remove his assailants. The street at this part was now filled with pillagers. A number of Europeans found refuge at the College, the doors of which were bolted and barred by the inmates. From the terrace above these were able to look down on the work of destruction.

About 5.30 a European in black clothes and apparently of good social position, covered with blood and with his trousers torn to rags, was seen running backwards and forwards, as if distracted. Just as he reached the corner of the Rue des Sœurs, a point guarded by two mustaphazin, a band composed of six or seven Arabs armed with sticks emerged from the street, rushed at once on the European, who was streaming with blood, and beat him on the head with their sticks. The two mustaphazin not only did not prevent the Arabs from ill-treating their victim, but, on the contrary, were seen to seize the wretched man by the arm, and laughing, thrust him into the midst of the band which was assailing him. Whether he subsequently escaped or not, is unknown.

One of these mustaphazin being remonstrated with, candidly replied, 'We are ordered to do it.'

In one spot in the Rue des Sœurs the bodies of three Europeans were found lying in a heap. One had a bullet-hole in the head, another was stabbed through the chest, and another with his skull fractured was lying on his face with his shoes and stockings stripped off.

The shops in the square now began to be broken into by pillagers armed, some with naboots, and a few with old swords. These proceeded to wreck the kiosques in the square itself. Next, crowds of looters were observed going back in the direction of Gabari, laden with goods from the neighbouring shops. These the mustaphazin allowed to pass without opposition; indeed, several of the mustaphazin were themselves carrying the stolen goods. The footway in front of the Hotel d'Europe was covered with blood. Soldiers were seen to take from Europeans, whose lives they spared, their watches and such valuables as they had about them. One person was thus despoiled of 175*l*., in coin, and 50*l*. worth of jewellery, with which he was trying to escape to the ships.

In the Strada Nuova the police and soldiers were observed encouraging the mob to break open shops, and each time this was done, the police and soldiers entered first, and had the first choice.

In another quarter two native policemen were observed attacking an Arab, who was carrying gold articles and a quantity of money, when a mounted soldier appeared on the scene, and he and the policemen shared the Arab's plunder between them, leaving the thief to go empty away.

In their selection of objects of plunder the mob were far from particular. A soldier was seen walking down the street with a glass chandelier on his head. Another was seen riding down the street on a toy horse.

The tobacco-shops suffered more severely than any others; wherever one of these was seen, it was invariably broken into, and the contents distributed among the crowd.

Wearing apparel, also, was in great request, and one of the native officers was observed sitting on the curbstone exchanging the trousers he was wearing for a new pair stolen from a neighbouring shop.

In the few cases where a native had not succeeded in obtaining any plunder for himself, he invariably turned to one of his more fortunate comrades, and helped himself to his stock. One man who was carrying off some dozens of slippers was stopped by no less than three of his fellow-countrymen, who made him wait whilst they selected those which fitted them best.

Whilst this was occurring similar scenes of violence were being perpetrated in another part of the town, namely, in the streets leading from the Place Mehemet Ali to the Marina, and to Ras-el-Tin.

A considerable number of Europeans had been

to visit the ships in the harbour. On their return, between 4 and 5 p.m., they found the Marina Street, Frank Street, and the adjoining thoroughfares, in the possession of a mob armed with naboots. What happened may be learned from the case of an English Baptist Missionary, Mr. H. P. Ribton, one of the victims.* Mr. Ribton, accompanied by his daughter, and Messrs. Allegretti and Von Rupp, were amongst those who had been afloat in the afternoon. On landing from the ships they found the city gate, leading from the Marina into the town, closed; but they were allowed to pass through by a door in the police-office. The shops were shut, and the streets were filled with soldiers. Mr. Ribton and party were in the rear of some other Europeans who had landed with them. Suddenly the soldiers called out in Arabic 'Quick! quick!' and all the Europeans commenced running. In a moment or two the Europeans in front wheeled round crying that the mob were coming. Mr. Ribton and his party turned at the same time, but the Arab soldiers with fixed bayonets drove them back, and in an instant they found themselves face to face with the mob who had already overwhelmed the Europeans in front.

The mob consisted of the lowest class of Arabs in the city; they were armed with clubs studded with nails, with which they beat the Europeans to death. As soon as the latter fell the Arabs dragged them out by the feet to the back streets, stripped their bodies and flung them into the sea. The Arab soldiers, so far from interfering to prevent the massacre, joined with and aided the mob, by bayoneting all who attempted to escape.

* *Vide* Petition of Mrs. Ribton to the Queen. Parliamentary Papers, Egypt, No. 4, 1883.

Mr. Ribton and his two male companions in vain attempted to shield his daughter from the blows. Mr. Ribton himself was twice felled to the ground and again staggered to his feet attempting to save his daughter. The third time he fell he rose no more, and when afterwards his body was found the head was so beaten as to be unrecognisable.* Mr. Ribton's two friends were also butchered by his side. His daughter was severely beaten about the head and shoulders, and as she was falling, almost insensible, she was seized by an Arab soldier, who, throwing her across his shoulders, carried her off to the Arab quarter. Here she was rescued by a friendly Sheik who had heard her screams, and who kept her in his house till nightfall, when he sent her home disguised in native clothes.

Amongst others who were slaughtered whilst returning from the harbour were Messrs. Dobson and Richardson, two British subjects, and a Mr. Cattowi, and a Mr. Rossi, of Cairo.

Some of the most atrocious acts of violence were perpetrated in immediate proximity to the Zaptieh, where is situated the Prefecture of Police. Here soldiers and Arabs, mixed together, pursued the Europeans who were passing on their way to the Marina, in the hope of escaping to the ships. One soldier was seen to kill with his sword a man who was already wounded with a club, but who might have got away. The native rabble struck the passers-by with their sticks without any restraint from the soldiers, and when the victims were felled to the ground the mustaphazin despatched them with their sword-bayonets.

Whenever a European appeared in sight the mob

* The actual murderer of Mr. Ribton was Hag Mohamed Ismail, who was subsequently convicted and hanged.

cried out in Arabic, 'Oh, Moslems, kill him; kill the Christian!'

Christodulo Andrea, master of a Greek merchantman, was forced by the police to descend from his carriage, and bayoneted on the spot.

A French subject, who was being pursued by the mob, applied to a soldier for protection, the latter responded by taking deliberate aim at him with his rifle.

A mustaphazin was seen holding a young man from behind, whilst a soldier shot him through the neck; his body was then maltreated, and, after being rifled, was thrown into the sea.

A man on guard at the Zaptieh was seen to shoot down a European who was running away from the mob, and who speedily reduced his body to pulp. The same witness saw the police at the next station, the Caracol Midan, adjoining the Place Mehemet Ali, breaking their rifle-stands, and distributing the pieces to the mob to be used as weapons.

Some Officers of H.M.S. *Superb*, Lieutenants Saule and Dyrssen, Dr. Joyce, and Mr. Pibworth, engineer, about 6 p.m., seeing the mob rushing towards them, attempted to obtain shelter at the Caracol Midan. The man on duty refused to admit them. They then ran to the Danish Consulate close by, where they were offered an asylum by the Consul, Mr. Dumreicher. As their ship was going to sea at 7 p.m. the officers were unwilling to stop, and, taking advantage of a carriage which had been secured, they proceeded towards the Marina by Frank Street. When about half-way down they found themselves in the centre of the mob, who, howling and shouting, seized the horses' heads and commenced striking the officers furiously with their sticks; several brandished knives, and one of them stabbed Mr. Pibworth, wounding him mortally, and attempted to stab the others. They then jumped from the carriage and managed to run through the crowd, receiving several blows in doing so. Mr. Pibworth was removed to the Police station, where he died half-an-hour afterwards.

A fireman of the P. & O. S.S. *Tanjore*, named Gardella, who was in a carriage with five of his companions, also on his way to the harbour, was stopped about 4 p.m. by the mob in the open piece of ground near the Zaptieh, and ordered to alight. They were then surrounded and beaten with sticks by the natives, some of the party receiving wounds from the swords of the mustaphazin drawn up there. The party tried their best to escape, but Gardella was dragged by the arm into the Zaptieh, where there were a few Greeks. Two minutes later Gardella saw one of his companions, named Chiavalire, brought in by a soldier. Almost at the same moment the guard on duty at the gate drew his sword and struck Chiavalire twice, splitting his skull with the first stroke, and severing his head from his body with the second. Gardella was detained for about three hours, and, according to his statement, all who were brought in during that time were slaughtered in the same manner.

Witnesses living near the Zaptieh have spoken to the cries and groans which came from the building at this period, and another witness has stated that from a window opposite he counted no less than thirteen bodies of Europeans, all denuded and disfigured, being dragged out and taken down a side street towards the sea.*

Amongst the natives who distinguished themselves in the work of slaughter, were two Syrian butchers named Selim Talekha and Abou Saleh. The first-

---

* Parliamentary Blue Book, Egypt, No. 10, 1882, page 17.

THE MASSACRE OF JUNE 11. 101

named killed his neighbour, a Greek subject, with the meat knife used in his trade, whilst the other was observed to kill no less than four persons with his chopper. The last, whilst thus engaged, shouted to the bystanders, ' You are not so clever as I am in finishing off these dogs of unbelievers.'

The rioting in the Rue des Sœurs, near the Caracol, was at its height at 4.30 p.m., and that in Frank Street about 5.30 or 6, and the two mobs of rioters marched on until they united in the Place Mehemet Ali.

The brutality of the mob extended even to the Arab boys and children. One of the latter was seen to go up to the dead body of a European and fire off a toy-gun at his head, and the boot-blacking boys in the Place Mehemet Ali were observed to beat out the brains of the wounded who lay groaning on the pavement. Mr. Cookson observed amongst his assailants boys hardly of the age of puberty who pierced his hands with sharp sticks as he was lying on the ground.

The conduct of the mustaphazin, or native police, has been frequently referred to. It is only right to do justice to another branch of the force, the European police, composed principally of Italians, under the command of M. Mark, who did their utmost to restore order, and a large number of persons owe their lives to this courageous officer. The force, however, under M. Mark, was too small, numerically speaking, to effect anything in the way of dispersing the mob, who consequently had things pretty much their own way.

Whilst all this was going on, the troops to the number of about 7000 remained at the different barracks under arms, waiting instructions to act. The Governor, about four in the afternoon, had asked Ismail Pasha Kamil, the Military Commandant of the town, to place at his disposal a battalion of the 5th Regiment, commanded by Mustapha Abdul Rahmi, at Ras-el-Tin; but the messenger returned saying the Colonel required an order in writing before he could move. Much valuable time was thus wasted. The Governor, however, then sent the written order demanded, and also sent an order to the Colonel of the 6th Regiment, at Rosetta Gate, to send a battalion of his troops into town without delay. He also, to prevent the disorder spreading to the Place Mehemet Ali and the Place de l'Eglise, sent a company of mustaphazin to each of those places.

The mustaphazin obeyed, but the soldiers still remained drawn up at the barracks. In spite of the Governor's request they refused to march without an order from the Minister of War.

Now came Arabi's opportunity. Arabi, it will be remembered, had a few days before been treated by Dervish Pasha as an ignoble rebel against the Sultan, and made to feel his inferiority. When the news of the massacre was telegraphed to Cairo the haughty Envoy himself was sent to fetch Arabi, and had, almost on his knees, to beg him to intervene. Arabi consented. He had attained his object, viz.: to show that there was only one Ruler in Egypt, and that was Arabi Pasha. The desired despatch was at last sent by telegraph from Cairo, and a little after 6 p.m., the soldiers began to march. It was not, however, till long after this time that they reached the scene of disturbance. As they advanced the mob gradually fell back, and then dispersed as if by magic. The tramping, shouting, and yelling suddenly ceased, and there was silence in the streets save for the groans of the wounded.

The behaviour of the troops was strictly in accordance with discipline. They had their orders to put an end to the disturbance, and they did so. One of them being asked if the massacre was finished, naïvely replied, 'Yes; the order has come to cease striking.'

Though before 8 p.m. all was quiet in the streets, it is said that the butchery went on at the Caracols until past midnight.

In the course of the afternoon hundreds of Europeans rushed off for protection to the different Consulates, where they remained with the gates closed and guarded. Every moment increased the number of fugitives. The British Consulate was literally crammed with officers, civilians, ladies, and children.

Telephonic communication was open with Admiral Seymour on board the *Helicon*. The Admiral's first idea appears to have been to land an armed force for the protection of the Europeans, for at 5.32 p.m. the *Helicon* made the general signal to the fleet, 'Prepare to land armed boats.' This order, however, was annulled five minutes later, in view of the danger which might arise to the Europeans in the event of the act being construed as one of hostility, and the troops and the mob uniting against the Christians. The captains of the English men-of-war were signalled to assemble on board the Flag-ship, when, after consultation, it was decided, as the only course open, to send boats round to the Eastern Harbour under cover of the guns of H.M.S. *Superb*, so as to be in readiness to embark those who had taken refuge in the Consulate; and boats were sent to the Arsenal and other landing-places to bring off the officers which remained on shore.

Mr. Cookson, being disabled by his wounds, Captain R. H. M. Molyneux, of the *Invincible*, was placed in charge of the Consulate. He at once put himself in communication with the Governor, and was visited by him and all the Consular body.

It had been arranged that the *Superb* was to take up a position off the Eastern Harbour, near the European quarter, and to have a force of seamen and marines ready for immediate service on shore, sending her boats as near as possible to the 'Café Paradiso,' which is on the beach, with a view to the removal from the town of all the women and children whom they might be able to find. The landing party, to be used only in case of need, was on a signal being made to clear the streets leading to the English Consulate.

Between 8 and 9 P.M. the Governor, to whom the arrangements were communicated, begged that the boats might not be sent, as their appearance would, in his opinion, excite the troops beyond control. He also stated that the disturbance had now been suppressed, and that he could guarantee the safety of everybody.

Under these circumstances, Captain Molyneux requested that the instructions to the *Superb* might be countermanded.

The night passed off badly enough at the Consulate. There were, however, no serious alarms until about 11.30, when an event happened which might have brought about a catastrophe.

One of the *Superb's* armed boats mistaking a bright light on the shore for the signal arranged in the event of the boats being required to land, answered the supposed signal with a blue light, and thus disclosed her position near the shore, hitherto concealed by the darkness. In an instant the bugles sounded the alarm, there was a call to arms all over the town, and a rush made by the troops towards the beach, showing that the Governor's fears were well founded, and that had the boats touched the shore, the troops, already much excited, would have been quite beyond the control of their officers. There was not a moment to be lost. Captain Molyneux at once sent off a peremptory order to the officer in charge of the boats to withdraw out of sight. Morice Bey, an English officer, Director of the Egyptian Coastguard, at considerable peril to himself, volunteered to carry the order, and went afloat in a small boat. But before the Bey was able to communicate, notice of the modification of the original arrangement had reached the officer, and the boats had withdrawn.

Most of the soldiers, seeing no further signs of a landing, withdrew to their posts, but the alarm occasioned by the incident again brought the Governor to the Consulate to protest against any troops approaching the shore, and saying that he could not accept any responsibility in case they did so.

The rest of the night passed without incident, detachments of soldiers with fixed bayonets, guarded the various Consulates, and stationed themselves at the corners of all the principal streets.

CHAPTER XIII.

AFTER THE MASSACRE.

Number of the Slain—Flight to the Ships—Arabi's Assurances—Consular Proclamation—Europeans Disarmed—Arabi's Proclamation—Flight of Europeans—Commission of Inquiry—The New Ministry—Arabi and the Sultan—Arabi keeps Order—The British Consulate—Native Feeling—Arrival of Ships of War—Continued Exodus of Europeans—Opinion in England—Feeling in the Fleet—Warlike Preparations.

THERE are no means of arriving at an accurate estimate of the numbers who perished on the 11th June, but they have been estimated, by competent persons, at one hundred and fifty Europeans, besides natives.* A great number of these last are known to have been carried off to the houses till nightfall and then secretly buried. The European doctors who visited the hospitals on the following day found forty-nine bodies—forty-four of which were Europeans. Thirty-seven were so battered as to be unrecognisable. Seventy-one persons were also found wounded; of these thirty-six were Europeans, two Turks, and thirty-three natives. Some of those killed or wounded had received stabs, as from a sharp instrument, on their bodies, but the majority had their injuries inflicted by naboots. One witness speaks to having seen several cartloads of bodies thrown, at night, into the sea near the Western Harbour, and it is quite possible that many were so disposed of. In a fluctuating population, such as that of Alexandria,

---

* It is only right to mention that the authenticated cases are less than half the number above given.

it is obvious that many persons might disappear and never be inquired for.*

During the night of the 11th, prayers were said to crowds of fanatics at the tombs of the Arab Saints, and menaces were uttered against the ' Unbelievers.'

The Governor, on the 12th, visited the sacked and looted quarters of the town, and took note of the houses injured. He also arrested and imprisoned between two and three hundred natives who had taken part in the riot of the previous day.

At daylight on the 12th, the women and children, who had taken refuge at the British Consulate, embarked under an escort provided by the Governor. Thousands of other Europeans of all nationalities also went afloat, and during the whole day the streets were blocked with fugitives. At first these were cursed and spat upon by the natives as they passed, but later on they were allowed to go by unmolested.

In Cairo a meeting was held at which the Khedive, Dervish Pasha, the Ministers, and the Consuls-General, were present. This was to obtain a reply to the demand of the Consular body, made to Dervish Pasha, that measures should be taken to insure the safety of Europeans. Arabi undertook to stop all inflammatory preaching, and to obey all orders given him by the Khedive. The Khedive engaged himself to issue orders immediately with the object of restoring public tranquillity. Dervish Pasha, on his part, consented to accept joint responsibility with Arabi for the execution of the orders of the Khedive. On the same day the Governor of Alexandria assembled the principal Egyp-

---

* One writer (Mr. John Ninet in his work *Arabi Pasha*) gives the number of natives killed on the 11th of June as 163. He relates that the bodies of 68 Europeans were found in the Hospital, and that seven bodies of Europeans were washed up on the shore on the 12th June.

tian officers, and asked them if they would answer for the safety of the town and public order, and they all answered in the affirmative. It was then decided to increase the number of patrols, and to reinforce the police-stations by troops, and an escort was provided for the overland passengers coming from India with the mails. Yacoub Pasha Sami, Under-Secretary of War, was sent from Cairo with two regiments of Infantry and some Artillery. Guards of soldiers were placed at the corners of the streets, and at night they lay down on the ground in the Place Mehemet Ali and other open spaces. In the course of the day a proclamation was issued by the Consular body to the Europeans, pointing out that the disorder had been suppressed by the army, and that its chiefs guaranteed public tranquillity. It further called upon the European population to remain in their dwellings, and to abstain from carrying fire-arms.

The effect of the proclamation in reassuring the inhabitants was simply *nil*. It may have been prudent to prohibit their going about armed, but after what had occurred the measure was not popular, and many persons who might otherwise have remained on shore betook themselves to the ships.

The process of disarming was carried out to the fullest extent. Not only were persons stopped in the streets and searched for firearms, but even walking-sticks were taken away.

Arabi next issued a proclamation couched in the following terms :—

'I demand of the public that every one goes about his business in all safety, and takes no notice of the rumours which circulate in the town, and which are only the inventions of intriguers.

'(Signed) AHMED ARABI.'

AFTER THE MASSACRE.

On the 13th the Khedive and Dervish Pasha arrived from Cairo. Their reception was anything but enthusiastic.

Alexandria remained quiet, the streets being still patrolled by soldiers night and day. The general flight of Europeans continued. The number seeking refuge on board the ironclads was so great that the ships would have been useless in the event of their having to act. Three hundred were on board the *Invincible*, the same number on board the *Monarch*, and all the smaller men-of-war were similarly crowded. On the Admiral's representation, merchant - steamers were chartered by the British Government, and employed to take the refugees to Malta; one of the Poste-Khedive steamers was, subsequently, taken up as a temporary refuge, and some hundreds of persons placed on board in charge of an English naval officer. Other steamers were thronged with passengers leaving for Cyprus, Constantinople, and other places; fabulous prices were charged the fugitives by the boatmen who took them off to the various vessels.

A Commission of Inquiry was next instituted by the Egyptian Government, with a view to discover the authors of the events of the 11th June. The President of the Commission, oddly enough, was Omar Pasha Loutfi, Governor of Alexandria, the official who was responsible for the maintenance of order on the day in question, and who was therefore himself, to some extent, on his trial. The Minister of Finance refused to sit on the Commission, alleging that, in view of the actual military supremacy, it would be impossible to bring to light the real facts of the case. The Commission, however, assembled, and much evidence was taken from the wounded and other witnesses. An English barrister, the late Mr. J. Keith Grosjean, attended as the delegate of the British Consulate. Before the inquiry had proceeded far, a difficulty arose as to the right to search the houses of policemen believed to have possession of stolen property. The Under-Secretaries of War and Justice, who represented the Egyptian Government on the Commission, insisted on a system of reciprocity, and demanded the right to search European houses. The inquiry proceeded to develop into mutual recriminations, and a pretext was afforded to the Government for bringing counter-charges against Europeans. Eventually Yacoub Pasha offered such determined opposition to the institution of a satisfactory inquiry, that the British delegate had to be withdrawn, and the Commission collapsed.

On the 15th the Khedive received an order from the Sultan to return to Cairo. He was at once informed by the English representative that if he did so, there was no power on the part of the English to protect him; and the Sultan was telegraphed to and asked to reconsider the matter. At all events His Highness did not go.

After the events of the 11th June it was impossible for the Khedive's Ministers to remain in power, and he accordingly charged Ragheb Pasha, an old and infirm politician, to form a new Cabinet.

On the 20th June a new Ministry under Ragheb was formed. In this, as before, Arabi figured as Minister of War. The men forming the Cabinet were not such, however, as to inspire confidence. Many of them were pronounced Arabists, and the rest were about fair specimens of the usual Egyptian Minister.

The programme of the new Ministry was as follows:—

1. General amnesty, except to those who have taken part in, or have been implicated in, the events of June 11th.

2. The government of the country to be carried

AFTER THE MASSACRE. 111

on under the terms of the rescript of August 28th, 1878.

3. No person to be punished except in virtue of, and by the law.

4. Relations with the foreign Powers to be carried on between them and the Minister of Foreign Affairs, and with no other functionaries of whatsoever degree.

Ragheb's first idea was to revive the extinct Commission of Inquiry into the events of the 11th June. The project, however, did not find favour with the English representative. It was obvious that the moment for going into any such investigation was not opportune, and the matter dropped.

Arabi, who had come to Alexandria at this time, now made a point of showing himself a good deal in public, driving out every evening, sometimes in the same carriage with the Khedive, and always attended by a cavalry escort. On these occasions great crowds of natives assembled, and showed unmistakably the interest they took in the *de facto* ruler of Egypt.

That Arabi and the Sultan were in perfect accord at this time is unquestionable. But if any doubt existed it was removed by the fact that on the 25th June the Sultan decorated with the Grand Cordon of the Medjideh the man who had plunged his country into revolution, and had been the cause of the 11th June massacre. The Order was presented to the Minister of War by the Khedive personally, who (Arabi declares) expressed his satisfaction and gratitude for Arabi's faithful services and attention to his duties.

The attitude of the Khedive on this as on other occasions, appears at first sight inexplicable. It may perhaps be accounted for on the hypothesis that His Highness, having just reason to doubt how far he could calculate on the sincerity of England and France, or on receiving help from them, was unwilling to cut himself altogether adrift from the National Party.

It is due to Arabi Pasha to say that during the period which elapsed between the day of the massacre and the subsequent bombardment, perfect order was maintained in Alexandria. It was not so in the interior, however, and on the 26th June, the British Acting Consul-General, Mr. Cartwright, reported that ten Greeks and three Jews were massacred at Benha, a town in the interior. In other provincial towns, Europeans were openly insulted by the natives, and began to join the fugitives taking flight to Europe. At Rosetta and Damietta, things grew so threatening, that even the European lighthouse-keepers had to be withdrawn, and their duties confided to natives.

At Alexandria, Mr. Cookson, the British Consul, disabled by the wounds which he received whilst courageously exposing himself on the 11th June, had, in consequence, to leave for Europe. Mr. Henry Hunter Calvert, the Vice-Consul, incapacitated by age, and suffering from the shock brought about by recent events, had also to depart. Most of the Consular clerks and employés likewise found it necessary to quit their posts, and Sir Edward Malet, overtaken at a critical moment by severe illness, had to betake himself to Europe. In this emergency, Mr. Cartwright was called upon to discharge the duties of Consul-General, assisted by the knowledge and local experience of Sir Auckland Colvin.

On the 29th June, Mr. Cartwright, the Acting British Consul-General, wrote to Lord Granville as follows :—

'The exodus of Europeans and the preparations for flight, after seeming temporarily to have abated, continue with increased vigour. The hotels are closing ; the shipping-agents, including the Peninsular and Oriental Company, have transferred their offices to the neighbourhood

AFTER THE MASSACRE.

of the port; and the banks which still remain open are preparing to transfer their staff to the ships. It is impossible to describe the collapse and ruin which have so suddenly overtaken the country ...... A large number of respectable Arabs are leaving the country. The departure of Turkish families is taking larger proportions, while 200 destitute Jews and Rayahs have been sent away at the expense of the Government itself.'

So important was the exodus of natives deemed, that Arabi laid before the Council of Ministers a proposal that all the property of Egyptians leaving the country should be confiscated.

Thrown out of employment by the exodus of Europeans, the greatest distress prevailed, and the Governor of Alexandria estimated that nearly 30,000 persons were left destitute.

Thus matters went on, until the measures taken by the Government in adding to the armament of the forts led to actual hostilities. On the side of the Europeans, there was, with a few exceptions, absolute panic. On the side of the natives, there was a vague feeling of disquietude. They realised that they had irretrievably committed themselves, and imagined that the day of retribution was drawing nigh.

Ships of war continued to arrive from all parts, until a squadron of twenty-six vessels belonging to the navies of England, France, Italy, Austria, Russia, the United States, Spain, Greece, and Turkey, lay off Alexandria.

Meanwhile, the crowd of fugitives continued to embark. The French and Greek Governments sent transports to remove their subjects *en masse*, and ships laden with British refugees left for Malta as fast as the vessels could fill up. Europeans arrived from Cairo and the interior, and the trains were thronged with passengers, many of whom rode on the roofs and steps of the railway-carriages. As many as 4000 arrived on one day, the 15th.

Alexandria, at this period, presented a curious spectacle. Beyond the business of transporting the fugitives, there was nothing else done. The shops were shut up, and the doors barred and padlocked. The banks were occupied in putting up iron shutters, and bricking up their windows. The few business firms which remained hired steamers, and removed their books and effects on board, so as to be ready for any eventuality. The streets in the European quarter presented a deserted appearance, the Arab soldiers being almost the only persons seen about.

In Cairo things were but little better, the whole of the foreign population had taken flight, together with most of the well-to-do Arabs. Preparations were made by the National Party in the event of the capital being attacked by an invading force. In such case it was arranged to collect in the citadel the families of the officers, and to offer a stern resistance. Provisions, arms, and ammunition, were accumulated with this object.

It is not too much to say that the events of the 11th June created a profound sensation in England. That a large number of unoffending Europeans, living in a civilised or quasi-civilised country, should have been without provocation suddenly attacked and slaughtered, was bad enough. But that this should have occurred at a moment when eight British ships of war, and nine others belonging to other Powers, were there, for the avowed purpose of protecting European life and property, was worse still.

The opportunity was not lost upon the Opposition. Indignation meetings were held throughout the United Kingdom, in which the conduct of Mr. Gladstone's administration was denounced in the strongest terms. Lord Salisbury, as the leader of the Opposition in the

AFTER THE MASSACRE.

House of Lords, was particularly vehement in his condemnation of a policy which had resulted in British subjects being 'butchered under the very guns of the fleet off Alexandria,' which 'had never budged an inch.'

On board the vessels of the British fleet, a similar feeling of indignation prevailed. When the bodies of the officer (Mr. Pibworth) and of the seamen massacred were on the 13th June taken out to sea for burial, officers and men alike clamoured for revenge. An insult had been offered to the British flag, which in their opinion ought to be avenged.

Public feeling became fully aroused, and Her Majesty's Government caused it to be intimated that it was their intention to demand reparation for the loss of life and property which had occurred. The Channel Squadron, consisting of the *Minotaur*, *Achilles*, *Agincourt*, *Northumberland* and *Sultan*, was despatched to Malta on the 15th, and placed under the temporary command of Admiral Seymour. More energetic measures still were in contemplation, but it was deemed unwise to decide upon them until the great body of Europeans should have had time to clear out of Egypt.

CHAPTER XIV.

HOSTILE PREPARATIONS.

Threat. Position of Affairs—Hostile Preparations of the Egyptian Authorities—Attitude of the Ministry—Admiral Seymour's Proceedings—Dervish Pasha's Proposals—Action of the French—Exchange of views between the Admiral and Egyptian Authorities—Conduct of the Khedive—Remonstrances of the Consuls-General—Admiral Seymour's Reply—Warlike Preparations continued—Lieutenant Dorrien—Admiral Seymour demands Surrender of Forts—Egyptian Overtures—Departure of the Khedive.

ON the 1st July, matters had become so threatening that the Consular archives and staff were ordered to be removed on board a Peninsular and Oriental steamer chartered as a place of refuge for the British subjects whose duties compelled them to remain in Egypt.

The same day Admiral Seymour telegraphed that there were upwards of 10,000 men in the forts and barracks of Alexandria, and that Arabi hoped to get the allied fleets into a trap by sinking stone barges in the Bar Channel.

On the 3rd, Admiral Seymour received the following instructions :—

'Prevent any attempt to bar channel into port. If work is resumed on earthworks, or fresh guns mounted, inform Military Commander that you have orders to prevent it; and if not immediately discontinued destroy earthworks and silence batteries if they open fire, having given sufficient notice to population, shipping, and foreign men-of-war.'

On the 4th, Dervish Pasha made a final attempt to get rid of Arabi and his party by diplomacy. The Turkish Envoy invited the Minister of War to go to Constantinople 'to live with the Sultan and other friends.'

HOSTILE PREPARATIONS. 117

Arabi, to his credit, refused to desert his followers, and replied that the people would not suffer him to leave, and that as they were attached to him he could not abandon them. The same day a telegram was sent to the Admiral as follows :—

'Acquaint Military Governor that any attempt to bar the channel will be considered as a hostile act which will be treated accordingly. Concert with Consul-General as to notice to Europeans if occasion arises. Before taking any hostile step, invite co-operation of French Admiral; but you are not to postpone acting on your instructions because French decline to join.'

On the same day the English Admiral telegraphed,

'Two additional guns placed in Pharos Castle last night. Parapet facing sea-wall was also strengthened. Consul-General would prefer I postponed operations until Thursday morning to allow time for people to quit Cairo. No change in the works bearing on the harbour. French Admiral has asked for orders. Have received reply from Military Governor, Arabi sending Egyptian Admiral to give assurance no channel obstructions contemplated.'

Admiral Seymour had now taken steps for strengthening the fleet, by ordering the ironclad *Sultan* from Malta. He had also received intelligence that two battalions had been ordered to Cyprus from Malta in ships of the Channel Squadron. He had, moreover, in concert with the Acting Consul-General succeeded in getting nearly the whole of the European residents out of the country. It only remained to see how far in the event of action becoming necessary, he could count on the support of the Power which had joined England in presenting the celebrated 'Joint Note.'

On the question being put to M. De Freycinet by Lord Lyons, the French Foreign Minister replied, that his Government had decided 'not to instruct Admiral Conrad to associate himself with the English

Admiral in stopping by force the erection of batteries or the placing of guns at Alexandria.'

The reasons given were, that such a step would be an act of war, which could not be resorted to without the consent of the Legislature, and that if the Government applied to the Chamber for sanction, they did not feel sure about obtaining it.

On the 6th, the French Ambassador called on Lord Granville and informed him, that in the event of a bombardment taking place, the French ships would go to Port Saïd.

On the 6th July, the English Admiral, finding that the warlike preparations on shore were continuing, wrote to the Military Governor of Alexandria, that unless such proceedings were discontinued, it would become his duty to open fire on the works in course of construction.

The following reply was received :—

'*To the Admiral of the British Fleet.*

'MY FRIEND ENGLISH ADMIRAL,

'I had the honour to receive your letter of the 6th July, in which you state that you had been informed that two guns had been mounted and that other works are going on on the sea-shore, and in reply I beg to assure you that the said assertions are unfounded, and that this information is like the intimation given to you about the blocking up of the entrance to the harbour, of the falseness of which you were convinced. I rely on your true feelings of humanity, and beg you to accept my respects.

'(Signed) TOULBA,
'Commandant of Forces.

'*Alexandria*, 20 *Shaban*, 1299.'

The Khedive during this period retained great self-possession and calmness. He realised perfectly the difficulties of his position, and sent for Sir Auckland Colvin, to whom he explained that should a bombardment be resolved upon he was determined to remain faithful to Egypt. He could not, he said, desert all those who had stood by him faithfully during the crisis, nor could he, merely to secure his personal safety, abandon Egypt when attacked by a foreign power. In the event of a bombardment taking place, His Highness announced his intention of retiring to a palace on the Mahmoudieh Canal, whither Dervish Pasha would accompany him, and added that the more rapidly the affair was conducted, the less danger there would be for himself personally.

On the 7th, the Consuls-General addressed Admiral Seymour, requesting to be informed whether he was satisfied with the reply of the Egyptian Government on the subject of the work on the fortifications. They (the Consuls-General) believed themselves able, in the event of the reply being incomplete, to obtain perfectly satisfactory assurances. They added that, in the event of the question not being settled, they wished to know how long a delay they could count on for the departure of their countrymen.

To this the Admiral replied the same day, that he thanked the Consuls-General for the offer they had kindly volunteered, and said that if their influence with the Military Commandant induced him to act with sincerity in forbidding the continuation of fortifications, the object aimed at would be attained ; but that mere written assurances were of little value. The Admiral pointed out that his operations, if rendered necessary, would be directed against the fortifications only. He added that in any case twenty-four hours' notice should be given.

On the 9th, Admiral Seymour telegraphed to the Secretary to the Admiralty that 'there was no doubt about the armament. Guns were being mounted in Fort Silsileh. He should give Foreign Consuls notice at daylight to-morrow, and commence action twenty-four hours after, unless forts on the isthmus and those commanding the entrance to the harbour were surrendered.'

The information upon which Admiral Seymour proposed to act was partly in the shape of a declaration made by Lieutenant Dorrien of the *Invincible*, and which (omitting immaterial parts) was as follows :—

'On the morning of the 9th day of July, 1882, at about 7.30 a.m., I drove through the Rosetta Gate, and .... reached the old quarantine station, where I .... proceeded on foot to the fort marked on Admiralty Chart "Tabia-el-Silsileh," and when within fifty yards of the said fort I observed inside two working parties of Arabs about 200 strong, under the superintendence of soldiers, parbuckling two smooth-bore guns—apparently 32-pounders—towards their respective carriages and slides, which were facing in the direction of the harbour, and which seemed to have been lately placed ready for their reception.'

On the 10th, the Admiralty telegraphed to Admiral Seymour directing him to substitute for the word 'surrendered' the words 'temporarily surrendered for the purposes of disarmament.'

On the 10th, the Admiral sent the following letter to Toulba Pasha, the Military Commandant :—

'I have the honour to inform your Excellency that as hostile preparations, evidently directed against the Squadron under my command, were in progress during yesterday at Forts Isali, Pharos, and Silsileh, I shall carry out the intention expressed to you in my letter of the 6th instant, at sunrise to-morrow, the 11th instant, unless previous to that hour you shall have temporarily surrendered to me, for the purpose of disarming. the batteries on the isthmus of Ras-el-Tin and the southern shore of the harbour of Alexandria.'

Besides the possible danger to his ships by the Egyptian preparations, it is probable that there was more than one reason which influenced the Admiral in hurrying on the bombardment. Amongst them may have been the knowledge that the Channel Squadron, under Admiral Dowell, was on its way to share the honours of the day. Besides these motives, the Admiral

HOSTILE PREPARATIONS. 121

commanding may have been desirous of allaying the growing impatience of the officers and men under his orders. Ever since the events of the 11th June, when an officer and two men belonging to the fleet were murdered in the streets of Alexandria, a good deal of dissatisfaction was expressed by the seamen under Admiral Seymour's command at the continued inaction of the Squadron.

This feeling was to some extent shared by the officers, who foresaw that the arrival of troops was only a question of a few days, and feared that in any operations undertaken, the navy would only be permitted to take a secondary part. The officers were reluctant, as they expressed it, to be employed merely ' to carry Sir Garnet Wolseley's baggage on shore,' and they felt that as what had taken place was an insult to the fleet, it was the fleet that should take the initiative. It is said that on the evening of the 9th July, a number of the commanding officers had put forward their views in a letter which they, on behalf of themselves and others, addressed to the Admiral's secretary. In this document they urged that the time had now arrived when the ships ought to commence the attack. Whether the letter was communicated to the Admiral or not, the writer is not in a position to say, but, as has been shown, on the following day, the Admiral issued his ultimatum.

On the receipt of Admiral Seymour's despatch of the 10th, a Cabinet Council was held at Ras-el-Tin. It was presided over by the Khedive in person. Dervish Pasha and Kadri Pasha were also present. It was decided to send a deputation to the Admiral to inform him that no new guns were being mounted in the forts, and to tell him that he was at liberty to send one of his officers, if he desired it, to test the truth of this statement. The deputation came back with the intelligence that the Admiral insisted on the disarmament of the forts.

The council again met at three p.m. and decided that the El Silsileh Fort and Fort Caid Bey (Pharos), and the guns placed in them on the *Eastern* Harbour, could not constitute any threat towards the vessels which were in the *Western* Harbour, and that the President of the Council should write to the Admiral in the terms of the despatch mentioned below. It was at the same time resolved that in the event of the Admiral persisting in opening fire, the forts should not answer until the fifth shot, when they were to reply.

'*Alexandria, July* 10*th,* 1882.
'ADMIRAL,

' As I had the honour to promise in the conversation I had with you this morning, I have submitted to His Highness the Khedive, in a meeting of the Ministers and principal dignitaries of the State, the conditions contained in the letter you were good enough to address this morning to the Commandant of the place, according to the terms of which you will put into execution to-morrow, the 11th instant, at daybreak, the intentions expressed in your letter of the 6th instant to the Commandant of the place, if before that time the batteries on the isthmus of Ras-el-Tin and the southern shore of the port of Alexandria are not temporarily surrendered to you, to be disarmed.

' I regret to announce to you that the Government of His Highness does not consider this proposition as acceptable. It does not in the least desire to alter its good relations with Great Britain, but it cannot perceive that it has taken any measures which can be regarded as a menace to the English fleet by works, by the mounting of new guns, or by other military preparations.

' Nevertheless, as a proof of our spirit of conciliation and of our desire, to a certain extent, to accede to your demands, we are disposed to dismount three guns in the batteries you have mentioned, either separated or together.

' If in spite of this offer you persist in opening fire, the Government reserves its freedom of action and leaves with you the responsibility of this act of aggression.

' Receive, Admiral, the assurances, &c., &c.'*

---

* This despatch was not delivered to the Admiral till the following day, as hereinafter related.

HOSTILE PREPARATIONS.

The previous day the Acting British Consul-General visited the Khedive and urged his removal to Ramleh. On the 10th Sir Auckland Colvin called to say farewell to His Highness, and used every argument to induce him to embark in one of the British vessels, but in vain. Tewfik remained firm, and announced his intention of standing by his country.*

At seven in the evening all the Consuls-General were warned to withdraw their subjects. The acting British Consul-General and Sir Auckland Colvin embarked on board the *Monarch*, and the few remaining British residents betook themselves to the P. & O. s.s. *Tanjore*.†

In the course of the day all the merchant-vessels in the harbour left, and these were followed by the foreign men-of-war. One by one the latter steamed slowly out, and as they passed the British flag-ship, her band struck up the different national airs. The last ship to leave was the Austrian frigate *Landon*, and when darkness closed in, the English ships of war were alone in the harbour of Alexandria.

At 9.20 p.m. the Admiral, in the *Invincible*, with the *Monarch* in company, weighed anchor, and steamed to a position outside the harbour. All lights were extinguished, and perfect silence was maintained as the ships cautiously felt their way through the water. At

---

* The Khedive so far yielded to the representations made to him that he removed to the Palace at Ramleh.

† There were however two exceptions which deserve to be mentioned. One was Mr. J. Easton Cornish, the English Manager of the Alexandria Water Works, who resolutely refused to desert his post. The other was the Director-General of the Egyptian Postal Administration, Halton Bey, likewise an Englishman, who, having a large number of European employés under his care, determined not to forsake them, and embarked at the last moment with them in a small steamer which remained moored alongside the breakwater during the bombardment.

10.10 both vessels came to an anchor off Mex, where their consort, the *Penelope*, was already lying.

In the meantime, all the ships had struck their upper masts, sent down top-gallant and royal yards, and got everything ready for action, and in this state they remained for the night.

CHAPTER XV.

THE SHIPS AND FORTS.

Position of Alexandria—The Fortifications—Their Armament—British Ships of War—Their Armament, Tonnage, Horse Power, and Crews.

IN order to give the reader an idea of the comparative strength of the opposing forces, it is necessary, in the first place, to give a short description of the fortifications of Alexandria, and their armaments.

Alexandria is situated on a strip of land between the Mediterranean and Fort Mareotis; a considerable portion of it stands on a promontory, which, jutting out from the rest towards the north-west, is bounded on the north-east by the new or Eastern Harbour, and on the south-west by the old or Western Harbour.

The fortifications, which were intended to protect the city from an attack, not only by sea, but also from the direction of Lake Mareotis, are said to have been planned in Paris, and executed under the direction of French engineers. The whole of the works were originally well built, but had fallen much out of repair.

The material used was a soft limestone but little calculated to withstand modern artillery. The parapets were of sand, covered with a thin coating of cement. The *escarps* and counterscarps were riveted with stonework. The rifled guns, without exception, fired through embrasures, and nearly all the smooth-bore guns fired over parapets.

The armament consisted of

	Weight of Shot.
RIFLED GUNS.	
10-inch M.L.R. Armstrongs	300 lbs.
9 ,, ,, ,,	250 ,,
8 ,, ,, ,,	180 ,,
7 ,, ,, ,,	115 ,,
40-Pounder B.L. Armstrongs	40 ,,
SMOOTH BORE GUNS.	
15-inch	450 ,,
10 ,,	135 ,,
6.5 ,,	36 ,,

MORTARS.
20-inch, 13-inch, 12-inch, and 11-inch.

The buildings were none of them bomb-proof; nor, except in the case of Fort Pharos, were there any casemated or covered batteries.

The forts on the sea face of Alexandria may be summed up as follows :—

WEST OF ALEXANDRIA.
1. Fort Marabout.
2. Fort Adjemi.
3. Fort Marza el Kanat.

SOUTH WEST OF ALEXANDRIA.
4. Citadel of Mex.
5. Old Fort of Mex.
6. Mex Lines.

SOUTH OF ALEXANDRIA.
7. Fort Kamaria.
8. Fort Omuk Kubebe.
9. Fort Saleh Aga.
10. Fort adjoining Battery.

NORTH OF ALEXANDRIA.

11. Light House or Ras-el-Tin Fort.
12. Lines of Ras-el-Tin (including the Hospital Battery.)
13. Fort Adda.
14. Fort Pharos.
15. Fort Silsileh ('Pharillon').

Of the above, Fort Adjemi took no part in the action, owing to it being impossible to train the guns in the the direction of the attacking vessels.

Fort Marabout ($7\frac{1}{2}$ miles distant by the coast line from Alexandria) had :—Three 9-inch M.L.R. Armstrongs, eight 10-inch S.B. guns, 17 6·5-inch guns, and seven mortars mounted.

The armament of these two forts is not included in the following tables.

The armament of the forts at Alexandria engaged is summarised in the following tables :—

RIFLED GUNS.

Forts, &c.	Mounted.					Un-mounted.		Total.
	10″ M.L.	9′ M.L.	8′ M.L.	7″ M.L.	B.L. 40 pr.	10″ M.L.	9″ M.L.	
Silsileh		1	1				2	4
Pharos	1	3	2		2			8
Adda	1	3	1					5
Ras-el-Tin Lines ...	1	3	2	2	1			9
Ras-el-Tin Fort ...	1	4	1					6
Omuk Kubebe			2					2
Mex Fort	1	1	3			2	4	11
TOTAL............	5	15	12	2	3	2	6	45
	_____ 37					_____ 8		

SMOOTH-BORE GUNS AND MORTARS.

Fort or Battery.	Guns.			Mortars.				Total.
	15'	10"	65"	20"	13"	12"	11"	
Fort Silsileh		3			1			4
„ Pharos		6	31		4			41
„ Adda		14			5			19
Ras-el-Tin Lines ...	4	15	11	1	6	1	2	40
Fort Ras-el-Tin ...	2	5	21		1		2	31
„ Saleh Aga ...		4	8					12
Battery		2	2					4
Fort Omuk Kubebe ...		6	10		1		1	18
„ Kamaria		2	3		1			6
Mex Lines	4	11	9					24
Fort Mex		4	5		3		2	14
TOTAL............	10	72	100	1	22	1	7	213
	182			31				

The British Squadron off Alexandria on the 11th July, 1882, consisted of the following vessels, viz.: the ironclads *Alexandra, Superb, Sultan, Temeraire, Inflexible, Monarch, Invincible* and *Penelope,* the torpedo vessel *Hecla,* the despatch boat *Helicon,* the gun-vessels *Condor* and *Bittern* and the gun-boats *Beacon, Cygnet,* and *Decoy.*

The *Penelope,* detached from the Reserve Squadron, and selected on account of her light draught of water, had only arrived from England on the 9th July.

The *Alexandra,* 12 guns, Captain Charles F. Hotham, is a central battery ironclad with twin screws, and the most powerful ship of her class in the British Navy. Her tonnage (displacement) is 9490, and her engines are of 8610 indicated horse-power. Her crew numbers 674 men. She has a battery containing two 11-inch 25 ton guns, and ten 10-inch 18 ton guns. Her battery is protected by 8-inch armour plating, and her hull by

THE SHIPS AND FORTS. 129

plates 12 inches in the centre, reduced to 10 inches at the bow, and 6 inches at the stern.

The *Superb*, 16 guns, Captain Thomas Le Hunt-Ward, is a central battery ironclad of 9170 tons and 6580 horse-power, and she has a crew of 620 men. Her battery contains sixteen 18-ton guns, and her armour is 10 inches thick on the battery, and 12 inches on the sides, reduced to $8\frac{1}{2}$ inches at the bow and stern.

The *Sultan*, 12 guns, Captain W. J. Hunt Grubbe, is a central battery ironclad of 9290 tons and 7720 horse-power, with a crew of 620 men. Her battery contains eight 18-ton and four $12\frac{1}{2}$-ton guns. Her armour is 9 inches thick in the centre, and 6 inches at the bow and stern.

The *Temeraire*, 8 guns, Captain Henry F. Nicholson, is an ironclad with a central battery of a different type from the vessels previously mentioned. Her tonnage is 8450, horse-power 7520, and her crew 530. Her distinguishing feature is that she carries the upper deck battery in two fixed turrets open at the top. At each end of the upper deck is a pear-shaped tower, containing a turn-table on which is a 25-ton gun, worked by hydraulic machinery. Her main-deck battery is divided. The foremost part contains two 25-ton guns, and the aftermost four 18-ton guns. The fore turret is protected with 10-inch, and the after one, as well as the battery, with 8-inch armour. She carries 11-inch armour amidships, reduced to 10 inches at the bow, and 8 inches at the stern.

The *Inflexible*, four guns, Captain John Fisher, the most remarkable vessel in the squadron, and the largest ship in the British navy, is a twin-screw double-turret ironclad of 11,407 tons, 8010 horse-power, with a crew of 440. She carries four 80-ton guns in two turrets. She possesses a central armed citadel, protected by

12-inch armour. The armour at the water-line is 24 inches, and above 20 inches in thickness. On the turrets it is 18.

The *Monarch*, 7 guns, Captain Henry Fairfax, is a double-turret ironclad of 8320 tons 7840 horse-power, with a crew of 530. She carries one 7-inch $6\frac{1}{2}$-ton gun, two 9-inch 12-ton guns, and four 12-inch 25-ton guns, the latter in the turrets. She is protected by 8-inch armour on the broadside, and by 10-inch on the turrets.

The *Invincible*, 14 guns, Captain R. H. Molyneux, is a central battery twin-screw ironclad of 6010 tons, 4830 horse-power, and has a crew of 480. Her armament consists of ten 9-inch 12-ton guns, and four 64-pounder 71-cwt. guns. Her armour is eight inches thick at the water-line, and six inches at the other parts.

The *Penelope*, 11 guns, Captain St. George, D. A. Irvine, is a central battery twin-screw ironclad, of 4390 tons, and 4700 horse-power. Her armament comprises eight 8-inch 9-ton and three 40-pounder 35 cwt. guns. Her armour is six inches thick on the battery aud broadside, and five inches at the bow and stern. She has a crew of 230 men.

The *Hecla*, 6 guns, is a torpedo-vessel of 6400 tons, and 1760 horse power, with a crew of 251 men. Her armament consists of five 64-pounder muzzle-loading guns, and one 40-pounder breech-loading gun.

The *Helicon* is a despatch vessel of 1000 tons, and carries two 20-pounder breech-loading guns.

The *Condor* and *Bittern* are gun-vessels of 805 tons, and carry each one 7-inch $6\frac{1}{2}$-ton gun, and two 40-pounder breech-loading guns, with crews of 100 men.

The *Beacon* is a gun-boat of 603 tons, and carries

one 7-inch 6½-ton gun, and one 64-pounder, with a crew of 80 men.

The *Cygnet* and *Decoy* are gun-boats of 455 tons and 430 tons respectively, are each armed with two 64-pounder muzzle-loading and two 20-pound breech-loading guns. They carry crews of 60 men.

In addition to the armament above given, the eight ironclads carried each from six to eight 20-pounder rifled breech-loading guns, and with the exception of the *Penelope*, from eight to twelve machine-guns.

There were also 880 supernumerary seamen and marines on board the fleet.

CHAPTER XVI.

BOMBARDMENT OF THE FORTS OF ALEXANDRIA.

Admiral Seymour's Orders—Overtures for Peace—Official Reports of the Bombardment—Observations on the Engagement—Casualties in the Fleet — Injuries received by Ships—Expenditure of Ammunition— Egyptian Account of the Bombardment.

THE orders given by Admiral Seymour to the fleet the day previous to the bombardment were, omitting certain details, as follows :—

'The Squadron under my command will attack the forts as soon as the twenty-four hours given to neutrals to leave the place have expired, which will be at 5 a.m. on the 11th. There will be two attacks.

'1. From the inside of the harbour in which the *Invincible, Monarch,* and *Penelope,* will take part.

'2. By the *Sultan, Superb, Temeraire, Alexandra,* and *Inflexible,* from outside the breakwater.

'Action will commence by signal from me, when the ship nearest the newly-erected earthwork near Fort Ada will fire a shell into the earthwork.

'On the batteries opening on the offshore squadron in reply, every effort will be made by the ships to destroy the batteries on the Ras-el-Tin peninsula, especially the Light-house Battery bearing on the harbour. When this is accomplished the *Sultan, Superb,* and *Alexandra,* will move to the eastward and attack Fort Pharos, and if possible the Silsileh battery.

'The *Inflexible* will move down this afternoon to the position off the Corvette Pass, assigned to her yesterday, and be prepared to open fire on the guns in the Mex Lines, in support of the inshore squadron, when signal is made.

'The *Temeraire, Sultan,* and *Alexandra,* will flank the works on Ras-el-Tin.

'The gun-vessels and gun-boats will remain outside and keep out of fire until a favourable opportunity offers itself of moving in to the attack of Mex.

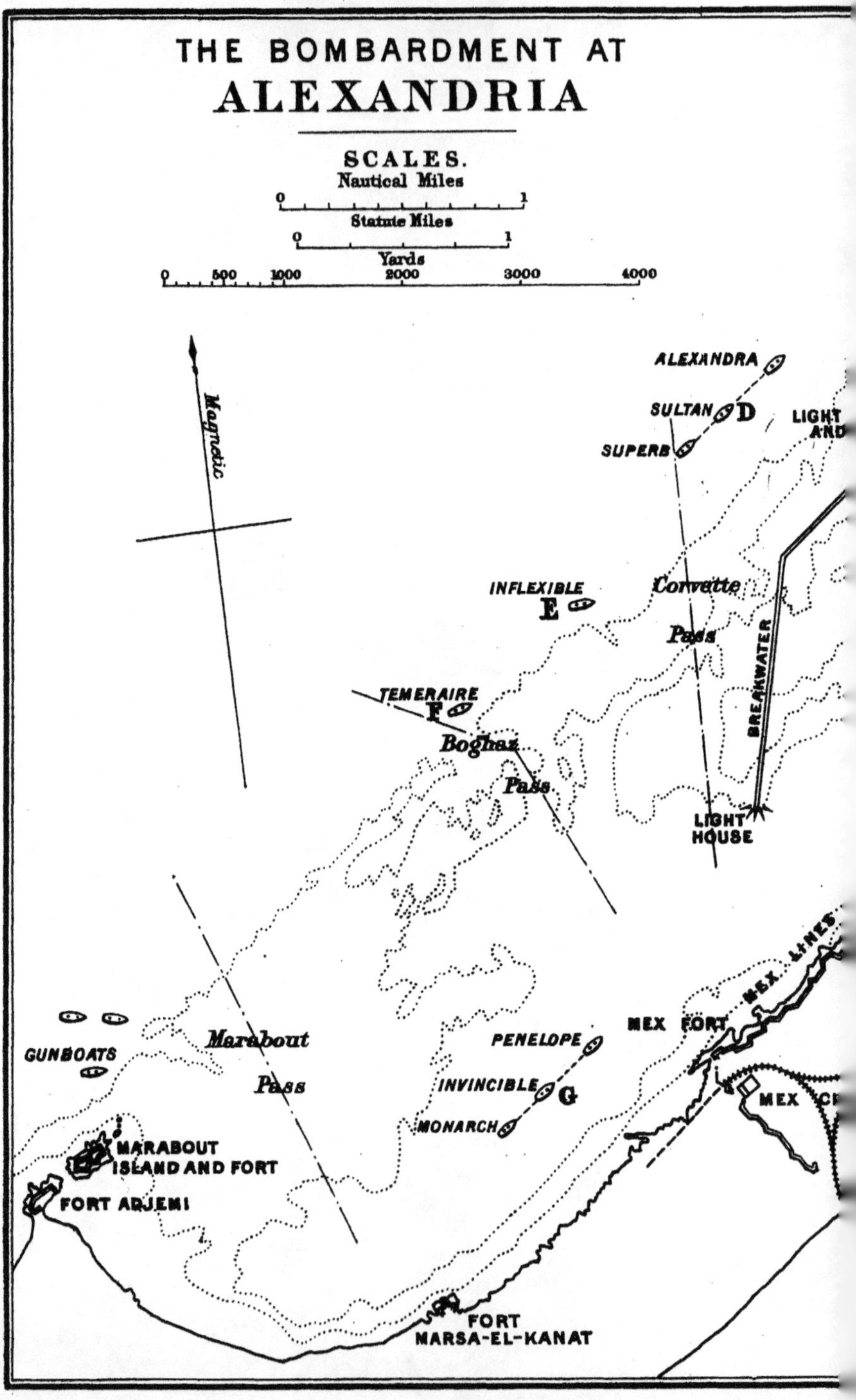
THE BOMBARDMENT AT
ALEXANDRIA
SCALES.
Nautical Miles
0
1
Statute Miles
0
1
Yards
0
500
1000
2000
3000
4000
Magnetic
ALEXANDRA
SULTAN
D
SUPERB
LIGHT
AND
INFLEXIBLE
E
Corvette
Pass
BREAKWATER
TEMERAIRE
F
Boghaz
Pass
LIGHT
HOUSE
MEX LINES
MEX FORT
MEX
GUNBOATS
Marabout
Pass
PENELOPE
INVINCIBLE
G
MONARCH
MARABOUT
ISLAND AND FORT
FORT ADJEMI
FORT
MARSA-EL-KANAT

London: Hu

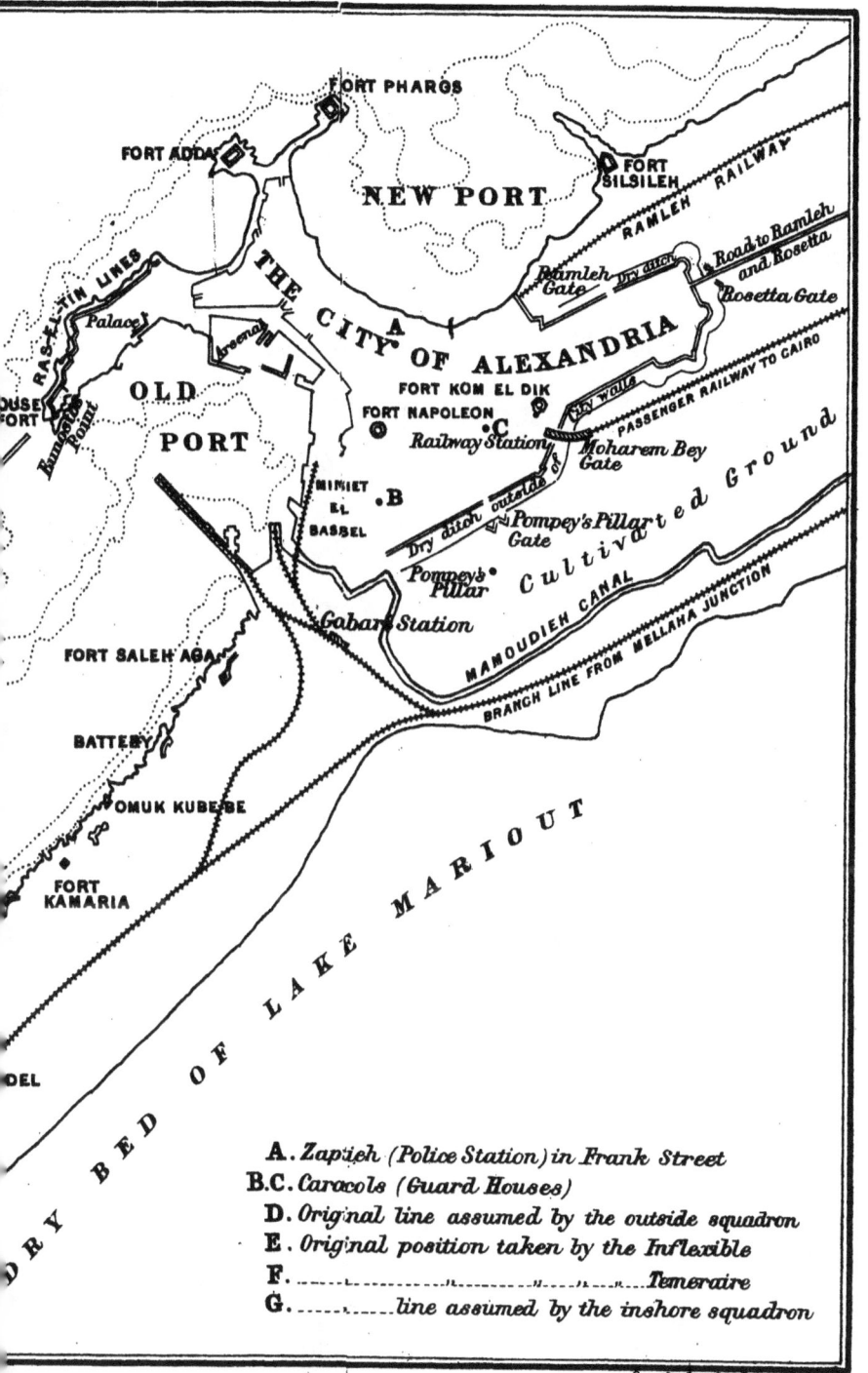

'Ships must be guided in a great measure by the state of the weather, whether they anchor or remain under way. If they anchor a wire hawser should be used as a spring.

'The inshore squadron will be under my personal command, the offshore ships under that of Captain Hunt-Grubbe, C.B., of the *Sultan*.

'The *Helicon* and *Condor* will act as repeating ships.

'Finally, the object of this attack is the destruction of the earthworks and dismantling of the batteries on the sea-fronts of Alexandria.

'It is possible that the work may not be accomplished under two or three days.'

In the early morning of the 11th, an incident occurred which might have rendered all the Admiral's arrangements unnecessary. A steam-launch, with an Egyptian Pasha and other officials on board, arrived alongside the *Invincible*, bringing the letter, the contents of which have been already given, from the President of the Council of Ministers.

The small steamer had been cruising about all night looking for the Admiral, but owing to his having removed from the *Helicon* to the *Invincible* the day before, had not been able to find him. At 2.40 a.m., it had arrived alongside the *Sultan*, the Captain of which ship had signalled to the *Alexandra*, 'Egyptian steam-launch with officers looking for Admiral. Do you think I can with propriety tell them?' Whether the steam-launch was directed to the *Invincible* or not, the writer is not in a position to say. Anyhow, it was not till some hours afterwards that the officials on board were able to put themselves in communication with the Admiral. The latter, on reading the despatch they had brought, replied as follows :—' I have the honour to acknowledge the receipt of your communication of yesterday's date, and regret that I am unable to accept the proposal contained therein.'

The official reports of the bombardment are as follows :—

'*Invincible* at Alexandria,
'*July* 20*th*, 1882.

'SIR,

'In continuation of my official report of proceedings, dated the 19th instant, I have the honour to submit, for their Lordships' information, a more detailed account of the action which took place on the 11th, between the squadron under my command and the forts which defend Alexandria, than I was enabled to forward at that time.

'As will be seen by the enclosed order of battle, a copy of which was supplied to each captain, I had decided to make two attacks, one by the *Sultan*, *Superb*, and *Alexandra*, on the north face of Ras-el-Tin, supported by the fire from the after-turret of the *Inflexible*, anchored off the entrance to the Corvette Pass, thus enfilading the Lighthouse Batteries; the other, by the *Invincible*, *Monarch*, and *Penelope*, from inside the reefs, aided by the fire of the *Inflexible*'s forward turret and the *Temeraire*, which took up a position close to the fairway buoy of the Boghaz, or principal pass leading into Alexandria Harbour. The *Helicon* and *Condor* were detailed for duty as repeating ships, and the *Beacon*, *Bittern*, *Cygnet*, and *Decoy*, were employed as directed by signal during the day. At 7 a.m. on the 11th I signalled from the *Invincible* to the *Alexandra* to fire a shell into the recently-armed earthworks termed the Hospital Battery, and followed this by a general signal to the fleet, "Attack the enemy's batteries," when immediate action ensued between all the ships in the positions assigned to them, and the whole of the forts commanding the entrance to the harbour of Alexandria. A steady fire was maintained on all sides until 10.30 a.m., when the *Sultan*, *Superb*, and *Alexandra*, which had been hitherto under way, anchored off the Light House Fort, and by their well-directed fire, assisted by that of the *Inflexible*, which weighed and joined them at 12.30 p.m., succeeded in silencing most of the guns in the forts on Ras-el-Tin; still some heavy guns in Fort Adda kept up a desultory fire. About 1.30 p.m. a shell from the *Superb*, whose practice in the afternoon was very good, blew up the magazine and caused the retreat of the remaining garrison. These ships then directed their attention to Fort Pharos, which was silenced with the assistance of the *Temeraire*, which joined them at 2.30 p.m., when a shot from the *Inflexible* dismounted one of the heavy guns. The Hospital Battery was well fought throughout, and, although silenced for a time by a shell from the *Inflexible*, it was not until 5 p.m. that the artillerymen were compelled to retire from their guns by the fire of the offshore squadron and the *Inflexible*. The *Inflexible*, with my flag, supported by the *Penelope*, both ships being at anchor, the latter on one occasion shifting berth, and assisted by the *Monarch*, under way inside the reefs, as well as by the *Inflexible* and *Temeraire* in the Boghaz and Corvette Channels, succeeded, after an engagement of some hours, in silencing

BOMBARDMENT OF THE FORTS OF ALEXANDRIA. 135

and partially destroying the batteries and lines of Mex. Fort Marsa-el-Khanat was destroyed by the explosion of the magazine after half an hour's action with the *Monarch*. About 2 p.m., seeing that the gunners of the western lower battery of Mex had abandoned their guns, and that the supports had probably retired to the citadel, I called in the gun-vessels and gun-boats, and under cover of their fire landed a party of twelve volunteers, under the command of Lieutenant B. R. Bradford, of the *Invincible*, accompanied by Lieutenant Richard Poore of that ship, Lieutenant the Honourable Hedworth Lambton (my flag lieutenant), Major Tulloch, Welsh Regiment, attached to my staff, and Mr. Hardy, midshipman in charge of the boat, who got on board through the surf, and destroyed, with charges of gun-cotton, two ten-inch M. L. R. guns and spiked six smooth-bore guns in the right-hand water battery at Mex, and returned without a casualty beyond the loss of one of their boats (*Bittern's* dingy) on the rocks. This was a hazardous operation very well carried out. Previous to this, after the action had become general, Commander Lord Charles Beresford, of the *Condor*, stationed as repeating ship, seeing the accuracy with which two 10-inch rifled guns in Fort Marabout were playing upon the ships engaged off Fort Mex, steamed up to within range of his 7-inch 90 cwt. gun, and by his excellent practice soon drew off the fire. I then ordered him to be supported by the *Beacon*, *Bittern*, *Cygnet*, and *Decoy*, the *Cygnet* having been engaged with the Ras-el-Tin forts during the early part of the day. I am happy to say during the action no casualties happened to those vessels, owing, in a great measure, to the able manner in which they were manœuvred, and their light draught enabling them to take up their position on the weakest point of the batteries. The action generally terminated successfully at 5.30 p.m., when the ships anchored for the night.

'The force opposed to us would have been more formidable had every gun mounted on the line of works been brought into action, but in the Ras-el-Tin batteries few of the large smooth-bores and fewer of the French 36-pounders, bought in the time of Mehemet Ali, were manned, the Egyptians preferring to use the English 10-inch, 9-inch, 8-inch, and smaller muzzle-loading rifled guns. These guns are precisely the same as those which Her Majesty's ships carry, and no better muzzle-loading guns can be found. They were abundantly, even lavishly, supplied with projectiles of the latest description—chilled shot, and the sighting of the guns was excellent. The same may be said of the guns in the Mex Lines, excepting that in them the 36-pounders were more used, and that one, if not two, 15-inch smooth-bores were brought into action in addition to the 10-inch, 9-inch, and smaller M. L. R. guns fired. Fort Marabout brought two 10-inch M. L. R. guns into action at long range, shell after shell of which came up towards the inshore squadron in an excellent line, falling from ten to thirty yards short.

Not one shell from the guns in the southern batteries burst on board H. M.'s ships during the day.

'I forward for their Lordships' perusal the official report of Captain Walter J. Hunt-Grubbe, C. B., A. D. C., of H. M.'s ship the *Sultan*, who most ably commanded the outside squadron, which bore the brunt of the action, as the accompanying statements of the damages sustained by the *Sultan*, *Superb*, and *Alexandra*, fully testify. I have no account of the damage sustained by the *Penelope*, as that vessel was shortly afterwards detached from my flag. The upper works of the *Invincible* and *Inflexible* were a good deal knocked about, but no serious injury was inflicted. No damage was done to the *Temeraire* or *Monarch*.

* * * * * * *

'It is quite impossible for me to account for the very small loss sustained by Her Majesty's ships on this occasion, considering the amount of shell and shot which struck them, and the injuries inflicted on the hulls of the *Sultan*, *Superb*, and *Alexandra*, and in a lesser degree on those of the *Invincible*, *Penelope*, and *Inflexible* ; but I may here express my deep regret that Lieutenant Francis Jackson and Mr. William Shannon, carpenter of the *Inflexible*, should have fallen. The wounded, who when last heard from were doing well, were sent to Malta in the *Humber*. I have, &c.,

'F. BEAUCHAMP SEYMOUR,
'Admiral and Commander-in-Chief.

'To the Secretary of the Admiralty.'

July 14th, 1882.

'SIR,

'In compliance with your memorandum of the 10th instant, I have great pleasure in reporting the successful manner in which the off-shore squadron, under my personal command, consisting of at first the *Sultan*, *Superb*, and *Alexandra*, and afterwards the *Temeraire* and *Inflexible*, attacked and silenced the earthworks and batteries on the 11th instant, comprising Forts Pharos and Adda, the batteries at Hospital Point, the new earthwork, which was of formidable nature, and the Light-house batteries bearing on the harbour.

'The action was commenced at 6.59 a.m. by the *Alexandra* firing a shell at the earthwork near Fort Adda, and a few minutes after all the forts replied, and the action became general.

'At this time I was steaming in close order, at about 1500 yards past the batteries and was turning in succession with a view to anchor in the order prescribed by you, but before doing so I again repassed. Finding, however, that the batteries were stronger than was anticipated, and that the Egyptian gunners were far from despicable, making, indeed, very good practice, I deemed it advisable to anchor and obtain the exact range. This was executed with great precision by the squadron, and we soon appeared to be dismounting their guns.

BOMBARDMENT OF THE FORTS OF ALEXANDRIA. 137

'At 10.30 a.m. the Light-house Battery, which had been, earlier in the day, severely handled by the *Inflexible*, ceased to return our fire, their last rifled gun being disabled, though not before it had given us much trouble.

'At 12.45 p.m. the *Temeraire* and *Inflexible* (you no longer requiring their services) began to assist in our attack, shelling Forts Pharos and Adda with great effect. By this time the fire was considerably less, but one rifled gun on the Hospital earthwork, which it was impossible to dismount, being invisible from the ship, did us great damage.

'At 1.32 p.m. a shell from the *Superb* blew up the magazine by Fort Adda and that fort and Pharos were hurriedly evacuated. After this the enemy's firing ceased, and on our side it was confined to dislodging parties of men, reported from time to time at the tops as reassembling in rear of the earthwork. The ships were handled, and fought in a manner reflecting great credit on their officers and ships' companies. I have, &c.,

'W. HUNT-GRUBBE, Captain.

'To Admiral Sir F. Beauchamp Seymour, G.C.B.,
'Commander-in-Chief.'

The weather was fine and the sea smooth during the bombardment. The wind and sun were both in the enemy's favour, and the smoke, which rose like a thick wall at times, prevented those on board the ships seeing the results of their fire.

It was at 9.40, and not at 10.30, as stated in Admiral Seymour's despatch that the *Sultan*, *Alexandra*, and *Superb*, came to an anchor, and by 10.30, with the aid of the *Inflexible*, they had silenced the Light-house Battery at Ras-el-Tin. In addition to helping the three outside vessels the *Inflexible* had meanwhile been engaging Mex Fort, and doing great execution with her 80-ton guns.

The *Temeraire*, at anchor, was all this time supporting the attack of the inside squadron on Mex, at a range of 3500 to 4000 yards, and making great havoc with her guns. Unfortunately Captain Nicholson, in anchoring, had got too close to the shoal water of the pass, and his vessel, in swinging round, grounded on the reef. Her situation was remarked by the Admiral, who signalled to her, 'What water have you got; you seem to be in a very dangerous position?' The Peninsular and Oriental Company's S.S. *Tanjore*, Captain Briscoe, then under way in the offing, gallantly offered to go to the assistance of the huge ironclad, but the offer was declined, and the *Condor* performed that service instead; eventually the ship was got off without injury.

Whilst this was going on, the inside squadron, under the Admiral's immediate command, was not idle. The *Invincible* and *Penelope*, at anchor, were engaging all the batteries about Mex at a range of from 1300 to 1500 yards. The enemy replied briskly both from their rifled and smooth-bored guns. The *Monarch*, under way, was firing at Mex Forts and Lines, Marsa-el-Kanat, and at Omuk-Kubebe, at various ranges. At 8.45 one of the *Monarch's* shells exploded the powder-magazine at Marsa-el-Kanat, and at 8.27 the Admiral signalled to her, ' Close nearer the forts, keeping as close to them as possible ; I want you to go a-head.' By 9 o'clock all the guns, except four at Fort Mex, had been silenced ; these four gave considerable trouble to the ships. It was difficult to hit upon the exact locality of the guns as they were dimly and occasionally seen through the smoke, and the elevation given to the ships' guns from time to time was at fault. At 9 the Admiral signalled to the *Penelope*, ' All your shell appear to fall short,' and a few minutes later to the *Monarch*, ' Your shot are falling short.' This was followed by the signal to the latter ship, ' Considerably over,' and by another, ' Very short.' By this time the Mex Batteries were completely silenced, and the Admiral signalled to the inside squadron, ' Cease firing.'

BOMBARDMENT OF THE FORTS OF ALEXANDRIA. 139

Fort Marabout had opened fire on the ships of the inside squadron at a range of 4200 yards, but they did not trouble to reply, as all the shot fell short. It was at 8 a.m. that Lord Charles Beresford performed his exploit with the *Condor* in taking the little vessel to Marabout. Here choosing a position upon which the enemy's guns could not be brought to bear, he engaged the fort at close range single-handed, the Admiral signalling, 'Well done, *Condor*.'

At 10.35 the flag-ship signalled to the *Monarch*, 'Steam close in to batteries we have silenced, and drop a few shell into them at close range.' This was followed by the signal, 'Go as close to forts as water will permit.' The *Monarch* then steamed in shore, and, having asked permission to fire a broadside, poured in a tremendous fire from all her guns. At 11.30, there being no return fire, she, as well as the *Inflexible*, ceased firing.

At 11.40 the gun-boats having returned from Marabout, the *Monarch*, which remained under way, was signalled to support them in an attempt to destroy the works, but ordered not to fire unless fired upon. All the gun-boats were at the same time signalled to close in to the batteries, and, remaining under way, to destroy their rifled guns. The *Condor*, ten minutes after, signalled that she had only 21 shell for each gun left, and received the order to cease firing. The gun-boats, supported by the *Monarch*, continued to fire on the works.

At 11.58, the *Monarch*, observing soldiers running back into the batteries, permission was given her to re-open fire.

Permission was also given to the *Penelope* to fire at the rifled guns in the batteries with her 40-pounder. At 12.20 p.m. the *Monarch* ceased firing, signalling that she had driven about 200 soldiers out of the works. At 12.50 p.m. the *Penelope* was ordered to get under way, and taking advantage of her light draught, to try to dismount the guns at Mex. She then weighed and proceeded in towards Mex Fort, firing at intervals. At 1.10 the windmills in the neighbourhood of the forts were seen to be full of soldiers, and the *Monarch* was ordered to open fire on them with her light guns. At 1.15 the gun-boats were ordered to take up position near the old fort at Mex to cover the landing-party from the *Invincible*. At 1.55 the landing-party left the flag-ship, and destroyed the guns at Mex Fort. At 3.25 the *Penelope* signalled to the Admiral that Fort Kamaria had its guns manned, though from her inshore position, the ship's guns would not bear on them. The Admiral, in consequence, directed the *Penelope* to change her position and open fire on the fort. About the same time soldiers were observed transporting light guns into one of the Mex Batteries, and the *Monarch* was signalled to again attack. Both vessels promptly responded, and steaming into position, poured in a devastating fire on the points indicated. At 5.30, there being no reply from the enemy, the inside squadron ceased firing.

To go back to the outside vessels: a little after ten the Harem buildings of the Ras-el-Tin Palace had been set on fire by a shell. As early as 10.30 the ships were beginning to run short of ammunition, and the *Sultan* signalled to the *Alexandra*, ' How many shell have you?' and received the answer ' Twenty.' At this time one of the *Alexandra's* guns was dismounted and rendered unserviceable.

At 12.30 p.m. the *Sultan* signalled to the *Inflexible*, whose work was now finished at Ras-el-Tin and Mex, ' Adda and Pharos are the only ones not silenced, all our filled shell are expended, and if you are going that way, one or two shell from your heavy guns would do much good, if you don't mind.' At 12.35 the *Sultan* added, 'Please silence Adda as well.' The *Inflexible* then stood across to Fort Adda, and at 12.40 opened fire. Shortly after, the *Temeraire* was signalled, 'Assist *Inflexible* in destroying Pharos and Silsileh.' The *Temeraire* then weighed, and steamed over to the position indicated.

At 1 the *Alexandra* signalled that she had only thirty common shell left, and was answered by the *Sultan* that she had none at all, and that the *Alexandra* had better use Palliser's, as the *Sultan* was doing.

At 1.32 Fort Adda ceased firing, on her magazine being blown up.

At 1.35, with the exception of the Hospital Fort, all the batteries from Fort Adda westward being silenced, the *Superb* signalled the fact to the *Sultan*, and suggested getting under weigh. The *Sultan* replied in the affirmative, adding, 'Can you touch up Pharos? *Temeraire* now on her way to assist *Inflexible* at Pharos. I have no shell filled, nor has *Alexandra*.' The *Superb* accordingly proceeded towards Fort Pharos and opened fire.

At two the *Sultan* signalled to the *Inflexible*, which was engaging the Hospital Battery and Fort Pharos, 'Proceed to Pharillon.'

A 2.55 a shot from the Hospital Battery struck the *Inflexible* aloft, carrying away the slings of the mainyards.

At 5 the Hospital Battery fired its last shot.

At 5.10 the *Inflexible* proceeded across to engage Forts Pharillon and Silsileh, all the other forts from Ras-el-Tin eastward, having been silenced.

At 5.15 the general signal, 'Cease firing,' was made, followed at 6.5 by 'Anchor in same position as last night.' This ended the operations for the day.

The casualties on board the ships were but slight, as appears from the list subjoined—

	Killed.	Wounded.
Alexandra	1	3
Superb	1	1
Sultan	2	8
Inflexible	1	2
Temeraire	0	0
Invincible	0	6
Monarch	0	0
Penelope	0	8
Hecla	0	0
Bittern	0	0
Condor	0	0
Beacon	0	0
Cygnet	0	0
Decoy	0	0
Helicon	0	0
	5	28

The expenditure of ammunition by the Squadron appears from the following table :—

Ship.	Common.	Pallisser.	Shrapnel.	Segment.	Empty Shell.	Shot.	Case.	Total.	Martini-Henry.	Nordenfe'dt.	Gatling.	Rockets.
Alexandra	379	23	1	..	..	4	..	407	..	4000	340	..
Superb	257	83	25	34	..	12	..	411	..	1161	880	..
Sultan	247	24	3	44	10	10	..	338	..	1800	2000	..
Penelope	241	..	45	32	..	62	..	380	5000	1672	..	..
Monarch	227	5	129	..	..	6	..	367	1800	3440	2680	21
Temeraire	139	70	13	6	..	..	..	228	..	160	..	..
Invincible	221	..	25	..	2	2	..	250	2000	2000	1000	..
Inflexible	139	21	11	37	..	..	..	208	..	2000	..	..
Beacon	21	..	..	1	61	18	..	101	320	..	..	3
Condor	162	..	8	..	31	..	..	201	1000	..	200	13
Bittern	66	7	1	..	..	12	3	89	..	..	..	..
Cygnet	72	..	..	..	71	..	..	143	..	..	..	..
Decoy	69	..	..	..	..	..	..	69	40	..	..	..
Helicon	6	..	..	..	..	..	..	6	..	..	..	..
Total	2246	233	261	154	175	126	3	3198	10,160	16,233	7100	37

There were 1731 shot and shell fired from the heavy guns, of these 88 were from the *Inflexible's* 16-inch guns. There were 117 12-inch shot, 184 11-inch, 752 10-inch, 224 9-inch, 231 8-inch, and 135 7-inch fired. The average of the number of rounds for the heavy guns was a little over twenty each.

A gallant deed was done by Mr. Israel Harding,* gunner on board the *Alexandra*. A lighted shell came through on the main deck, and the officer picked it up and immersed the burning fuse in a bucket of water.

The hits received by the fleet were as follows :—

Alexandra. Twenty-four shot and shell penetrated the ship above the armour-plating, injuring several of the cabins. Several shot and shell struck the armour, of these, one which fell on the upper edge, made indentations on the plate of from five inches to one inch in depth. The foremost funnel was struck in three places, the standing rigging in eight, and the running rigging in twenty-one places. The total number of hits was about sixty.

Sultan. Number of hits, twenty-seven; of which two struck the armour, denting two plates, and starting one. One shot went through the after funnel. The holes made in the side were as follows :—one sixteen inches by twelve inches; another fifteen inches in diameter; and a third fourteen inches in diameter. The rigging was cut in several places, and a hole sixteen inches by ten made through the mainmast.

Superb. Fourteen hits, of which seven were on the hull, and seven on the upper works and spars. A ten-

---

* For his conduct on this occasion Mr. Harding received the Victoria Cross. Without wishing to detract from Mr. Harding's merits it may be mentioned that the composition of a fuse supplies its own oxygen, which permits it to burn as well under water as above, and therefore the fuse, if really burning at the time, would have been wholly unaffected by its immersion.

inch shell struck the port side, and bursting, tore a hole in the side ten feet by four feet, within three feet of the water-line. The armour-plating on the port side was struck by two shells, of which one indented the armour three inches, and the other burst, starting a plate, and breaking fourteen rivet-heads. Some of the standing and running rigging was shot away, and a hole twelve inches in diameter was made in the foremast. Two other holes in the side were as follows :—one ten inches in diameter, four feet above the water-line; the other twelve inches in diameter (made by ten-inch shot), five feet above the water-line.

Penelope. Received eight hits, of which three were on the armour, making little or no indentation. Of the others, one passed through the after embrasure on the starboard side, doing no special damage; another hit the starboard quarter gallery; the third struck the starboard gangway, hit a nine-pounder gun, carried off the sight and damaged the carriage; the fourth hit the mainyard, port side; and the fifth struck the muzzle of one of the eight-inch guns, then broke up and destroyed the transom plate of the carriage. The gun and carriage were put out of action. Some of the rigging was shot away.

Invincible. Eleven hits, six of which passed through the side. A large dent was made in the armour by a shot which also started a plate. The foreyard was struck, and the fore royal braces were shot away.

Inflexible. About six hits altogether. One shot from Eunostos Point struck the unarmoured part of the hull, and penetrating, damaged the bollards and did other injury. Other shots damaged the upperworks, but the armour-plating was not struck. One shot carried away the slings of the jeers of the mainyard.

The *Monarch, Temeraire, Hecla,* and gun-boats received no hits.

BOMBARDMENT OF THE FORTS OF ALEXANDRIA. 145

The account of the bombardment, published in the Arab paper, *El Taif*, in Cairo, was as follows :—

'WAR NEWS.—On Tuesday, 25 Shaban, 1299, at twelve o'clock in the morning (July 11th, 7 a.m.). The English opened fire on the forts of Alexandria and we returned the fire. At 10 a.m. an ironclad foundered off Fort Adda. At noon two vessels were sunk between Fort Pharos and Fort Adjemi. At 1.30 p.m. a wooden man-of-war of eight guns was sunk.

'At 5 p.m. the large ironclad was struck by a shell from Fort Pharos, the battery was injured, and a white flag was immediately hoisted by her as a signal to cease firing at her, whereupon the firing ceased on both sides, having lasted for ten hours without cessation. Some of the walls of the forts were destroyed, but they were repaired during the night. The shots and shells discharged from the two sides amounted to about 6000, and this is the first time that so large a number of missiles has been discharged in so short a time.

'At 11 a.m. on Wednesday the English ships again opened fire and were replied to by the forts, but after a short time the firing ceased on both sides, and a deputation came from Admiral Seymour and made propositions to Toulba Pasha, which he could not accept.

* * * * * * *

'No soldiers ever stood so firmly to their posts under a heavy fire as did the Egyptians under the fire of twenty-eight ships during ten hours.

* * * * * * *

'At 9 a.m. on Thursday an English man-of-war was seen to put a small screw in place of the larger one which she had been using, and it was then known that her screw had been carried away by a shot from the forts. On examining other ships it was observed that eight had been severely battered on their sides, and that one had lost her funnel.'

CHAPTER XVII.

EFFECTS OF THE BOMBARDMENT.

Fort Marabout—Fort Adjemi—Marsa-el-Kanat—Old Fort of Mex—Kamaria—Omuk Kubebe—Saleh Aga—Ras-el-Tin—The Lines of Ras-el-Tin—Hospital Battery—Fort Adda—Fort Pharos—Fort Silsileh.

WITH regard to the effects of the bombardment on the various forts, it is proposed to give a short account, taking them in the same order in which they were first presented to the reader.*

1. *Fort Marabout.*—A small store was burnt. There were several hits on the scarp, but none of the guns were in any way injured.

Fort Adjemi.—Uninjured.

3. *Marsa-el-Kanat.*—No injury was done to the fort, but a store of gun-cotton, intended for use in the neighbouring quarries, was exploded.

4. The citadel of Mex had several breaches made in the works, but no guns were dismounted.

5. *Old Fort of Mex.*—Parapets were uninjured, but the buildings in the rear were almost swept away. A small store in front of magazine was levelled to the ground. A shell, falling inside, levelled the walls, which fell in one piece. The large store was riddled with shot, but the magazine was untouched. The barracks were much damaged. The fort was found to contain many fragments of shell, and the loss of life among the

---

* The writer is indebted for much of the following information to the able report of Captain N. L. Walford, R.A.

defenders was probably considerable. The damage to the guns was as follows :—a 10-inch Armstrong gun was struck in the second coil by a shell which cut a groove of an oval shape in the metal. The coil was shaken out of place and cracked, but the gun was left serviceable. A Nordenfeldt bullet hit this gun obliquely, and penetrated 1·25 inch, and a shell also burst under the left trunnion doing no damage. A 9-inch Armstrong gun was struck by a shell on the right side of the breach, and received an oval graze 1·25 inch in depth. In the right portion of the battery, a 10-inch S. B. and two 8-inch Armstrong guns were struck by from nine to twelve shrapnel bullets, and the fifth gun from the left, an 8-inch Armstrong, was struck on the second coil by a shell. The blow dismounted gun, carriage and slide. The metal of the gun was ripped off for eighteen inches, and the trunnion ring was also started by the force of the blow. There was on the left of the breach the mark of a Nordenfeldt bullet. The remaining guns, 36-pounders, were uninjured,

Left Flank Battery.—Left gun, 10-inch S. B. This gun was hit on the right of the carriage by a splinter, the gun is uninjured. No. 3 gun, 10-inch S. B. This was hit by a shell on the muzzle, and the carriage was struck by thirteen shrapnel bullets. Both gun and carriage were uninjured.

6. The Mex Lines armed with S.B. guns were not fought and the works escaped injury.

7. *Fort Kamaria* was not much injured. A 10-inch S.B. gun was dismounted by a shell.

' In view of the tremendous fire to which Fort Mex was subjected and the comparatively short range at which all the ships except the *Temeraire* engaged it, it is almost impossible to believe that not a single gun here was disabled or dismounted during the action proper. The 8-inch gun which was dismounted was bowled over by the *Penelo*pe long after the fort had ceased firing, and from a distance stated to be about 300 yards. The successful shot was the thirtieth of this series, and was aimed by the gunnery lieutenant.

'Mex Fort was the only fort which could not have resumed action on the following day, in consequence of the injury done by the landing-party by exploding gun-cotton and spiking the guns.'*

8. *Omuk Kubebe.*—The effects of the bombardment were considerable, though they were due less to the number of hits than to the size and weight of the 16-inch shells which caused most of the injuries. The effect of three of these shells from the *Inflexible* was worthy of note. One shell having burst on the top of the scarp made an almost practicable breach. Two others, within a few feet of each other, hit the parapet, 24 feet thick, and almost pierced it. They appear to have struck the exterior slope, and having cut a trough in the parapet about 11 feet in width, burst after penetrating 17 feet, and formed craters 16 feet in diameter, and 5 feet and 4 feet 6 inches in depth, respectively. With regard to the ordnance, the only damage was the destruction of a 36-pounder S.B. gun. A 10-inch (blind) shell, fired by one of the ships, was found lying in the centre of an arched passage, 24 feet in length. It is impossible to say how it came there, as the seaward entrance to the passage was covered at a distance of only 8 feet by a high traverse battery adjoining.

9. *Saleh Aga.*—One 10-inch and one 6·5 S.B. gun were dismounted, and one of the 6·5-inch S.B. guns was destroyed, though not dismounted.

10. The adjoining battery received only slight injuries.

11. *Light-house Fort or Fort Ras-el-Tin.*—The barracks to the north of the fort were riddled with shell,

* Report of Lieutenant Commander Goodrich, U.S.N.

THE EFFECTS OF THE BOMBARDMENT. 149

and in many parts left in ruins. The parapets on the west side were so scored with shell that it was difficult to estimate the number of hits, but at no point had they been pierced. The scarp also suffered severely, both at the bastions and on the curtain; and the right face of the bastion was much marked by shrapnel bullets. On the west front the parapet showed about twenty-three hits, and the scarp twenty-four. The two stores were burnt, and the rifled-shell store was riddled with shell. The Light-house itself was hit by several shells, and the buildings round its base were reduced to ruins. Right gun 9-inch.—This gun was sent back to the end of the slide, and breaking the ties was tilted up on its breech with the muzzle in the air. Left gun 9-inch.—This was struck by two shells, and gun and carriage were both destroyed. The former was hit on the trunnion ring, which had been partially carried away, the carriage was in pieces, and the brackets were torn off and broken. The gun was thrown about twelve feet to the rear and crushed several of the gunners, ten bodies having been found beneath it. In the left bastion, a 10-inch Armstrong gun was hit on the muzzle, but the tube was not damaged. The sockets of the levers were broken by use, the tackle shot away, and the shot-crane broken and useless. A 9-inch gun was run back and tilted up on the breech in the same manner as the 9-inch gun in the right bastion. There was no sign of other damage to the gun, and it is doubtful if the result was in any way attributable to the fire of the fleet. The rear truck was hit by a shell. An 8-inch gun was struck in reverse by shells. The gun and carriage were capsized on the left side, but uninjured. One truck of the slide was cut away. The embrasure and parapet in front of the gun were wrecked, and the gun was found resting on a block of concrete, on which was the print of a Nordenfeldt bullet, 4½ inches deep, and the cascable of the gun was also scored by a similar projectile. The Light-house Fort suffered more severely than either Pharos or Adda, since there was not one of the rifled guns which could bear on the fleet left fit for service.

12. *The Lines of Ras-el-Tin.*—Harem Battery. The effects of the bombardment on the fort were small, but the loss of life must have been considerable, as many shells burst in it. The rear face of the tower was in ruins. Right gun 8-inch Armstrong. A 9-inch Palliser shell struck the lower side of the gun and burst on the breast of the carriage with the following results : the gun beyond being indented for a distance of 8 inches in length was uninjured, but had been thrown about 10 feet from its original position. Both brackets of the carriage were torn away. The entire carriage was a wreck. Centre gun 8-inch Armstrong.—The right-front truck of the carriage was broken, and the gun was struck by a splinter on the chase. The gun and the carriage, however, suffered no serious injury, though the left bracket of the latter was pierced by a splinter. The centre battery in the interior was almost uninjured, though the parapet was deeply scored in all directions by shells. The embrasure of the left gun (9-inch) was choked up by the ruins of the cheeks, whilst the rivetment on each side of the neck was swept away. The condition of the guns was as follows :—10-inch Armstrong gun. The right-front truck of the carriage was carried away, and the buffers of the slide were much damaged by the recoil of the gun. 9-inch Armstrong gun.—The gun and carriage were uninjured except that the lever of the elevating gear was bent, and the holdfast was rising off the pin. 9-inch left gun.—This was hit on the left trunnion

EFFECTS OF THE BOMBARDMENT. 151

by a shell which tore off the cap square, and also by a second shell, on the right bracket six inches in the rear of the trunnion hole. The gun and carriage were, however, practically uninjured. This battery in the early reports of the bombardment was miscalled the Moncrieff Battery, but there was in it no gun mounted on that system. The Moncrieff gun, 180 yards to the westward, was hit on the left side by a splinter of a shell, and a bolt in the rear of the left bracket was also cut out by a Nordenfeldt bullet. Beyond this it was unhurt, and remained perfectly serviceable.

The Hospital Battery.—The effects of the bombardment here were overwhelming. The entire gun portions were so entirely destroyed that it was difficult to discover where the original crest had been. The injuries to the guns were as follows :—Right gun 7-inch Armstrong.—The cheeks of the embrasure were driven in on the gun, and the trucks were jammed, otherwise the gun and carriage were uninjured. The former was, however, scored with forty-nine hits from a 10-inch shrapnel shell, the greatest depth of any hit being 5 inches. Left gun 7-inch Armstrong.—A shell burst under the front racer on the left side of this gun, tore it up and bent it into a vertical plane, twisting the truck and forcing it off the racer. The slide was also jammed by the ruins of the rivetment. The gun-carriage and slide were otherwise uninjured, and were left fit for service.*

13. *Fort Adda.*—The barracks and stores, especially on the east side of the fort, were very much injured, but the batteries were not materially damaged. The only shell which entered, that on the southern half of the western side, blew up the magazine. The loss of life from the explosion was probably very great, and the

---

* In August 1882 they were removed to Ramleh for the purpose of firing on the enemy's lines.

entire space between the magazine and the gate was covered with stones, timber, and broken shell. Another battery to the north of the last was uninjured, as was also the low sea battery in front. The injury to the guns was as follows:—A 10-inch S.B. gun was dismounted by a shell which threw the gun and carriage to a distance of about fifteen feet from the slide. Another 10-inch S.B. gun was similarly dismounted, whilst a third was struck on the left side of the platform by a shell which had previously cut off the cascable of the second gun to the left; the beams of the platform were completely shattered, and the gun with its carriage was overturned and wrecked.

14. *Fort Pharos.*—The west tower and front were breached in many places; the minaret was partly knocked down, and the whole of the west front of the Keep with its two turrets, were in ruins. The south-east corners of the fort were also much shattered by the shells which passed over the west front. The stores and barracks suffered severely, and the destruction of so much masonry must have added considerably to the moral effect of the fire of the ships. With regard to the sea front, the parapet was hit in several places (seven in all), but only in three cases did a shell enter the battery. The corners of the traverse to the right of the 8-inch Armstrong guns were carried away by two shells, a third shell pierced the sole of the embrasure of the 10-inch Armstrong gun, and threw the large granite block which formed the sill on to the platform of the gun. The gun might be said to be out of action. Of the S. B. guns, one heavy 10-inch on the west tower, was dismounted, gun and carriage, by a 16-inch shell from the *Inflexible*, one 10-inch gun on the west front was capsized, and put out of action, and it is not unlikely that another, with its carriage, fell into the crater formed by a shell.

THE EFFECTS OF THE BOMBARDMENT. 153

On the rear face, a 36-pounder having been hit on the cascable by a chance shell, was thrown completely over the parapet, and left standing on its muzzle at a distance of thirty feet from its original position. Another gun was also unserviceable, owing to the partial destruction of its carriage by a shell. But it was in the casemates below that the fire of the ships inflicted the greatest injury. The front wall of the casemates, which is faced with masonry two feet in thickness, was in many places torn away under the stress of fire, leaving only six feet of rubble as a protection to the guns. Through the latter, the heavy shells pierced with ease. The results were as follows :—Under west tower, casemate penetrated, gun not disabled. In casemates Nos. 1 to 12, just one half of the guns were disabled. Of the casemates on the right sea front, No. 17 was the only one in which there was no gun hit. The loss of life in the casemates must have been out of all proportion to the effect produced by the feeble guns (six 5-inch S. B.), mounted within; yet their defenders continued to fight them after the rifled battery above had been silenced.

On the scarp of casemates, Nos. 1 to 12, there were about thirteen hits, of which seven pierced the wall.

15. *Fort Silsileh.*—The fire does not appear to have in any way injured the guns or stores of this fort, though fragments of at least two shells lay around the rifled guns. In the ditch, in the rear of the work lay two blind 10-inch shells, of which one was fitted with a percussion fuse, while that of the other was blown out. The total number of guns dismounted was, four M. L. R. guns, sixteeen S. B. guns, and one mortar.

CHAPTER XVIII.

OBSERVATIONS ON THE BOMBARDMENT.

Mode of Attack by Ships on Fortifications—Ships keeping under Way or Anchoring—Disproportion between Injuries received by the Ships and inflicted by them—Faults of the Defence—Accuracy of Fire of the Ships—Conflicting Opinions—Failures of the Shells to burst—The Egyptians overmatched—Their Losses—Summary of Armaments of Forts and Ironclads.

THE following general observations on the bombardment may not here be out of place.

The most obvious mode of attack on forts by a fleet would be for the ships to form in line ahead and steam past the batteries, each ship delivering her fire in succession as her guns would bear. Having thus passed the line of defences, the ships would turn and repeat the process with the other broadside. By manœuvring in this manner the forts, which have the advantage of fixed gun-carriages, would suffer from the disadvantage of having moving targets. On this principle, for two and a half hours, the bombardment of the forts from Ras-el-Tin to Pharos was conducted by the *Sultan*, *Superb*, and *Alexandra*, which began the action at a minimum distance of about 1500 yards from the forts. Afterwards this system was changed for one which consisted in moving from time to time so as to obtain a concentration of fire from stationary ships on individual forts. From the time of the adoption of the latter plan the fire of the ships improved much in accuracy. The advantage of knowing the range exactly prevailed over the increased risk of being hit. This alteration in the mode of attack was, curiously enough, accompanied by a simultaneous diminution of accuracy in the fire of the enemy. It is a fact that the majority of the shells which struck the three vessels named were received by them during the time they were under way. That their fire should improve as soon as the vessels became stationary is intelligible enough; but that the enemy should make better practice against a movable than against a fixed target is difficult to understand. The naval officers engaged have, with some humour, suggested that the vessels, in manœuvring from time to time, steamed across the Egyptian line of fire and so got struck. But probably the fact is to be accounted for by the increased state of demoralisation of the Egyptian Artillerymen as the ships, after having anchored, made more accurate practice.

In the inshore squadron the flag-ship *Invincible* was anchored for the most part at 1300 yards from Mex, and was kept broadside to the wind on one side, and to the batteries on the other, by a kedge carried out to windward. The *Monarch* and *Penelope* remained under way, passing and repassing the forts. The *Penelope* adopted the plan of steaming out three-quarters of a mile towards the reef, and then drifting towards the shore broadside on until within about 700 yards, whilst the *Monarch* kept more way on, moving in a line parallel with the shore. These ships exchanged a few shots with Fort Marabout, but at so great a range that they could neither inflict nor receive any damage. Later in the day, when the outside squadron moved to the eastward to attack Fort Pharos, these two ships passed inside the breakwater and shelled Saleh Aga and the battery between it and Omuk Kubebe.

The enormous disproportion between the amount of

damage sustained by the ships and the batteries respectively may be accounted for partly by the inferior construction of the works, and partly also by the inferior practice of the gunners by whom they were manned. There were other faults in the defence; amongst them were the following :—

1. The batteries were so placed as to be unable to support each other.
2. There was no bomb-proof cover.
3. There was too small a stock of ammunition in readiness.
4. The men who should have been employed as reliefs for manning the rifled guns wasted their efforts with the smooth-bores, which were practically useless.

With regard to the fire of the fleet generally, a variety of opinions has been expressed. One authority states that, with the exception of the *Inflexible* and *Temeraire*, the English gunners did not greatly distinguish themselves. Many of the shells of the *Monarch*, *Inflexible*, and *Superb*, fell short. The fire also was said to have been too slow, thus giving the enemy's artillerists time to recover themselves. The fire of the *Inflexible* was stated to have been particularly disappointing in this respect. That of the *Alexandra* was much more rapid than that of the others, as her much greater expenditure of ammunition shows. Foreign naval officers who were present, on the other hand, are nearly unanimous in the opinion that the squadron fired with great precision. Probably the truth will be found to lie between the two views.

If one considers the great size and weight of the majority of the projectiles used against the fortifications, and further realises the velocity at which these masses of metal were travelling at the moment of impact, as well as the capacity of the shell and the consequent amount of

OBSERVATIONS ON THE BOMBARDMENT. 157

their bursting charges, one can hardly fail to be astonished at the small effect produced on the sand parapets, especially when it is remembered that the latter were in many cases, according to modern theory, too weak to afford any real protection. It is a fact, and one on which too much stress cannot be laid, that in only one instance was any one of the parapets pierced by a shell from the fleet.

One remarkable feature of the fire from the fleet was the enormous number of shells which failed to burst, and this has never been satisfactorily accounted for. An American writer says:—

'Of the fuzes used by the British the greater part were the general service percussion. It is impossible to exaggerate the misbehaviour of this fuze on the occasion of the bombardment. The most careless witness of the action could not help noticing the frequency of premature explosions, and of failures to explode at all.

'It is not beyond the limits of fair estimation to set down the number of the latter as reaching several hundred, while some British officers think the proportion no less than four-fiths of all fired. As a result of the unreliable nature of these fuzes, it may be mentioned that one of the *Penelope's* 8-inch shells was afterward found lying harmless in a magazine containing over 400 tons of powder!'*

The Egyptians, it must be allowed, were overmatched both in the size and number of the guns brought into action, but the way in which they responded to the heavy fire was marvellous. When the *Inflexible's* 1700 lb. projectiles struck the scarp of the Light-house Fort immediately underneath an embrasure they threw up a cloud of dust and fragments of stone as high as the Light-house itself. To the looker-on, it seemed impossible to live under such a fire, yet after a few minutes the dust would clear away and the gun's crew would pluckily toss another shell back at their huge opponent.

* Lieutenant Commander Goodrich.

The Egyptian forces were under the immediate command of Toulba Pasha. From the best sources of information accessible, it is gathered that the defences contained no less than 2000 artillerymen, and of infantry and civilian volunteers there was no lack.

The disposition of these troops has not been accurately ascertained, but it is known that the important post of Mex was commanded by an adjutant-major, who had with him one captain, three lieutenants, and 150 men. Of this small number one lieutenant was mortally wounded, 50 men were killed, and 48 wounded.

Omuk Kubebe, as already mentioned, was subjected to the *Inflexible's* fire during the afternoon. Its garrison consisted of 75 artillerymen aided by a considerable number of Arab volunteers. Eighteen of these were wounded by splinters of masonry. In all, along the southern or inside line, from Saleh Aga to Marabout, 65 men were killed, and from 150 to 200 wounded. Among the latter, were several officers.

In the northern line of defences, one officer was killed in the Light-house Fort, and one in the lines of Ras-el-Tin. In each of the foregoing, and also in Fort Adda, one was wounded. At least 50 men are believed to have been killed and 150 wounded in these lines, but the record is very vague. Stray pieces of shell are reported by the chief of police to have killed and wounded between 150 and 200 citizens, but this statement must be accepted for what it is worth.*

* Mr. John Ninet, in his work, *Arabi Pasha*, puts the number of Egyptians killed during the bombardment at 680. General Stone, an American officer, serving as the Khedive's Chief of the Staff, estimates them at 700.

OBSERVATIONS ON THE BOMBARDMENT. 159

The ordnance *mounted* in the Forts was as follows:—

Fort or Battery.	R. Guns.	S. B. Guns.	Mortars.	Total.
Fort Silsileh	2	3	1	6
„ Pharos	8	37	4	49
„ Adda	5	14	5	24
Ras-el-Tin Lines...	9	30	10	49
Fort Ras-el-Tin ...	6	28	3	37
„ Saleh Aga ...	...	12	...	12
Battery	...	4	...	4
Fort Omuk Kubebe	2	16	2	20
„ Kamaria ...	...	5	1	6
Mex Sea Lines ...	...	24	...	24
„ Fort ...	5	9	5	19
TOTAL.........	37	182	31	250

The guns on board the ironclads may be seen from the accompanying table:—

Ships.	Guns.									
	in. 16	in. 12	in. 11	in. 10	in. 9	in. 8	in. 7	pr. 64	pr. 40	Total.
Alexandra ...	...	...	2	10	...	...	...	...	...	12
Inflexible ...	4	...	...	...	...	...	...	...	...	4
Superb ...	...	...	...	16	...	...	...	...	...	16
Sultan ...	...	...	...	8	4	...	...	...	...	12
Temeraire ...	...	...	4	4	...	...	...	...	...	8
Invincible ...	...	...	...	...	10	...	...	...	...	10
Monarch ...	...	4	...	...	2	...	1	...	...	7
Penelope ...	...	...	...	...	...	8	...	...	3	11
TOTAL...	4	4	6	38	16	8	1	4	3	84

This does not include the six to eight 20-pounder guns and eight to twelve machine-guns carried by each vessel.

CHAPTER XIX.

THE DAY AFTER THE BOMBARDMENT.

Burial of the Dead—Movements of the Ships—Attack on Marabout—The Ships open Fire—Flag of Truce—The Helicon sent to treat with the Authorities—Outbreak of the Fire—Alexandria in Flames—Mr. John Ross and Landing Party—Embarkation of Refugees—Council of War—Admiral Seymour's Hesitation—Landing decided on—Deficiency of Ammunition for Ships—The Khedive at Ramleh.

THE following day, the 12th July, there was dull, gloomy weather off Alexandria, with a haze hanging over the city. There had been a strong breeze from the sea during the night, and it was still blowing fresh from the N.N.W., causing the ironclads forming the outside squadron to roll somewhat.

At 5 a.m. the *Beacon* took on board the bodies of those killed the previous day, and buried them at sea. The *Humber*, store-ship, appeared in sight, and the Admiral signalled to all the ships, except the *Temeraire*, to send working parties to her for ammunition.

At 7.20 a.m. the *Inflexible* and *Temeraire* were sent to engage Fort Pharos. At 9 they weighed anchor, prepared for action, and steamed off to Eunostos Point and Fort Pharos.

At 9.20 the signal was made to the *Sultan, Superb*, and *Alexandra* to prepare to weigh anchor. The *Alexandra*, in reply, made the signal, 'We have two guns disabled,—they are split.' At 9.50 the Admiral signalled to the *Penelope* and *Sultan*, 'Weather having moderated, Admiral intends to attack Marabout and Adjimi; approach with *Sultan*.' And at the same time

THE DAY AFTER THE BOMBARDMENT. 161

it was signalled to the *Penelope*, *Superb*, and *Alexandra*, 'Will send gun-boat to south side to summon them to surrender.'

At 10.15 the *Temeraire* reported that the Hospital Battery was prepared, that two large rifled guns were ready with guns' crews about them, and that numbers of men under arms were in the barracks and covered way. The *Inflexible* at the same time signalled that a large body of men was in the rear of the Hospital earthworks, all armed with rifles. In reply, the *Sultan* signalled to the *Inflexible* and *Temeraire*, 'Close, and open fire with shell.' At 10.40 the two ships, having taken up position, fired twelve shells, to which there was no reply, and the men were observed leaving the batteries.

At 10.48 flags of truce were displayed at the Lighthouse Battery, and at Fort Adda. At the same time, a boat bearing a white flag came out towards the *Inflexible*. This being noticed, the two vessels were ordered to cease firing. The boat then returned to the shore without communicating.

At 11 the *Sultan*, *Alexandra*, *Temeraire*, and *Superb*, were ordered to proceed to Marabout, where the Egyptian flag was still flying.

At 11.10 the *Bittern* was sent with a flag of truce to communicate with the Egyptian authorities.

At 11.15 the squadron was reinforced by the arrival of the ironclad *Achilles* belonging to the Channel Squadron.

At 2.50 p.m. the *Bittern* returned, and signalled, 'Negotiations have failed, have informed authorities you will engage batteries at 3.30 precisely.' At 3.40 the *Bittern* hauled down her flag of truce, and it was reported that the flag of truce at Ras-el-Tin was also taken down, though this was subsequently found not to have been the case.

At 3.50 the Egyptian flag at Marabout having been hauled down, the squadron was recalled, and the Admiral signalled to the Captain of the *Sultan*, ' Engage batteries off Pharos and Ras-el-Tin with your squadron.' At the same time the *Invincible* fired a shot into the Mex Forts, but got no reply.

At 4.40 a general signal was made to the ships to ' take up position for engaging batteries, anchoring as convenient ; ' and at 5 the *Alexandra, Temeraire, Achilles, Superb,* and *Sultan,* weighed anchor, and proceeded in line towards Fort Pharos. None of the ships, however, opened fire, as the flag of truce at Ras-el-Tin was discovered to be still flying.

At this time the *Condor* reported that a good many soldiers had come back to the batteries bearing S. by W. from her and were getting in behind them, also that there were soldiers in the other forts. In reply, the Admiral signalled, ' Flag of truce is flying.'

At 5.40 the *Helicon* was sent into harbour with a flag of truce. The instructions of Lieutenant Morrison in command were to inform the authorities that if they wished to treat with the Admiral they could do so by returning in the *Helicon*, and that if they did not do so, no more flags of truce would be respected.

At 5.50 the signal was made for the squadron to anchor for the night.

The *Helicon*, pursuant to orders, steamed up the harbour and lay off the Arsenal wall, whilst Lieutenant Morrison went on board the Khedive's yacht *Maharoussa* expecting to find some one to treat with ; but not a living person was on board. After waiting half-an-hour, he signalled that he had been unable to find any authorities to communicate with, and returned at 8.20 p.m. As early as four o'clock a part of the town was observed to be on fire, and this soon after was seen to spread rapidly.

During the night the fires on shore continued to extend, and it became evident that it was the richest part of Alexandria, the European quarter, which was being destroyed.

The spectacle as viewed from the ships was grand, but awful in character. The sky on the land side was lighted up with a fierce red glare, and columns of smoke covered the greater part of the city.

The Admiral's first idea was to send a landing-party to save the town. He, however, hesitated on account of the risk to his men. Eventually, to discover the state of things on shore, he landed at midnight a party of fifteen men in charge of Lieutenant Forsyth, of the *Invincible*. Mr. John Ross, of Alexandria, Contractor to the Fleet, with great courage volunteered to accompany the party and place his local knowledge at their disposal. On arriving at the landing-place he disembarked, and whilst the steam-pinnace pushed off and awaited his return, went alone for some distance into the town, as far as the Zaptieh. The streets he found completely deserted, and all was silent save for the roar and crackle of the flames and the sound of falling beams and walls. Finding his passage barred by the burning ruins, Mr. Ross returned and made his report at three a.m., on the 13th.

Daylight revealed the town still wrapped in flames, and an immense cloud of smoke hung over its whole extent.

At 5.40 a.m. the *Invincible*, *Monarch*, and *Penelope* left their anchorage off Mex, and steamed into the outer harbour, with the *Beacon* and *Bittern* in company. At 5.50 the *Helicon*, which had again gone in to pick up refugees, embarked and brought 170 of them for distribution amongst the ships outside; many came from the Anglo-Egyptian Bank. They were of all classes and nationalities, and included several women and children. They had passed through the streets unmolested, and reported Alexandria deserted, and that all the troops had left the previous day, after setting fire to the town. It was believed that part of the soldiers had gone to Rosetta, and part to Damanhour. The *Helicon* reported that there were a great many more refugees, women and children, inside the mole waiting for an opportunity to come off.

In the meantime the Admiral held a consultation with some of the Captains and officers under his command as to what was best to be done. On the one hand, there was the certainty that unless some step should be taken, a great part, if not the whole, of Alexandria, would be destroyed. On the other, it was uncertain how far Arabi's troops had retired, and one report was that they were massed to the number of 9000 outside the town, no further off than Moharrem Bey Gate. The number of men that could be landed without disabling the ships was not large. The Admiral found it difficult to decide. Already he must have begun to realise the error he had committed in opening fire with such precipitation. The Channel Fleet (of which, as already stated, the *Achilles* had arrived) were known to be on their way from Malta, as well as the *Orontes*, troop-ship, with troops from Gibraltar. The *Tamar*, too, with 1000 marines was at Malta. The ships of the Channel Fleet alone could have furnished a contingent of 1800 men in addition to those which Admiral Seymour could have disembarked from his own squadron.

The bombardment, so long delayed, might well have been retarded for the short period necessary to enable the reinforcements to arrive. What had occurred was not altogether unforeseen. Arabi had, before the bombardment, declared that if the ships opened fire he would burn the European quarter; and the fulfilment of his threat would have not only gratified his thirst for revenge, but would have also covered the retreat of his forces. Regrets, however, were too late; it was necessary to act.

At 8.35 a.m. the general signal was made, 'Prepare to land marines,' followed ten minutes later by the order, 'Prepare to land brigade of seamen.' The *Helicon*, *Bittern*, and *Beacon*, were despatched to the outside squadron to bring in as many men as possible, whilst the *Condor* and *Cygnet* were told off to take the seamen and marines from the inshore vessels. At 9.5 the *Alexandra* was detached to reconnoitre off Rosetta Gate, and the remaining vessels of the outside squadron were directed to take stations for bombarding, in case the landing should be resisted.

At 10.30 the landing-party left the ships. The force consisted of four hundred men, including all the marines of the squadron; it was under the command of Commander Hammill of the *Monarch*, and had with it a Gatling gun.

The *Invincible*, at the same time, sent ashore and spiked the guns at Fort Saleh Aga, and the other vessels landed men to destroy the guns in the Lighthouse Fort at Ras-el-Tin.

Whilst Commander Hammill's force was disembarking, large bodies of soldiers were seen moving towards Fort Silsileh, apparently accompanied by field-pieces, and the *Sultan*, *Temeraire*, and *Achilles*, were ordered to watch that point, and to bombard if necessary.

In the intervals between carrying out the above-mentioned operations, the larger ships were engaged in recruiting their exhausted stock of ammunition from the store-ship *Humber*. In this matter a most unexpected difficulty arose. Through some unpardonable blunder, the ship had been despatched from Malta without a single filled common shell on board, and actually without powder to fill the empty shells she had brought with her, and most of which were of an obsolete pattern and unserviceable. Further than this, she had brought no fuzes, and as the vessels of war had no reserves of powder, they would, had hostilities been resumed, have been speedily reduced to a state of comparative impotence.

In the course of the day, anxiety being felt for the safety of the Khedive, the *Condor* was sent to cruise off the Palace at Ramleh.

Further parties of men were landed in the town, making the total force disembarked about 800 men. They took with them a day's provisions, Gatling guns, and ammunition. At 2.15 the P. and O. S. S. *Tanjore* signalled that the marines were engaged in street-fighting.

At 3.25, the *Temeraire* signalled that great activity was observed about Ramleh Palace, and that Dervish Pasha was supposed to be there.

At 4.43, the *Temeraire* having reported that Fort Pharos did not appear to be entirely deserted, had permission given her to send a party to spike the guns there

At 5, the *Bittern* was directed to take a guard of fifty marines to the Palace of Ras-el-Tin, for the protection of the Khedive, who was expected from Ramleh.

What had been taking place on shore in the meantime is reserved for another chapter.

CHAPTER XX.

ALEXANDRIA DURING THE BOMBARDMENT.

Exodus of Native Population—Aspect of the City—Arabi's Movements—Europeans left on Shore—Murder of M. Ternant—The Dead and Wounded—The Danish Consulate—M. Dumreicher—Retreat of the Soldiers—The Morning of the 12th July—Exodus continued—Position of Europeans—Withdrawal of the Soldiery—Arab Looting—The Fire —Retreat of Europeans to the Ships—The Anglo-Egyptian Bank—M. Dumreicher's Party.

AFTER the preceding narrative of events from a naval point of view, it may be convenient to relate what was taking place at the time in Alexandria itself.

During the whole of the night preceding the 11th July, the native population had been leaving the town in crowds, some in carts and others on foot, the women uttering loud lamentations. Towards daylight the movement slackened. From three a.m. troops were marching through on their way to Ras-el-Tin; at five the last detachment passed.

The morning dawned on the city without a cloud in the heavens. There was a gentle breeze from the northwest, all was quiet as the sun gilded the tops of the domes and minarets of the various mosques, and lighted up the acacia-trees of the Place Mehemet Ali and the Place de l'Eglise. In the streets the soldiers, who had passed the night on the door-steps of the houses, on the marble benches of the square, or on the ground, slowly roused themselves, and, yawning, looked about them in a somnolent way. The streets were being watered as usual, the 'bowabs,' or door-keepers, were tranquilly smoking their cigarettes at the house-doors, and the Arab women were going about selling milk as if nothing unusual was about to happen. With the exception of these few indications of life, the streets were deserted. The military posts were relieved at six o'clock as usual, each soldier carrying a linen pouch full of cartridges.

The clock of the church of St. Catherine struck seven, and before the sound had died away out of the bell, the thundering boom of the first gun from the *Alexandra* startled the city, and the few civilians who were about sought refuge in their dwellings. The Egyptian soldiers remained at their posts.

There was a solemn silence which lasted some minutes. Then the bombardment with all its horrors began. The English ships were seen in the distance vomiting volumes of fire and smoke, whilst the forts in their turn thundered forth a reply. The scene was of the grandest description. The immense ships of war appeared to cover the sea around Alexandria, and the shrieks of the projectiles as they flew overhead, mingled with the boom of the cannon, which echoed and re-echoed on all sides. The report from the huge eighty-ton guns of the *Inflexible* was easily distinguishable above the general roar.

At a little before eight a large shell fell in the Arab quarter, behind the Ramleh railway station, causing a panic, which forced many of the inhabitants into the forts close by.

Arabi, who had from an early hour stationed himself at the Ministry of Marine in the Arsenal, finding the missiles from the fleet falling thickly there, left with Toulba Pasha and an escort of cavalry, and at eight o'clock drove to the fortifications behind Fort Kom-el-Dyk, where he remained till four p.m.

By nine o'clock the streets were totally deserted except by the soldiers. At that time the cannonade slackened, and sounds of rejoicing came from some of the Arab cafés, where it was reported that two ironclads were sunk and five were disabled. At about nine o'clock a shell fell on the terrace of a house alongside the Palace Menasce in the Rosetta Road. At the same time another burst over the German Consulate. The discharges averaged about two per minute. The soldiers commenced to send patrols to the houses of the Europeans who were ashore, to prevent any signalling they might attempt with the English squadron.

The number of Europeans ashore at this period amounted to about 1500. Of these some 100 were at the College of the 'Frères,' a great number in the Greek Church, and in the Greek and European Hospitals.* The German Hospital at Moharrem Bey also sheltered a large number of nurses, invalids, and refugees. The Anglo-Egyptian Bank, in the Rue Cherif Pasha, was held by Mr. George Goussio, the manager, and a determined party of about twenty (subsequently increased to eighty-two), amongst whom was Madame Goussio, who, with heroic courage, determined to brave the terrors of the bombardment. The bank of Messrs. Caprara in the same street was also occupied by its proprietors and a small band of defenders. The Danish Consul-General, M. Dumreicher, had himself fortified the Danish Consulate, where a large number of people, including many women and children, found a refuge.

There were other Europeans, mostly of the poorest class, hidden away in their dwellings in various parts

---

* In the last-named were 75 invalids, besides an equal number of children from the Foundling Hospital.

of the town, and to all these the movements of the patrols naturally occasioned serious disquietude.

Early in the forenoon, an Egyptian officer mounted the roof of the 'Credit Lyonnais' Bank, and commenced cutting away the telephone wires. Shortly afterwards, a gang of boys in the same street began pulling down all the wires they could reach, raising at the same time the wildest shouts.

At nine, a shell fell in the Rue Copt, in the stables of M. Zervudachi, and for a quarter of an hour the neighbourhood was enveloped in a cloud of dust. At ten, a shell fell in the Franciscan Convent, where a great number of persons were assembled, but as it did not burst did no injury beyond destroying one or two of the walls.

Shortly afterwards a shell fell into the house of M. Antoniadis, in the Rue Cherif Pasha, making a large hole. Another pierced the wall of the Jewish Synagogue. Another hit the Zaptieh, and a fourth struck a house in Frank Street. As the missiles fell, the soldiers sought shelter in the doorways of the houses, but did not entirely desert their posts.

At eleven o'clock, the natives spread the report that only three ironclads remained afloat, and great rejoicings took place in the Arab cafés.

Half-an-hour later, an officer and a detachment of soldiers stationed themselves opposite the Anglo-Egyptian Bank, and insisted on mounting to the roof to satisfy themselves that there was no signalling going on. They also went to the central Telephone Office, and to the Telegraph Offices, and cut the wires. At the office of the Eastern Telegraph Company, they found one of the employés, M. Ternant, a French subject, who had refused to go afloat, and murdered him on the spot. At noon, a shell in passing over the house of Mr. Friedheim, carried away a piece of wood which fell at the feet of two of the soldiers outside ; they, imagining that it was a projectile thrown by the Europeans inside, called to the soldiers near and directed them to the house, where they endeavoured to compel the inmates to come forth.

At this period, isolated firing from a westerly direction was all that was heard ; otherwise the silence of death prevailed throughout the town.

At half-past twelve, two shells, one following the other in quick succession, struck the Khedivial Free Schools, in the Rosetta Road, and bursting, destroyed the south-western angle of the building.

Soon after the cannonading commenced, a number of empty carts and drays was seen going towards the Marina. During the forenoon, these, as well as some cabs, began to return laden with dead artillerymen. The first load passed up soon after ten in the morning, the bodies being stripped and tied in with ropes. A little later, the wounded began to arrive in great numbers, some in carriages and some in carts, many of the men showing ghastly wounds. Crowds of women followed them uttering cries of distress and lamentations.*

At one p.m., a crowd of native children carrying a green flag passed down the Rue Cherif Pasha beating petroleum tins and calling on God and the Prophet. During the day many of the houses in which Europeans were seen on the terraces or roofs watching the bombardment, were surrounded by soldiers, who, under the pretext that the inmates were signalling to the fleet, required them to descend and accompany them to the police-stations. Eight or ten Europeans were dragged

---

* The dead were taken along the Boulevard de Rossette to the native hospital, where the bodies were at once interred.

from their dwellings and set upon in the streets by the mob. As soon as they fell into the power of the latter, they were forced along by soldiers towards the Moharrem Bey Gate, and struck with the butt ends of their rifles, and received blows from naboots. As they passed along they were subjected to every species of ill-usage. On their arrival, covered with blood and in a wretched condition, fresh troubles awaited them. They were cast indiscriminately into cells with natives, and during their captivity endured the vilest usage. Happily, their gaoler, more humane than the rest, took pity on the captives, and sent a message to M. Mark, of the police, and he came to their assistance.

This courageous official, under the pretext of taking them to the Zaptieh, found means to place them in carriages, and some at least were enabled to return, though in dilapidated condition, to their homes.

A mob of natives in the course of the day broke into the German Hospital, where there were many Europeans, as well as the patients. The inmates ran for the cellars, where the invalids had already been placed for safety. The Secretary of the German Consulate was the last to flee, and as a final effort he fired a shot from his revolver. The effect on the crowd was magical. They drew back, and contented themselves with demanding that the flag which was flying over the hospital, and which they imagined was being used for signalling to the fleet, should be given up to them. This was acceded to, and they then dispersed.

The Danish Consulate was surrounded by soldiers and a mob of Arabs, who required M. Dumreicher to haul down the flag flying over the house. This he courageously refused to do, and whilst the dispute was at its height, three Arabs were killed by shells almost at his door, and the rest fled.

At three, the fire of the ships which had in the

meantime slackened, was resumed with great vigour. One shell burst at Moharrem Bey Gate, and killed two officers and six men of the police, and a horse in a carriage standing by.

According to Arabi's statement, he received during the day several messages from the Khedive congratulating him on the behaviour of the troops. Shortly after four o'clock Arabi left the town in a carriage with an escort of soldiers, taking the route by the Rosetta Gate.

About this time, two of the English ironclads* were observed to approach Fort Pharos and reopen fire on the batteries there, the ships themselves being nearly end-on to the fort, so as to expose themselves as little as possible to the return fire. A great number of the British shells were seen to strike the rocks, raising clouds of *débris*, and bounding in repeated ricochets over the face of the water. Towards five o'clock the picturesque mosque in the fort fell, burying in its ruins a large number of the wounded who had taken refuge behind the walls. The two ships at the same time pitched a few shells at Fort Silsileh; as several of the missiles struck the water, they threw up fountains sixty feet in the air. The firing continued, at intervals, until past five o'clock, when it ceased altogether.

As soon as the cannonade was over, the exodus of natives from the town re-commenced, and the streets were again filled. The desire of all was to escape from the town as soon as possible. Along the banks of the Mahmoudieh Canal, and along the line of the railway to Cairo, was one vast stream of fugitives, which only ceased as night fell.

Then a great stillness came over Alexandria.

* The *Inflexible* and *Temeraire*.

The night was calm. The gas was not lighted, and the city, plunged in darkness, resembled a vast necropolis. The only sounds heard from time to time were the plaintive howlings of forsaken dogs. A few fugitives ventured into the streets, and encountered only the sentries and patrols.

On the morning of the 12th, the movement of the natives recommenced. All the Arabs who had remained in the Ras-el-Tin and other quarters, endeavoured to get out of the town with their luggage and effects. It was rumoured that the bombardment was to recommence, and the terror of the people was indescribable. The trains from Moharrem Bey Station were thronged with fugitives, who not only rode inside, but on the roof, the steps, and even the buffers of the carriages.

In the Place Mehemet Ali a regiment of infantry was scattered about, the men, with arms piled, seated or lying on the ground, tranquilly smoking their cigarettes. A few of the bowabs were seen going to the bazaars and returning to the houses with small stores of meat and other provisions. Amongst the Europeans, the greatest anxiety prevailed, and everyone was asking when the English disembarkation would begin. The soldiers on duty became more and more threatening, and the supplies of provisions began to run short. Gangs of disorderly Arabs from time to time appeared and made violent demonstrations in front of houses known to shelter Europeans.

From early morning, bands of natives ran through the streets with soldiers at their head looking for any Europeans who might be concealed. At a quarter to eleven the cannonade recommenced, and a dozen reports were heard coming from the westward. There was then a silence, and all wondered what was to come next.

As soon as the cannonade ceased, the troops at Moharrem Bey and Rosetta Gates precipitated themselves into the streets calling on the natives to flee, as the dogs of Christians were going to disembark and massacre the Mussulmans.

The news soon after spread that the convicts in the Arsenal had been let loose, and were going to pillage and fire the town.

An hour later part of the garrison left the town by the Rosetta Gate, taking the road to Ramleh. The first 500 marched in fours in pretty good order; they were followed by 1500 more, who passed in gradually increasing disorder, until they became confused with the rabble of fugitives who crowded the roads. At this time soldiers drew up in front of the Anglo-Egyptian Bank in the narrow alley separating Caprara's Bank from the Tribunal buildings; and they occupied the Bourse street, and surrounded the Bank. Crowds of natives carying large bundles, and straggling soldiers, moved up the Rue Cherif Pasha towards Rosetta Gate.

At one o'clock the soldiers in the street received the order to eat their midday meal, and, each opening his haversack, set to work with an appetite indicating hours of abstinence. When the men had finished their repast, mounted mustaphazin and officers, amongst whom was Soleyman Sami, appeared, and gave hurried orders to the soldiers at the various posts. It appears that these orders were for them to abandon the town, and to retire to the outside. The military at once formed at certain given points, such as the Place Mehemet Ali, the Place de l'Eglise, and the Place de la Mosque d'Attarin, and shortly after the evacuation commenced, the greater part of the soldiers proceeded to the Mahmoudieh Canal.* Then arose a general

* On the 13th the troops removed to Esbet Horshid, 5000 metres south of Milaha junction on the Cairo railway, so as not to be exposed to the fire of the ships. On the 14th they moved to Kingi Osnan and Kafr Dowar, where they entrenched themselves.

cry of 'Death to the Christians!' People were heard hammering at the doors and windows of the houses. This was followed by the sound of falling shutters, and the crash of broken glass. Infuriated crowds appeared on the scene, armed with heavy sticks, with which they carried on the work of destroying and plundering the shops and dwellings. The soldiers, too, broke from the ranks and joined in the looting, and with the butt-ends of their rifles assisted in forcing open doors and windows.

Continuous lines of soldiers and civilians staggered past laden with plunder. In a short time the streets were literally blocked by the mob.

The order was given to the natives to quit the town, and from two p.m. a constant stream of fugitives flowed out of the Rosetta and Moharrem Bey Gates. When outside the town, they were met by Bedouins, who, in many cases, fought with them for the spoil. One eye-witness stated that a common handkerchief changed hands in this way no less than three times whilst he was looking on. Not only furniture, looking-glasses, and such things, were carried off, but horses and carriages as well. The soldiers in many instances undressed themselves and wrapped round their bodies all sorts of rich stuffs, such as silks and satins. Some brought gilt chairs and sofas with them, but, finding the articles too cumbersome, broke them to pieces, and tore off the velvet coverings, leaving the remainder in the road.

The large open space between the water-works and the European cemeteries was crowded by a huge mob of pillagers fighting and struggling amongst themselves for the plunder. Those who could get away with their spoils took them either by the road to Ramleh, or by that leading to Hadrah and the Mahmoudieh Canal.

The wildest disorder prevailed, and amongst the fugitives were Turkish women and children of good position from the different harems. On arriving at the gates of the town the women were attacked by the mob and outraged. The marauders, in their haste to get possession of the jewellery which the women were wearing, even cut their ears and wrists, and to silence their cries stunned them with blows from their sticks. Soon afterwards several of the soldiers were seen returning to the town, apparently to share in the pillage, and struggling to force their way through the gates against the stream of pillagers and fugitives going the other way. Many of those coming out encumbered with heavy loads were upset in the mêlée, and several of the soldiers, finding it impossible to re-enter the town, contented themselves with joining the Bedouins in seizing the loot of the fugitives.

About four p.m. volumes of smoke, accompanied by the crackling of flames, were observed in the neighbourhood of the British Consulate. These indications increased every instant, and as the sun went down the whole sky became lighted up with a lurid glare. This was accompanied by the shouts and cries of the Europeans, who were either burned out or dragged from their dwellings by ruffians, who, with sticks and knives in their hands, spared few of the Christians whom they could meet with. A small number found refuge in the houses as yet untouched by the fire and guarded by Europeans, but most of the rest fell victims. Amongst those who humanely opened their doors to the fugitives was M. Dumreicher, who sheltered no less than 150.

It was a night to be remembered.

From the terraces of the houses the flames were observed extending in the direction of the Rue Cherif

Pasha. The French Consulate, the Okella Nuova, and other parts of the Place Mehemet Ali, were already wrapped in flames.

During the night nothing was heard but the crackling of the flames, mingled with the cries of the incendiaries and the occasional fall of a heavy building. The volumes of smoke filled the air with the most nauseating vapours. In some cases cotton soaked in petroleum and set on fire was thrown into the houses, whilst in others tins of paraffin were poured over the furniture and ignited. Where ingress to the dwellings could not be obtained, bedding soaked with petroleum was piled up on the outside and fired. On every side the smell of petroleum was distinguishable.

The night passed without slumber for those on shore and on the morning of the 13th Alexandria presented the appearance of a vast bonfire. The Europeans, who remained on shore, saw the flames gradually closing in on them. The pillagers and assassins had disappeared, but the atmosphere had become unbearable. There was further a fear that the Arabs, seeing that no force was being landed, might return to complete the work of massacre.

All hope of a disembarkation appeared as remote as ever. Two of the ironclads had indeed been seen to approach Fort Pharos and send their boats ashore, and for a moment it was thought help was coming. The idea was a vain one. The landing was only for the purpose of spiking the Egyptian cannon, and this having been accomplished, the ships steamed away.

The courageous garrison of the Anglo-Egyptian Bank, seeing there was no help to be expected, resolved to make a sortie, and early in the morning they all sallied forth together, the women and children were put in the middle of the troop, and thus they marched towards the Marina. On their way there they were joined by others in the same condition as themselves. They passed, without encountering any opposition, over masses of burning and smouldering ruins. They broke open the gates at the Marina, and seizing some native boats rowed out to H.M.S. *Helicon.*

M. Dumreicher and his party still held on, but the situation becoming worse and worse, at three in the afternoon, they too evacuated their stronghold, and having secured the attendance of M. Mark of the police, marched to the shore, having more than once to go out of their course to avoid the falling houses. On reaching the Custom-House Quay, they met the landing-party under Commander Hammill. The fugitives passed the night in safety on board the Porte-Khedive S.S. *Charkieh,* and were the next day taken off to the vessels outside.

CHAPTER XXI.

THE KHEDIVE AT RAMLEH.

His Surroundings—Reinforcements demanded—Arabi sent for—Arrival of Bedouins at the Palace—Renewal of Bombardment threatened—Courage of the Khedive—Plot at Rosetta Gate to kill the Khedive—Protestations of Loyalty—Return of the Khedive to Alexandria.

On the day of the bombardment the Khedive was at his Palace at Ramleh, abandoned by all but a few faithful followers; amongst them were General Stone, Federigo Pasha, Zohrab Bey, Tonino Bey, De Martino Bey, and Tigraine Bey.

His Highness was kept badly posted up in the progress of the bombardment, and amongst those who came and went with despatches were a number of spies, who, from time to time, went off to Arabi to inform him of what was passing at the Palace.

At 8.30 a.m., Hussein Bey, aide-de-camp of His Highness, arrived with the news that a considerable number of the Egyptian gunners were killed, and that several guns had been dismounted. On the part of the Commandant he begged the Khedive to order reinforcements to be sent. The greatest excitement reigned. There were no artillerymen available, so the Minister of War was directed to despatch a force of infantry.

In the course of the forenoon Ragheb Pasha, in high spirits, brought the news that the forts were offering a stout resistance, and that serious damage was being inflicted on the English fleet. Ragheb appeared to be greatly pleased at the intelligence of which he was the bearer.

Late in the afternoon news was received that the forts were destroyed, and incapable of offering further opposition.

No further accounts arriving, the Khedive sent for Arabi, his Minister of War, about seven o'clock in the evening. Arabi came from Alexandria where he had been during the bombardment, and on his arrival told the Khedive that the forts were destroyed, and that it was no longer possible to defend them. 'We must,' he added, 'either have recourse to other measures, or else come to terms with the Admiral.' The Khedive thereupon demanded a detailed report of the action, and of the actual condition of affairs; to which Arabi replied that it was impossible to give one. Dervish Pasha, who was present, expressed his astonishment that Arabi should refuse to make such a report after having sworn obedience to the Khedive, and reproached Arabi for not having followed his (Dervish's) advice to dismantle the forts and comply with the Admiral's demands. After some further consultation, and more or less vehement discussion, it was decided that Toulba Pasha should be sent to the Admiral to confer.

On the morning of the 12th July about 500 Bedouin Arabs appeared before the Palace with the intention (as they said) of assuring the Khedive of their fidelity, and with offers of assistance in case of need; but after a slight demonstration of loyalty they retired.

Shortly after mid-day Toulba returned and announced that the Admiral had said that, unless he was allowed peaceably to land his men at three points on the coast, he would recommence the bombardment at two o'clock.

To this demand Toulba said he had objected, as it gave him no time to obtain instructions, but that the Admiral had refused to allow further delay. A hurried consultation took place, and it was decided to send Toulba Pasha and two Beys to the Admiral to tell him that Egypt had no power to authorise the landing of foreign troops on her shores without the consent of the Porte.

Toulba proceeded as far as the Arsenal, and it being after two o'clock, the time fixed by the Admiral for recommencing the bombardment, and being alarmed at the signs of pillage and desertion he saw around him, refused to go any farther, and returned to the Palace, where a flag of truce was flying. On the road he noticed that pillage had been commenced by officers and soldiers, but he made no attempt to restrain it, or even to remonstrate with the officers.

Shortly after Toulba's departure the Ramleh Palace was surrounded by cavalry and infantry, about 400 men in all; the first thought was of the loyal Bedouins, who had been there in the morning and declared their fidelity; but it was soon discovered that Arabi's agents had distributed 2000*l*. amongst these and other loyalists to secure their absence; that the force was a hostile one, and that the Khedive was left helpless with his handful of attendants.

Panic spread in the Palace, and the numerous domestics were beside themselves with fear; the Khedive showed complete self-possession and calmness, and ordered a rifle to be brought to him. Dervish Pasha followed his example, and, with tears in his eyes, declared his intention of dying with His Highness. The Khedive then sent to the Commander of the troops to ask what he wanted; he replied that his orders were to guard the Palace. It became known afterwards that his real orders were to set fire to the Palace, and shoot any one who should attempt to escape. The Khedive then sent Sultan Pasha to Arabi to ask the meaning of this proceeding.

Arabi was at Rosetta Gate, and, it is said, had given orders to pillage and burn the town. With him were Mahmoud Sami, Omar Rahmy, and Soleyman Sami. Omar Rahmy, in Arabi's presence, ordered Soleyman Sami to go to Ramleh immediately and kill the Khedive. Soleyman replied that he could not do this, upon which the others were very angry. Soleyman asked if he was to go alone, or take soldiers with him. They replied that soldiers were already there. Mahmoud Sami then took Soleyman Sami aside and asked him what reasons he had for refusing to obey the order. Soleyman answered that it was impossible for him to commit such an act, and that Mahmoud Sami had better do it himself. He asked Soleyman to what regiment the soldiers at Ramleh belonged; and Soleyman told him to his (Soleyman's), and offered to give Sami an order, in writing, to the soldiers to obey his orders. Arabi then became very angry, and ordered Soleyman to go to his regiment. At this moment Sultan Pasha arrived with the message from the Khedive.

After some delay Toulba Pasha reappeared at the Palace with some of the Ministers, who endeavoured to explain that the surrounding of the Palace was a mistake, and that the officer in command should be punished. This was, subsequently, discovered to be untrue, and that similar steps for the destruction of the Khedive had been taken at 'No. 3 Palace,' on the Mahmoudieh Canal.

The situation remained unchanged until seven o'clock, when it was observed that the cavalry were preparing to depart; orders, it appears, having been given that all the troops should follow Arabi. One officer, however (Munib Effendi by name), remained behind with about 250 men. A General Council was called at the Palace to consider the situation. Dervish Pasha advised that they should escape to Benha and thence to Suez. Others were in favour of going to Cairo.

It was finally determined to inform Admiral Seymour of the situation, and if possible to get the Khedive within reach of the fleet. This state of uncertainty and anxiety continued till the next morning, when the officer left in charge of the 250 men came to His Highness and declared himself to be loyal to the Khedive. The Khedive made him a firm and impressive speech, which brought tears into his eyes. The other officers of his company were called up, and all swore loyalty and devotion, and kissed His Highness's hand. A distribution of decorations followed, and confidence was restored.

Zohrab Bey was then sent to inform the Admiral that the Khedive wished to return to Ras-el-Tin, and at one returned with the news that the Admiral had sent a guard to assist him.

The Khedive then started for Ras-el-Tin Palace, and in driving into the town had to make a *détour* so as to enter by the Moharrem Bey Gate. He was escorted by sixty or seventy cavalry, and preceded by a group of outriders carrying white flags on the points of their sabres. He had to pass *en route* numerous bands of pillagers and incendiaries, and on reaching the Palace was received by Admiral Seymour, and a force of marines.

CHAPTER XXII.

THE DESTRUCTION OF ALEXANDRIA.

Landing of Commander Hammill's Force—The March into the Town—The Portions of the City Destroyed—The Pecuniary Loss—The Responsibility for the Catastrophe—Admiral Seymour.

COMMANDER HAMMILL's party of 250 blue jackets and 160 marines landed without opposition. They reached the Palace of Ras-el-Tin at 10.30 a.m., seized the western end of the Peninsula, and threw out a line of sentries north and south extending from shore to shore. At 12.30 p.m. a small party of marines and a Gatling's crew from the *Monarch* pushed on towards the town and guarded the streets in the immediate neighbourhood, making prisoners of natives who were seen looting inside the gates, and firing upon those more remote. In Frank Street they found every shop looted and burnt. The looters retreated before them and dropped their plunder. Women were seen setting houses on fire with petroleum.

The streets were strewn with the most miscellaneous articles ; broken clock-cases, empty jewel-boxes, and fragments of all kinds. Every now and then the party had to run up a side street to avoid the fall of a house or wall. Bodies of Europeans, stripped and mutilated, were seen in the Place Mehemet Ali in an advanced state of putrefaction.*

* The Commander of the German gunboat, *Habicht*, who disembarked on the 14th, on his road to the German Hospital, found a dozen bodies of Europeans of different nationalities.

The scenes on every side were of the most appalling description.

The parts of Alexandria which were found to have been destroyed, or which were destroyed in the next two days, included not only the Grand Square, or 'Place Mehemet Ali,' in which three buildings only remained, but all the streets leading from it to the sea, the Rue Cherif Pasha and the Rue Tewfik Pasha, with the adjoining streets. In the Place itself the statue of Mehemet Ali on horseback in the centre remained untouched. One side of the Place de l'Eglise, one side of the Rue de la Mosque d'Attarine, a portion of the Boulevards de Ramleh and de Rosette, and the whole of the northern portion of the Rue de la Bourse, were also consumed. In addition to these, most of the houses in the following thoroughfares were destroyed: Rue Osman Pasha, Rue de l'Attarine, Rue des Sœurs, Rue de l'Enchère, and Rue du Prophète Daniel. The French and Austrian post-offices were burned, together with the Hotel d'Europe and the Messageries Hotel; also the English, French, Greek, Portuguese, and Brazilian Consulates, the Mont de Piété, and one police-station.

Such of the European dwellings as were not burnt were looted from top to bottom: articles of furniture not easily removed were wantonly injured or destroyed. Several of the Arab houses and shops also suffered in the general looting carried on. Almost the only European dwellings untouched were those in which Europeans were known to have remained.

The English Church was struck by a shell, but not otherwise injured; the German, the Coptic, the Catholic, and the Israelitish churches were also uninjured, except that the last-named received one shell. The theatres, the banks, and the tribunals, escaped injury.*

* Of the pecuniary loss sustained through the pillage and incendiarism

In considering the question of responsibility for all this destruction, there are one or two important matters to be taken into account. It must be admitted that had Admiral Seymour promptly landed only a small force, such as, the bombardment being then over, his ships could easily have supplied, there would have been no conflagration at all. The Arab soldiers, utterly demoralised by the fire of the squadron, loaded with plunder, and but little disposed to renew the fight, would have promptly dispersed, and the whole of Alexandria would have been saved; and even when the fire broke out, on the afternoon of the 12th, a prompt landing would have saved the greater part of the town.

It cannot be too often repeated that the destruction of Alexandria was the work, not of the ships, but of the native population. The aim of the vessels, directed solely on the forts, had been so true, that the damage done to the town by the half-dozen or so of shells which struck it was insignificant, and, with the exception of the Harem buildings at Ras-el-Tin, the British missiles did not create a single conflagration.

The Admiral's reluctance to disembark his men has been explained in more than one way. It has been said that, because the Constantinople Conference was then sitting, the disembarkation of a British force in Egypt would have been inconsistent with the understanding under which the Conference had been convoked. Next, it has been alleged that the Admiral's action was simply

some idea may be formed from the statistics subsequently furnished by the International Commission of Indemnities. The total sum awarded was 106,820,236 francs, or 4,341,011*l*. Of this sum 26,750,175 fr., or 1,070,007*l*., was given for house property destroyed, and 34,635,050 fr., or 1,385,402*l*., for furniture, and 43,395,061 fr., or 1,735,806*l*., for merchandise. When one bears in mind that the decree appointing the Commission expressly excluded claims for money, jewellery, securities, and works of art, it will be obvious that the total value of property stolen or destroyed must have considerably exceeded the sums above quoted.

of a defensive character and limited to the destruction of the forts which were considered to menace the fleet. Further, the material objection has been urged that the Admiral had not at his disposal a sufficient number of men, to these three reasons we will reply *seriatim*.

1. That since the assembling of the Conference the whole situation had been changed by the aggressive attitude adopted by Arabi and his colleagues towards the British Fleet, and this left Admiral Seymour free to take whatever steps, he, in consequence, deemed necessary.

2. That allowing that it was necessary as a defensive measure to bombard the forts, it was not only proper, but incumbent on Admiral Seymour to take such precautions as would render that proceeding as little injurious as possible to the thousands of subjects of neutral Powers in Alexandria, even if this involved a temporary occupation of the town.

Whether Admiral Seymour's actions were intended by Her Majesty's Government to be merely of a defensive character, we may judge from their having placed under the Admiral's orders the Channel Squadron, besides troopships and marines, a force which for the purposes of a bombardment undertaken merely in defence was clearly superfluous.

3. As to the Admiral not having the required force at his disposal, it was his duty before undertaking an operation of such importance as the bombardment, to have seen that he was provided for all contingencies.

It would be childish to suppose that Arabi's preparations constituted any real danger to the fleet, or that the emergency was so pressing that it was impossible for him to delay the bombardment until the additional ships of war and troopships should have arrived.

What took place was, as has been already said,

THE DESTRUCTION OF ALEXANDRIA.

exactly what was foreseen and had been threatened by Arabi.

It was moreover, considered, from a strategic point of view, precisely the right step for Arabi to have taken. He thereby not only gratified the vengeance of his followers, but covered the retreat of his troops to Kafr Dowar.

Regarded from any point of view, the responsibility for the burning of Alexandria rests with Admiral Seymour just as much as if his shells instead of the torches of the Arabs had set fire to the town, and it is submitted that it is not too much to say that the bombardment of the forts without the movement being followed by an immediate landing was one of the gravest errors ever committed by any military or naval commander in modern times.

CHAPTER XXIII.

OCCUPATION OF ALEXANDRIA.

Further Disembarkations —Patrolling the Town—Landing from *Achilles* and *Sultan*—Captain Fisher takes Command—Disposition of the Land Forces—Landing from German, American, and Greek Vessels of War; also from *Tanjore*—Incendiaries—Fire Brigade—Rumoured Attack— Preparations—Re-embarkation of Greek and American Sailors—Bedouin Attack—Night Alarm—Arrival of Sir A. Alison—Suspension of Arabi —Attempt to seize Locomotives—Return of Natives—Further Reinforcements—Scarcity of Provisions.

On the 13th July Admiral Seymour received a telegram from the Admiralty, as follows :—

' On invitation or concurrence with the Khedive, or in his absence of any Egyptian authority in Alexandria, you may land seamen and marines for police purposes to preserve order, acquainting Commanders of European ships of war if any present, and inviting their co-operation.'

During the afternoon the marines of the *Superb*, *Inflexible*, and *Temeraire*, were added to the forces on shore.

The patrolling of the city was begun, and a company of Royal Marine Artillerymen, armed as infantry, marched through the European and the Arab quarters of Alexandria.

They shot some natives caught in the act of setting fire to houses, and also three of the native police who were pillaging a house after having maltreated the Berberine door-keeper.

In the evening, the marines were landed from the *Achilles* and the *Sultan* ; and Captain Fisher of the *Inflexible* took command of the forces on shore.

OCCUPATION OF ALEXANDRIA.

The *Inflexible*, *Temeraire*, and *Achilles*, were stationed off Ramleh to command the land approaches to Alexandria from the southward and westward.

On the 14th, the *Penelope* with Admiral Hoskins left for Port Saïd.

Of the events of the 14th Admiral Seymour says, 'Employed during the whole of the day landing as many men as we could spare from the Squadron, and by evening we had occupied the most important positions.'

Alexandria, being a walled town, the distribution of the force at Captain Fisher's disposal had to be governed by this fact, and was practically as follows:—At the Ramleh station were marines from the *Monarch*. At the Rosetta Gate were marines from the *Temeraire*. At the Moharrem Bey Gate were marines from the *Alexandra*. At Fort Kom el Dyk Gate were marines from the *Sultan*. At Pompey's Pillar Gate and Dead Gate were marines from the *Superb*. At the Gabari Caracol Gate were marines from the *Achilles*. At the Gabari railway station were marines and blue jackets from the *Alexandra*. At the Zaptieh and Arsenal were marines from the *Invincible*.

As the streets were gradually explored the bodies of many Europeans were discovered, others were found floating in the harbour. The corpses found in the streets were buried as quickly as possible. During this time the town was still being fired and looted in places.

On the 15th the *Minotaur* arrived with Admiral Dowell, in command of the Channel Squadron, and a brigade of seamen and marines from her was at once disembarked. Fort Napoleon was occupied by gunners from the fleet. Fort Kom-el-Dyk, which it was reported had been mined, was also occupied by blue jackets. A party of men from the *Alexandra* destroyed the guns at Fort Silsileh with gun-cotton.*

The German, American, and Greek ships of war landed men to assist in restoring order. Commander Briscoe of the Peninsular and Oriental Company's S.S. *Tanjore*, also patrolled the town at the head of an armed force from that vessel. Lord Charles Beresford was appointed Chief of Police, and persons found pillaging or setting fire to the houses were brought before him and summarily dealt with. Those guilty of pillaging were flogged, and incendiaries were sentenced to be shot. The American marines rendered much service in promptly disposing of incendiaries, and in blowing up houses with gunpowder to check the conflagration.†

In consequence of a rumour that Arabi intended to attack the town, a large number of blue jackets and marines, with Gatling guns, were landed, each ship reinforcing its detachment on shore. The *Minotaur's* marines strengthened the post at the Ramleh Gate, and her blue jackets the weak part of the defence between Pompey's Pillar Gate and Minit-el-Bassel; and the *Alexandra's* blue jackets were stationed in the latter quarter to guard the bridge over the Mahmoudieh Canal.

As a fact, Arabi was busy entrenching himself at Kafr-Dowar, and had no more thought of attacking the British forces than these last had of making an onslaught

---

* This wanton and useless work of destruction was repeated at all the forts bearing on the sea. The light guns (6½ inch S.B.) were hove off their carriages, and the rifled guns treated with gun-cotton. Hundreds of tons of gunpowder were ruined, and scores of valuable guns rendered useless. The object of this destruction is hardly evident. It is the more incomprehensible as on 13th July Admiral Seymour had received a despatch from the Admiralty in the following terms: 'Opposition having ceased, do not dismantle forts or disable guns.'

† A regular Fire Brigade Service was organized under an Englishman, Mr. John Wallace, C.E., and was the means of saving much valuable property.

on him. This, however, was not known to the British Admiral, who, at eleven p.m. telegraphed to the Admiralty as follows :—' Arabi Pasha reported to be advancing on Alexandria. I have telegraphed to Port Saïd to intercept ships from Cyprus, and order them to call here on their way back.'

On the 15th the Khedive summoned Arabi to Alexandria, which was a little like ' calling up spirits from the vasty deep;' and Arabi telegraphed from Kafr Dowar, by way of response, that ' His Highness would be glad to hear that recruits were coming in to assist him to fight the English.'

At the Khedive's suggestion the Admiral, on the 16th, despatched two ships to command Aboukir in case Arabi should attempt to cut the dyke there and let in the sea.

The same day it was found necessary to re-embark the Greek marines who had been landed to restore order. The Americans and the others, excepting the Germans, likewise re-embarked. The Germans remained on shore some days later, and were most useful.

On the 16th the Tribunals were occupied by bluejackets. Fresh fires broke out in the town, and a party of Bedouins, 150 strong, appeared at Gabari Gate, bent upon looting. They succeeded in capturing a donkey, when they were fired on by a midshipman of the *Alexandra* and twelve seamen, and two of their number were killed.

At 10.30 p.m. it was rumoured that official information had been received that Arabi was marching back, and would arrive in two hours. Between one and two on the following morning loud reports of explosions were heard, and the electric lights flashing from the ships tended to increase the prevailing alarm. Eventually it transpired that Arabi's forces were nowhere near, and that the explosions were attributable to the blowing up by the Engilsh of the bridge near Rosetta Gate.

On the 17th further reinforcements arrived. The *Tamar* arrived with 1000 marines and marine artillery from Cyprus. The *Agincourt* and *Northumberland* (ironclads) arrived from Port Saïd with the 38th (Staffordshire) Regiment, 860 strong, and a battalion of the 60th Rifles, 1700 in all. The *Salamis*, with General Sir Archibald Alison and staff, also arrived, and the General assumed the command of the land forces, now numbering 3686 men.

On the same day, Commander Maude of the *Temeraire*, accompanied by Mr. J. E. Cornish, of the Water-works, with four blue-jackets and four of the Khedive's guards, rode out to within 300 yards of Arabi's position at Kafr Dowar. They encountered a number of natives at the railway bridge over the canal. These last were unfriendly, and hustled two of the sailors who formed the advanced guard, and who were only released on the rest of the party coming up and preparing their revolvers.

At Millaha Junction, Commander Maude found several human bodies lying about in various stages of decomposition. There were signs of loot in all directions, and the bodies were evidently those of looters who had in their turn been robbed by the soldiers. One of the natives of Commander Maude's party deserted, and rode straight for Arabi's camp. It was not thought prudent to attract attention by firing at him, and the rest of the expedition returned.

The camp was reported to consist of 6000 men, with six batteries of rifled guns, one battery of Gatlings, and 300 marine artillery, besides Bedouins. They were entrenching themselves behind earthworks on the line of railway.

OCCUPATION OF ALEXANDRIA. 195

The Khedive now announced that Arabi had been suspended from his functions as Minister of War. The Ministry of Foreign Affairs, in communicating to the Admiral the dismissal of Arabi, stated that 'the publication of the decree was deferred for fear of seeing reproduced in Cairo and other towns the fearful disorder which had taken place in Alexandria.'

An attempt was made to carry off the locomotives and rolling stock from the Government railway, to Arabi's lines, together with 3000 tons of coal, but was cleverly frustrated, mainly through the efforts of Mr. Cornish, already mentioned. Mr. Cornish, on the morning of the 17th, on going on board Admiral Seymour's flagship, found a party going to Gabari to cut the railway line to prevent Arabi's friends carrying off the rolling stock there, and recollecting that there were six or seven engines and a number of carriages, at the other station at Moharrem Bey, which might also be taken, informed the Admiral of the fact. He ordered Lieutenant Anson and a party of marines to accompany Mr. Cornish to the spot. Mr. Cornish found that the most convenient place for cutting the line was under a bridge outside the station, where, sitting in the shade of the bridge, were several Arab platelayers; they set to work at once, in accordance with his directions, and with their help, the Marines soon lifted two pairs of rails on each line, and so cut the communication, and saved the rolling stock.

Whilst this was being done, an Effendi came out from the station, and begged the party to wait five minutes until the Pasha's engine, which was getting up steam, came out. All this while Zeki Pasha, the native administrator of the Egyptian railways, was on the platform eating a water melon, and expecting to start as soon as steam was up, doubtless intending to take the rest of the engines and rolling stock with him. However, when he found how matters stood, he changed his plans, got into a carriage, drove to Ras-el-Tin, and arranged things so well with the Khedive's party, that within a fortnight he was made Governor of Alexandria. After this, all the locomotives were brought down to the Mole so as to be under the protection of the ships.

Lieutenant Aplin of the *Hecla* was unfortunately killed by the accidental explosion of his revolver at Moharram Bey Gate. At the same place, the German guard coming from the Deaconesses' hospital at night, and not answering when challenged, were fired on by the English forces. The Germans returned the fire, but happily no one was hurt on either side.

A reconnaissance was made to Ramleh, and this pleasant suburb of Alexandria was found to have been in most quarters looted.

On the 18th, the troopship *Orontes* arrived from Malta, but through some unaccountable blundering of the authorities, she came without a single soldier.

By this time order was beginning to be re-established in Alexandria; the fires, too, had either burnt themselves out or been extinguished. The Egyptian Post Office, under the Director-General, afterwards Halton Bey, was reopened in the town, and the work of clearing the streets was proceeded with rapidly. For this purpose many natives and others out of employment were utilised.

The first day's work in street-clearing was marked by the first public execution. A negro, who had been caught setting fire to some houses, was, after a court-martial, tied to a tree in the Place Mehemet Ali, and shot by a party of sailors. The people too began to return to the town. These, however, required to be watched, as they were almost to a man Arabists, and ready to resume the work of incendiarism and plunder on the first opportunity. Looters were still to be found lurking in odd corners, notably in the Minet-el-Bassel quarter, where there were many stores containing sugar and grain.

The sanitary condition of the town now began to give rise to apprehension. Disagreeable odours, indicating the presence of dead bodies, were perceived proceeding from many of the houses. These were no doubt the victims of the pillagers, left to lie where they fell.

On the 18th the 3rd battalion of the King's Royal Rifle corps (late 60th Foot), which had reached the outer roads the day before in the *Agincourt*, went to Moharrem Bey Gate, relieving the posts of the 38th, which concentrated at Rosetta Gate. The land defence of the city was now definitely assumed by the army, assisted at the Rosetta Gate by the marines from the *Alexandra*, *Superb*, and *Temeraire*, and elsewhere by the blue-jackets with their Gatling guns. The other bodies of marines landed from the ships were employed in patrolling and policing the town.

The whole of the marines on shore were under the command of Lieutenant-Colonel F. G. Legrand, R.M.L.I., who had come out from England for this purpose. These carried on the duties of constables, cases being tried at the Tribunals and Zaptiehs, and then sent to the Arsenal for punishment. Strong measures had to be adopted to keep the large native population in order, especially in view of the great temptations and opportunities for looting. Efforts were made to secure a native police force as a substitute, but the unsettled condition of things, and the difficulty of getting trustworthy Egyptians, rendered this a long and tedious process.

At this period it was found that the supply of provisions in Alexandria was running short, and steps had to be considered for stopping the return of the European fugitives.

CHAPTER XXIV.

THE SITUATION IN EGYPT.

Departure of Dervish Pasha—Proclamation of Admiral Seymour—Executions—Omar Pasha Loutfi's Report—Massacres in the Interior—Situation in Cairo—General Council summoned—Arabi's Preparations—Decree against Arabi—Arabi's Proclamations against the Khedive'—The Force at Kafr Dowar—Raouf Pasha—Decision of the Great National Council.

ON the 19th July, Dervish Pasha, the Sultan's Envoy, whose pacifying mission to Egypt had so signally failed, left Alexandria for Constantinople.

On the 20th a proclamation was issued by Admiral Seymour, with the permission of the Khedive. It announced that 'Orders had been given to officer commanding patrols to shoot any person taken in the act of incendiarism; that any person taken in the act of pillage would be sent to the Zaptieh to be tried and punished; that any person taken a second time for the same offence would be shot; and that no person would be allowed to enter or leave the town after sunset.'

On the 23rd three natives and one Greek were shot for incendiarism.

Omar Pasha Loutfi, Governor of Alexandria, returning from Cairo, reported that he had seen Europeans massacred, and their houses pillaged, at Damanhour, Tantah, and Mehalleh. The Governor stated that he had seen a European and his wife murdered at the Tookh Station, half-an-hour distant by rail from Cairo.

According to an inquiry made by the Prefect of Police at Tantah, the number of Europeans murdered, and subsequently buried, in that town, amounted to fifty-one, and there were about an equal number who were massacred and thrown into the Canal. At Kafr Zayat, six persons were killed, a young French engineer named Alexandre, a British subject, two Copts and two Jews. Ten Greek and three Jews were murdered at Benha. Disturbances also occurred at Zagazig, but no persons were killed there, although a German was wounded. At Galioub, a family was taken out of the train, put under the carriages, and crushed by the wheels. The inspector of the 'Cadastre,' at Mehalleh Kebir, reported that fifteen Europeans were killed there. At Kafr Dowar also, some Europeans were massacred. The exact number is not known. Five Europeans were killed at Mehalla-Abou-Ali.

In Cairo, Omar Pasha Loutfi found that the greatest excitement and panic prevailed. The Prefects of Menoufieh and Garbieh, and the Mudir (or Governor) of Galioubieh, were imprisoned in the citadel for obeying the Khedive.

A general Council had been summoned at the Ministry of the Interior to consider the question of continuing the military preparations. It was attended by about a hundred Pashas, Ulemas, and merchants. After a number of violent speeches against the Khedive, the Coptic Patriarch remarked that the assembly had as yet heard only one side of the question, viz., that of Arabi, and that before coming to any decision it was necessary to hear the Khedive's side as well. The views of the Coptic Patriarch were adopted by the majority of the assembly, which proceeded to nominate a delegation to carry out the vote.

The delegation consisted of Ali Pasha Moubarek,

(a former Minister) and five others, who were directed to proceed to Alexandria to see the Khedive, and ask His Highness what truth there was in the charges of the Arabists; they were also directed to ascertain whether all the Ministers were really in prison as had been stated.

As regards the rebel military preparations, Mahmoud Pasha Sami had been appointed Commander-in-chief of the army corps stationed in the neighbourhood of the Suez Canal. Arabi demanded that one-sixth of the male population of every province should be called to Kafr Dowar. All old soldiers of every description were called upon to serve again, and horses and provisions were everywhere requisitioned for the army.

'Arabi's chief strength,' wrote Mr. Cartwright, the Acting British Consul-General, 'lay in his unscrupulous and barbarous mode of warfare.' At the moment, there was such a terrible dread among the officials at the Palace of what might happen to their property in Cairo and elsewhere, that the Khedive's action was paralysed, and His Highness was deterred from denouncing Arabi as a rebel by his unwillingness to incur the consequences of Arabi's retaliation. At an interview with the Khedive, Mr. Cartwright had endeavoured to represent to him the moral effect which such a proclamation would produce, and the encouragement which it would afford to those who remained faithful to His Highness.

On the 22nd the Khedive published a Decree dismissing Arabi from his post of Minister of War, and proclaiming him a rebel. Omar Pasha Loutfi, formerly Governor of Alexandria, was appointed in his place.

The reasons for Arabi's dismissal as set forth in the Decree were the insufficient resistance offered to the British Fleet, the loss of 400 guns, allowing the

English to land without resistance, the retreat to Kafr Dowar, and the disobedience of Arabi in not coming to the Khedive when summoned.

Considering the relations existing between the Khedive and the British forces at this time, the Decree, issued at a period when Tewfik was no longer under any sort of coercion, is as curious a specimen of an Oriental document as generally comes to light.

The proclamation itself may be regarded as a reply to one issued by Arabi against the Khedive, and transmitted to the Governors of the various provinces in Egypt.

On the 26th Arabi telegraphed to the Sultan protesting his fidelity to the Khalifate, and saying, 'That being provoked into a war, he was in possession of all that was necessary to overcome his enemies, thanks to the Divine assistance and the abundance of the land.' He added, 'That he did not believe, that, as the enemies of his country and religion asserted, he would find Ottoman troops on his path, which would place him under the cruel necessity of treating as enemies his brethren in the faith.'

Aly Pasha Moubarek succeeded in reaching Alexandria. He reported that at Kafr Dowar a Holy War had been proclaimed, and through the influence of the sheikhs large numbers of soldiers were flocking to Arabi from the villages, arms were being distributed to all comers, and a total force of 30,000 men had been got together. Raouf Pasha, however, who came from the camp a few days later, gave the number of Arabi's men as only 15,000, and related that much sickness prevailed amongst them.

On the 3rd August the official journal of Cairo published the decision of a great National Council of the week before, to the effect that—

'In consequence of the occupation of Alexandria by foreign troops, of the presence of the English squadron in Egyptian waters, and finally of the attitude taken up by Arabi Pasha for the purpose of repulsing the enemy, Arabi Pasha was to be upheld as Minister of War and Marine, intrusted with the general command of the Egyptian army, and full authority in all that concerned military operations, and that the orders of the Khedive and his Ministers would be null and void.'

The document bore the signatures of the three Princes Ibrahim, Ahmed, and Kamil (cousins of the Khedive), of seven Princes of the Yegan family, of the Sheikh of the El Khazar Mosque, of the Grand Cadi of Egypt, of the Coptic Patriarch, of the Grand Cadi of Cairo, besides those of the Ulemas and Judges, and in fact all the notabilities left in Cairo.

CHAPTER XXV.

OPERATIONS AT ALEXANDRIA.

Reinforcements ordered—Despatch of the British Expeditionary Force—Details—Sir Garnet Wolseley's Instructions—The British Government—The Khedive—Request for Assistance—Works at Alexandria—Fresh Fires—The Water Supply—Mr. Cornish—The Mahmoudieh Canal Dammed—Salt Water let into the Canal—Looting of the Palace at Ramleh—Looting generally by the Soldiers.

ON the 19th July, at the request of the Foreign Office, additional troops were ordered to Malta and Cyprus to bring up the forces there to 15,000 men; and the next day the British Cabinet had so far realised the gravity of the situation, as to decide on the despatch of an English expedition to Egypt, with or without the consent of the Powers.

The vote of credit for the expedition, 2,300,000*l*., was asked in Parliament on the 24th July, Mr. Gladstone carefully explaining that the country '*was not at war.*'

The Scots Guards sailed for Alexandria on the 30th July, the head of a column of ships and regiments which from that time until the occupation of the Suez Canal on the 20th August, never ceased to stream towards its ultimate point of destination.

The force was originally fixed at 21,000 men, composed as follows:—cavalry, 2400; infantry, 13,400; artillery, 1700; Hospital and other non-combatant services, 3700, with a reserve of 3100, to sail at a later period. The entire force was to be under the command

OPERATIONS AT ALEXANDRIA.

of General Sir Garnet Wolseley, G.C.B., with General Sir John Adye, K.C.B., as second in command, and Lieutenant-Generals G. H. Willis, C.B., and Sir E. B. Hamley, as divisional commanders.

One hundred men of the 24th Middlesex (Post Office) Volunteers were chosen to accompany the forces, and take charge of the postal arrangements during the campaign.*

Sir Garnet Wolseley's instructions were to take command of the army ordered for service in Egypt in support of the authority of the Khedive to suppress a military revolt in that country. He was told that Her Majesty's Government did not wish to fetter his discretion as to the particular military operations which might be necessary, but that the main object of the expedition was to re-establish the power of the Khedive. He was empowered, after successful operations against Arabi and those in arms against the Khedive, to enter into any military convention which the circumstances might warrant, but to make no arrangements involving a political settlement.

In despatching the British expedition, Mr. Gladstone's Government made a final plunge in the direc-

---

* The reinforcements, which were prepared after the despatch of the first corps, amounted to 280 officers and 10,800 men, so that the total force despatched, or in the act of being despatched, to the end of the war from Great Britain and the Mediterranean stations amounted to 1290 officers and 32,000 men. The Indian Contingent, including a small reserve left at Aden, consisted of 170 officers and 7100 men. Some of these, consisting of depôts, and drafts, and one infantry battalion, were stopped at the last moment, but on the whole not far short of 40,000 men were sent. The troops despatched from India were the 1st Seaforth Highlanders and the 1st Manchester, two Bengal and one Bombay battalions of Native Infantry, with one 9-pounder field battery and one mountain battery, each of six guns, and three regiments of Bengal cavalry, with some sappers and miners from Madras. The force was accompanied by about 3500 followers, including transport drivers, 1700 horses, 840 ponies, and nearly 5000 mules, some for regimental and others for general transport purposes. The first battalion left Bombay on the 22nd July. The rest of the force received their orders on the 24th July, and began to leave on August 5th. The Government engaged 71 transports in England and 54 in India during the war in 1882.

tion which they had from the first wished to avoid. No one can say that their intervention came too soon.

The Khedive on the 19th had sent for Sir Auckland Colvin, who was the right-hand man of the Acting British Consul-General, and begged him to urge Her Majesty's Government to take further action without delay. He pointed out that it was most necessary, as Arabi's power had become so great as to spread terror and consternation in the minds of all the natives. His possession of the country, and especially of Cairo, His Highness added, left at his mercy the families and property of all who remained loyal to the Khedive. His Highness concluded by saying he should be glad to receive an intimation as to the steps which were contemplated. Those steps, as has been seen, culminated in the despatch of the British expedition.

The means by which the British Government was gradually induced to adopt a resolute attitude in regard to Egypt, and the degrees by which it arrived at a decision, will appear later on.

The general feeling of uneasiness at Alexandria was augmented by Omar Pasha Loutfi's report. It was further known that Arabi's forces were daily increasing, and scouts ascertained that his outposts had been advanced in the direction of Alexandria. Repeated rumours of intended attacks from time to time prevailed, and scarcely a night passed without an alarm of one kind or another.

The British authorities now began to employ themselves seriously in looking to the defences of the town, and on the 20th Major Ardagh and the engineers proceeded to repair the drawbridges, to mend the walls at Kom-el-Dyk, to mount guns at Rosetta Gate, to secure the railway station, and to place Gatlings in position. Three 9-pounder rifled guns were mounted in Fort Kom-el-Dyk, as part of the permanent defences of the city, and manned by blue-jackets from the fleet.

On the 19th, a brisk wind fanned the embers of some of the ruins into flames, which occupied the fire-brigade several hours to subdue.

The water supply of Alexandria, of this time, began to be a source of anxiety. The supply to the town comes from the Mahmoudieh Canal, which joins the Rosetta branch of the Nile at Atfeh, forty-five miles distant. The canal itself adjoins the position taken by Arabi at Kafr Dowar. Throughout the bombardment, and subsequently, the town had been abundantly supplied by the efforts of Mr. Cornish. When, previous to the bombardment, as has been mentioned, all his countrymen, and the great mass of Europeans sought safety afloat, he refused to desert his post. He contrived an elaborate system of defence for the waterworks. It comprised an arrangement for throwing jets of steam at any possible band of assailants, as well as a line of dynamite bombs, capable of being exploded by means of electricity. The upper part of the engine house was converted into a kind of arsenal, into which he and his men could retire as a last resort, and where rifles and ammunition were in readiness. During the bombardment, the works happily escaped injury. On the morning of the 11th July, the day of the bombardment, Mr. Cornish visited the auxiliary pumping station on the canal, more than a mile distant, as usual. From the roof of the engine-house Mr. Cornish and his companions (nine Europeans in all) watched the progress of the bombardment, until the shot and shell which whistled overhead from the vessels firing at Fort Pharos, compelled them to descend. Meanwhile, the pumps were kept going as in ordinary times. When, on the afternoon of the 12th, the mob of rioters left the town, the majority of them passed a few yards from the Works, and indulged in curses and execrations at the 'Christian dogs' within. With humane forethought, two large jars of water were placed in front of the gate and kept supplied from within. Thousands of thirsty natives coming from the dust and smoke of the town, stopped to drink, and after cursing Mr. Cornish passed on. To whatever cause it may be attributed no attack was made on the works, and their courageous director survived to receive the congratulations of the Khedive and of his own countrymen.*

Arabi's position at Kafr Dowar placed the water supply of Alexandria at his mercy, and he was not long in taking advantage of the circumstance. On the 21st July, the water in the Mahmoudieh Canal was observed to be rapidly falling. Arabi had made a dam, at a point called Kinje Osman, between Kafr Dowar and Alexandria, by which all further flow from the Nile was stopped. Assuming that his operations were limited to this, the great quantity of water in the Alexandria end of the canal ensured a supply for about twelve days. It was rumoured, however, that he had broken the banks of the canal on the Alexandria side. This would, of course, have soon cut off the supply altogether, and have caused much suffering among the population, beside forcing the troops to rely on the distilled water from the ships. In view of the emergency, Admiral Seymour appointed a Commission to sit every day to consider the measures to be adopted. Steps were taken to stop all the steam-engines and 'Sakeah' (or water-

---

* Mr. Cornish had the decoration of the C.M.G. conferred on him for his conduct on this occasion.

wheels), taking water from the canal for irrigation purposes, arrangements were made for clearing out and filling the old Roman water-cisterns of Alexandria, and for regulating the supply to the inhabitants, and H.M.S. *Supply* was ordered from Malta with the necessary apparatus for distilling water.

On the 21st, Arabi caused salt water to be let into the Mahmoudieh Canal, by cutting the dam separating it from Lake Mareotis, thereby considerably aggravating the difficulty of the water supply.

A rumour was started that the Khedive's Palace at Ramleh had been looted by the English soldiery. Major Ardagh was instructed to hold a searching inquiry, the result of which was that the report was found to be utterly without foundation. The soldiers, individually, were searched and no loot was discovered. The Palace had, indeed, been looted to a large extent; none of the Khedive's servants had been left in charge, and from the time of his evacuating it till the 24th, it was wholly unguarded.*

* It is only fair to the British army to say that but very little looting was ever proved against them during this period. Isolated cases of breaking into houses and carrying off wines and spirits occurred, but these were almost the only instances. The foreign population of Alexandria and Ramleh have frequently borne testimony to this effect, as well as to the perfect impartiality with which British cellars, as well as those of other Europeans, were requisitioned in an informal manner.

CHAPTER XXVI.

OPERATIONS AT RAMLEH.

Troops under Sir Archibald Alison move out to Ramleh—Skirmish—Ramleh Occupied—The Ramleh Lines—The Position on the Mahmoudieh Canal—The Ironclad Train—Mr. De Chair—Rumoured Attack on the Town—Bedouin Attacks—The Reconnaissance to Kinje Osman, and Engagements of 5th August—Earthworks at Mandara.

On the 21st July Sir Archibald Alison moved two regiments of infantry and a squadron of mounted men out to Ramleh in the direction of Arabi's entrenchments. They went as far as 'Water-Works Hill,' a commanding position from which a good view of the Egyptian lines at Kafr Dowar could be obtained.

On the morning of the 22nd a force of 250 men of the Rifles was pushed forward beyond Millaha Junction, on the Cairo railway, to blow up the line. They met Arabi's cavalry and exchanged shots with them. The Egyptians fled, leaving two dead on the field. Having finished the work entrusted to them the Rifles then withdrew. A strong patrol was the same day sent to Ramleh.

On the 24th, the troopship *Malabar* having arrived the previous day from Gibraltar and Malta with the 46th (Duke of Cornwall's Light Infantry) Regiment, a wing of the 35th, and a Battery of Artillery, in all 1108 men, Sir Archibald Alison, at 3 a.m., sent mounted infantry to the position intended to be occupied in front of the Ramleh Barracks. The General followed by the train of the Alexandria and Ramleh Railway with the 60th Rifles, two 7-pounder naval guns, and some sappers. On arriving the General found the ridge, running from the Palace to the Mahmoudieh Canal, occupied by the mounted infantry, and he at once took possession of the Water-Works Tower on the ridge, a strongly defensible building, and established outposts at the railway bridge, and at the front of the canal bend. Shortly after the British troops were in position a small force of Arabi's cavalry, followed by infantry, advanced towards the railway bridge, across the canal, within 400 yards of the Rifles. After exchanging shots for some time, the cavalry retired rapidly on the Mahmoudieh Canal. The enemy's advance then became more decided. A considerable force of cavalry with two horse-artillery guns pushed on rapidly, the guns coming briskly into action. The infantry followed, and the movements of a considerable body of troops were observed on the high ground behind. A fight ensued which lasted about an hour; several of the enemy being observed to drop. The attack, however, was not pushed home, and the firing gradually ceased. There were no casualties on the English side.

Ramleh was from this day occupied and held by the British forces. The work of fortifying it was begun at once, and prosecuted with vigour, for the force opposed to the English far outnumbered the latter at all times, and the need of the moment was to hold on until the army corps under General Wolseley could be collected and transported to Alexandria.

It may be here mentioned that Ramleh is not a village or town, but a species of summer resort for the European residents of Alexandria, who have built houses and villas upon the sandy neck of land lying between Lakes Mareotis and Aboukir on the one hand, and the Mediterranean on the other. The houses are distributed over a length of some miles, and are mostly surrounded by high walled enclosures, with, in many cases, luxuriant gardens. Between these scattered country places the sand lies everywhere ankle-deep. There is an occasional pretence of a road, but, generally speaking, communication between any two points is in the straightest possible line, and through the sand. To supply the needed transit to and from the city, a private company has constructed the Alexandria and Ramleh Railway. This has no connexion, material or otherwise, with the Government lines. An incidental advantage due to the occupation of Ramleh was the protection enjoyed by the Ramleh Railway, and by the owners of other property in this quarter.

The water-works at Ramleh contain the pumping-engines which deliver the fresh water for distribution from the Mahmoudieh Canal to the tower and reservoir just behind them on higher ground. These two points, the water-works and the water-tower, were the centre of the defence. A strong detachment was always maintained at the former, whilst the head-quarters were established at the latter. An elevation immediately in rear of the Water-works Tower was strengthened, a trench dug, and a number of guns, viz., five breech-loading 40-pounders and two 12-pounders, were mounted on the 26th by seamen from the *Alexandra, Monarch, Sultan*, and *Superb*, under the command of Commander Thomas, of the *Alexandra*, subsequently relieved by Commander Hammill of the *Monarch*. A magazine was also sunk. At first working parties ran a shelter trench along the crest of the rising ground, and this was gradually converted into a musketry parapet four and a half feet high. In this places were arranged for the guns, the platforms being of railway-sleepers and the parapets revetted with sand-bags and timber. Small musketry redoubts were thrown up upon the flanks of the position. To the east and west were entrenched infantry camps. Two nine-pounders of the Naval Detachment were mounted in the adjoining earthwork. The extreme eastern picket was placed in a fortified house, a mile and a half distant. Its object was to serve as a feeler in the direction of Aboukir. The Egyptians could advance from Kinje Osman either by the road on the canal bank or by the railway embankment. The outpost on the former line was called 'Dead Horse Picket;' on the latter no regular picket was maintained beyond the iron railway bridge over the Mahmoudieh Canal, although vedettes were constantly thrown out in the direction of Millaha Junction.

As a barrier against a movement along the southern branch of the railway, that coming from the Gabari Station, a strong force was established at the Villa Antoniadis on the canal, with orders to hold on whether reinforced or not. The men's tents were pitched on the roadway along the Canal, outside the garden, the horses and mules being picketed at a stable-yard, and a tower of the villa was utilised as a station for signals and look-outs. From this point signals could be exchanged with the head-quarters at the Ramleh water-tower, while the view it commanded extended across the bed of Lake Mareotis to Kinje Osman, and swept on the left to Ramleh. Inside the entrance to the villa garden was a semi-circular breastwork facing the villa, and reaching across the gateway. Two B. L. R. 40-pounder guns were permanently mounted. These commanded the approach along the railway embankment. Other stockades were built across the road to protect the rear, and temporary bridges were built across the canal. The walls of a deserted Arab village on the other side were loopholed and otherwise defended. On the roofs of the houses sand-bags were piled for breastwork. The garrison at this point was composed of five companies of the 35th (Royal Sussex Regiment), first battalion, under Lieut.-Colonel Hackett, and 75 artillerymen.

The general defence profited by the presence of the Mahmoudieh Canal, with its high banks, and by the railway embankment, which stretched from the Antoniadis garden towards Ramleh. For night-work an electric light was placed on the roof of a house at Fleming Station, so as to illuminate the approaches from Aboukir and Kafr Dowar.

An ingenious device for reconnoitring was at this time adopted, in fitting out an armour-clad train in which to make reconnaissances towards Arabi's lines. One of the Government locomotives was armed under the direction of Captain Fisher, of the *Inflexible*, with a 40-pounder gun, and fitted with boiler plates, iron rails, and bags of cotton to protect the vital parts. This, accompanied by two or three open carriages filled with blue jackets rendered considerable service. It was frequently brought into action, and whilst able to considerably harass the enemy's forces at Kafr Dowar, never sustained any injury in return.

At this time, Mr. Dudley De Chair, midshipman of the *Alexandra*, was captured and taken to Arabi's lines. He had been ordered to proceed with despatches from Alexandria to the British post at Ramleh following the line of rail. Unfortunately, he went by the wrong line and found himself at Mandara, some miles beyond his destination, where, meeting some natives, he inquired his way, and they undertook to direct him to the British lines, but taking advantage of his ignorance of the locality, they led him to an Arab outpost where he was made prisoner.*

On the 27th July, at 8.45 a.m., the following message was signalled from the signal station at Fort Kom-el-Dyk to the flag-ship. 'Colonel Thackwell reports the enemy advancing in force, three guns drawn by horses. I hope Gordon has warned the 40th and 35th to be held in readiness.' At nine, it was reported that the enemy had halted at entrenchments.

It subsequently appeared that the supposed enemy was nothing more serious than an immense flock of pelicans, which with the aid of the mirage bore in the distance the appearance of Egyptian soldiers.

On the 31st July, the Bedouins who had been pillaging the neighbouring houses, attacked the night pickets at Ramleh with considerable energy, but were beaten off. In one of these skirmishes, what was taken to be the figure of a Bedouin was seen under the palm-trees. A whole volley was fired at the supposed enemy which proved to be only a pump. When examined closely the next morning the pump was found not to have received a single bullet.

On the following night, the Bedouins returned and attacked a picket of the 60th Rifles, under the command of Major Ward, posted at the extreme limit of the British position on the Mahmoudieh Canal. The picket, uncertain of the strength of the attacking force, fired a single volley and fell back on the pumping-station a mile distant. Reinforcements were sent and the position was re-occupied.†

* Mr. De Chair was sent by Arabi to Cairo, where, a report having been circulated that Admiral Seymour was being brought a prisoner to the capital, great crowds of natives assembled. Mr. De Chair was lodged in a building at Abdin used as a school for the sons of officers of the army and well treated, and at the conclusion of hostilities he was released.

† The picket on this occasion retired with some precipitancy, and the circumstance was taken advantage of by one of the London newspapers to publish a highly coloured account of the affair, which was however shortly after contradicted.

On the 3rd August an alarm of an impending rising of the natives and of a massacre of Europeans was raised. The patrols were ordered to use increased vigilance and activity, and all bludgeons and sticks in the hands of the natives were confiscated. Criers proceeded through the native quarter enjoining the people to remain in their houses at three in the afternoon, this being reported to be the hour fixed upon for the massacre, and the garrison was confined to barracks.

The same day an attack upon Fort Mex was expected, a force was therefore moved down on the railway, and the whole country round to the left of the fort was patrolled. The reconnaissance covered a large tract of ground, but only small parties of the enemy's infantry were seen, and these retired quickly on the approach of the English troops. The same afternoon, the 38th Regiment made a reconnaissance five miles beyond the Ramleh outposts.

On the 5th August, the first serious engagement of the campaign took place, when Sir Archibald Alison, being desirous of ascertaining the enemy's true position and strength, made a reconnaissance towards Kinje Osman. A half battalion of the Duke of Cornwall's Regiment and a half battalion of the 38th (South Staffordshire) Regiment, 800 in all, with one 9-pounder gun and the whole of the mounted infantry, numbering 80, were told off to advance along the east bank of the Mahmoudieh Canal. Six companies of the 60th Rifles, about 500 strong, with one 9-pounder gun, formed the centre, and were to advance along the west bank. These constituted the left attack. They were to follow the line of the Canal till they reached a house in a grove of trees towards the point where the Cairo Railway approaches nearest to the Canal. Along the line of rail a strong battalion of marines, 1000 in number, was to come up by train to Millaha Junction, preceded by the armoured train carrying one 40-pounder, two 9-pounder guns, a Nordenfeldt, and two Gatlings, and formed the right attack. The train was to stop at Millaha Junction. The marines were ordered to *detrain* there and advance by the railway line, accompanied by the two 9-pounders and covered by the fire of the 40-pounder from the train.

The ground beyond Millaha Junction between the canal and railway was occupied by native houses and gardens, and traversed in all directions by small irrigating canals or ditches. Here were the Egyptian outposts, the point to attack. It was a place admitting of very thorough defence, and it gained in practical value by the fact that the attack was divided by the Mahmoudieh Canal into two parts, which could only pass from one side to the other with great difficulty and at considerable risk. An enemy on the alert might have routed the extreme left column before any assistance could have been rendered by its neighbours.

The left column commenced its advance from the Ramleh out-picket station at 4.45 p.m., moving by both banks of the canal. It soon came into action with the enemy, who were strongly posted in a group of palm-trees on the eastern side, and a strong defensible house and gardens on the western side, of the canal. The Egyptian fire was very inaccurate, most of their bullets passing harmlessly overhead. Both positions were carried.

At this time Lieutenant Howard Vyse, of the Rifles, was killed.

The enemy then took up a position half a mile in the rear of the first upon the east bank of the canal, amongst high crops and houses, and behind the irregular banks of the canal. From this position also they were driven back.

General Alison accompanied the right column himself. The marines and nine-pounder guns, dragged by blue jackets, were placed to the west and under cover of the railway embankment, and moved forward as rapidly as possible, and quite out of sight of the enemy engaged with the left column, with a view to cutting off their retreat. After a time this movement was perceived, and the enemy opened fire with artillery on the right column. General Alison pushed on as rapidly as possible to the spot where the railway approaches nearest to the Mahmoudieh Canal. He then opened fire with musketry from the railway embankment upon the enemy lining the banks of the canal. The two nine-pounders were dragged on to the embankment and came into action against the enemy's guns, the forty-pounder from the train firing overhead against the point where the enemy were beginning to appear. Fixing his right upon both sides of the embankment, General Alison then threw forward two companies to carry a house near the canal, and followed up this movement by throwing some four companies still more to his left on the banks of and across the canal. The left column, it appears, had orders to seize a certain white house on the canal, but its commander, Lieut.-Colonel Thackwell, of the 38th, mistook the first white house reached for the one intended. In consequence, the left of the marines was uncovered, and the substantial benefits of the fight lost. Had the two wings joined many prisoners would have been secured, and two guns, if not more, been captured. Signals were made to the left wing to advance, but the smoke of the battle and the failing light prevented their being understood. As it was, Sir Archibald Alison succeeded in taking up a position forming a diagonal line across both the canal and the railway, the enemy falling back slowly before him. The fire of their seven and nine-pounder guns was soon got under by the fire of the English blue-jackets. Desirous of inducing the Egyptians to develop their full power before withdrawing, the General held his position for about three-quarters of an hour, until dusk was drawing on. The order to retire was then given. The movement was carried out with the most perfect regularity and precision by the marine battalion under Colonel Tuson, and the men fell back by alternate companies with the regularity of a field-day. Every attempt of the enemy to advance was crushed by the excellent practice of the forty-pounder and nine-pounder naval guns under Commander Morrison. The right column was quickly *entrained* at the Junction, and slowly steamed back to Alexandria; at the same time the left column withdrew along the banks of the canal to the Ramleh lines unmolested.

The British loss in the engagement was one officer and three men killed and twenty-seven men wounded. The Egyptian loss was given by a Circassian who, four days later, made his way from Arabi's camp to Alexandria, as three officers and seventy-six men killed, and a large number wounded.

According to the prisoners' statements, which had to be received with some caution, the Egyptian force engaged was 2000 strong.

The Egyptians next erected earthworks at Mandara, between Ramleh and Aboukir. They, however, overlooked the fact that the place was accessible from the sea, and the *Superb* having been sent round, shelled them out without difficulty.

CHAPTER XXVII.

THE CONFERENCE.

The Twenty-four hours Council—Withdrawal of Turkish Troops demanded—Retrospect—The Conference—The 'Identic Note'—The Sultan proposes to go to Egypt—The 'Note' Presented—Instructions to English Admiral at Port Saïd—French Government refuses to issue similar Orders—Proclamation against Arabi demanded—Proposals for Protection of Canal—Replies of the Powers—Turkey joins the Conference—The Vote in the French Chamber.

It is now necessary to go back a little, to consider the diplomatic steps taken by the Powers in view of the crisis in Egypt.

On receiving the news of the bombardment, the Sublime Porte was so impressed with the gravity of the situation that a Council sat continuously for twenty-four hours at the Palace, and separated without arriving at any conclusion.

On the 15th July, however, the Sultan's advisers had so far recovered themselves that the Turkish Ambassador was instructed to protest, and to demand of the English Government the withdrawal of the forces disembarked.

In reply Lord Dufferin stated that the bombardment was an act of self-defence, and that the seamen and marines were landed for the purpose of restoring order, and with no view to a permanent occupation. 'They were, and continued to be necessary for the defence of the Khedive,' said his Lordship, 'in the absence of all steps by the Sultan to maintain his own authority and that of his Highness.' Lord Dufferin concluded by observing that 'Her Majesty's Government were desirous to maintain the Sovereignty of the Sultan over Egypt, but that if his Majesty took no steps to vindicate his authority, and objected to the provisional measures taken by England and the other Powers, it would be difficult to find arguments for the continuance of the existing arrangement.' In order to understand what were ' the provisional measures ' referred to, it is necessary to consider the proceedings of the Constantinople Conference, which had in the meantime assembled.

When in May, France and England had at length agreed to send their vessels of war to Alexandria, it was at Lord Granville's suggestion proposed that if it was found advisable that troops should be landed, Turkish troops should be called for, but France objected and the proposal dropped.

When the Khedive and his Ministry became reconciled the Porte addressed a circular to its representatives abroad, arguing that the Egyptian Ministry having submitted to the Khedive, the crisis no longer existed, and the naval demonstration was unnecessary. Lord Dufferin was instructed to calm the apprehensions of the Sultan as to the character and objects of the naval demonstration. He succeeded so well that Said Pasha stated that His Majesty was willing to discuss with the Western Powers any arrangements that they might suggest for the maintenance of the *status quo* in Egypt, upon the understanding that the presence of the fleets should be restricted to the shortest possible period.

Lord Granville, on the Dual Note demanding the retirement of Arabi from Egypt being rejected, asked the Sultan to summon the three military leaders to Constantinople, and requested the other Powers to concur.

When Admiral Seymour complained of earthworks

being thrown up alongside his ships, the French Government on the 30th May proposed an immediate Conference on Egyptian affairs. This proposal was accepted by Lord Granville, and invitations to the Conference were issued the same day.

Considerable delay ensued in regard to the meeting of the Conference, owing to the opposition of Turkey, which refused to join, and persisted in maintaining that the mission of Dervish Pasha having effected a satisfactory settlement, there was really nothing left to discuss.

Eventually the Conference met on 23rd June at Constantinople, without the participation of the Porte.

The Powers were represented by the different Ambassadors at Constantinople, and Lord Granville, in the apparent desire to tie the hands of the British Government as much as possible, irrespective of future eventualities, succeeded in getting all the Powers represented to sign a self-denying protocol by which each engaged 'not to seek in any arrangement which might be made in consequence of the concerted action for the regulation of the affairs of Egypt any territorial advantage, nor any concession of any exclusive privilege, nor any commercial advantage other than those which any other nation might equally obtain.'

On the 27th June the position of Admiral Seymour with regard to the forts in course of being armed by Arabi, being explained to the Conference, it was, on the proposal of the Italian representative, agreed that so long as the Conference lasted the Powers should abstain from isolated action in Egypt, with the reservation of *force majeure*, such as the necessity for protecting the lives of their subjects.

On the 30th the Conference met again, when the critical state of the situation in Egypt was dwelt upon, and the English representative explained that under the words *force majeure* he should include any sudden change or catastrophe which menaced British interests.

Notwithstanding the pressure put upon the Sultan at this time to induce him to send a force to Egypt, he still hesitated. His anxiety seemed to be to avoid doing anything himself, and at the same time to prevent intervention by any one else. He reminded the English Ambassador that at his request the Porte had ordered the Egyptians to discontinue the fortifications at Alexandria, and in return asked that the warlike preparations of the British Fleet should be stopped.

On the 6th July, the Conference met again and agreed on the terms of an 'Identic Note' to be addressed to the Porte fixing the conditions on which the Porte should be invited to send Turkish troops to Egypt as a provisional measure to restore order.

On the 8th the Sultan's Minister of Foreign Affairs begged the English Ambassador from considerations of humanity to enjoin Admiral Seymour not to do anything precipitate at Alexandria. Lord Dufferin replied that ' the Egyptian authorities had the matter completely in their own hands. They had only to do what was required of them and not a shot would be fired.' Lord Dufferin added the question, ' Why was the Sultan not there with his troops to keep them in order?'

On the 9th the Porte was so far alarmed at what was going on at Alexandria as to send a despatch to Musurus Pasha pointing out that Admiral Seymour's statements respecting the Alexandria armaments were denied by the Egyptian authorities, and begging that the British Admiral might be directed to adopt a line of action more in conformity with the peaceful and conciliatory feelings which animated the Imperial Government and the Court of St. James.

On the 10th Lord Dufferin intimated to the Porte that it was the intention of Admiral Seymour to open fire upon the batteries of Alexandria unless there was a temporary surrender of the forts for the purpose of disarmament. The Sultan replied that he would send a categorical answer on the following day. At the same time he requested that the bombardment might be delayed.

Said Pasha called on Lord Dufferin in the middle of the night (2 a.m. on the morning of the 11th), urging him to send a telegram to the British Government to order the bombardment to be arrested. The British Ambassador transmitted the message. It arrived too late. The bombardment had already taken place. As Lord Dufferin, in a letter to Said Pasha in the course of the following day, observed, 'When such grave issues were at stake, it was unwise to run things so fine.'

On the following day the Sultan's Prime Minister, in ignorance of what was taking place at Alexandria, promised Lord Dufferin 'a satisfactory solution.'

On the 12th the Minister informed His Lordship that the bombardment having added to the gravity of the situation, he was not in a position to make the promised communication, but that the Council was still deliberating as to the course to be pursued. This was the Council referred to at the beginning of the present chapter, which sat for twenty-four hours, and decided nothing.

On the 15th Said Pasha asked if an intimation to the Powers of the Sultan's intention to go to Egypt would be well received. Lord Dufferin said in reply that at one time he was certainly of that opinion, and that even then it might not be too late, provided His Majesty would authorise a Commissioner to enter the Conference. Said Pasha then wanted to know if it

THE CONFERENCE. 225

could not be managed without Turkey joining the Conference, and, receiving no encouragement on that point, the matter dropped.

On the 15th all the Powers represented at the Conference presented an Identic Note to the Porte, inviting it to send troops to Egypt to assist the Khedive to re-establish order. The conditions proposed were, 1st. That the stay of the Imperial troops in Egypt should be limited to a period of three months; 2nd. That the expenses of the occupation should be borne by Egypt.

The Sultan, on receiving the Note, observed that if the Imperial Government had not up to the present decided on its own initiative to send troops to Egypt, it was because it was convinced that measures of force could be dispensed with. He also announced that his Government now consented to take part in the Conference.

On the 16th July Lord Lyons was instructed to inform M. de Freycinet that in view of the uncertainty which prevailed as to the movements of Arabi and his forces Her Majesty's Government had telegraphed to the British Admiral at Port Saïd, authorising him to concert with the French Admiral for the protection of the Suez Canal, and to act in the event of sudden danger. In reply, the French Minister stated that the French Admiral should be instructed to concert measures with the English Admiral for the protection of the Canal, but that the French Government could not, without the sanction of the Chambers, authorise him to act.

On the 17th appearances became still more threatening. The Admiralty received a despatch from Admiral Hoskins reporting the arrival at Port Saïd of Ali Pasha Fehmy, whom Arabi had nominated Governor-General of the Suez Canal. This was followed by another, announcing that Arabi had called upon all Mussulmans to rise. Lord Granville thereupon urged the French Government to give their Admiral at Port Saïd full discretion by telegraph in view of any emergency. In reply, M. de Freycinet informed the British Minister that he regretted very much to be unable to comply, but that it was out of the power of the French Government to do so without the previous sanction of the Chambers.

On the 19th the news from Egypt assumed a yet more serious character, and Lord Dufferin was instructed to inform the Sultan that after the delay which had occurred he could only hope to recover the confidence of Her Majesty's Government by the immediate issue of a Proclamation in favour of the Khedive, and denouncing Arabi as a rebel.

Whatever might have been the Sultan's views with regard to Arabi, he was not at the time disposed to comply with the Ambassador's request. Accordingly, His Majesty said that the issue of such a Proclamation as was suggested might not be a bad thing, and then turned the conversation to some other subject.

The same day news came of the blocking of the Mahmoudieh Canal, of the issue of Proclamations against the Khedive by Arabi, and of the military preparations being made by him; and orders were given for a British force of 15,000 men to be collected in Malta and Cyprus.

On the same day, at a meeting of the Conference, the English and French Ambassadors presented proposals relative to the measures to be adopted *for the protection of the Suez Canal*, and asked the Conference to designate the Powers who should be charged in case of need to take the measures specially necessary for the purpose.

The four other representatives reserved to themselves

the right of referring the matter to their respective Governments.

On the 20th July Her Majesty's Government decided on the despatch of the expedition to Egypt.

On the 21st the Austrian Government declined to join in giving to other Powers the *mandat* proposed for the defence of the Canal.

On the 22nd Lord Granville, feeling the necessity for doing something, made the following proposal to the French Government:—

'1. Unless the Porte sends an acceptance of a kind immediately available, the English and French representatives should be instructed to say to the other Ambassadors that England and France can no longer rely upon Turkish intervention; and as they consider immediate action necessary to prevent further loss of life and continuance of anarchy, they intend, unless the Conference has any other plan, to devise with a third Power, if possible, military means for procuring a solution.

'2. To ask Italy to be that third Power.

'3. To consult immediately upon the division of labour.

'4. The Suez Canal may be included in the general scheme of allied action.'

M. de Freycinet, in reply, cautiously stated that the French Government understood that the measures to be taken by them for the protection of the Canal would not extend to any expedition into the interior of the country, but would be limited to naval operations, and to the occupation of certain points on the Canal itself; and that although they would not object to an expedition by England into the interior of Egypt, they could not themselves take part in any such expedition. He added that before giving an official answer, he must bring the matter before the Council of Ministers.

The German Chargé d'Affaires stated to Lord Dufferin and the French Ambassador in very positive terms, that the northern Governments would never agree to a mandate, that it would be better for England to go forward at once by herself, and that everyone admitted that the reserve made under the term *force majeure*, would cover anything that she might be obliged to do in Egypt.

On the 23rd July the Sultan determined to allow Said Pasha and Assim Pasha to represent him at the Conference. At the meeting, the following day, the two Ottoman delegates both took their seats, and the other delegates, having given the Turkish representatives to understand that a formal answer was expected to the Identic Note of the 15th July, the Turkish Minister declared that 'he accepted in principle the despatch of Ottoman troops to Egypt.'

This statement made at the eleventh hour was not without its effect on the different great Powers. As a fact, with the exception of England, and possibly France, none of them desired to meddle either directly or indirectly in Egyptian matters, and were glad of the pretext to let England settle Egypt alone.

The Austrian Government notified that 'in case the Sultan refused to send his troops to Egypt, Austria would be even less disposed to join in asking other Governments to act as European "mandataires," for the maintenance of order, than to do so for the protection of the Suez Canal.'

On the 24th July Italy was invited to co-operate with England and France in the steps to be taken for the protection of the Canal. The Italian Minister, M. Mancini, thanked Her Majesty's Government for the proof of confidence and friendship afforded by their invitation to her, but thought that at the moment when Turkey had accepted all the conditions of a Note to which England and Italy were parties, it would appear to be a contradiction for those two Powers to enter into engagements as to another form of intervention. His Excellency admitted that the position of England was different from that of Italy and the other Powers. England had already got her troops in Egypt, and he quite understood her having a sufficient force there to control the conduct of the Turks; but for Italy to enter at that moment into an agreement with England such as that suggested, would be for her a new departure, which would not be justified by the circumstances.

On the 25th M. de Freycinet, being pressed for a formal answer to the proposal made for the joint military intervention, answered that for the moment the French Government could not go beyond the projected co-operation for the protection of the Suez Canal.

On the 24th July a Bill was brought into the Chamber of Deputies to enable the French Government to carry into effect the arrangements they had made with England for a joint protection of the Canal. The amount asked for was 9,410,000 francs. The result was a most stormy debate, which was adjourned amid much excitement.

CHAPTER XXVIII.

THE PORTE AND THE POWERS.

Said Pasha announces that Turkish Troops will leave immediately—Declaration of Views of England and France—Lord Dufferin's Reply—The Views of the Powers—The Debate in the Chamber of Deputies—Co-operation of Turkey accepted—The Proclamation against Arabi—Orders sent to prevent Landing of Turkish Troops—Turkish Military Preparations—Negotiations continued—Sailing of Sir G. Wolseley for Suez Canal.

On the 26th July Said Pasha formally announced that the Sublime Porte, resolved to give effect to its incontestable Sovereign rights over Egypt, had decided to send immediately a sufficient number of troops. This was communicated to the Conference at its sitting the same day.

Said Pasha admitted, on being pressed, that the despatch of the troops could only be the result of an understanding arrived at between the Powers. The British and French ambassadors then made the following declaration :—' France and England have communicated to the Conference their views, which have also been communicated to the different Cabinets, and their proposals having encountered no objections, either on the part of those Cabinets, or of their representatives in the Conference, the two Powers are at present agreed that in the present state of affairs they are ready, if necessity arises, to employ themselves *in the protection of the Suez Canal*, either alone, or with the addition of any Power which is willing to assist.'

At a meeting on the 27th, the representatives of

the Porte communicated a declaration to the effect that having again informed the members of the Conference that the Imperial Government was on the point of sending troops to Egypt, the Government earnestly hoped that, in face of this determination, the existing foreign occupation of that country would be abandoned as soon as the Ottoman troops should arrive at Alexandria.

In reply, Lord Dufferin was instructed to say that Her Majesty's Government could neither withdraw their troops, nor relax their preparations; adding that the arrival and co-operation of Turkish forces in Egypt, would be accepted by England, provided the character in which they came was satisfactorily defined beforehand.

At this period it must be borne in mind, that the British Expeditionary forces had already started, and the Ministry of Mr. Gladstone had now no desire to have the Turkish troops, for which they had professed so much anxiety. It was, however, necessary to keep up appearances, and to find from time to time plausible pretexts to prevent the Sultan from carrying out his determination.

In effecting the desired object Lord Dufferin, as will be seen, found means to throw such difficulties in the way as to prevent the despatch of a Turkish army to Egypt.

The views of Germany were also at the same time communicated to Lord Granville, and were stated to him, as being that the Sultan had the first claim to exercise the proposed protection. In the event of his being unwilling or unable to do so, the Powers interested in the Canal would be justified in acting themselves. If those Powers had the intention of protecting their own interests in the Canal, Germany could not take upon herself any responsibility for the measures to be taken for this purpose. Finally Austria, Russia, and Italy, adopted the same view as Germany.

On the 28th the adjourned debate on the vote of 9,410,000 francs for the despatch of French troops to Egypt for the protection of the Canal, took place in the French Chamber of Deputies. The force, it was explained, was to be 8000 men and two gunboats. The Ministers pointed out that all that was intended was to occupy one or two points on the Canal. France would be charged with the 'surveillance' of the Canal between Port Saïd and Ismailia, and England of the part between Ismailia and Suez.

The vote was violently opposed, and in the end rejected by a majority of 341 against the Government.

The debate was wound up by a remarkable speech from M. Clemenceau, who said,—' Messieurs, la conclusion de ce qui se passe en ce moment est celle-ci, L'Europe est couverte de soldats, tout le monde attend, tout les Puissances se reservent leur liberté pour l'avenir; reservez la liberté d'action de la France.' Lord Granville, seeing that all hope of French cooperation was gone, intimated to M. de Freycinet that although Her Majesty's Government accepted the cooperation of Turkey, it would nevertheless proceed with its own measures. 'That then,' said the French Minister, ' is *intervention à deux*.'

On the 31st July the Russian Government intimated 'that the delay, or alleged refusal, of the Porte to send troops to Egypt, had confirmed His Majesty in the opinion that the position in which the Conference was placed was inconsistent with his own dignity, and he had therefore decided that his representatives should abstain from attending the Conference.'

On the 1st August Lord Dufferin informed the Turkish Minister, in reply to his request that the British Expedition should be countermanded, that it was useless for him to base any of his calculations on the supposition either that the troops would be countermanded, or that the British 'Corps d'Armée' would leave Egypt until order had been completely re-established.

The Minister said with reference to the proclamation against Arabi, that he thought it would be advisable to defer it until after the Turkish troops were landed.

Lord Dufferin answered that if the proclamation was not previously issued, no Turkish troops would be allowed to land in Egypt. The Ambassador said, 'If the Sultan desired to co-operate with England it was necessary he should first clearly define the attitude he intended to assume towards Arabi and the rebellious faction.' It was then promised that such a proclamation should be officially communicated to the embassy before the troops started.

On the same day the Ottoman plenipotentiaries delivered to the other members of the Conference the reasons for the Porte not issuing the desired proclamation declaring Arabi a rebel. The principal passage was as follows:—'It is, therefore, quite natural to suppose that a proclamation which would accuse a subject of His Imperial Majesty the Sultan, who, at a moment when he showed fidelity and devotion to his sovereign, was the object of honorary distinctions, would derive its force from the immediate presence of the material factor, the absence of which at the time of its publication would render its provisions barren.'

On the 2nd August the Russian delegates were again authorised to attend the sittings of the Conference.

Orders were sent to the English Admiral that until the Porte should have entered into an agreement with Her Majesty's Government for the issue of a proclamation by the Sultan in support of Tewfik Pasha, and denouncing Arabi as a rebel, and should have signed a military convention for the co-operation of the Turkish troops, no Turkish troops could be allowed to land in Egypt.

On the 5th Lord Dufferin formally notified to the Ottoman delegates, that unless the Ottoman Government consented to conclude the Military Convention, the Turkish troops would not be allowed to disembark. Said Pasha intimated that he fully understood the grave nature of the communication.

On the 2nd two large Turkish transports started at night from Constantinople, one for the Dardanelles and Salonica, the other for Salonica direct, with stores, provisions, and details of troops to complete the battalions at Salonica to war strength. Two other steamers left the same night, one for Smyrna, the other for the Dardanelles. On the 3rd other transports with soldiers on board left also at night, and two more transports commenced taking on board stores, ammunition, &c. On the 5th two transports with men and stores left the Golden Horn for Suda Bay in Crete. A third was to leave the same evening. It became known that Dervish Pasha was to command the force, taking four other Generals with him. They were to leave in the *Izzedin* for Salonica. The fleet was to rendezvous either at Rhodes or Suda Bay.

In consequence of the foregoing, Admiral Seymour was instructed, if any vessel with Turkish troops appeared at Port Saïd, Alexandria, or elsewhere, to request the officer in command, with the utmost courtesy, to proceed to Crete or elsewhere, and apply to the Turkish Government for further instructions, as Admiral Seymour was precluded from inviting them to land in Egypt. Admiral Seymour was further instructed to prevent their landing if they declined to comply with his advice.

On the 7th the Ottoman delegates made the

following declaration to the Conference : 'The Sublime Porte accepts the invitation for a Military Intervention in Egypt made to it by the Identic Note of the 15th July, as well as the clauses and conditions contained therein.'

On the 8th Said Pasha informed Lord Dufferin that the Sublime Porte was disposed to issue the proclamation against Arabi, and that he, the Minister, was authorised to negotiate the Military Convention.

He also stated that by reason of the importance of the events in Egypt, the Ottoman troops would leave on the 10th.

Lord Dufferin, on the 9th August, received the ideas of the British Government as to the Military Convention. Lord Dufferin was instructed to inform the Sultan's Government that before any other step was taken, such as the conclusion of a Military Convention, the British Government adhered to the necessity for the issue of a properly-worded proclamation. On the 9th the Draft of the proposed proclamation was sent to Lord Dufferin.

On the 15th Sir Garnet Wolseley arrived at Alexandria.

At the meeting of the Conference on the 14th August, the President, having reopened the discussion with regard to the Italian proposal respecting the Canal, all the members of the Conference having replied that they accepted it, the Italian Ambassador made the following proposition :—' The Commanders of the naval forces on the spot shall be charged by their Governments, with the establishment of the rules to be adopted in order to execute the proposition that the Conference has adopted.' All the members accepted this proposition. The representatives of the Powers having expressed their opinion that the moment had come to suspend the labours of the Conference, the Ottoman delegates, apparently still anxious to be on the opposition side, stated that they did not share in this opinion, and reserved the right of informing the others of the date of the next meeting.

On the 16th August Lord Dufferin was informed, with reference to the negotiations for the Military Convention, that Her Majesty's Government would have no objection to a part of the Turkish troops being landed at Damietta or Rosetta, should the Turkish Government desire it.

On the next day the Turkish Government, instead of accepting at once the Military Convention, began to make efforts to get it laid before the Conference. These failed, however, thanks to Lord Dufferin, who contended that the engagement was one between England and Turkey alone. Further, the Sultan struck out the clause requiring the consent of England to the landing of the Turkish troops, and demanded that Alexandria should be named as the port of disembarkation.

The foregoing brings the narrative of events down to the eve of Sir Garnet Wolseley's sailing for the Canal.

CHAPTER XXIX.

EVENTS AT ALEXANDRIA.

Another Proclamation of the Khedive—His Promise to indemnify the Sufferers by recent events—Return of Europeans—Alexandria filling with Troops—Arrival of Sir Garnet Wolseley—The Situation—Embarkation of Troops—Departure for Aboukir—*Ruse de Guerre*—Arrival of Expedition at Port Saïd.

ON the 7th August the Khedive issued a proclamation against Arabi and the rebels generally.

The same day the Khedive addressed a letter to the President of the Council of Ministers announcing his intention to indemnify the sufferers by the recent events.

At this period the European population was flocking back to Alexandria in such numbers that Mr. Cartwright deemed it necessary to make strong representations on the subject to the representatives in Egypt of the several Powers. A system of examination of passports was now established, and people of suspicious character, or who were unable to show that they had some employment, or other means of subsistence, were forced by the authorities to re-embark.

Alexandria was now fast filling with British troops, and fresh detachments were disembarking daily. On the 10th August Sir John Adye, Chief of the Staff, arrived at Alexandria, with the Duke of Connaught. The whole of the Brigade of Guards had arrived in the transports *Orient*, *Iberia*, and *Batavia*, two days later, and astonished the people by their size and martial appearance as they marched through the town to

Ramleh. The Duke of Connaught rode at their head. Egypt had never seen such soldiers before; and loud were the expressions of admiration on all sides. The stalwart bag-pipers particularly impressed the natives.

The Brigade consisted of the 2nd battalions of the Grenadier and Coldstream Guards, and the 1st battalion of the Scots Guards. The force was encamped on a piece of desert land at Ramleh, near the sea, and between the stations of Bulkeley and Fleming on the line of the Ramleh railway.

Sir Garnet Wolseley reached Egypt on the 15th in the *Calabria*. He had made the voyage by sea on account of his health.

Major-General Sir Evelyn Wood arrived the same day. Other transports were coming in rapidly, and everything pointed to an immediate advance upon Kinje Osman and Kafr Dowar. The following is a list of the principal officers in the expeditionary force:—

General-Commanding-in-Chief:—General Sir Garnet J. Wolseley, G.C.B., G.C.M.G.

Chief of the Staff:—General Sir John Adye, K.C.B., R.A.

Officer commanding Royal Artillery:—Brigadier-General W. H. Goodenough, R.A.

Officer commanding Royal Engineers:—Brigadier-General C. B. P. N. H. Nugent, C.B., R.E.

Command of base and lines of communication:—Major-General W. Earle, C.S.I.

1st Division:—Lieutenant-General G. H. S. Willis, C.B. 1st Brigade:—Major-General H.R.H. the Duke of Connaught, &c., &c. 2nd Brigade:—Major-General G. Graham, V.C., C.B., R.E.

2nd Division:—Lieutenant-General Sir Edward B. Hamley, K.C.M.C., C.B., R.A. 3rd Brigade:—Major-

General Sir Archibald Alison, K.C.B. 4th Brigade:—
Major-General Sir H. Evelyn Wood, G.C.M.G,, K.C.B.

Garrison of Alexandria: — Major-General G. B. Harman, C.B.

Cavalry Division: — Major-General D. C. Drury-Lowe, C.B.

Sir Garnet Wolseley lost but little time after landing. He made a hasty inspection of the position at Ramleh, and gave his orders.

On the 18th August the Guards Division, the Household Cavalry, the 60th Rifles, and the 46th Regiment, marched in from Ramleh and commenced embarking, the troops of the Second Division taking their places at Ramleh. The Manchester Regiment landed and took over police duty in the town, relieving the Berkshire Regiment which joined General Wood's Division at Ramleh.

At 11.15 a.m. the greater part of the British force was embarking. The troops selected were the First Division under Lieutenant-General Willis. Several transports the same day steamed out of harbour, and anchored off the Boghaz Pass. The following day, the 19th, the transports, escorted by the ironclads *Alexandra*, *Inflexible*, *Minotaur*, *Superb*, and *Temeraire*, steamed away in a stately procession to the eastward. Both Sir Garnet Wolseley and Admiral Seymour accompanied the force.

It was given out that Aboukir was to be the place of attack, and at 3.30 p.m. on arriving off the bay, the ships, with the exception of the *Alexandra*, *Euphrates*, *Rhosina*, and *Nerissa*, which pushed on to Port Saïd, anchored in regular lines according to a pre-arranged plan, the men-of-war being nearest the shore. The ironclads struck their topmasts, and made other preparations for an attack. Every facility had been given to newspaper correspondents to obtain such details as might prudently be made public without exciting too much suspicion of a *ruse de guerre*. It succeeded perfectly. Not only the Europeans, but the enemy, were completely deceived. The gunners in the forts at Aboukir stood to their guns, expecting every moment the fleet would open fire. After dark the troopships moved off to the east, followed later on by the men-of-war. When day broke the whole fleet had disappeared.

As rapidly as possible the fleet steamed for Port Saïd. The transports *Rhosina* and *Nerissa* had singularly bad luck, the last two breaking down *en route*. The delay was not serious, for their escort the *Alexandra* towed the *Nerissa* at the rate of twelve knots an hour, whilst the *Euphrates* helped the *Rhosina*.

The next morning the whole fleet arrived at Port Saïd, when they found the entire Maritime Canal in the hands of the British Navy.

CHAPTER XXX.

PORT SAÏD, SUEZ, AND ISMAILIA.

Events at Port Saïd—Patrolling the Canal—French Neutrality—Admiral Hoskins' Instructions—The Fleet at Port Saïd—Events at Suez—Events at Ismailia—Captain Fitz-Roy's Preparations—Council of War.

IT may now be convenient to refer to what had in the meantime been taking place on the Canal.

On the 9th July Mr. J. E. Wallis, the British Consul at Port Saïd, received instructions to warn British subjects to embark. Next morning a large number of British, French, Italian, Greek, German, and Austrian subjects took refuge in vessels in the harbour. A report was spread of troops being ordered from Damietta, and some alarm prevailing, the Governor issued to the Consuls a circular assuring them there was no danger.

On the 11th, whilst the bombardment was going on at Alexandria, the Port Saïd refugees remained on board ship. The town was quiet and orderly. The British despatch vessel *Iris* acted as guardship during this period. The Egyptian corvette *Sakha* had arrived from Alexandria a day or two previous to the bombardment. Her captain was an Arabist of the most pronounced type. Immediately after her arrival telegraphic information reached the authorities and the Canal Company's officials that the *Sakha* had a considerable quantity of dynamite on board, intended to be used against vessels entering the Canal. The *Iris*, which had taken up a berth inside the harbour, shifted berth, and her commander, Captain Seymour, moored his ship opposite the *Sakha*, the better to watch her movements. A great noise was observed on board the Egyptian vessel at night, the men moving up and down as if transporting heavy cases. The next morning Captain Seymour called on her captain, and on inquiring the reason of the commotion, was informed that the men were 'practising.' Captain Seymour replied that considering the troubled state of the country, practising at such an unusual hour was calculated to create alarm on shore, and expressed a hope that it would be discontinued. 'I am the only master on board my own ship,' was the Egyptian commander's reply. 'In that case,' Captain Seymour replied, 'I shall be under the painful necessity of either seizing your ship or of sinking her.' From that moment no further night exercise was indulged in, and hostilities were avoided, though both ships remained with their guns pointed at each other. The commander of the *Iris* took the further precaution of placing a torpedo in a position which would enable him to blow up the Egyptian vessel at any moment. After this, nothing of importance occurred for some days.

The naval force at Port Saïd was strengthened by the arrival of the *Penelope*, the flagship of Admiral Hoskins, and the *Monarch*, *Agincourt*, and *Achilles*.

On the 13th July the British Government notified that British merchant-ships might go through the Canal if clear. On the 14th British gunboats commenced to convoy vessels. On the 15th the French Government authorised their gunboats to be employed on similar service. This was followed by the like arrangements on the part of Germany and Italy.

The English ironclad *Orion*, Captain R. O. B. Fitz-Roy, carrying four 25-ton guns, arrived from Alexandria *en route* to Ismailia, on the 26th, and at once attempted to enter the Canal. Several objections were made by the Suez Canal Company to her doing so. More than once she got under way, and was stopped under various pretexts. The last objection was that the *Coquette* being already in Lake Timsah, there was no room for another vessel of war. Eventually, having embarked 142 officers and men from the *Agincourt*, the *Orion* entered the Canal, ostensibly bound for Suez.

Captain Fitz-Roy had orders to stop at Kantara to cut the telegraph wire from Cairo to Constantinople, but just as his vessel was nearing Kantara a torpedo-boat overtook her, and delivered an order from Admiral Hoskins, countermanding the cutting of the wire, and directing that the small-arm men from the *Agincourt* should not be landed. At three p.m. on the 27th the *Orion* reached Lake Timsah. Captain Fitz-Roy took his ship out of the hands of the pilot and anchored her about 800 yards from the town of Ismailia.

On the 28th July the Governor and Sub-governor of Port Saïd, fearing that their lives were in danger from the military party, took refuge on board the P. and O. S.S. *Poonah*. The town of Port Saïd was, in consequence, left completely in the hands of the supporters of Arabi. Nevertheless, though considerable anxiety prevailed no outbreak took place.

On the 29th the German gunboat *Move* was ordered to take part in the patrolling of the Canal.

On the 31st July Admiral Hoskins telegraphed that the French Admiral at Port Saïd was ordered to suspend action, and the French ironclad *Thetis* was directed to leave Ismailia. Rigid neutrality was to be observed.

On the 3rd August Admiral Hoskins was directed for the present to confine his operations on the Suez Canal to maintaining the *status quo*, and not to land except for the protection of British subjects, or in the event of any attempt being made to block the Canal, as to which he was allowed discretion. This reserve, he was informed, was only temporary and was contingent upon future military requirements.

On the 5th the ships of war off Port Saïd comprised the *Penelope*, *Agincourt*, *Monarch* and *Northumberland* armoured ships, the *Tourmaline* and *Carysfort* wooden sloops, and the *Ready* and *Beacon* gun-vessels. The *Don* and *Dee*, iron river gun-boats, arrived a day or two later.

What had been taking place at Suez was reported in a letter from Mr. West, the British Consul, to Lord Granville, from which the following are extracts :—

'The whole of the British residents, with one or two exceptions, had taken refuge afloat, and were living in great discomfort on board boats, barges and lighters in the open roadstead. Her Majesty's ship *Euryalus* arrived on the 29th.

'Admiral Sir William Hewett, who, on the 2nd instant, had under his command in the Suez Roads the following ships of Her Majesty's fleet, viz., the *Euryalus*, flying the flag of the Rear-Admiral, the *Eclipse*, the *Ruby*, which had arrived in the early morning, the *Dragon*, the *Mosquito* and the *Beacon*, which had just come in from Ismailia, and was about to return following the steamer *Peshawur*, with the homeward India mail from Bombay, then decided to act, and I went on shore with his Secretary, Mr. Henry C. Gibson, with a Proclamation to be delivered to the Acting Governor, informing him that the place had been occupied by British forces, which occupation was effected without opposition or resistance on the part of the native soldiers. The town was then occupied by the marines and blue-jackets, about 500 men in all. The few native soldiers in the place got away in the train that was about to leave Suez with more fugitives. The Governor's dwelling and public offices were guarded by marines; the Victoria Hospital, and commanding positions in the environs of Suez, were also held by the British forces.'

To return to Ismailia, where, as above stated, the *Orion* had arrived on the 27th July. The place was found perfectly tranquil, but the telegraph being in the hands of Arabi's people, Captain Fitz-Roy could get no news or telegrams. H.M.S. *Coquette* was anchored by Captain Fitz-Roy's orders off the lock-gates of the Fresh Water Canal, with orders to report everything going in and coming out. By this means information that Arabi was receiving daily several boat-loads of coal was obtained.

On the 29th the *Carysfort*, Captain Stephenson, arrived from Port Saïd and anchored. Lake Timsah was patrolled at night by a steam-launch with an armed crew, which moved about twice in every watch. The *Orion's* electric light was also used during the first and middle watches of the night, and turned on the Arab guardhouse outside Ismailia.

On the 2nd August Egyptian troops estimated at about 800, arrived at Nefiché Junction and encamped outside the railway station.

On the 4th the Governor Ali Bey Yaffa came on board the *Orion* and claimed protection. He had, he said, been recalled by Arabi to Cairo, and another Governor put in his place.

From the 6th torpedo and picket boats were employed to keep up communication with Suez and Port Saïd. The guns of the different vessels were cleared for action every night, and the marines and small-arm men kept in readiness to land.

On the 8th the detachment of men from the *Agincourt* was relieved by a draft from the *Northumberland*.

On the 16th the Egyptian force at Nefiché was largely increased. Several more refugees came off to the ships.

On the 17th Captain Fitz-Roy was summoned to a council of war at Port Saïd, and returned on the following day.

On the 19th the compass-bearing and distance of the camp at Nefiché were taken during the day from the masthead of the *Carysfort*, and one of the *Orion's* 25-ton guns was laid accordingly. To secure sufficient elevation to carry the projectile over the intervening sand-hills, the vessel's port boilers were emptied and shot removed so as to give the ship a strong list to starboard. The same night the crews of the vessels were mustered at 8 o'clock in working rig, with ammunition and provisions all ready for landing.

The foregoing narrative brings the history of events down to the eve of the British forces taking possession of the Canal.

CHAPTER XXXI.

M. DE LESSEPS AND THE SUEZ CANAL.

Ships warned not to enter the Suez Canal—Protest—M. de Lesseps forbids Hostilities—Neutrality of Canal—M. de Lesseps at Port Saïd—M. de Lesseps and Disembarkation—The French Government disavows M. de Lesseps—The latter decides to oppose Operations—Complaint to French Government—Circular Letter to the Powers—Lord Lyons and the new French Premier—Instructions to Admiral Seymour—The Khedive's Proclamation—M. de Lesseps and Admiral Hoskins—M. de Lesseps' Acquiescence dispensed with.

THE history of events having now been brought down to the time when the British Expedition arrived at the entrance of the Suez Canal, it may be interesting to consider the attitude of M. Ferdinand de Lesseps, the President of the Canal Company, and of the other agents of that concern, in view of the impending military operations of Great Britain.

To do this it is necessary to go back a little, and start with the events immediately preceding the bombardment at Alexandria. When that step was impending, Admiral Seymour was instructed to warn British ships not to enter the Suez Canal in case of hostilities. In consequence of this warning eleven ships were stopped at Port Saïd and Suez on 10th July. M. Victor de Lesseps, the Company's agent at Ismailia, thereupon protested against what he termed 'this violation of the neutrality of the Canal.'

On the same day M. de Lesseps, then in Paris, communicated to the British Ambassador there, and to all the other representatives of the Powers, a copy of the telegraphic instructions which had on the 8th July been sent to the *Agent Supérieur* of the Company at Ismailia. Their effect was that any action or warlike demonstration in the Canal was forbidden, and that 'its neutrality had been proclaimed by the Firman of Concession, and had been recognised and acted upon during the two last wars between France and Germany, and Russia and Turkey.'

As this question of the neutrality of the Canal was raised at the outset, and was persistently asserted by M. de Lesseps until the end of the military operations in Egypt, it may be desirable to devote a little space to the subject, and to examine the basis on which it rests.

M. de Lesseps has always claimed that the neutrality of the Canal was secured by a clause in the Concession, in which it was declared by the Sultan to be a neutral highway for the ships of all nations.

It remains to consider whether this clause has the effect which M. de Lesseps contended for. To commence with, it may be observed that it is not competent for the sovereign of a country to thus neutralise any part of his territory by an *à priori* declaration irrespective of future eventualities. Whether any particular country is neutral or not may depend upon a variety of circumstances. It may be neutralised by the ruler himself refusing to take part in any hostilities which may be in progress with other Powers, and taking steps to prevent this neutrality being infringed. But in any case there must be no hostilities carried on in the country which declares itself a neutral state.

Hostility and neutrality are opposite terms. Once granted that hostilities are being carried on in a country, no declaration of neutrality can have any effect; nor can the sovereign exempt his territory, or any part thereof, from belligerent operations.

What was the situation in Egypt? Arabi Pasha as the *de facto* ruler of the country was practically carrying on war with the British nation, and his forces were occupying places in the neighbourhood of the Canal, and even on the Canal itself. Theoretically it was competent for the Sultan, as the supreme ruler of the country, to put an end both to Arabi and the revolt. That, however, he did not do. The result was that England found herself in Egypt, with authority of the Khedive, engaged as a belligerent against the rebel leader. This state of things conferred on her belligerent rights so far as regarded the occupation of any Egyptian territory necessary for military operations.

Further, by the terms of the Canal Company's Concessions, the Khedive's authority over the Canal was expressly reserved. Although a Concession for the Canal in Egyptian territory was accorded to M. de Lesseps, the country through which it ran remained none the less a portion of Egyptian territory, and the right of the Khedive to interfere to maintain order there was one of the clauses of the Concession.*

Whether the Khedive intervened by himself or by his agents, which in this case were the British Government, was the same thing. Sir Garnet Wolseley was acting under the direct authority of the Khedive. Of what then had M. de Lesseps to complain? What took place was a simple matter of police.

But apart from any express reservation in the Act of Concession, to assert that the Khedive was not at

* Article 9 of the Concession of the 22nd February, 1866, is as follows:—
'The Maritime Canal and all its dependencies remain subject to the Egyptian Police, which may act freely as on any other point of the territory in a way to ensure good order, public security, and the execution of the laws and regulations of the country.' Article 10 is as follows:—'The Egyptian Government will occupy in the limits of the lands reserved as dependencies of the Maritime Canal every position or strategic point which it shall judge necessary for the defence of the country. This occupation shall not cause obstacles to the navigation.'

liberty to suppress a revolt in his own dominions would be too startling a proposition for even M. de Lesseps to propound. Had Arabi been the recognised sovereign of a foreign state, other than Egypt, engaged in hostilities with Great Britain, it would, of course, have been competent for the ruler of Egypt (but not for M. de Lesseps) to have objected to the Canal as a portion of Egyptian territory being selected as the battle-ground. Such, however, was not the situation.

The precedents evolved by M. de Lesseps from the Franco-German and the Russo-Turkish wars, in reality, were worth nothing. When France and Germany were at war, Egypt was at peace, and her neutrality had to be respected ; neither Turkey nor Egypt being in any way mixed up with the dispute. As regards the Russo-Turkish war, it is incontestable that if Russia in the exercise of her undoubted rights as a belligerent had seized on the Canal as a piece of Egyptian territory, no other power would have had reason to complain. Whether by doing so Russia would have made an enemy of England, and so have caused her to take part against her, was another matter; and influenced probably by considerations of this kind Russia was induced to abstain. This, however, in no way affects the principle involved.

It is difficult to understand on what grounds M. de Lesseps could seriously contend that a mere trading concern like the Suez Canal was neutralised.

From motives of self-interest it was natural that the Canal Company should claim for it a neutral character, but that M. de Lesseps could have been so ignorant of International Law as to believe that his work really was what he assumed it to be, no sane person can imagine.

It is unnecessary to comment on M. de Lesseps' conduct in taking upon himself the position of a Sovereign

State, and issuing a circular note to the representatives of the European Powers. In dealing with the matter, M. de Lesseps from first to last appears to have misunderstood the situation, and that of the commercial concern over which he presided. Not only was it not neutral in the sense in which the word is generally understood, but equally it had none of the international character which he claimed for it. It was, indeed, no more international than a railway, or a dry-goods store, to which the citizens of all nations could have access on paying for the accommodation or for the goods received. Viewed in this light, the pretensions of the President of the Company seem simply ridiculous, and in any less distinguished individual would be laughed at. The Suez Canal is a commercial enterprise, founded by French promoters, and carrying on business in Egypt. It is, moreover, subject to the jurisdiction of the local Tribunals; where then is its claim to an international character? It fails entirely as does its claim to neutrality.

In treating this question of neutrality, it must be owned that the British Government acted with the utmost consistency in steadily denying M. de Lesseps' pretensions.

On the 19th July M. de Lesseps arrived in Egypt with his son Victor, and proceeded at once to Port Saïd, and from thence went through the Canal, returning again as far as Ismailia. According to the official journal of the Canal Company (*Le Canal de Suez*), which, however, must not in all cases be accepted as an accurate record of events, M. de Lesseps found the native and European population at Port Saïd much disturbed at the idea of a possible landing, and he called a meeting of the native Notables and Ulemas to reassure them. After this incident, according to the same authority, he received from Arabi a telegram, of which the following is a translation :—

'Thank you for what you have done to prevent the landing of foreign troops at Port Saïd, and for your efforts to give tranquillity of mind to the natives and the Europeans.—(Signed), MINISTER OF WAR AND MARINE.'

According to the same journal, the object of M. de Lesseps' communication with Arabi was to ensure protection for the emigration of 120 Greeks abandoned in a village, and to prepare transport under escort from Cairo to Ismailia, for the sick and the staff of the European Hospital, namely, thirty-five sick, eleven Sisters of Charity, a doctor, and four hospital attendants. His object also was the maintenance of order in the province of Zag-a-Zig, where numerous French and Italian subjects were residing.

On the 22nd July, the following telegram was sent by the Admiralty to Admiral Seymour :—

'It may be necessary to occupy Port Saïd and Ismailia immediately. Admiral Hoskins should be prepared to accompany French ironclad with *Penelope* and gunboats to Ismailia if ordered, and sufficient force should be available to hold Port Saïd. Report what force would be required to hold Nefiché if ironclads are at Ismailia. Instruct Admiral Hoskins as follows. If preparations at Fort Gemil threaten Port Saïd you may inform Commandant that unless it is evacuated it will be destroyed, and in the event of refusal send ships to destroy it.'

M. de Lesseps on the 26th, sent off a telegram, of which the following is a translation :—

'M. F. de Lesseps to C. de Lesseps.
                                                    '*Ismailia, 26th July.*

'The English Admiral having declared to me that he would not disembark without being preceded by the French Navy, and a disembarkation being possibly ruin to Port Saïd, I have had to reassure the numerous Arab population without whom we should be forced to suspend our works. In the presence of the Ulemas and Notables, I have sworn that not a Frenchman shall disembark whilst I am here, and that I will guarantee public tranquillity and the neutrality of our Universal Canal. The Government of my country will not disavow me.'

On the 29th, M. de Lesseps sent to M. Charles de Lesseps another telegram, of which the following is a translation,—

'*Ismailia, 29th July,* 1882.

'To disembark at Ismailia, where there is not a solitary Egyptian soldier, is to determine to take possession of our Canal. The only persons here are a Chief of native police and some Agents. The inhabitants are our employés, their families, and some refugees. The invaders will find us unarmed at the head of our *personnel* to bar their passage with "protests." '

On the 31st the French Government, in reply to the communication already referred to from Lord Lyons, stated that M. de Lesseps had not received any mandate from the French Government, and in consequence could not bind the Ministry. On the same day, the French Admiral was directed to remain at Port Saïd, but to preserve a strict neutrality, to cease convoying vessels through the Canal, and to send the ironclad *Thetis* from Ismailia to Port Saïd, and the ironclad *Alma* to Athens.

On the 4th August M. de Lesseps telegraphed to M. Charles de Lesseps as follows :—

'The English Admiral at Port Saïd writes me that he has decided to take, in spite of my protests, such measures as he judges necessary to occupy the Canal. I have decided to oppose any warlike operation on the Canal.'

On the same day, M. de Lesseps went on board the *Orion* at Ismailia. He was in evening dress, and wore his Order of the Star of India, and was attended by his son Victor and M. de Rouville, the Canal Company's agent. He demanded the intentions of the English towards the Canal, and protested most energetically and with much excitement against any landing as 'a violation of international rights.'

Captain Fitz-Roy received his visitor with perfect politeness, but gave him but little information.

On the day following, M. de Lesseps telegraphed to M. Charles de Lesseps, in Paris, as follows:—

'The English Admiral having announced the occupation of Ismailia, I went yesterday on board the *Orion* with Victor. We have signified verbally our resolution to resist, to prevent serious disorder and interruption in navigation of the Canal. We have obtained a declaration that a landing should only take place on our demand.'

In consequence of M. de Lesseps' telegram, Admiral Hoskins was desired to report on the statement that he had promised only to land a force on the Canal upon being asked by him. The Admiral replied that Lesseps' statement was 'quite unwarranted.'

The Council of the Canal Company assembled on the 5th August, and passed resolutions supporting their President, and declaring that 'the Company could not lend itself to the violation of a neutrality which was the guarantee of the commerce of all nations.'

Lord Granville then complained to the French Government that active opposition to the operations of the British Government in Egypt, by obstruction of the Suez Canal, in the event of British forces being landed at any stations at or near the Canal, had been threatened by M. de Lesseps, against whose proceedings, as an eminent French citizen, and Chairman of the Canal Company, Her Majesty's Government would be unwilling to take any measures without absolute necessity. 'Her Majesty's Government hoped,' said his Lordship, 'that any such necessity would be avoided by those representations on the part of the French

Government to M. de Lesseps, which, from the friendly relations, and the identity of interests in the Canal and in Egyptian affairs generally, of both Governments, Her Majesty's Government felt sure they might confidently expect.'

M. Charles de Lesseps on the 7th August, addressed a Circular letter to the representatives of the Great Powers in Paris on the threatened violation of the neutrality of his Canal.

On the 8th August Admiral Hoskins was instructed by the Khedive to occupy such points of the Isthmus of Suez as he might deem useful for the free traffic on the Canal, and the protection of the towns and populations situated in the neighbourhood.

On the 12th, Lord Lyons having had an interview with the new French Premier, wrote to Lord Granville as follows :—

'*Paris, August* 12, 1882.

'I spoke this afternoon to M. Duclerc respecting the proceedings of M. de Lesseps in Egypt. His Excellency promised to write to-day to M. de Lesseps with a view to inducing him to take another line, but his Excellency added that he trusted that Her Majesty's Government would show great patience (*longanimité*) in dealing with a man who enjoyed in France so high a reputation and so extensive a popularity as did M. de Lesseps. I answered that Her Majesty's Government and Her Majesty's officers on the spot had shown the utmost consideration for M. de Lesseps, and the greatest forbearance towards him, and that they earnestly desired to continue to do so, but that it must be remembered that we were engaged in military operations, and that M. de Lesseps seemed to be unhesitating in his efforts to thwart our operations and to help and encourage our adversaries.'

On the same day, the following telegram was sent to Admiral Seymour :—

'When force goes to Canal you will yourself precede it by a few hours, and request Canal authorities to give temporary precedence to transports over merchant-ships, and keep sections clear for time you think necessary. Assure them interruption to traffic, if any, will not exceed a certain time, the shorter the better. If authorities refuse, naval officers must assume duty of giving preference to transports and keeping Canal clear. Authorities should be treated with forbearance, and informed action necessary because of their opposition to measures necessary for obeying Khedive's orders to restore order and public security on Canal. Report date of despatch of force to Canal.'

On the 15th the Khedive issued a proclamation declaring that the Commander-in-Chief of the British forces was authorised to occupy all points on the Isthmus necessary for the operations against the rebels.

On the 19th Admiral Hoskins gave orders that no ship or boat was to enter the Canal, and announced that he was prepared to resort to force to prevent any attempt to contravene these orders. M. de Lesseps replied that he protested against 'this act of violence and spoliation.'

On the 20th August Lord Lyons telegraphed Lord Granville as follows, omitting irrelevant passages :—

'We communicated to M. Charles de Lesseps last night a memorandum in the terms of your Lordship's despatch to us of the 14th instant; and we requested, at the same time, that the transports should pay dues at Ismailia, and that the regular traffic through the Suez Canal should be suspended during the short period necessary for the passage of these vessels. M. Charles de Lesseps declined to express any opinion of his own, but it was plain to us that he did not expect that the wishes of Her Majesty's Government would be acceded to by his father.'

As the sequel showed, M. de Lesseps' acquiescence was not deemed by the English Government essential to the carrying out of the operations decided on.

M. de Lesseps, ever since his arrival in Egypt, had continued to assure Arabi that if he let the Canal alone the English would also respect it. His theory was, 'Le Canal est la grande route ouverte à tous les pavillons. Y toucher amenerait contre nous l'Europe, le monde entier.' Towards the end of July, M. de Lesseps, having learned that the blocking of the Canal had been decided at the Egyptian camp, had telegraphed to Arabi to do nothing with it, adding the words, ' *Jamais les Anglais n'y péné-*

treraient jamais, jamais!' Nevertheless, secret orders were given to Mahmoud Pasha Fehmi to prepare everything for the military occupation of the Canal jointly with Mahmoud Choukri Bey, another able engineer of the National Party. This was on the evening of the 17th August.

On the 20th, after an attack by the British on the lines of Kafr-Dowar, intended to cover the expedition to Port Saïd, Arabi's look-outs signalled a great movement of the English fleet in the direction of the Canal.

The day following, M. de Lesseps having been informed of the presence of thirty-two English ships of war and transports in the waters of Port Saïd, sent to Arabi a telegram, the substance of which was as follows:—

'Make no attempt to intercept *my* Canal. I am there. Not a single English soldier shall disembark without being accompanied by a French soldier. I answer for everything.' On receipt of this message, a new Council of War was held, which, with the exception of Arabi, who still hesitated, unanimously decided to act. The answer to M. de Lesseps was as follows:—

'Sincere thanks, assurances consolatory, but not sufficient under the existing circumstances. The defence of Egypt requires the temporary destruction of the Canal.' The despatch ordering the destruction of the Canal was sent by a roundabout route by way of Cairo, and when men and material were ready for the projected work, the English were already in occupation of the Canal, in spite of M. de Lesseps' positive declarations. The fifteen hours' delay caused by M. de Lesseps' communication, prevented the execution of the orders of the Council.*

---

* The details here given are from *Arabi Pasha*, by John Ninet.

CHAPTER XXXII.

SEIZURE OF THE SUEZ CANAL.

Official Report of Admiral Hoskins—The Canal secured—Report of Captain Fairfax—The Operations at Port Saïd—Canal Company's Office occupied—Report of Commander Edwards—Report of Captain Fitz-Roy—The Capture of Ismailia—Proceedings in southern half of the Canal—Official Reports—Observations—Steps taken to preserve the Canal—The 20th August at Port Saïd—Arrival of the Expedition at Ismailia.

THE official reports of the operation of taking possession of the Canal are quoted at length.

'H. M. S. *Penelope*,
'*Port Saïd, August* 23*rd*, 1882.

' SIR,
' I have the honour to make the following report of my proceedings after I left Alexandria in the *Iris*, on the evening of the 16th instant, with the plan of operations agreed on between Sir Garnet Wolseley and yourself.

' I arrived at Port Saïd the next morning (Thursday) at ten o'clock, and immediately sent the *Nyanza*, condenser-steamer, with tents, provisions and 100 men of the *Northumberland* to Ismailia, as a reinforcement to Captain Fitz-Roy.

' On Friday morning, the 18th instant, Captain Fitz-Roy joined me from Ismailia, and after discussion with him I gave him orders with reference to the occupation of that place.

' I also arranged for the occupation of Port Saïd by Captain Henry Fairfax, of H. M. S. *Monarch*, to whom I gave instructions.

' On Friday evening I brought in two companies of the battalion of Marines from the *Northumberland*, and placed them on board of the *Monarch* and *Iris*.

' M. Victor de Lesseps, who is the working head of the Canal Company at Ismailia, came on board on the 17th instant and entered into a long discussion, presenting a series of arguments against any possible intention on our part to disembark in the Canal, and disputing the grounds of my intimation that I considered Ismailia, both town and port, to be Egyptian. He left with the conviction, I feel sure, on his part, that we sooner or later should use the Canal for a military purpose, while I had imbibed a conviction that no remonstrance on our part would induce Count Ferdinand de Lesseps to willingly accept the position and withdraw his opposition to our doing so.

'I considered, therefore, that to insure the safe passage of our troops, it was absolutely necessary that the barges and dredgers, &c., should be occupied along the whole line of the Canal to Ismailia; and further, that it was most desirable that the Kantara telegraph station should be seized, and our through telegraphic communication be restored, while Arabi's communication with Syria should be stopped.

'For this duty I selected Commander H. H. Edwards of H.M.S. *Ready*, as an officer thoroughly conversant with the Canal, and in whose judgment I had confidence.

'He started at 8 p.m. on Saturday evening, the 19th instant, taking the necessary telegraphists, and left the parties told off for each post as he passed up.

'At the same time I brought in the remaining three companies of the battalion of Marines, under Lieutenant-Colonel Graham, from the *Northumberland*, and towards daylight transferred them to the *Ready* and *Dee*, with two launches from the *Penelope*, to facilitate their landing on arrival at Ismailia.

'The *Falcon*, which had just arrived from Alexandria, was sent an hour before sunset on the 19th to an anchorage off the coast half-way between Port Saïd and Ghemil, and the *Northumberland* anchored during the night off Ghemil Fort, the object being to check an exodus of the Arab coal-heavers from Port Saïd, and to create an impression that our intention was to attack that work.

'About 4 o'clock a.m. on the 20th the movement was executed simultaneously along the line with complete success, the rebels being completely taken by surprise; telegraphic communication was restored between Ismailia, Kantara, and Port Saïd, and the Syrian telegraph was under our control. It was found, however, that the latter had been previously disconnected.

'On your arrival in the *Helicon*, about 8 a.m. on the 20th, I had intended to proceed at once to Ismailia to reinforce Captain Fitz-Roy, who was exposed to the possibility of attack by a large force of the enemy moving down on him by rail.

'Circumstances, however, as you are aware, necessitated my remaining at Port Saïd to see the First Division of Transports into the Canal, and by their entering I was precluded from going on for some time in my flag-ship. When night fell, therefore, I went up to Ismailia in a picket-boat, and arrived about 4 a.m.

'I immediately landed and joined Captain Fitz-Roy, and inspected the position he had taken up. It appeared to me to have been admirably chosen, and the works thrown up for the protection of our men by Captain Stephenson's party, with the advantage of Major Fraser's, R.E., advice, to have been thoroughly satisfactory.

'It is known that three trains full of soldiers were moved down by the rebel general from Tel-el-Kebir, with the view to attempt to retake the place, but he was deterred from making an attack, probably by the shell-fire on the Nefiché Station, and after some time spent in observation of our position the trains ran back in the direction from whence they came.

'I would here draw your particular attention to the effective fire maintained by the *Orion* and *Carysfort* on a position which could only be seen from the mast-head of the latter at over 4000 yards' distance; a fire by which a train standing on the rails at the station was twice struck, and the carriages and trucks secured for our own uses.

'I enclose reports from Captains Fairfax and Fitz-Roy and Commander Edwards of their respective shares in the operation, and desire to express my sense of the judgment, zeal, and ability shown by them in the performance of the difficult and delicate duties which devolved on them. I have, &c.,

'A. H. HOSKINS, Rear Admiral.

'To Admiral Sir F. Beauchamp Seymour, G.C.B., &c.,
  'Commander-in-Chief Mediterranean.

'P.S.—My report would not be complete without my mentioning that I employed Captain Seymour, of the *Iris*, on the delicate duty of securing the Canal Company's office at Port Saïd, and in preventing any information being conveyed through it to their other stations, or to the rebels, a duty which was performed, as have all others on which I have employed Captain Seymour, entirely to my satisfaction.'

In obedience to the orders given, the whole length of the Canal was quietly secured on the night of the 19th–20th August. The occurrences at Port Saïd are thus described by Captain Fairfax, of the *Monarch* :—

'H.M.S. *Monarch*,
'Port Saïd, August 21st, 1882.

'SIR,
'In pursuance of your order dated the 19th instant, that at 3.30 a.m., on the 2t0h, I was with the force named in the margin to occupy the town of Port Saïd, and, if possible, to surprise and capture the soldiers whilst in the barracks, and before they had any time to commit any acts of incendiarism, I made the following disposition of the force under my command.

'Lieutenant A. Cook, R.N., with *Iris*, naval brigade, a Gatling

SEIZURE OF THE SUEZ CANAL.

gun, and a company of the Royal Marine battalion under the command of Captain R. P. Coffin, R.M.L.I., were to land abreast of the *Iris* and double down the beach, the company of Marines turning down the street in which the barracks are situated, and halting immediately opposite them. The men from H.M.S. *Iris* advancing along the beach till they reached the narrow neck of land which separates the European from the native town, there to place sentries across from the sea to the road that passes down the centre of it.

'Commander T. F. Hammill, with two companies of seamen from the *Monarch*, was ordered to land abreast from the ship, and doubling through the southern part of the town (leaving half a company to protect the block of buildings in which the British Consulate is situated), to push on to the neck of land and form a line of sentries from Lake Menzaleh to the road, thus completing with the *Iris* men a chain of sentries right across from the lake to the sea, and barring escape from the town.

'The company of the Marine battalion under Captain F. M. Eden, R.M.L.I., and a Gatling from the *Monarch* under Lieutenant Charles Windham, R.N., were to proceed up the centre of the town and halt on the other side of the barracks to that occupied by the other company of Marines.

'Arrangements were made that the force should fall in with the least possible noise so as not to alarm the sentries on the quay. A lighter was planked over, and after dark placed alongside the ship; this a few minutes before landing was hauled to the shore, and with the launch formed a floating bridge over which the men were able to pass.

'The Khedive's Governor, who had been living on board the P. & O. steamer, came on board the *Monarch* at 3 a.m. and landed with me.

'Major Tulloch, of the Royal Welsh Fusiliers (who gave me much valuable information) landed with six Marines, and secured three out of four sentries on the quay.

'At 3.30 commenced landing, and succeeded in getting on shore without observation, and all the arrangements made were carried out in every particular. I was accompanied by Major James W. Scott, R.M.L.I., commanding the two companies of the Royal Marine battalion, who posted his men in such a way that escape from the barracks was impossible.

'The soldiers, who when we arrived appeared to be asleep, were ordered to surrender. Shortly after 160 fell in and laid down their arms. The Governor, having addressed them, they swore allegiance to the Khedive, and his Excellency then requested that I would permit them to return to their barracks; but two officers were arrested and sent on board H.M.S. *Iris*.

'On Monday afternoon I received a request from the Governor

that I should make prisoners of the soldiers, as he found that they were leaving the town, and some were trying to incite the Arabs against the English. I therefore ordered two companies to arrest them in barracks, where only fifty-two were found. They were marched down to the quay, where they were embarked and sent off to H.M.S. *Northumberland*.

'I am much indebted to Commander T. F. Hammill and Major J. W. Scott, R.M.L.I., for the able way in which they executed my orders, the silent and orderly manner in which the work was done contributing very much to the success of the undertaking.

'The conduct of the officers and men landed gave me entire satisfaction. 'I have, &c.,

'H. FAIRFAX, Captain.

'To Rear-Admiral Anthony H. Hoskins, C.B., &c.,
'Senior Officer.'

It should be added that the *Monarch* had been so moored off the town, that her forward turret guns commanded the main street leading to the quay, whilst the *Iris* was to seaward of the *Monarch*, where she could shell the beach and the Arab town. At eleven on the night of the 19th, the ship's companies were called on deck and warned that they would be landed at 3 a.m. The strictest silence was enjoined. So well was this order carried out that those on board the French ironclad *La Gallissonière*, moored close astern of the *Monarch* and to the same buoy, knew nothing of what was going on. Of the arms surrendered by the Port Saïd garrison, but one piece was loaded. The military commandant was absent, and the Egyptian sentries were asleep at their posts.

Captain Seymour occupied the office of the principal transit agent of the Canal Company, and a midshipman not more than fifteen years of age, was told off with a party of blue-jackets to take possession of the Company's telegraph apparatus. The Company's employés stood aghast with solemn faces. Such an act of desecration had never been even dreamt of. Presently the Company's Telegraph Agent arrived full of dignity and importance, and, apparently unconscious of what had taken place, walked towards his office. He was stopped at the entrance by the small midshipman, who said with a very good French accent, ' On ne passe pas.' The Frenchman (all the important posts in the Company are filled by Frenchmen) looked at the diminutive object in front of him with dignified astonishment, and demanded, ' Qui êtes vous? Que voulez vous ici ? ' ' Je suis içi pour empêcher le monde d'entrer,' answered the midshipman. The Frenchman, quite bewildered, looked round, and from the long faces of his colleagues was able to guess the truth. His anger and humiliation at first prevented his uttering a word. It was not so much that his office had been seized, but that such an important mission should have been confided to so small a midshipman. This was the bitterest sting of all. Had he but been suppressed by a troop of soldiers with fixed bayonets, his dignity at least would have been saved, though the result might have been the same. ' Ces sacrés Anglais veulent se moquer de nous en nous envoyant un gamin comme cela,' was his remark to his brother officials.

Resistance was, however, in vain, and the Company's staff had to submit to the inevitable.*

The work done in the Canal between Port Saïd and Lake Timsah is thus reported by Commander Edwards of the *Ready* :—

'H.M.S. *Ready*.
' At Ismailia, August 22nd, 1882.

' Sir,

' I have the honour to report my proceedings in carrying out your orders, dated 19th August, in connexion with the occupation of certain points on the Suez Canal. Learning that it was very important that the dredger stationed at the ninth mile should be secured, I placed Lieutenant Davies, of the *Penelope*, with twenty men, in charge of her.

---

* Port Saïd was held by the ship's marines and blue-jackets until 16th September, when they were relieved by 200 Royal Marine Light Infantry and 100 Royal Marine Artillery sent from England.

Proceeding up the Canal, I informed all vessels bound to Port Saïd, also the gare keepers, that it would be necessary for the ships to remain in gare until they received further instructions. I detached Sub-Lieutenant Blomfield in *Tourmaline's* steam-cutter, with six additional hands, to insure the above instructions being complied with, having previously obtained a promise from the English shipmasters that they would obey them. After occupying Kantara, as instructed, I detached Lieutenant Barnes-Laurence in *Iris* torpedo-boat to insure the Canal being kept clear. He reports that, on his return to the gare at Kilometer No. 34, he found the Messageries Maritimes steamer *Melbourne* leaving, and that, on remonstrating with the Captain, he was informed that the steamer should only be stopped by armed force, and that the first man stepping on board would be the signal to let go the anchor and leave the ship in his hands.

'Lieutenant Barnes-Laurence, not considering that his instructions warranted the use of force, left to report to me, and sent the *Tourmaline's* steam-cutter to warn ships coming up from Port Saïd. Shortly after leaving he observed the British steamers *Rossshire* and *Counsellor* weigh and follow the Messageries steamer, upon which he chased them and compelled them to haul into the next gare; and having cautioned the masters, who had reiterated their promise, he left to rejoin me. Mr. Blomfield informed me on his return, that directly the *Iris* torpedo-boat was out of sight the English ships appear to have again left the gare, as he met them steaming down the Canal at a point where it was useless to stop them. The other duties assigned to the party under my command were all punctually executed, and on Sunday, the 20th instant, all who could be spared were employed lightening the steamer *Kaiteur*, aground in the Canal, but she could not be moved. In conclusion, I beg to express my thanks to all the officers, especially Lieutenant Barnes-Laurence of the *Iris*, Sub-Lieutenant R. G. H. Blomfield of the *Tourmaline*, and Mr. A. H. Freeman, midshipman, of the *Monarch*, for their zealous attention to my orders. Also my great satisfaction with the behaviour of the men during nearly forty-eight hours of continuous hard work.

'I have, &c.,
'H. H. EDWARDS, Commander,
'To Rear-Admiral A. H. Hoskins, C.B.,
Second in Command.'

Of course, the vital point to be seized was Ismailia, but the proximity of the Egyptian force at Nefiché, rendered the operation dangerous in the extreme. The preparations made by Captain Fitz-Roy have

SEIZURE OF THE SUEZ CANAL.

been already referred to. His official report, showing how they were carried into effect, is as follows :—

'H. M. S. *Orion*, *Lake Timsah*,
'*August* 21*st*, 1882.

' SIR,

'I have the honour to report that in accordance with your secret orders of the 18th instant, I took possession of Ismailia, the Arab town, and advanced sufficiently towards Nefiché to cover the weir. The force landed consisted of 565 officers and men, comprising forty marines, one 9-pounder gun's crew, one Gatling, a torpedo engineer party, and twelve riflemen from *Orion*; one Gatling and one rifle company from *Northumberland*; one 7-pounder gun, *Coquette's*; landing party, with twenty-one Royal Marine Artillery of *Northumberland* and *Carysfort*, under Captain Stephenson, C.B., including a company of Marines under Captain Gore, also one hundred seamen and marines, from the *Nyanza*, troop-ship, belonging to the *Northumberland*. The enemy were known to have a strong picket at the Arab town, several patrols, and a guard at Ismailia, about 2000 men, and six guns encamped at Nefiché, and a considerable number of Bedouins in the neighbourhood.

' At 3 a.m. in perfect silence, the *Orion's* and *Coquette's* men landed, the *Carysfort's* shortly following, and advanced. The silence was so perfect that Commander Kane surrounded the lock-guard before we were discovered. The lock-guard fired their rifles and so did our men, and here Commander Kane was wounded by a rifle bullet on the left cheek.

' The Governor's guard laid down their arms to Lieutenant Lennox Napier, and the Royal Marine Artillery, under Lieutenant Swinburne. No further resistance was experienced in the town. Commander Kane seized the railway and telegraphs, the *Orion's* men the canal lock-bridge, town generally, and Government House (with the Governor), where I established my head-quarters. Captain Stephenson and his party had slight skirmishing in advancing, and in the Arab town some of the enemy were killed. The ships, at 3.40 a.m. bombarded the guard-houses at the Arab town, firing five rounds of shell each. By 4 a.m. the whole place was occupied as ordered. By intercepted telegrams and reports, I ascertained the enemy were making arrangements to forward a large force to Nefiché to at once attack Ismailia and the ships. Considering this, the small force at my disposal, and that the inhabitants were getting alarmed, I determined to dislodge the enemy from Nefiché and destroy their camp and any trains running; therefore *Orion* and *Carysfort* commenced a slow bombardment at 11 a.m. at a distance of 4200 yards. By noon the camp was destroyed and enemy retreating towards Cairo; also one train running south severely hit and stopped for a time. The bombardment was stopped for a short time, but at 4 p.m., as another train was seen arriving and discharging men from Cairo way, it was continued, wrecking the train, jamming and apparently overturning trucks on the line, driving every one away, and from the position of the train on the Suez line, completely blocking Arabi's communications with his forces between Nefiché and Suez by railroad. This was most satisfactory. The Squadron was in charge of Commander Moore, Lieutenant Royds having charge of the *Carysfort* and her guns, under Commander Moore's orders. Her mast-heads were the reconnoitring and look-out places. The bombardment then ceased until 10 p.m., after which shells were fired at Nefiché, at intervals of half-an-hour, until daylight, to prevent the railway being cleared and to check troops coming by train from the west. My position was still an anxious one. At 6 p.m. 340 marines arrived, 200 reinforced Commander Kane, 140 Captain Stephenson, who had with the assistance of Major Fraser, intrenched himself in advance of the Arab town. Lieutenant Napier had secured his admirable position in the Khedive's palace, and I reinforced him with twenty seamen of *Northumberland*, and an officer. I have since heard that on this afternoon Arabi with 3000 men in three trains did advance to within a few miles of Nefiché, but retired again.

'During the night the search lights were worked as necessary.

'At 10.30 p.m. General Graham arrived with the advance guard of the army, reinforced the different positions and assumed military command. I was directed to retain command in Ismailia until 4 p.m. the 21st August, 1882, when Sir Garnet Wolseley relieved my guards.

'At 8 a.m. to-day I sent a Gatling gun and crew, under Lieutenant Adair and Lieutenant King-Harman, torpedo engineer party, with General Graham, to occupy Nefiché, where they now remain. I have also a steam-cutter and the jolly-boat working on the Fresh Water Canal to Nefiché. The officers and men did their work perfectly. I have to thank Captain Stephenson, Commander Kane, Commander Moore, Major Fraser, R.E., Lieutenants Napier, Royds, and King-Harman (who destroyed the railway approaches to my west front in two advanced positions); also my first Lieutenant Cross, who had, with a gun, charge of the canal bridge and town approaches specially.

'Seven prisoners, Arabi's soldiers, were taken near lock-bridge and Arab town, sent on board *Orion* for two days, and, being disarmed, were allowed to proceed on shore. I had every reason, on the evening of the 20th August, 1882, to expect a night attack in force, so I placed the *Ready* and the *Lee*, that had arrived with the marines, close in shore in a position that would cover a retreat on our part through the town.

'Captain Stephenson brings to my notice the services of Lieutenant Langley, the senior Lieutenant of the *Carysfort*, with the landing-party. I have great pleasure in also specially mentioning this officer to you.

SEIZURE OF THE SUEZ CANAL.

'I have the honour to enclose herewith a report from Captain Stephenson.

'I have, &c.,
'ROBT. O'B. FITZ-ROY,
'Captain.

'To Rear Admiral H. Hoskins, C.B.,
'Senior Officer.'

The official report of the occupation of Ismailia is so complete that it remains only to add a few details.

The shelling of Nefiché was a case of firing at a target invisible from the gun. Commander Moore, of the *Orion*, was left in charge of the squadron, with orders to shell the enemy's camp. Lieut. Langford directed the operation on board the *Orion*. The ships opened fire and woke up the town just as the landing-party had reached the Lock Bridge. Fifteen rounds were fired from the *Orion*, the last being at 8 a.m., on the 21st August. The *Carysfort* also fired, with less results, due to the smaller size of her guns, the largest being 7-inch M. L. R. The fortunate shot that wrecked the train was, according to one account, fired just at daybreak.

There was only one European injured. The brother-in-law of the Dutch Consul happened to be walking by the lock, and, not stopping when challenged, was unfortunately shot in the left arm. This was subsequently amputated, but the man died.*

When the railway station was secured, the telegraph wires in connexion with Cairo were worked by an English *employé* of the Egyptian Telegraph Administration, who sent off a message to Arabi stating that 5000 English were landing with many guns, and asking what was to be done. This *ruse* succeeded and an answer was received, stating that reinforcements would be sent to

* His mother received compensation from the British Government.

Nefiché. All day the men were employed throwing up entrenchments, and loopholing the houses facing the desert.

At 10 p.m. Captain Fitz-Roy made a complete inspection, and satisfied himself that everything was ready to resist the night attack, which according to two Egyptian officers, who came in under a flag of truce, was being prepared. In addition, the *Orion* was ordered to fire a shell every quarter of an hour into the desert beyond Ismailia. She commenced at 10.30 p.m., and continued firing till 4 a.m. the next day.

Thanks, doubtless to the precautions taken, no night attack took place.

In the southern half of the Canal from Lake Timsah to Suez, the events of the day were on a smaller scale, but none the less interesting. It will be remembered that Suez had been in the possession of the British navy for nearly three weeks, and that the advanced guard of the Indian Contingent and the first battalion of the Seaforth Highlanders, under Lieut.-Col. Stockwell, had arrived from Aden.

The following is the report of Rear-Admiral Sir William Hewett, Commander-in-Chief of the naval forces in the East Indies, the bulk of whose squadron had assembled at the southern end of the Suez Canal. A few immaterial passages only are omitted.

'H. M. S. *Euryalus at Suez, August* 21, 1882.

'SIR,

'On Friday last, the 18th instant, I had the honour of receiving, through Rear Admiral Hoskins, C.B., a copy of the plan of operations in the Suez Canal, agreed to between yourself and Sir Garnet Wolseley, and your telegram of the 17th instant gave me authority to act on it.

'In the course of the same afternoon the rebels were observed intrenching themselves in our front, and movements of Bedouins on our left flank also called for our attention. I consulted with Brigadier-General Tanner, C.B., who commanded the troops, and we agreed

SEIZURE OF THE SUEZ CANAL.

that the Naval Brigade would be too weak to hold the place by itself if attacked by a large force, such as we knew to be in our vicinity. I therefore, with the concurrence of the Brigadier-General, telegraphed to you that 100 of the Seaforth Highlanders would be detained at Suez until the arrival of the troops from India.

'Later on, Captain Hastings, whom I had sent in the *Sea Gull* to reconnoitre the banks of the Canal, returned with a report that showed the information sent me from time to time by Captain Fitz-Roy of the movements of the enemy in our direction, to be fairly correct; and the Brigadier-General then agreed with me that it would not be prudent to send any of the Highlanders away without previously reconnoitring the neighbourhood; for, as I have already stated in my telegram, the collection of military stores at Suez represented a considerable value, and a matter of still more serious consequence, was the fact that the town had recently become crowded with women and children, Copt Christians, who had sought refuge at Suez from the brutalities of the surrounding Bedouins.

'On Friday night I caused the telegraph wires to be cut between Suez and the first Canal station, and on Saturday morning notices were issued that from that date, the 19th instant, until the prohibition was formally removed, no ships or boats would be allowed to pass into the Canal from the Suez side without my special permission. The damage to the wire on the above occasion was soon repaired, but on the following night I caused the poles which conveyed the line across the creek close to the Company's offices to be cut down, and placed a guard over them to prevent their being restored.

'At the time when it was decided to retain the Highlanders, the regiment was already on board the *Bancoora*. This was on Saturday night, and their disembarkation on Sunday must have had a very puzzling effect upon the officials of the Canal Company and others who were interested in our movements. It must, also, have had the happy effect of qualifying any reports that may have reached the rebels that our troops were about to enter the Canal.

'On Sunday morning at daylight, 400 Highlanders, under Lieutenant-Colonel Stockwell, were disembarked from the transport, and marched eight miles in the direction of Chalouf to make a feint attack in our front. Brigadier-General Tanner, C.B., accompanied this force, and at the same time I sent my flag-captain, Captain A. P. Hastings, in the *Sea Gull*, with the *Mosquito* in company, and 200 of the Seaforth Highlanders, to Chalouf by the Maritime Canal. The party, under Lieutenant-Colonel Stockwell, returned to Suez at about four p.m. without having touched the enemy; but later in the day Captain Hastings returned in a steam-pinnace to report very successful operations from the gun-vessels. It appears that the first that was seen of the enemy along the Canal was a small cavalry patrol about three miles this side of Chalouf, and on arrival at Chalouf, his presence in force was only discovered by a few heads appearing over the railway embankment on the other side of the Sweet Water Canal; this embankment forming a natural intrenchment behind which it was afterwards discovered there was some 600 infantry ready to resist our advance. These men were extremely well armed and accoutred, and had a plentiful supply of ammunition with them.

'The manner in which the position was taken reflects the highest credit on Captain Hastings, and I recommend him to your favourable notice. The coolness and dash of the Highlanders, and the excellent fire from the ships' tops, seem to have been the chief causes of success, and the conduct of all concerned, appears to have been in every way creditable.

'I am in hopes that the action taken at Chalouf will do much to secure the safety of the Canal, and as the Indian forces are now arriving, the Highlanders will go to Serapeum to-morrow.

'I have, &c.,
'W. HEWETT,
'Rear Admiral and Commander-in-Chief
'on the East Indies Station.

'To Admiral Sir F. Beauchamp Seymour, G.C.B.,
'Commander-in-Chief on the Mediterranean.'

From the accounts received of this affair it appears that the Egyptian soldiers engaged were mostly old men belonging to the Reserve, many of whom had been brought down from the interior in chains. With such soldiers it is hardly to be wondered at that the aim should have been indifferent. They held their pieces at arm's length above the head, and discharged them vaguely over the embankment, behind which they had taken shelter. To this method of shooting may be attributed the slight damage done to the standing and running rigging of the gunboats in the Suez Canal. The crossing of the Fresh Water Canal ought to have been almost impossible, the boats being so small as to convey but seven or eight men at a time; and the Canal being so full of reeds as to render swimming difficult and dangerous. The dash of the English forces, however, more than counterbalanced the disadvantages of numbers, and of an attack on a position of great natural strength. With the exception of the Serapeum portion between Lake Timsah and the Bitter Lakes, where no annoyance or interruption of traffic was expected, the whole of the Maritime Canal was in the possession of the British navy by nightfall of August the 20th. On the following day the *Tourmaline* and the *Don* moored permanently at Kantara, where a caravan road to Syria crosses the Canal, and there established a strongly defended post; while the gunboats in the southern half completed the link which perfected the chain from Port Saïd to Suez.

Having seized the Canal the English prepared to protect it. Between Ismailia and Suez this was effected by the *Mosquito* and *Sea Gull*, which patrolled it constantly, no force being permanently landed. In the northern half the *Tourmaline* and *Don* held Kantara and the gares adjoining on either side. Strong detachments of sailors from the fleet at Port Saïd with Gatlings were landed at the other gares. Breastworks were thrown up and regular camps established each night on the left. At Port Saïd a camp was pitched between the European and Arab towns, where never less than 500 blue-jackets and marines were kept. Intrenchments were thrown up across the Isthmus from Lake Menzaleh to the Mediterranean, and field-pieces mounted. In the Canal itself steam-picket boats, launches, &c., with armed crews were used as patrols. The fast Thorneycroft torpedo launches of the *Iris* and *Hecla* were employed as despatch boats, making the passage between Port Saïd and Ismailia in about four hours and a half.

Sunday, August the 20th, was a busy day at Port Saïd. As already stated the whole of the immense fleet of transports arrived early in the forenoon. There was some little delay until the way was clear. During this delay, to provide against possible trouble, 300 of the York and Lancaster Regiment were put on board the gun-vessel, *Falcon*, and a similar number of the West Kent Regiment was embarked on board the gun-vessel, *Beacon*, to form the advance. These vessels arrived at Ismailia in the evening of the same day.

Early in the afternoon the *Nerissa* led the transport fleet into the Canal, followed by the *Rhosina*, the troopship *Euphrates*, and the rest. Ismailia was reached that night or early next morning. Although the ships were unprovided with pilots, they were so skilfully navigated by their own officers, that very little difficulty arose, almost the only exception being the grounding of the *Catalonia*,* with some of the West Kent Regiment on board. She grounded on the west bank at a distance of seven miles from Lake Timsah, and caused a temporary block; but did not for long interrupt the passage of the other vessels. M. Ferdinand de Lesseps was seen standing on the steps of the Empress's Chalet at the entrance to Lake Timsah, watching the long line of British vessels-of-war and transports arriving from the Canal. The vessels as they entered the lake were moored bow and stern under the direction of Staff-Commander Petch of the *Orion*. Rear-Admiral Hoskins' flag-ship was one of the first to take up her position. Sir Garnet Wolseley arrived in the despatch vessel *Salamis* at nine a.m. the same day.

At ten a.m. on the 21st Sir Garnet Wolseley sent off the following telegram from Kantara on the Suez Canal:—

'Reached Port Saïd yesterday morning. Found, in compliance with orders previously issued, that all commercial traffic was stopped,

---

* This vessel was one of the few vessels which had a pilot (formerly in the Canal Company's service) on board.

SEIZURE OF THE SUEZ CANAL.

and Port Saïd, Kantara, and Ismailia successfully occupied by navy at daybreak, and telegraph seized at Ismailia. Small skirmish had taken place, and enemy bombarded in his camp at Nefiché. Hope that Serapeum may be occupied by troops from Suez to-day.'

The following proclamation was issued by order of the Khedive :—

'PROCLAMATION TO THE EGYPTIANS.

'The General in command of the British forces wishes to make known that the object of Her Majesty's Government in sending troops to this country is to re-establish the authority of the Khedive. The army is therefore only fighting against those who are in arms against His Highness. All peaceable inhabitants will be treated with kindness, and no violence will be offered to them. Their religion, mosques, families, and property will be respected. Any supplies which may be required will be paid for, and the inhabitants are invited to bring them. The General in command will be glad to receive visits from the Chiefs who are willing to assist in repressing the rebellion against the Khedive, the lawful Ruler of Egypt appointed by the Sultan.

'G. J. WOLSELEY, General,
'Commander-in-Chief of the British Army in Egypt.'

CHAPTER XXXIII.

M. VICTOR DE LESSEPS' NARRATIVE OF OPERATIONS ON THE SUEZ CANAL.

Admiral Hoskins—His Unwillingness to be convinced—The Ball at M. Poilpré's at Ismailia — The Disembarkation — Women and Children fired on — Attempt to embark them — The 'Personnel' ordered to remain — Contradiction of M. de Lesseps' Report—The French Press.

THE account given of the operations in the Canal and at Ismailia, by M. Victor de Lesseps in his official report, differs somewhat from the foregoing.

It is, however, not without interest, if only for the flights of fancy occasionally indulged in by the writer; and for this reason a translation of some of the more important passages is given below.

'On the 17th I had an interview with Admiral Hoskins. I ought to say that if I have only to speak well of my reception by Admiral Hewett, it has been altogether the reverse with Admiral Hoskins. Whilst Admiral Hewett has listened with attention and courtesy, Admiral Hoskins clearly showed his intention to remain deaf to all arguments. I shall not expatiate on the explanations which I gave him for more than an hour to prove that Lake Timsah and Port Saïd were, like the Canal itself, in the waters of the Company, and that at Port Saïd, as well as in the Canal, all ships, without distinction of nationality, were subject to the strict observance of our Rules.

'The Admiral would listen to nothing, interrupting me brusquely at every instant, and limiting himself to two sentences,—" M. de Lesseps is the enemy of England. I see here the Egyptian flag."

'All my efforts to convince him that we were not the enemies of England, and that the fact of seeing the Egyptian flag at Port Saïd did not give a right to the British Navy any more than to others to disregard our Rules, were in vain. It was evident that the Admiral had decided that we were the enemies of England, and that Port Saïd and Lake Timsah were Egyptian waters, where he was free to act as he pleased.

. . . .

'During the night of the 19th to 20th all the European population, the *personnel* of the Company, and the principal Egyptian functionaries, were assembled at the house of M. Poilpré, Chief Agent of the Domain, at one of the gayest of balls, enlivened by the presence of the officers of the Spanish and Austrian ships of war. At two in the morning, everyone went home, and commenced to sleep, when, towards 3 o'clock, in the middle of a very dark night, the streets resounded with warlike cries, mingled with the sound of musketry, and of the rolling of gun-carriages dragged at a walking pace.

'It is the English sailors who disembark without having warned the inhabitants that they might be exposed to be killed in the streets. On what are they firing?—on whom?—no enemy is before them. The camp of the Egyptians is at Nefiché, three kilomètres from Ismailia. There are in the town only some soldiers of police, very peaceable people, inhabiting Ismailia for a long time, and who have never dreamed of anything but maintaining order.

'Shortly after the embarkation, the cannon thunders. It is the *Orion*,—it is the *Carysfort*,—which are sending their shells on to Nefiché, or in the desert.

'The musketry fire continues in the streets of Ismailia. At daybreak it ceases in the town, after having happily made only made one victim.

'It is a European, a Dutchman, M. Bröens, who, not answering clearly to the challenge of a seaman, received a rifle bullet, which, traversing his body, broke his left arm. M. Bröens lies between life and death. The doctors regard his condition as hopeless.

'The English sailors direct their steps towards our Arab village, inhabited by our native workmen with their families, and where they find no enemies to reply. Nevertheless, they fire on the women and children,* who flee into the desert; heart-rending cries from the terrified population reach even us. Some Police Agents are made prisoners without any of them having tried to defend themselves.

'One of them is killed from behind, whilst trying to escape with his family.

'Towards eight in the morning the musketry fire ceased. The cannon thunders still, and will thunder until the morning of the 21st.

'On landing, the English have cut our telegraph wires to Suez and Port Saïd. Captain Fitz-Roy occupies the Port Office, and our boats are seized. Ismailia is blocked, and we know nothing of what is passing on the rest of the line.

'In the afternoon we think of putting the families of our *personnel* in safety. For 300 seamen only occupy the town, and during the night the Egyptians of Nefiché may attack. It is prudent to make the women and children sleep on the Lake. As to the *personnel* and M. Ferdinand de Lesseps, they have decided not to quit the town.

* Of this there is absolutely no proof.

'The families betake themselves to the landing-place. Captain Fitz-Roy opposes their departure.* I then write him a letter. M. Fitz-Roy answers me verbally at seven in the evening, when the night commences, that the families are free, but that M. de Lesseps and all his *personnel* shall pass the night in the town, for he expects to be attacked. There will be a battle in Ismailia, and he wishes that M. de Lesseps and all his *personnel* should be there. " I am the master, uow," says he.

'These odious words were quite gratuitous, since M. de Lesseps and all the *personnel*, chiefs and employés, had declared that they would not go out of the town, and there had never been a question except as regards their families.

'A part of the families preferred to return to town; the other part was enabled to embark in the boats sent by Don Carlos Ruiz, Commander of the ironclad Spanish frigate *Carmen*, and by M. Bonfield, Commander of the Austrian gun-boat *Albatross*.

'The night, happily, passed without any incident; the silence was broken only by the shells thrown by the *Carysfort* and *Orion* on Nefiché. At daylight Ismailia woke up in the midst of several thousands of English soldiers of the army. The Lake is full of transports and ships of war.

'We learn then that in the night of the 19th to the 20th the English have disembarked at Port Saïd, but peaceably, and that Admiral Hoskins has taken possession of our offices, from whence M. Desavary, Principal Transit Agent at Port Saïd, had been expelled. Ships of war and transports entered the Canal without pilots, and without paying their dues.†

'During the 20th and 21st the movement without pilots of the English vessels of war gave rise to complete confusion. The greater part got ashore, and several were obliged to disembark their troops on the bank before arriving at Ismailia, being incapable of extricating themselves by their own resources. Admiral Seymour has been forced to recognise this, and the hurry that he was in on the 21st to hand back the working to us is the proof of it.‡

'It is desirable to add that the British Naval Authorities tried to obtain the services of several of our pilots behind the backs of their superiors, and that all the pilots without exception refused to move without the order of the Company.§

* But see letter from the Secretary to the Admiralty, page 277.
† These dues were, with unnecessary liberality, paid subsequently by the British Government.
‡ On the contrary, the ships in general were navigated by their own officers and almost without accident.
§ Several ex-employés of the Company offered their services to the British Admiral, and some few were engaged. They proved, however, of little use.

'During all this crisis no *defaillance* has been produced in all the *personnel* from Port Saïd to Suez. The Company may well be proud of it.'

The substance of M. Victor de Lesseps' account of the occupation of Ismailia being telegraphed to the *Standard* newspaper, the Lords of the Admiralty thought the matter of sufficient importance to be noticed, and on the 1st September, communicated to the Foreign Office as follows :—

'From these reports* they are able to give the following account of the occurrences of that day : Ismailia was garrisoned by rebel troops; guards were placed at the lock, the Governor's house, and the Arab town. The lock was surrounded by a party under Commander Kane, R.N. The guard fired and wounded that officer slightly. Their fire was returned, and it is believed that it was here that a brother of one of the employés of the Canal was unfortunately wounded, who died on the 29th ultimo in the British hospital. The guard at the Governor's house laid down their arms. The Arab town was occupied by Captain Stephenson; the guard retreated and were fired upon, and two men killed. A few rounds of shell were also fired from the ships at the guard-houses in the Arab town.

'Sir Beauchamp Seymour also reports that he saw on the 21st ultimo many women on board the Spanish ship *Carmen;* that he was told by the Captains that they took refuge on board of her and the Austrian ship *Albatross* on the 20th. It appears that Captain Fitz-Roy permitted two large Canal boats to be used for their embarkation, although he did not consider it consistent with his duty to allow Canal officers to leave Ismailia.'

The action of England in taking possession of the Suez Canal, naturally gave rise to comments in the French Press.

The *Siècle* said :—

'The English seized on the Suez Canal like thieves. They not only appropriated the Canal, which does not belong to them, but also the plant, the dredging-machines, and steamers. They even indulged in a little bombardment in order to keep their hands in, and are everywhere acting as if they were the masters. They are cutting the telegraph wire; they have done even more—they have placed the Canal under an interdict, prohibiting ships from passing through.'

* Despatches from the Captains of the *Orion* and *Carysfort*.

In like manner the *France* exclaimed :—

'Honest England has seized on the Suez Canal. She has trampled under foot the principles and interests which the "bandit" Arabi Pasha had recognised and respected. Prince Bismarck's famous maxim " Might overrides right," has rarely had a more striking illustration. . . . A nation which could not put 100,000 men into the field, taking possession of a great highway, necessary for the traffic of all the Powers ; the chief of a civilised army seizing on private property, and adopting measures which his Mussulman adversary had deemed derogatory ; the European Governments looking silently on these manœuvres and undergoing the decrees of the Gladstone Cabinet. . . . What a spectacle !'

The *Télégraphe* went further, and pressed the Canal Company to sue England for damages before the Paris Appellate Court. It did not explain how the defendant could be forced to appear, or how damages could be recovered. It added, ' It would be well if, after the high-handed robbery committed in Egypt, justice pronounced condemnation on the offenders, and if its voice was audible at Paris.'

The *Soir*, which still regretted the fall of M. de Freycinet, pointed out that things would have happened differently had the Vote of Credit been passed, but as matters stood it deprecated any Platonic protest, and thought France could only be a silent spectator of national injustice and selfishness.

The Gambettist *Paris* naturally drew a moral in favour of M. Gambetta's policy, which, it contended, would have safeguarded the Canal's neutrality. That policy would, it thought, have resulted in the speedy quelling of the insurrection, and have spared France the humiliation of seeing the results of so much French industry transformed in a moment into a branch of St. George's Channel.

Of the Reactionary papers, the *Liberté* alone really discussed the question ; the others scarcely did more than confine themselves to stating the facts. The

Français in one paragraph explained the efficacy of Sir Garnet Wolseley's occupation of the Canal as a strategical move, and said that 'the question of the Canal's neutrality has thus been rudely solved ; England has not only taken military possession in order to establish her operations at Ismailia, but she has closed the Canal to all the ships of other nations. A more haughty contempt for so-called international rules, and less consideration for the feelings and interests of others, could not have been shown.'

CHAPTER XXXIV.

TEL-EL-MAHUTA.

Description of Country—The Advance on Nefiché—Transports at Ismailia—Engagement at Tel-el-Mahuta—Sir Garnet Wolseley's Despatch—Observations on the Engagement—Disproportion between the English and Egyptian Forces—The dam in the Canal.

THE country between Ismailia and the Delta is so monotonous that a few words only are needed to give a notion of its character. It is a desert of sand, across which run the Fresh Water Canal and the railway, side by side. To the northward of these the ground is, as a rule, somewhat higher, sloping in a southerly direction across the Canal. From these elevations occasional peeps can be obtained of the blue waters of Lake Timsah, and of the violet-tinted hills of Gebel Attakeh, in the distance. The surface is occasionally diversified by low hammocks and mounds, and is dotted at intervals by tufts of scrub called 'camel grass.' The soil is a deep light shifting sand near Ismailia, but it gradually increases in firmness towards the westward; and at Tel-el-Kebir, especially on the upper crests of the hills, is a fairly compact gravel over which progress is comparatively easy.

The sky is here rarely cloudy, so that the sun beats down with full force during the day; while at night the radiation is so great that the air becomes cool and almost chilly even in summer. Shelter is needed against the sun in day-time, and at night a blanket is indispensable, both on account of the low temperature and the dews.

By reason of the absence of rain and the dry temperature stores of all kinds could be freely piled up uncovered in the open air, without fear of injury. The Fresh Water Canal joining the Nile just below Cairo, furnished the necessary water, of fair quality when once the mud held in suspension was got rid of. The Egyptian flies, the worst of their species, made life almost unendurable. They disappeared with the sun, only to be relieved by countless hosts of mosquitoes.

No time was lost after the landing at Ismailia. The advance commenced the day following the occupation.

At 11 a.m. on the 21st August, Major-General Graham started from the town with 800 men, and a small naval contingent under Captain Stephenson of the *Carysfort*, and marched across the heavy sand, arriving in position at Nefiché at 1.30 p.m.

The Egyptian camp was found completely deserted, the enemy having retired up the Fresh Water Canal. A few tents were left behind, and about thirty railway trucks full of provisions and ammunition. The remains of the wrecked train which had been struck by the *Orion's* shell, were also lying about. The locomotive, however, which was badly wanted, was gone, and the telegraph wires were cut. The entire force bivouacked here and the position was at once placed in an efficient state of defence. Shelter trenches were thrown up, one Gatling was placed to command the railway from Suez, the other the railway from Zag-a-Zig. Later in the day a reconnaissance was made towards the westward, and the presence of the enemy, about four miles distant, was revealed.

The troops had carried with them two days' rations, and it was necessary to accumulate a small stock of stores before continuing the advance. In consequence, the next two days were devoted to preparations. Transports continued to arrive daily in Lake Timsah, and landing went on rapidly. On the 22nd twenty-six transports, besides vessels of war, were moored off Ismailia. Sir Garnet Wolseley, who, as already stated, had arrived on the 21st, took up his quarters in the Governor's house. At 4 p.m. on this day all the blue-jackets from the fleet re-embarked, except three Gatling-gun crews and the torpedo party who had advanced with General Graham to Nefiché.

On the 23rd there was great activity in Ismailia, several transports arrived from Suez with portions of the Indian Contingent. The Khedive's Palace was turned into a hospital. Lines of rail were laid down by the Royal Engineers from the landing-place to the station, and stores were disembarked in great quantities and moved up to the front.

On the day following commenced a series of engagements, which, with some intervals, continued until the dispersal of the Egyptian army at Tel-el-Kebir.

The operations on the 24th are best described in the official report quoted below :—

'*Ismailia, August* 26*th,* 1882.

' Sir,

'I have the honour to supplement my telegraphic despatch of the 24th instant with a detailed report of the events which took place on that date in the neighbourhood of Abu Suer, and of Tel-el-Mahuta, on the Sweet Water Canal, about nine miles west of Ismailia.

' A gradual but continuous decrease of level in the Canal determined me to push forward my available cavalry and artillery (very little of which had landed as yet) together with the two infantry battalions, which I had advanced to Nefiché Junction on the 21st instant, with the object of seizing and occupying a position on the Canal and railway, which would secure possession of that part of the water supply of the desert lying between Ismailia and the first cultivated portion of the Delta, which I had reason to believe was the most vulnerable to damage at the hands of the enemy. The paramount importance of this object, as affecting all my future operations, induced me to risk a cavalry movement with horses which had been less than two days on shore after a long sea-voyage, and also neutralised the objections, which I must otherwise have entertained, to placing the strain of a forward movement upon the recent and partially organized supply service. Accordingly, at 4 a.m. on the 24th, I advanced with the troops marginally noted,* whom I placed for the day under the command of Lieutenant-General Willis, C.B., commanding 1st Division, reached Nefiché at daybreak, and, following the general line of the railway, arrived at 7.30 a.m. on the north side of the Canal, at a point about midway between the spot marked El-Magfar on the map and the village of Tel-el-Mahuta. At this point the enemy had constructed his first dam across the Canal, and after some skirmishing with his scouts and light troops, in which two squadrons of Household Cavalry charged very gallantly, I took possession of it. From this point the enemy could be observed in force about one and a half miles further on, his vedettes holding a line extending across the Canal, lining the crest of a ridge which curved round to my right flank at a general distance of about 2000 yards from my front. The canal and railway at Tel-el-Mahuta are close together, and both are there carried through deep cuttings, with mounds of sand and earth on both sides of them. These were strongly intrenched and crowds of men could be seen at work there. At Mahuta the enemy had constructed a very large embankment across the railway and a wide and solid dam across the Canal, which afforded him easy communication from one side to the other.

'From the statement of some prisoners taken by the mounted troops, as well as by the length of front covered by the enemy, it was apparent that he was in force at Mahuta, and I could see by the smoke of his locomotives, which kept constantly reaching his position throughout the forenoon, that he was being largely reinforced from Tel-el-Kebir. I could perceive that the enemy's force in my immediate front was large; I estimated it at 10,000 men and ten guns, but I have since found that it consisted of one regiment of cavalry, nine battalions of infantry (about 7000 men), twelve guns, and a large but indefinite number of Bedouins. Although I had but three squadrons of cavalry, two guns and about 1000 infantry, I felt it would not be in consonance with the traditions of Her Majesty's Army that we should retire, even temporarily, before Egyptian troops, no matter what their numbers might be. I decided, therefore, upon holding my ground until evening, by which time I knew that the reinforcements I had sent for to Nefiché and Ismailia would reach me. I consequently took up a position, suited to the numbers at my disposal, with my left resting on the captured dam over the Canal, and the cavalry and mounted infantry covering the right.

'It was now 9 o'clock a.m. The enemy had kept gradually reinforcing his left, showing considerable skill in the method with which he

---

* Household Cavalry; Mounted Infantry; 2 Guns Battery, N.-A. (N battery, A brigade), R.H.A.; York and Lancaster; Marines.

swung round his left, moving along the reverse slope of his position, and showing only his light troops upon the sky line.

'The two guns of N Battery, A Brigade, Royal Horse Artillery, only reached me at 9 a.m., although the officer in command had made every effort to push his way as rapidly as possible through the deep sand over which our route lay. They took up a good position on a sandy hillock near the railway embankment, from which a good view of the enemy's position was to be obtained. By this time the enemy had opened a heavy artillery fire upon us, and his infantry advanced in very regular attack formation, halting and forming a line of shelter trenches about 1000 yards from our position. On my left he had pushed his infantry along the Canal to within about 900 yards of the dam held by the York and Lancaster Regiment, but the steady and well-directed fire of this battalion easily checked his movement upon that side.

'From 10 to 11 o'clock the enemy continued to develop his attack upon my centre and right. His guns were served with considerable skill, the shells bursting well amongst us. Fortunately, they were common shells with percussion fuzes, which sank so deep in the very soft sand before bursting, that few splinters flew upwards; when he did use shrapnel the time-fuzes were badly cut.

'Feeling complete confidence in my ability to drive back any close attack the enemy might make, I did not allow our guns to open fire for some time after they were placed in position, hoping he might thereby be the more readily induced to advance to close quarters, under the notion that we had no artillery with us. When, however, he brought twelve guns into action, to relieve the Household Cavalry, into whose ranks and those of the Mounted Infantry he was throwing his shell with great accuracy, our two guns opened upon his twelve guns with marked effect, our practice being very good.

'The Household Cavalry and Mounted Infantry were skilfully manœuvred by Major-General Drury-Lowe on the extreme right, to check the enemy's advance on that side; but the horses, just landed from a long sea-voyage and fatigued by their march across a desert deep in sand, were in no condition to charge.

* * * * * * *

'About noon two Gatlings, with a party of sailors, under command of Lieutenant King-Harman, and belonging to H. M. S. *Orion*, arrived and took up a position for action. The manner in which the sailors brought these Gatlings into position, and the energy shown by them and by the Marine Artillery, deserve the highest commendation.

'The fire opened by the enemy on my right was as accurate as that which he had already directed against my front; but although many shells continued to drop in and around the hillock where our two guns were in action, causing loss to the overworked men of N Battery, A Brigade, Royal Horse Artillery, they continued to work their two guns with great steadiness during many hours; exposed to a concentrated fire from twelve guns, and under very trying conditions of heat, glare, and sunshine.

* * * * * * *

'At 3.30 p.m. the Household Cavalry, under General Lowe, and the Mounted Infantry, again moved forward on my right, causing the enemy to partially withdraw his attack on that flank.

'At 1 p.m. the Second Battalion of the Duke of Cornwall's Light Infantry had arrived from Nefiché.

'About 5.15 p.m. the enemy again advanced his left, pushing four guns across the ridge and moving his cavalry with a considerable force of infantry some distance down the slope, but not near enough to come within effective infantry or Gatling fire.

'At this time our reinforcements began to arrive rapidly. Colonel Sir Baker Russell, with 350 sabres of the 4th and 7th Dragoon Guards, reached the field, and at 6 p.m. the brigade of Guards, under His Royal Highness the Duke of Connaught, arrived. It was now too late to begin an offensive movement; the troops I had with me were tired by their exertions during the early part of the day, and the brigade of Guards, which had moved from Ismailia at 1.30 p.m., had suffered much from the great heat of the desert march. Shortly after sunset the entire force bivouacked on the field which they had so tenaciously held all day, and the enemy withdrew across the ridge to his position at Mahuta.

* * * * * * *

'I have, &c.,

'G. J. WOLSELEY, General.'

Shortly described, the events of the 24th may be said to have been a successful attempt to seize the dam, and so secure the water supply, and the retaining by Sir Garnet Wolseley of the position gained, in the face of overwhelming numbers.

Up to noon the English forces were 1000 infantry, three squadrons of cavalry, and two guns. The forces opposed to them were not less than 8000, with twelve guns.

That Sir Garnet's little force should have been able to hold their own says wonders for their discipline and steadiness. The first reinforcements were thirty-five seamen of the *Orion*, under Captain Fitz-Roy, with the two

Gatlings. The 46th, Duke of Cornwall's regiment, which had pitched its tents the night before at Nefiché, was the next to arrive. When the Dragoon Guards and the brigade of Guards arrived between five and six, the safety of the British position was secured.*

The fight began with a skirmish between the advanced guard and an Egyptian detachment engaged in destroying the railway. After a short engagement the enemy's force was driven back, and twelve persons were taken. The rest of the fight appears to have been mainly between the gunners, the infantry on either side never coming to close quarters; of actual hard fighting there was none. It was a question of endurance under a galling fire, and a fierce sun, which injured more men than the enemy's shells.

The Egyptian artillery practice was good, the first shell bursting only twenty yards from Sir Garnet Wolseley and his staff, killed an artillery horse and wounded one man.

---

* The dam, which by threatening the water supply had necessitated the advance of the 24th, was found to have been made of bundles of reeds cleverly lashed together with telegraph wire, with sand thrown over each layer. All the next day the blue jackets, assisted by a fatigue party of soldiers, were at work up to their necks in the water trying to cut through the dam. Little or no impression, however, was made upon it. It was then operated on with gun-cotton, which had but little effect on the sand. A large hole was made, but it instantly filled up again. Pickaxes and shovels were then set to work, but it was not until the 27th that the dam was at last cleared away and the Canal opened to navigation.

CHAPTER XXXV.

MAHSAMEH.

Arrival of Reinforcements—The Line of Battle—Advance to Tel-el-Mahuta—Sir Garnet Wolseley's Report—Naval Brigade—March of the Marines—The British Losses—Capture of Mahmoud Pasha Fehmy—The Lock on the Fresh Water Canal occupied.

DURING the night of the 24th August, reinforcements from Ismailia continued to arrive, and at daybreak line of battle was formed in the following manner :—Beginning on the left, was General Graham's brigade, or rather such of its component parts as had reached the front. It consisted of the 84th, York and Lancaster regiment, the Duke of Cornwall's Light Infantry, and the Marine Battalion. Then came four guns of Battery A 1, then the Guards' Brigade, then six guns, N. A., of the Royal Horse Artillery, then the Cavalry, 4th and 9th Dragoon Guards, then two guns of Battery A 1, then the Household Cavalry, and lastly, the mounted Infantry. Battery N. A. was strengthened by two guns, each of N. 2. Royal Artillery, and battery G. B. Royal Horse Artillery, which came up during the advance.

Early on the 25th, another short advance was made and Tel-el-Mahuta was occupied. The following is the official report :—

'*Ismailia, August* 27, 1882.
'SIR,
'I have the honour to inform you of the events which took place on the 25th instant in the neighbourhood of Tel-el-Mahuta, and further along the line of the Canal and railway as far as the station of Mahsameh.

'The attack on the enemy's intrenched post at Tel-el-Mahuta, which was deferred on the 24th instant in consequence of the lateness of the hour at which the reinforcements could arrive, and also because of the fatigue undergone by the troops in action, was successfully carried out shortly after daybreak on the 25th instant.

'Accompanied by General Sir J. Adye and the head-quarters staff, I left Ismailia at 3 a.m., and reached the scene of yesterday's fighting at 5.30 o'clock. I took with me the remaining squadron of the 1st Cavalry brigade, most of whom had only landed the previous day. The 1st division, including the troops marginally noted,* had by that time quitted their bivouack, and had advanced towards the enemy's position in the following order : the Cavalry and Mounted Infantry formed the extreme right, thrown well forward upon the desert ridges over which the enemy had on the previous day carried out his flank movement. The Artillery moved on the left of the Cavalry, towards the summit of the high ground overlooking the line of railway between Ramses and the Mahsameh station. The Infantry, on the left of the Artillery, advanced in echelon from the right upon Mahuta, the brigade of Guards leading.

'When the summit of the ridge was gained the enemy was observed to be abandoning his earthworks at the last-named place, and to be retiring his forces along the canal banks and the railway line towards Mahsameh. His railway trains were also to be seen in motion towards the same place.

'At 6.25 a.m. our Artillery came into action against the enemy's Infantry and guns which were posted on the canal bank to the west of Mahuta. As it was of great importance to obtain possession, if possible, of some of the enemy's locomotives, I ordered the Cavalry to push forward with all speed and attempt to cut off the retreating trains. The Cavalry and eight guns moved as rapidly as their horses, which were in no condition for hard work, would permit. The ground was much better and harder than that moved over yesterday. The enemy offered considerable resistance in the neighbourhood of Mahsameh, but nothing could stop the advance of our mounted troops, tired even as their horses were. Mahsameh, with its very extensive camp left standing by the enemy, was soon in our possession. Seven Krupp guns, great quantities of ammunition, two large trains of railway waggons loaded with provisions, and vast supplies of various kinds, fell into our hands. The enemy fled along the railway and canal banks, throwing away their arms and equipments, and showing every sign of demoralization. Unfortunately there was not at this time in the whole Cavalry brigade a troop that could gallop, their long march and rapid advance having completely exhausted the horses, who were not yet fit for hard work after their long voyage from England.

'The results of the operations, extending over two days, have been

* Household Cavalry; 4th and 7th Dragoon Guards; battery N.A., R.H.A.; 3rd Battalion Royal Rifles.

most satisfactory. The enemy has been completely driven from the position at Tel-el-Mahuta, which he had taken such pains to fortify and upon which he had by force compelled 7000 peasants to labour. The Canal has been cleared for more than half the distance intervening between Ismailia and the Delta and the water supply completely secured to us.

'The railway line is in our possession for more than twenty miles from this place, and the vigour, dash, and energy displayed by the troops in the sudden forward movement, made with horses out of condition and from a base hastily organized, and where we are still contending with all the difficulties incidental to rapid disembarkations, have assured to the army an important strategic position, the possession of which cannot fail to influence the future operations of the campaign. Amongst the prisoners taken was Mahmoud Fehmi Pasha, who was chief engineer to Arabi Pasha, a very important personage among the rebel chiefs.

'The enemy were commanded by Rashid Pasha, and the force he had collected at Mahuta and Mahsameh consisted of ten battalions of Infantry (at least 8000 men), of six squadrons of Cavalry and twenty guns, besides a large force of Bedouins. Owing to the result of the action of the previous day (24th instant) many of his troops had retreated during the night, and upon our guns opening on his works early on the morning of the 25th instant, the 7000 labourers ran away. Rashid Pasha then issued orders for a general retreat.

'Military operations in Egypt at this season of the year are very trying to the soldiers engaged, and the complete absence of anything approaching the nature of a road renders all movements most difficult and fatiguing. Owing to the fact of this advance being made before the railway or the telegraph lines had been repaired, or the canal cleared of obstructions, or any regular system of transport had been effectually organized, considerable exposure without tents, and severe privations as regards food have been imposed upon all ranks. These hardships have, however, been cheerfully borne, and the conduct of the troops has been everything I could wish.

'The troops engaged were, upon both the 24th and 25th instant, under the immediate command of Lieut.-General Willis, C.B., who carried out my views in a most satisfactory manner. My advanced troops, under Major-General Graham, now hold the Kassassin Lock.

'I am, &c.,

'G. J. WOLSELEY, General.'

To the foregoing account it may be well to add that a small naval detachment took part in the operations of the day. It was composed of two Gatlings and 70 marines from the *Carysfort* and *Orion*, and was commanded by Captain Fitz-Roy of the latter vessel.

The Marine Infantry Battalion, under Lieutenant-Colonel Howard S. Jones, had left Ismailia at 4 p.m. the previous day, and had reached El Magfar at 1.30 a.m. of the 25th. It started again at 4.30 a.m. with the general advance, and at 5 p.m. was able to march into the Egyptian Camp at Mahsameh, which had been seized by the Cavalry in the morning; so good a piece of work deserves to be recorded. The Guards and the Duke of Connaught were, unluckily, unable to get up in time, although they struggled manfully through the deep sand.

The extreme right of the British line was on a ridge about a mile and a half from the centre. When Mahsameh Station was in full sight the two guns of Battery A 1 came into action and shelled the fugitives, the Cavalry and Mounted Infantry dashing in and capturing the camp and station which they occupied until the advance on Tel-el-Kebir.

The canal had been filled with dead bodies, and the banks were still strewn with them, probably with the idea of making the water undrinkable. It was here that one of the English artillerymen having offered to fetch water for a wounded Egyptian was shot by the latter whilst doing so.

The stock of provisions captured was a most welcome addition to the stores in hand, and in particular the grain left on the ground in large quantities was invaluable, for the horses had been for several days on an extremely short allowance of forage.

It will be remarked that the operations of the day hardly attained to the dignity of an engagement, the Egyptians offering practically no resistance, but falling back on Tel-el-Kebir, where a large camp had been established north of the railway, and where extensive entrenchments were begun along the crest of a range of hills running north and south.*

The losses on the side of the British were small— only five killed and twenty-five wounded, but the cases of sunstroke were unfortunately numerous, the 4th Dragoons having sixteen, and the York and Lancaster Regiment twenty-five men disabled from this cause.

On August the 26th a small force of the Dragoons occupied the lock on the Fresh Water Canal at Kassassin without opposition. This was a most important step, because the possession of the lock gave Sir Garnet Wolseley control of the water in the upper reach of the canal. That it could have been accomplished so easily is but another indication of the ignorance or carelessness of the enemy.

Later in the day the Duke of Cornwall's Light Infantry, the 84th York and Lancaster Regiment, as well as two guns of the Royal Horse Artillery, were marched to the lock where they established themselves, the Cavalry withdrawing to Mahsameh, a mile and a half to the eastward. A large house on the left bank of the canal was occupied by General Graham and his staff, who remained in charge of the advanced guard; and strong outposts were thrown out, as it was known that the enemy was not far off, and the Cavalry scouted by day and night.

* Mahmoud Pasha Fehmy, who was captured, was the Chief of the Staff of the Egyptian Army. He missed the train and was found strolling apparently unconcerned about the railway station at Mahsameh. As he was in the ordinary Egyptian dress with a 'tarboosh' and white umbrella, he would probably have got away unobserved had he not been recognised and denounced by a wounded Egyptian soldier.

CHAPTER XXXVI.

KASSASSIN.

The Question of the Commissariat—Serious Attack by the Egyptian Forces—General Graham's Despatch—General Drury Lowe's-Despatch—Further Details—Loss of the Captured Guns—Results of the Action—Arabi's Telegrams—The Field of Battle.

THE British force had now outrun its Commissariat, and for two days the men had lived from hand to mouth. To secure the water supply it had become necessary to push forward a force into the Desert nearly 20 miles from the base of operations at Ismailia. The question arose how the troops were to be supplied with food, and the want of a proper organization for the transport of provisions began to be severely felt. The men, weakened by prolonged exertion under a terrible sun, were forced to live for two or three days on biscuits and muddy water, flavoured only with the dead bodies of Egyptian men and horses. The English horses also were short of forage and showed signs of fatigue and exhaustion. The question of supply became an anxious one. Mules were not forthcoming, the railway had been cut, and no rolling stock was available, and the British force was for days almost without food.

On the third day, owing to the vigorous efforts of the navy, some stores were forwarded to the front by the Fresh Water Canal, but the prospects were, to say the least, gloomy. The men were compelled to live on pigeons, water-melons, &c., looted out of the neighbouring village. On the 27th, however, a daring foraging party was conducted into the country by the transport officer, and some fourteen head of cattle were driven in, besides some sheep and turkeys. The General ordered them all to be paid for, and this rule was observed on subsequent occasions.

The distribution of the force was approximately as follows:—At Kassassin Lock, were a squadron of the 19th Hussars, the York and Lancaster Regiment, the Duke of Cornwall's Light Infantry, the Royal Marine Artillery Battalion, and two guns of Battery N. A. At Mahsameh, the Household Cavalry, the 4th and 7th Dragoon Guards, the 2nd Bengal Cavalry, and 13th Bengal Lancers, the Mounted Infantry, and the Royal Marine Light Infantry Battalion. At Tel-el-Mahuta, the 1st Brigade of Guards, the Rifles, the 26th Company Royal Engineers, and Battery A 1 of the Royal Artillery. At Nefiché, the West Kent Regiment. At Ismailia, the 7th, 8th, and 18th Companies of Royal Engineers, besides many other corps landing from the transports.

On the 28th, the Egyptians made an effort to regain their lost ground by a serious attack upon General Graham's force at Kassassin, as narrated in the official reports given herewith.

'FROM MAJOR-GENERAL GRAHAM TO SIR GARNET WOLSELEY.

'*Kassassin, August* 29*th*, 1882.

'SIR,

' I have the honour to report that an important engagement with the enemy took place here yesterday, the 28th inst., in which, though attacked by a vastly superior force numerically, tried seriously by exposure to the sun and previous privations, the troops I have the honour to command finally drove back the enemy at all points ; and, with the aid of the cavalry under Major-General Drury-Lowe, C.B., inflicted severe chastisement.

'The position the advanced brigade occupied at Kassassin is not the best for defence. We are astride the Canal (which runs nearly east and west), and hold the bridge and locks. Taking the west as our proper front, on our right the Desert rises to a ridge, with an elevation of from 100 to 160 feet; at a distance of from 2000 to 3000 yards, there is the millet and palm-covered plain of the Ouady, intersected by a disused branch of the Canal. This ridge on our right is obviously a source of danger to a force too weak to occupy it, as I have already observed in a previous report.

'About 9.30 a.m., on the 28th inst., the enemy's cavalry appeared in force, on our left front, on the north side of the Fresh Water Canal, and I at once heliographed to Major-General Drury-Lowe at Mahsameh. The force under my command, consisting of 57 Cavalry, 70 mounted infantry, 1728 infantry, and 40 artillery with two 13-pounders, as detailed in margin,* were at once posted by me under cover, fronting to the north and west, the cavalry and mounted infantry being thrown out on the flanks to observe the enemy's movements, while I awaited the development of his attack. About eleven a.m. it was reported that a large force of cavalry, infantry, and artillery, were being moved round towards our right, behind the ridge. At twelve the enemy opened fire from two heavy guns on our left front, at least 4000 yards off, the shot from which fell short.

'The enemy's attack seemed to languish, and about three p.m. the officer commanding the mounted infantry reported the enemy retiring.

'The men had been suffering very much from their long exposure to the heat of the sun without food, so I ordered them back to their camps. Major-General Drury-Lowe brought a brigade of cavalry within two or three miles of the camp, and about three p.m. withdrew them to Mahsameh, as I had previously requested him not to engage them unnecessarily.

'At 4.30 p.m. the enemy advanced his infantry in great force, displaying a line of skirmishers at least a mile in length with which he sought to overlap my front on the left, supported by a heavy and well-directed fire of artillery, with which he searched the camp, wounding a sick officer in the house where I had established my head-quarters, but which, as the best building, was now given up as a hospital. My dispositions to meet this attack were as follows: On the left, the Marine Artillery were directed to take up a position on the S. bank of the Canal, where (secure from being turned themselves, the Canal being

---

* Royal Horse Artillery, 40 officers, non-commissioned officers, and men, and 2 guns; 4th Dragoon Guards, 15 officers, non-commissioned officers, and men; 7th Dragoon Guards, 42 officers, non-commissioned officers, and men, Duke of Cornwall's Light Infantry, 611 officers, non-commissioned officers, and men; York and Lancaster, 690 officers, non-commissioned officers, and men; Mounted Infantry, 70 officers, non-commissioned officers, and men; Royal Marine Artillery, 427 officers, non-commissioned officers, and men.

5ft. to 6ft. deep) they could check the enemy's advance by a flank fire. (The Royal Marine Artillery, therefore, gave fire to W. and N. W.)

'In the centre, the 2nd Battalion Duke of Cornwall's Light Infantry extended a fighting line of three companies, facing W. by N., about 800 yards to the right rear (E.N.E.) of the Royal Marine Artillery. The supports and reserves of the Duke of Cornwall's Light Infantry were under cover of the railway embankment, facing N.

'The 2nd Battalion York and Lancaster extended the fighting line of the Duke of Cornwall's Light Infantry with two and a half companies, keeping the remainder in support and reserve.

'The position of the Infantry, therefore, was an irregular echelon, right thrown back. The troop of the 7th Dragoon Guards was kept on this flank, and the two 13-pounders, now reinforced by two others, took up a position on the ridge. Unfortunately these guns had only got their ammunition in their limbers, and had soon to cease firing for want of a further supply, though they did good service while it lasted. The Mounted Infantry and detachment of the 4th Dragoon Guards occupied a portion of the gap between the Royal Marine Artillery, and Duke of Cornwall's Light Infantry, and all the persistent efforts of the enemy to break through at this point were unavailing, owing to the steady fire of the Royal Marine Artillery and the gallant resistance of the little band of Mounted Infantry and detachment of the 4th Dragoon Guards dismounted and employed as Infantry. The enemy made great efforts to overcome this resistance, putting a number of men across the Canal; and three times his guns were kept from advancing by their horses and men being shot, when trying to press past. In order to support the left, the companies on the left of the Duke of Cornwall's Light Infantry facing N. were spread out along the line of railway embankment, and a fresh company from the right half battalion was moved to the left to prolong the line.

'Feeling secure on my left, I turned my attention to the right flank. On the first notice of the attack (4.30 p.m.) I had sent a message to Major-General Drury-Lowe by heliograph and by a mounted officer to Mesameh three or four miles distant, requesting him to move up the Cavalry brigade to cover my right flank and to send forward the Royal Marine Light Infantry.

'At five p.m., thinking I saw the Cavalry advancing I sent an order to Major-General Drury-Lowe to bring round his Cavalry under cover of the hill, fall upon the left flank of the enemy's skirmishers and roll up his line. This order was received and gallantly executed. For an account of this part of the action I beg to refer to Major-General Drury-Lowe's own report.

'At five p.m. I observed reinforcements coming to the enemy by train, and fearing a charge of cavalry on our exposed right, directed the officer commanding the Reserve Company of York and Lancaster to prepare to receive them in line. Near the right of our position, on the line of railway, a Krupp gun, taken from the enemy at Mahsameh, had been mounted on a railway truck and was being worked by a gun detachment of the Royal Marine Artillery, under Captain Tucker. This gun was admirably served and did great execution among the enemy. As the other guns had to cease firing for want of ammunition, Captain Tucker's gun became the target for the enemy's artillery, and I counted salvoes of four guns opening on him at once with shell and shrapnel; but although everything around or in line was hit, not a man of the gun detachment was touched, and this gun continued to fire to the end, expending ninety-three rounds.

'At 6.45 p.m., I ordered an advance, with the object of closing on the enemy's infantry, about the time of the expected cavalry charge. The advance was made very steadily, by the fighting line, in echelon from the left, about 600 yards to our west front, when the line fired volleys by companies, the reserves following in rear of the railway embankment.

'On arriving at the point held by the Mounted Infantry a message reached me that the Royal Marine Light Infantry had come on to the ground on our right; and, galloping back, I at once directed them to advance in order of attack. This advance was continued for about two or three miles, supported by the Duke of Cornwall's Light Infantry on the left, the York and Lancaster being left behind in reserve, the enemy falling back, only one attempt being made at a stand on our left which broke at the first volley of the Royal Marines.

'About 8.45 p.m. I first heard of the cavalry charge from an officer of the 1st Life Guards who had lost his way.

'We had now been advancing for an hour and a half in the moonlight, and my two aides-de-camp had had narrow escapes in mistaking detached bodies of the enemy for our own troops. Fearing some mistake might be made and seeing no further chance of co-operation with the cavalry, I ordered the Marines and Duke of Cornwall's Light Infantry to retire at 8.45 p.m. On approaching the camp I called in the other troops.

'During the night the enemy made no sign, and this morning at daybreak I rode out over the battlefield, and have had all the wounded that were found brought in.

'I append a detailed list of killed and wounded, an abstract of which is given in the margin.* The corps which suffered most heavily was the Royal Marine Artillery, under Lieutenant-Colonel Tuson, whom I would beg to bring especially to your notice. The Mounted Infantry

---

* Cavalry, killed or dangerously wounded 1 (exclusive of force under Major-General Lowe's command); Royal Marine Artillery, killed or dangerously wounded 7, wounded 25; Mounted Infantry, wounded 7; Duke of Cornwall's Light Infantry, killed or dangerously wounded 1, wounded 34;

also suffered heavily, and early in the action were deprived of the services of their gallant leader Lieutenant Piggott, an officer who deserves especial mention. Another valuable officer of this corps, Lieutenant Edwards, was also wounded. The services of the Mounted Infantry have been invaluable to me, in the absence of a sufficient force of cavalry. I have also to bring to your notice the admirable steadiness of the 2nd Battalion Duke of Cornwall's Light Infantry under fire, and during their advance under Colonel Richardson. The 2nd Duke of Cornwall's Light Infantry were effectively supported by the 2nd York and Lancaster under Colonel Wilson, to whose careful personal leading ably supported by the officers under him, much credit is due. The Royal Marine Light Infantry, although they arrived too late to take any decisive share in the action, showed by the promptitude of their march to the field and the steadiness of their advance under Colonel Jones, that they are well capable of sustaining the high character of their corps.

'In general, I cannot too highly express my opinion of the steadiness of the troops under fire, and the ready alacrity with which they carried out my orders. Although exposed for two hours to a heavy fire of artillery, the lines I advanced were full of cheerful confidence and eager to close with the enemy.

'I may also mention that the five hours' exposure to the sun in the morning, expecting an attack, had been most trying to the men, and that the Duke of Cornwall's Light Infantry had not had time to eat their dinners before they were ordered out to meet the enemy.

'I estimate the enemy's force at 1000 cavalry, 8000 infantry, and twelve guns.

'I have, &c.,

'GERALD GRAHAM, Major-General, Commanding
'Advanced Brigade.'

'FROM MAJOR-GENERAL DRURY-LOWE TO MAJOR-GENERAL WILLIS, C.B.

'*Mahsameh, August* 29, 1882.

'SIR,
'Having received information from Major-General Graham, at Kassassin, that the enemy were advancing on his position, and having been told by Colonel Keyser that his signallers had been withdrawn, I turned out the following troops of the 1st Cavalry Brigade, under Brigadier General Sir Baker Russell, viz., Household Cavalry, 7th Dragoon Guards, and four guns N Battery A Brigade Royal Horse

York and Lancaster Regiment, killed or dangerously wounded 1, wounded 11; Army Medical Department, killed or dangerously wounded 1. Total killed or dangerously wounded 11, wounded 67.

Artillery, and advanced towards the enemy's left. A distant and ineffective artillery fire was being directed against General Graham's position, but beyond this nothing was taking place. I remained some hours communicating with General Graham and withdrew my brigade about 4.30 p.m. About 5.30 Major Molyneux arrived from Kassassin, and gave me a message from General Graham that the enemy was advancing in force; I again, at 5.30 p.m., turned out the brigade and moved to the sound of the heavy firing that was now taking place. *En route*, a galloper reached me from General Graham, who stated that the General desired to say "that he was only just able to hold his own, and that he wished me to attack the left of the enemy's infantry skirmishers." The sun had now set and a bright moon was shining. The light, however, was not good owing to the haze and we were guided by the flash of guns and musketry. I made a wide circuit to turn the enemy's left, and the brigade arrived without being noticed, near this portion of their line. As we approached a heavy fire of shells and musketry was opened upon us, which was practically harmless, as it was very high. I cleared the front of our guns by a retirement of the first line, whilst the Household Cavalry on their right formed line. After a few rounds from our guns, Sir Baker Russell led a charge of the Household Cavalry under Colonel Ewart against the enemy's infantry which had commenced to advance. Moving most steadily towards the flash of the rifles, the charge was right gallantly led and executed. The enemy's infantry was completely scattered and our cavalry swept through a battery of seven or nine guns, which in daylight must have been captured, but, unfortunately, their exact position could not be found afterwards, and they were no doubt removed during the night, after our retirement. The enemy's loss was heavy, the ground being thickly strewn with their killed, and quantities of ammunition, &c. I beg to attach a list of casualties sustained by the brigade, which considering the nature of the attack, was not heavy.* The greatest praise is due to the Household Cavalry for their behaviour throughout, and I have to thank Brigadier-General Sir Baker Russell and the officers and men of the brigade for their gallant conduct.

'I have, &c.,
'DRURY-LOWE, Major-General, Commanding Cavalry Division.'

The Egyptian attack is described by eye-witnesses as heavy and direct, and their fire rapid. General Graham's forces, although greatly outnumbered, stood

* Three killed and sixteen wounded.

their ground with coolness, expending their ammunition effectively and deliberately, and holding the enemy in check for two hours, when his retreat began. This movement appears to have been accompanied by very little fighting, and to have been conducted in good order.

Two batteries of field artillery arrived from Mahuta, but too late to take part in the action.

It will be remarked, that General Graham's report mentions a Krupp gun having been worked on a railway waggon on the line. Though continuously under fire for nearly two hours, the detachment of Royal Marine Artillery which worked the gun received no injury. Captain Tucker, who commanded the detachment, attributed this immunity to the constant shifting of the position of the gun on the rails. The gun itself was protected by a breastwork of sand-bags.

The reason of the scarcity of ammunition for the artillery was the heaviness of the road from the base to the front. Efforts were made to get up a proper supply, but the waggons stuck in the sand and so arrived late.

The message referred to by General Drury-Lowe as being delivered to him about 5.30, to the effect that General Graham wished to say that 'he was only just able to hold his own,' was, it appears, not sent by the General, but was merely the appreciation of the aide-de-camp who conveyed the order for the cavalry to advance. There is little doubt, however, that it correctly represented the situation at the time.

In spite of General Graham's report, there is reason to believe that the cavalry charge took place after the enemy had begun their retreat, and between 8 and 9 p.m. From one account,[*] it appears that at this time some of the enemy were observed making a move on

---

[*] Commander Goodrich's Report, page 137.

General Drury-Lowe's right. The cavalry advanced, the 4th Dragoon Guards on the left, the Household Cavalry on the right, and four guns of Battery N. A. Royal Horse Artillery, in rear of the former. Approaching within 500 or 600 yards of the Egyptians, the guns were unmasked by the cavalry, and brought into action, ceasing fire only when the Household Cavalry crossed in front to ride down the enemy.

This moonlight charge was the most dramatic as it was one of the most gallant episodes of the campaign. The Household Cavalry and Dragoons rushed on at full gallop, swept through the Egyptian guns, and made fearful slaughter among their defenders. Whether the charge, brilliant as it was, occurring so late in the engagement had any real effect upon the fortunes of the day has been much discussed by military men. One thing, however, is to be regretted, viz., that in the impetuosity of the charge no one seems to have thought of securing the captured guns, instead of leaving them on the field to be subsequently removed by the enemy.

It may be remarked that, small as was the force employed, the results of the engagement at Kassassin were of the greatest possible importance. Arabi evidently felt himself strong enough to act on the offensive and thus to attempt to regain the prestige which he had lost in the previous encounters.

In the next place, it showed the British Commander that the campaign was likely to be something more than a parade across the Desert, and that the enemy was willing to come within range and hold his own for hours together.

The position occupied by General Graham was not favourable for defence. His troops were astride the Canal, and although a bridge existed, the separation of right and left wing was partial in any case, and complete if the force had either to advance or retire. Moreover, on the right of the position the Desert rose to a ridge some 150 feet high, which might easily conceal the movements of an outflanking force. The British left, being well supported by the Canal and its banks, the most obvious move on the part of the attack was to double up their right and force them back into the Canal, cutting off communication with their rear. The Egyptians had no commander capable of realising the importance of this move, and in consequence the main attack was in front, and the flanking movement, weak and, as has been seen, unsuccessful.

The following are Arabi's telegrams reporting the action :—

'August 28th.—Our victorious troops have worsted the enemy, and made him retreat to Mahsameh, by the strength and power of God. At the present moment, the two armies are facing each other at a distance of about 5000 metres from Mahsameh, and after a little rest, and when the horses have been watered, there will be a charge, please God. Give us the aid of your pure prayers in asking for succour from the Lord Almighty.

'August 28th, 7.40 p.m.—The fighting has begun again. Cannon have been firing since 4 p.m. till 7.30 p.m., and still continue. I pray God for help against His enemies. Pray God to help His true believers.

'Till this hour the fighting continues with cannon and musketry. I thank God for the endurance He has given us, and pray for perfect help and victory. Pray to Him that He may help His servants, the true believers, and disappoint our treacherous enemies. It is now twenty minutes past eight in the evening.

'August 28th, 11.15 p.m.—Thanks be to God, the fighting has ceased on both sides, after a serious engagement with musketry and cannon, followed by a charge by our cavalry on that of the enemy, when they were in a mêlée and used their swords against each other, after which they separated. God is the best protector.'

The burying parties next morning found that many of the bodies had been shockingly mutilated during the night. The circumcised had all been left untouched. The persons committing these outrages followed a fixed plan which they applied to the uncircumcised corpses of both armies. Of these they had lopped off the feet, hands, and other members, and deeply gashed the abdomen and the upper part of the forehead.

CHAPTER XXXVII.

ENGAGEMENT AT KASSASSIN.

Difficulties in the way of a Further Advance—The Water Supply—Arrival of the Highland Brigade and the Indian Contingent—Preparations—Action of 9th September at Kassassin—Sir Garnet Wolseley's Despatch—Details of the Action—Repulse of the Egyptians—Retreat on Tel-el-Kebir—The Egyptian Plan of Attack—Arabi's Account of the Action.

THE engagement referred to in the last chapter may be regarded as terminating the first part of the campaign.

There was then necessarily a pause in the military operations. A further advance was beset with many difficulties. The railway was damaged in many places, and blocked in others. There were no locomotives to haul the trucks containing stores from the base to the front, and the army transport had in great measure broken down.

The draught animals were few and in poor condition; pack-mules in sufficient numbers were lacking, and camels were almost entirely wanting. The strong regulation carts, suitable for use on European roads, were so heavy as to stick hopelessly in the sand. A waggon, designed for two horses, required not less than six to move it under existing conditions.

The navy, it is true, was doing its best to make up for the defects of the army transport. The boat service on the Canal had been definitely organized under Commander Moore of the *Orion*, and rendered most valuable service in getting provisions and stores to the front.

Notwithstanding all that the boats could do, it

became doubtful whether even the few troops at the front could be maintained, and every effort had to be made to keep them supplied with the food requisite to enable them to exist. The men bore their privations and discomforts cheerfully until the arrival of locomotives from Suez made it possible to supply the army properly. The water too was the reverse of good, the only supply practically being from the Canal, and this at times was simply loathsome.

In addition to this discomfort, there was always the possibility of the railway or Canal being intercepted by marauding parties of the enemy. Either of these contingencies would have seriously imperilled the troops at the front.

In the meantime, the 3rd Brigade, 2nd Division, composed of Highlanders, under the command of Sir Edward Hamley, arrived at Ismailia from Alexandria.

Three more transports with Indian troops also turned up, making the total number of transports in Lake Ismailia no less than 93, besides men-of-war. The 3rd Brigade was not landed at once, but remained on board the troopships, pending the solution of the transport problem.

The state of affairs at this period appears from a telegram from Sir Garnet Wolseley to the Secretary of State for War, and which was as follows :—

'*Ismailia, September* 1, 1882.

'In reply to your inquiry of 29th ultimo, circumstances have forced me ahead of transport, but it is rapidly becoming efficient. The necessity of securing a sufficient supply of fresh water in the Canal rendered it imperative to push on as quickly as possible. My successes on the 24th and 25th and retreat of the enemy have enabled me to seize (the) two important positions on the Canal of El Magfar and Kassassin Lock, the latter about twenty miles from this place. I am, therefore, in a more forward and favourable position generally, than I had anticipated, and am only now waiting till my transport arrangements are more complete, to enable me to make a further movement.

'In the absence of roads, I had always calculated on partially using the Canal and railway in sending supplies to the front, but the enemy having blocked the former by two large dams, and the latter by an embankment, and the partial removal of rails, it has been necessary to get these obstructions removed. I have one engine on the line, and expect a second from Suez to-night, and am preparing the land transport companies, some of which are now landing, to supplement the other means above indicated.

'A supply of mules has arrived from Cyprus. I expect 400 more from Malta and Italy to-morrow; and the large supply collected at Smyrna and Beyrout at last released by the Ottoman Government are on their way. In a desert country like this part of Egypt, it takes time to organize the lines of communication.'

By the 2nd September, the whole of the Indian Contingent, except the 6th Bengal Cavalry, had reached Suez, and many of its troops had gone to the front.

Except for an occasional reconnaissance, bringing about an interchange of shots and for one real attack, the period now entered upon was one merely of preparation for a further advance. With this object, stores first, and then men, were gradually being accumulated at Kassassin.

On the 9th September the Egyptian leaders apparently began to realise the fact that Sir Garnet Wolseley's force was daily increasing in size and importance, and that if any attempt was to be made to crush him there was no time to be lost. Accordingly an attack was made on that day on Kassassin. The official report of the engagement is as follows:—

Camp, Kassassin, September 10th, 1882.

'SIR,

'I have the honour to acquaint you that the enemy made a combined attack yesterday morning upon this position, one column advancing from the north from the Salahieh direction, the other from Tel-el-Kebir. Arabi Pasha was on the ground, but the attacking troops were commanded by Ali Fehmi Pasha, Rashid Pasha being, it is asserted by prisoners, in disgrace for having lost his camp and guns in the fight of the 25th ultimo at Mahsameh Station. The enemy's force was about thirty guns, of which we took four, and seventeen battalions of infantry, several squadrons of cavalry, and a few thousand Bedouins. From the information I have obtained from prisoners, it would seem that the enemy expected an easy victory, thinking the force here was only a weak advance guard. The troops in camp when the attack began were under the command of Lieutenant-General Willis, commanding 1st Division. With these he immediately moved out, attacked and drove back the enemy, who retreated with loss within their line of works at Tel-el-Kebir, from which they opened an angry but harmless fire upon our troops, which had been halted byond the range of their guns.

'Our troops moved with great steadiness, and Major-General Graham has especially brought to my notice the dashing manner in which two Krupp guns were taken by the battalion of Royal Marine Light Infantry, and the excellent manner in which that battalion was handled by its commanding officer, Lieutenant-Colonel Jones. Our casualties were three men killed, and two officers and seventy-eight men wounded. Lieutenant Purvis of H.M.S. *Penelope*, is amongst those who were severely wounded. He was in command of the naval detachment that was serving the 40-pounder which is mounted on a railway truck. He is a very good officer and I have to regret very much the loss of his valuable services with this army. With the exception of five, who were too severely injured to be moved by railway, all the wounded were sent to Ismailia last night, and those five were sent there this evening by the Fresh Water Canal.

'I have, &c.,
'G. J. WOLSELEY,
'General.'

The Egyptian attack was meant to be from two sides. On the west by an advance of the garrison of Tel-el-Kebir, and on the north by a body, variously estimated at from 1500 to 5000 men, from Salahieh.

There is very little doubt that the British force came very near being surprised. Early in the morning Colonel Pennington, of the 13th Bengal Lancers, going out to the westward to post vedettes, found the Egyptians advancing in force. Although he had but fifty men with him he dismounted them behind a ridge, and opened fire on the advancing enemy, and when hard pushed charged some squadrons of cavalry, killing ten men, and capturing five horses. Warning of the impending danger was thus given to the camp, enabling a line of battle to be formed.

By 7 a.m. Arabi had succeeded in posting most of his guns on an eminence known as Ninth Hill, 2000 yards to the British right front, whilst his infantry deployed for attack, with the right resting on the Canal, and then advanced to within 1200 yards. A few of his troops got south of the Canal, with a view to a flank movement.

No sooner were the Egyptian guns posted than they opened fire. The practice was very accurate, shot after shot falling admirably into the British camp and lines. The shells, however, burst so rarely as to neutralise the excellence of the aim.

The British artillery batteries and the guns on the railway replied vigorously with shell and shrapnel. The 25-pounders did excellent work on the enemy's right on both sides of the Canal, sending their projectiles over the heads of the British infantry until the advance was begun. Batteries A 1 and D 1 shot down the men working two of the guns mentioned in the despatch as having been captured, and the guns were seized by the infantry as they advanced. The other two were captured by the Marines in their forward march. Their battalion, in regular formation for attack, came upon a battery of four guns which was playing briskly upon the Marines at a distance of 1400 yards. Without returning the fire they kept on their way until within 400 yards, when they began firing volleys by half companies, still continuing the march. This steady work proved too severe for the Egyptian gunners, who broke and ran, leaving two of the four guns behind.

The infantry also engaged, holding its ground for an hour and a half, no forward movement being permitted until it was ascertained that no danger was to be apprehended from the direction of Salahieh.

At 8.30 it was deemed prudent to assume the offensive, and the line was ordered to advance; the right being always kept in reserve. The 46th (Duke of Cornwall's), 84th (York and Lancaster), and 50th (West Kent) regiments, which had been stationed on the south bank of the canal to check any flank movement of the enemy, were ordered to retire across the Canal bridge, and crossing the plain in front of the camp to form up with the rest. The infantry with the four batteries of artillery on its right, moved forward about 1000 yards and re-engaged the enemy who by this time had retired.

To prevent any attempt to overlap the right of the position, the 46th was advanced in this direction over the hills. The attack in this quarter, however, resolved itself into nothing. At 9.30 the general advance was resumed amid a smart musketry fire, and the enemy broke and retired with precipitation upon Tel-el-Kebir. The Cavalry and Royal Horse Artillery ran them very close. The fortifications being approached as near as from 5000 to 6000 yards, more for the purposes of observation than with any idea of an assault.

The repulse did not take the form of a rout, although little doubt can be entertained that the retreating army would not have stopped at Tel-el-Kebir had a vigorous assault been attempted. Both the officers and men of the British force were extremely anxious to continue the advance, but Sir Garnet Wolseley would not give his consent, and ordered the withdrawal of the army to Kassassin.

The British Artillery proved its value in this action, and received just praise for the way in which it was handled. The Infantry had less opportunity of distinguishing itself, for the Egyptians were unwilling to engage at short range. The contingent from Salahieh was late in arriving on the scene of action.

'The Egyptian plan of attack,' according to a work already quoted,* 'was perfect. At two in the morning the Egyptian right and left columns, supported by a strong centre, were to advance simultaneously on the English lines. To the astonishment of the Nationalist Generals Ali Pasha Fehmi and Rashid Pasha they at one o'clock came across the enemy's pickets, and in a place where Bedouin spies alone could have conducted them. These two excellent officers fell wounded at the outset of the action; and the day, at first victorious, was lost later on for want of competent chiefs to lead the men under fire.'

A full and detailed plan was found by General Willis in Arabi's tent. By this it appears that the force at Salahieh was to join the force from Tel-el-Kebir, and to move round the flank of the British troops as far back as Mahsameh, and thus cut the line of communications. The Commander at Salahieh, however, had not been able to unite with the troops from Tel-el-Kebir, owing to the difficulty of dragging his guns so far through the heavy sand. When he did at length arrive near the field he was met by the Cavalry division, under Major-General Drury-Lowe, in the desert north of the lines. Seeing the impossibility of joining Arabi in the face of the force thus unexpectedly encountered, the Commander withdrew without fighting, losing a field-gun in his retreat.

The failure of the movement was attributed by the Egyptians to their having kept too far to the eastward. The Egyptian versions of the affair are worth reading.

---

* *Arabi Pasha*, by John Ninet.

They are contained in the following telegrams sent by Arabi to the Ministry of War in Cairo:—

'September 9th.—Last night some mounted Arabs of the province of Sharkieh, belonging to the tribes of Nakiat, Tamailat, Ayad, and Haim, rode out towards the enemy at two a.m. under the command of Ali Bey Ismet, Superintendent of the Arabs, and with them Captain Abdul Hamid Effendi Hamdy and forty cavalry soldiers. They went forward as far as the enemy's outposts, rode at them and fired a volley, which made them retire, and then the Arabs found forty-five oxen grazing, which they drove off, while some of the party remained to keep back the enemy. At sunrise, the enemy came out with infantry, cavalry, and artillery and firing began, and continued on both sides for about an hour. Then the Arabs charged like lions, displaying a courage and bravery which enabled them to drive back the enemy, who were much more numerous than themselves. Then they followed the enemy, driving them until they had killed 100 of them (about), and dispersed the rest, driving them back into their tents. The Arabs captured the oxen, about 500 metres of torpedo wire, and other military stores, and they returned to their posts victorious. This engagement, including the attack and pursuit, lasted about six hours. Thanks be to God, not one of the Arabs, nor of the soldiers, was wounded. Give the news to those under your administration.'

And in a second telegram dated the same day, the veracious Arabi reports:—

'On this day, September 9th, an engagement took place with the enemy at five a.m. Our force was composed of infantry, cavalry, and artillery, in the two directions of Ras-el-Ouady and of Salahieh. After the enemy had hidden himself behind his entrenchments at the bridge of Kassassin, our troops retired to their posts in perfect order, and when there was a considerable distance between them, the enemy came out of his entrenchments and endeavoured to cut off our troops. The engagement lasted till five p.m., when the enemy retreated defeated with great loss, to Kassassin. Thanks be to God, our losses were very small in comparison with those of the enemy. We and our officers and the conquering army, his Excellency Mahmoud Pasha Sami, and his officers and soldiers, are all in perfect health, and our two divisions being at their post in perfect condition of readiness; and we pray God to give us the victory over our enemies, and to strengthen our courageous men against them, for the sake of the Lord of the beginning and of the end. Amen. O Lord of the Universe!'

ENGAGEMENT AT KASSASSIN.

Having had time to consider the matter, Arabi gave a third account three days later, as follows :—

'September 12th.—I give you good news, which will cause you joy, and will delight each individual of the people, namely, that the engagement of Saturday (9th September) was the most serious battle that has yet taken place between us and the English, for the force of both armies was very great, and the fighting lasted for twelve hours, with impetuosity and daring, while the cannonade and the discharge of musketry were unceasing, pouring down like rain on the field of battle. Still we lost only thirty-one men, martyrised, and 150 were slightly, not dangerously, wounded, according to the official returns presented by the various regiments, with great exactness and precision. It had been thought that our casualties would have been double that number, owing to the seriousness of the engagement and its long duration. Moreover, from true observations, it has been proved to us that the number of the enemy killed and remaining on the field of battle is about 2500, and their carts were insufficient for carrying off the wounded.'

CHAPTER XXXVIII.

TEL-EL-KEBIR.

Head-quarters moved to Kassassin—Preparations—12th September, British Forces concentrate at Kassassin—Reconnaissances at Tel-el-Kebir—Camp left in charge of General Nugent—The Advance—Description of Tel-el-Kebir—The Egyptian Position—The Entrenchments—Sir Garnet Wolseley's Despatch—Was Tel-el-Kebir a Surprise?—The Polygonal Redoubt—Summary of the Battle—The Egyptian Losses—Sir Garnet Wolseley's Tactics.

ON the 9th September, Sir Garnet Wolseley who had been to the front during the engagement of that day, and had made a reconnaissance towards the enemy's lines at Tel-el-Kebir, established his head-quarters at Kassassin.

The same day the Highland Brigade, under Sir Archibald Alison, commenced its march from Ismailia to the front. The Guards were also brought up. The 10th, 11th, and 12th, were occupied in bringing forward troops and stores. His staff had been increased by the undermentioned officers named by the Khedive to accompany him in the field :—

Colonel Zohrab Bey, Colonel Morice Bey, English ; Lieutenant-Colonel Thurneysen, Austrian ; Lieutenant-Colonel Yusuf Bey Diah ; Lieutenant-Colonel Dulier Bey, Belgian ; Captain Tewfik Effendy.

At 2 p.m. on the 12th, the army was concentrated at Kassassin, the Royal Irish Fusiliers being the last battalion to arrive.

To remain behind and guard the line of communication, the following force was detailed :—At Ismailia 800 of the Manchester Regiment, and 500 of the Native Infantry. At Nefiché 50 of the West Kent Regiment, 150 of the Native Infantry, and one troop of 19th Hussars. At Mahuta 100 of the West Kent Regiment, 50 of the Native Infantry, and one troop of the 19th Hussars. At Mahsameh 100 of the West Kent Regiment, and one troop of the 19th Hussars. At Kassassin 200 of the West Kent Regiment, and the 24th and 26th Companies of the Royal Engineers. This left available for the forward movement, 11,000 Infantry, 2000 Cavalry, and 60 guns.*

Reconnaissances were made daily in the direction of Tel-el-Kebir, but serious engagements were forbidden. On the occasion of one of these reconnaissances, Colonel Buller, V.C., of the Intelligence Department, managed to get round the enemy's flank as far as El Karaim, and to ascertain that his outposts at night were withdrawn to very near the trenches.

At 5 p.m. on the 12th, the men's knapsacks and all

* The following table gives the disposition and enumeration of the Egyptian forces at this time.

Place.	In command.	Infantry.		Artillery.		Cavalry.		Irregulars and Bedouins.	Total.
		Regiments.	Men.	Guns.	Men.	Regiments.	Men.		
Tel-el-Kebir	Arabi Pasha, Ali Rubi Pasha	8	24,000	60	1000	2	1000	2500	38,500
Kafr Dowar	Toulba Pasha	2	6000	40	800	...	...	6000	12,800
Mariout	Halil Khamil	...	...	18	350	...	200	5000	5500
Aboukir and Rosetta	Khoutshid Pasha	3	9000	18	350	...	200	5000	14,550
Salahieh	Mahmoud Sami Pasha	...	...	12	200	...	...	5000	5200
Damietta	Abdul Al Pasha	2	5500	...	...	...	...	...	5500
Cairo	...	4	12,000	...	...	...	...	...	12,000

Total regulars, say 60,000; total irregulars, say 34,000; grand total, about 94,000 men.

baggage were stacked alongside the railway. After sunset no bugles were allowed to be sounded. After dark all the tents were struck and piled near the railway. The camp was left in charge of General Nugent, Royal Engineers. The camp fires were left burning. The troops formed in order of battle. The batteries of artillery were all placed by 10 p.m., and the other corps formed on them. The men then rested on their arms waiting for the word to advance. At half-past one on the 13th, the famous march on Tel-el-Kebir was begun.

Tel-el-Kebir, signifying in Arabic 'the great mound,' is the name of a peaceful Arab village on the south side of the railway leading from Ismailia to Cairo, and on the banks of the Fresh Water Canal. On the opposite side of the railway and canal stands the 'mound,' an elevation of considerable height, near which Arabi had for some weeks past been entrenching his forces.

Tel-el-Kebir had for many years past been used as a military station and camp, and it was here that Arabi had been exiled with his mutinous regiment in the autumn of 1881.

The position selected by the Egyptians for a final stand was by nature the strongest it was possible to find in that flat section of country.* Near the station of Tel-el-Kebir there is a general and gradual rise of the ground towards the west, culminating in a range of hills that stretch from a point on the railway about a mile and a half east of the station, northward to Salahieh. Roughly parallel to the Fresh Water Canal is a second series of hills intersecting the first about two miles

---

* Tel-el-Kebir and Kafr Dowar are the two great strategical points to be held in defending Lower Egypt. This will at once be seen on referring to a map of the Delta.

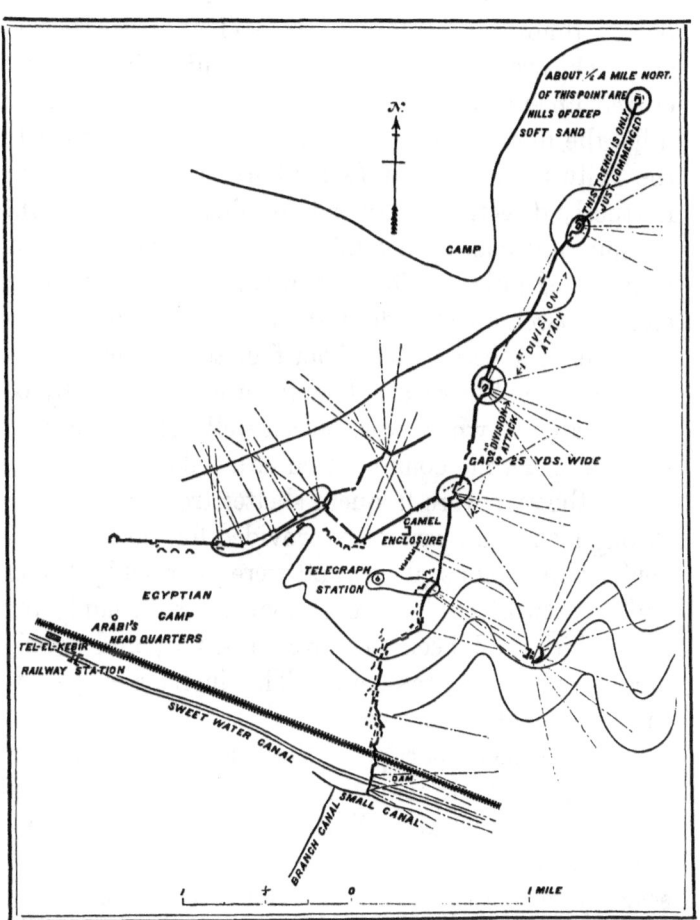

THE LINES OF TEL-EL-KEBIR.

distant from the railway. Viewed from the railway, this east and west range appears as a moderate hill. Its real character, however, is that of a table-land sloping away to the northward with a rather steep descent towards the south. The ground is generally even, and barren almost to desolation, the soil consisting of sand and rock, producing only a small scrub. The Egyptian entrenchments were laid out along the crests of these hills, the lines running north and south, starting from the railway and canal (see plan), and running in a northerly direction for over two miles beyond the intersection, and making a total frontage to the eastward of nearly four miles. The plan included a dry ditch from eight to twelve feet wide, and from five to nine feet deep, in front of a breastwork from four to six feet high with a 'banquette' in rear. The trace was broken by occasional salients, where were placed well-designed redoubts, possessing a wide command on either flank.

In the rear were frequent shelter trenches. Passages through the parapet were provided for field-pieces and vehicles in various places, and were guarded by traverses and breastworks. The revetment differed mainly in the care which had been bestowed upon it, and consisted mostly of reeds, grass, &c. The interior slopes were the only ones thus treated.

The southern portion of the defences was practically completed at the time of the battle. Here the revetment was neatly finished. Work was in progress on the northern and western lines, their extremities being scarcely more than laid out. The extent of these defensive works, which was enormous in comparison with the number of troops at Arabi's disposal, would seem to imply an inordinate reliance upon mere ditches and breastworks to keep out an enemy however vigorous. It led as a necessary consequence to the excessive spreading out of the defenders, and the fatal weakening of the force which could be gathered at any given point. Had the same amount of labour been expended in several concentric lines it would have resulted in a position of great strength, permitting the retiring, if necessary, from one line to the next, and an almost indefinite prolongation of the fight.

The batteries were along the front, and were thus distributed at the southern end of the line. There were two well-built redoubts, mounting each three guns, on either bank of the Canal. Connecting the two, and stopping the flow of water in the Fresh Water Canal, was a stout dam. On each side of the railway was one gun.

In front of the lines running north and south, and distant about 1100 yards, was a formidable outwork standing on rising ground. This was a polygonal redoubt, and mounted six guns. In the rear of this redoubt and on the lines was a 4-gun battery, behind which was a look-out and telegraph station, the wire running back to Arabi's head-quarters near the railway station, and in the midst of a large camp. The diminished size of the ditch from this point northwards is very noticeable. The attack was evidently hoped for at and near the railway.

Following the lines in a northerly direction, the next battery is at the intersection of the two lines of entrenchments. This was the most elaborately finished of all the redoubts, and mounted five guns. Still further in the same direction was another formidable battery of five guns.* Beyond this there were two other incomplete redoubts, further still to the northward, but this part of the line was hardly begun.

* This was turned by the Highlanders, who passed to the south.

As regards the east and west line, intersecting the lines running north and south, its object was to afford a defence in the event of the enemy succeeding in breaking through those lines at the northern end, their weakest part.*

To the eastward of the lines and in the direction of Kassassin was a desert of tolerably level smooth sand and pebble, without cover of any kind.

The account of the battle of Tel-el-Kebir, contained in Sir Garnet Wolseley's report, is as follows. The omitted paragraphs relate to events subsequent to the action, and are quoted elsewhere :—

'Cairo, September 16.

'Sir,

'I have already had the honour of reporting by telegraph to you that I attacked the entrenched position of Tel-el-Kebir a little before sunrise on the morning of the 13th instant, completely defeating the enemy with very great loss, and capturing fifty field-guns, vast quantities of ammunition, military stores, and supplies of all sorts.

*   *   *   *   *

'From the daily reconnaissance of the position at Tel-el-Kebir made from our camp at Kassassin, especially from the good view I obtained of the enemy's works on the 9th instant when our troops drove back within their entrenchments the force of thirteen battalions five squadrons, and eighteen guns that had attacked our camp in the morning, it was evident their works were of great extent and of a formidable character. All the information obtained from spies and prisoners led me to believe that the enemy's force at Tel-el-Kebir consisted of from sixty to seventy horsed guns, which were mostly distributed along their line of works, of two Infantry divisions (twenty-four battalions) of about 20,000 men, and three regiments of Cavalry, together with about 6000 Bedouins and Irregulars, besides a force of about 5000 men, with twenty-four guns, at Salahieh,† all under the immediate command of Arabi Pasha. I have since been able to verify these numbers, which are certainly not overstated, except as regards the number of guns at Tel-el-Kebir. which I believe to have been fifty-nine, the number we took in the works and during the pursuit.

---

* This work was absolutely useless in the battle, being taken by the Highlanders in the rear and by the 2nd Brigade in the flanks.
† 25,000 rations were served out to the Egyptian Army on the 12th September.

'Owing to the numerous detachments I was obliged to make for the defence of my long line of communication from Suez to Ismailia and thence on to Kassassin, and owing to the losses incurred in previous actions, I could only place in line about 11,000 bayonets, 2000 sabres, and sixty field-guns.

'The enemy's position was a strong one; there was no cover of any kind in the desert lying between my camp at Kassassin and the enemy's works north of the Canal. These works extended from a point on the Canal $1\frac{1}{2}$ miles east of the railway station of Tel-el-Kebir for a distance, almost due north, of about $3\frac{1}{2}$ miles.

'The general character of the ground which forms the northern boundary of the valley, through which the Ismailia Canal and railway run, is that of gently undulating and rounded slopes, which rise gradually to a fine open plateau from 90 to 100 feet above the valley. The southern extremity of this plateau is about a mile from the railway, and is nearly parallel to it. To have marched over this plateau upon the enemy's position by daylight our troops would have had to advance over a glacis-like slope in full view of the enemy, and under the fire of his well-served artillery, for about five miles. Such an operation would have entailed enormous loss from an enemy with men and guns well protected by entrenchments from any artillery fire we could have brought to bear upon them. To have turned the enemy's position either by the right or left was an operation that would have entailed a very wide turning movement, and therefore a long, difficult, and fatiguing march, and what is of more importance, it would not have accomplished the object I had in view, namely, to grapple with the enemy at such close quarters that he should not be able to shake himself free from our clutches except by a general fight of all his army.

'I wished to make the battle a final one; whereas a wide turning movement would probably have only forced him to retreat, and would have left him free to have moved his troops in good order to some other position further back. My desire was to fight him decisively where he was, in the open desert, before he could retire to take up fresh positions more difficult of access in the cultivated country in his rear. That cultivated country is practically impassable to a regular army, being irrigated and cut up in every direction by deep canals. I had ascertained by frequent reconnaissance that the enemy did not push his outposts far beyond his works at night, and I had good reason for believing that he then kept a very bad look-out. These circumstances, and the very great reliance I had in the steadiness of our splendid Infantry, determined me to resort to the extremely difficult operation of a night march, to be followed by an attack before daybreak on the enemy's position; the result was all I could have wished for. At dawn on the morning of the 12th instant, accompanied by all the Generals and Brigadiers, I inspected the enemy's works and explained to them my intended plan of attack, and gave to each a sketch showing the formation in which it was to be effected. As soon as it was dark, on the evening of the 12th instant, I struck my camp at Kassassin, and the troops moved into position near "Ninth Hill," where they bivouacked. No fires allowed, even smoking was prohibited, and all were ordered to maintain the utmost silence throughout the night's operations. At 1.30 a.m., on the morning of the 13th instant I gave the order for the advance of the 1st and 2nd Divisions simultaneously. The night was very dark and it was difficult to maintain the desired formation, but, by means of connecting files between the battalions and brigades, and between the first and second lines, and through the untiring exertions of the Generals and the Officers of the Staff generally, this difficulty was effectually overcome.

'The Indian Contingent,* under Major-General Sir H. Macpherson, and the Naval Brigade, under Captain Fitz-Roy, R.N., did not move until 2.30 a.m. To have moved them earlier would have given the alarm to the enemy, owing to the number of villages in the cultivated land south of the Canal. Telegraphic communication by means of an insulated wire was kept up through Kassassin all through the night between the Indian Contingent on the south of the Canal and the Royal Marine Artillery, with which I moved in rear of the 2nd Division.

'In moving over the desert at night there are no landmarks to guide one's movements; we had, consequently, to direct our course by the stars. This was well and correctly effected, and the leading brigades of each division both reached the enemy's works within a couple of minutes of one another.

'The enemy were completely surprised, and it was not until one or two of their advanced sentries fired their rifles that they realised our close proximity to their works. These were, however, very quickly lined with their Infantry, who opened a deafening musketry fire, and their guns came into action immediately. Our troops advanced steadily without firing a shot, in obedience to the orders they had received, and when close to the works went straight for them, charging with a ringing cheer. Major-General Graham reports, "The steadiness of the advance of the 2nd Brigade† under what appeared to be an overwhelming fire of musketry and artillery will remain a proud remembrance."

'The 2nd Brigade was well supported by the Brigade of Guards, under H.R.H. the Duke of Connaught. On the left the Highland Brigade,‡ under Major-General Sir A. Alison, had reached the works

---

* 7—1 Royal Artillery (mountain battery), 1st Battalion Seaforth Highlanders, 3rd Battalion Native Infantry, made up of detachments of 7th Bengal Native Infantry, 20th Punjaub Infantry, and 29th Beloochees.

† 2nd Battalion Royal Irish Regiment, Royal Marine Light Infantry, 2nd Battalion York and Lancaster Regiment, 1st Battalion Royal Irish Fusiliers.

‡ 1st Battalion Royal Highlanders, 1st Battalion Gordon Highlanders, 1st Battalion Cameron Highlanders, 2nd Battalion Highland Light Infantry.

a few minutes before the 2nd Brigade had done so, and in a dashing manner stormed them at the point of the bayonet without firing a shot until within the enemy's lines. They were well supported by the Duke of Cornwall's Light Infantry and the 3rd Royal Rifles, both under the command of Colonel Ashburnham of the last-named corps. In the centre, between these two attacks, marched seven batteries of Artillery, deployed into one line, under the command of Brigadier-General Goodenough; and, after the capture of the enemy's works, several of these batteries did good service, and inflicted considerable loss upon the enemy, in some instances firing canister at short ranges. On the extreme left the Indian Contingent and the Naval Brigade, under the command of Major-General Sir H. Macpherson, V.C., advanced steadily and in silence, the Seaforth Highlanders leading, until an advanced battery of the enemy was reached, when it was most gallantly stormed by the Highlanders, supported by the Native Infantry battalions. The squadron of the 6th Bengal Cavalry, attached temporarily to General Macpherson, did good service in pursuing the enemy through the village of Tel-el-Kebir.

‘The Indian Contingent scarcely lost a man—a happy circumstance, which I attribute to the excellent arrangements made by Major-General Macpherson, and to the fact that, starting one hour later than the 1st and 2nd Divisions, the resistance of the enemy was so shaken by the earlier attacks north of the Canal, that he soon gave way before the impetuous onslaught of the Seaforth Highlanders. The Cavalry Division, on the extreme right of the line, swept round the northern extremity of the enemy's works, charging the enemy's troops as they endeavoured to escape; most of the enemy, however, threw away their arms, and, begging for mercy, were unmolested by our men. To have made them prisoners would have taken up too much time, the Cavalry being required for the more important work of pushing on to Cairo.

‘Such is the general outline of the battle of Tel-el-Kebir. All the previous actions of this short campaign were chiefly Cavalry and Artillery affairs, but that of the 13th instant was essentially an Infantry battle, and was one that, from the time we started at 1.30 a.m. until nearly six a.m., when it was practically over, was peculiarly calculated to test, in the most crucial manner, the quality of the fighting discipline of our Infantry. I do not believe that at any previous period of our military history has the British Infantry distinguished itself more than upon this occasion. I have heard it said of our present Infantry regiments that the men are too young, and their training for manœuvring and for fighting, and their powers of endurance, are not sufficient for the requirements of modern war. After a trial of an exceptionally severe kind, both in movement and in attack, I can say emphatically that I never wish to have under my orders better infantry battalions than those whom I am proud to have commanded at Tel-el-Kebir.

'Our casualties have been numerous, but not so many as I had anticipated. Her Majesty has to deplore the loss of many gallant men, who died as became the soldiers of an army that is proud of the glorious traditions it has inherited.

'It would be impossible in this despatch to bring to your notice the services of those officers whom I consider especially worthy of mention. I shall do so in a subsequent despatch; but I cannot close this without placing on record how much I am indebted to the following officers who took part in the battle of Tel-el-Kebir, and who, by their zeal and ability, contributed so largely to its success:—General Sir John Adye, K.C.B., Chief of the Staff; Lieut.-Generals Willis and Sir E. Hamley; Major-Generals Sir A. Alison, H.R.H. the Duke of Connaught, Drury-Lowe, Sir H. Macpherson, and Graham; Brigadier-Generals Goodenough, R.A., Sir Baker Russell, the Hon. J. Dormer; Deputy Adjutant-General Tanner and Colonel Ashburnham, who temporarily commanded a brigade during the action; and to Captain Fitz-Roy, who commanded the Naval Brigade.

'Brigadier-General Nugent, R.E., remained during the action in command of the staff left at Kassassin, to cover the rear of the army operating in his immediate front, and to protect that position, with all its stores and depôts from any possible attack from the enemy's force at Salahieh. He rejoined me in the evening at Tel-el-Kebir, having carried out the orders he had received.

'The medical arrangements were all they should have been, and reflect the highest credit upon Surgeon-General Hanbury. In the removal of the wounded on the 13th and 14th instants to Ismailia the Canal boat service, worked by the Royal Navy under Commander Moore, R.N., did most excellent work, and the army is deeply indebted to that officer and to those under his command for the aid he afforded the wounded, and for the satisfactory manner in which he moved a large number of them by water to Ismailia.

'No exertion has been spared on the part of Major-General Earle, commanding the line of communications, and of Commissary-General Morris, to supply all the wants of this army during its advance from Ismailia. To the Head-Quarter Staff, and the officers composing the Staff of each division, my best thanks are due for the able manner in which they performed their duty.

'In conclusion, I wish to express my deep sense of the high military spirit displayed throughout the battle of Tel-el-Kebir, and during all our previous engagements, by commanding officers, by all regimental officers, and by every non-commissioned officer and private now serving in Egypt. I have also the honour to enclose a roll of the casualties which occurred at the battle of Tel-el-Kebir.

'Major George FitzGeorge, 20th Hussars, the senior member of my personal Staff, is the bearer of this despatch, and I have the honour to recommend him to your favourable consideration.

'I have, &c.,
'G. J. WOLSELEY, General.'

'The following is a summary of the killed, wounded, and missing, in the action at Tel-el-Kebir on the 13th September, 1882 :—

'Staff, Army Corps—One officer wounded.

'Staff, 1st Division—One officer wounded.

'2nd Battalion Grenadier Guards—One non-commissioned officer and man killed, one officer and nine non-commissioned officers and men wounded.

'2nd Battalion Coldstream Guards—One officer and seven non-commissioned officers and men wounded.

'1st Battalion Scots Guards—Four non-commissioned officers and men wounded.

'2nd Battalion Royal Irish Regiment—One officer and one non-commissioned officer and man killed, two officers and seventeen non-commissioned officers and men wounded.

'Royal Marine Light Infantry—Two officers and three non-commissioned officers and men killed, one officer and fifty-three non-commissioned officers and men wounded.

'2nd Battalion York and Lancaster—Twelve non-commissioned officers and men wounded.

'1st Battalion Royal Irish Fusiliers—Two non-commissioned officers and men killed, thirty-four non-commissioned officers and men wounded, three non-commissioned officers and men missing.

'19th Hussars—One officer wounded.

'2nd Battalion Duke of Cornwall's Light Infantry—One officer and five non-commissioned officers and men wounded.

'Royal Artillery—Two officers and seventeen non-commissioned officers and men wounded.

'1st Battalion Royal Highlanders—Two officers and seven non-commissioned officers and men killed, six officers and thirty-seven non-commissioned officers and men wounded, four non-commissioned officers and men missing.

'1st Battalion Gordon Highlanders—One officer and five non-commissioned officers and men killed, one officer and twenty-nine non-commissioned officers and men wounded, four non-commissioned officers and men missing.

'1st Battalion Cameron Highlanders—Thirteen non-commissioned officers and men killed, three officers and forty-five non-commissioned officers and men wounded.

'2nd Battalion Highland Light Infantry—Three officers and fourteen non-commissioned officers and men killed, five officers and fifty-two non-commissioned officers and men wounded, eleven non-commissioned officers and men missing.*

'3rd Battalion King's Royal Rifles—Twenty non-commissioned officers and men wounded.

'1st Battalion Seaforth Highlanders—One non-commissioned officer and man killed, three non-commissioned officers and men wounded.

'Native Troops—One non-commissioned officer and man killed, nine non-commissioned officers and men wounded.

'Chaplains—One wounded.

'Total—Nine officers and forty-eight non-commissioned officers and men killed, twenty-seven officers and 353 non-commissioned officers and men wounded, twenty-two non-commissioned officers and men missing. Grand total of casualties, all ranks, 459.

'List of officers killed in the action at Tel-el-Kebir on the 13th September, 1882 :—

'2nd Battalion Connaught Rangers (attached to 2nd Battalion Royal Irish Regiment)—Captain C. N. Jones. Royal Marine Light Infantry—Major H. H. Strong, Captain C. J. Wardell. 1st Battalion Royal Highlanders—Lieutenant Graham Stirling, Lieutenant J. G. McNeill. 1st Battalion Gordon Highlanders—Lieutenant H. G. Brooks. 2nd Battalion Highland Light Infantry—Major Colville, Lieutenant D. S. Kays, Lieutenant L. Somervelle.

'List of officers wounded in the action at Tel-el-Kebir on the 13th September, 1882 :—

'Staff, Head-quarters—Lieutenant Wyatt Rawson, Royal Navy. Army Corps Staff, First Division—Lieut.-General G. H. S. Willis, C.B. 2nd Battalion Grenadier Guards—Lieut.-Colonel R. Balfour, severely. 2nd Battalion Coldstream Guards—Lieut.-Colonel G. B. Sterling, slightly. 2nd Battalion Royal Irish Regiment—Lieutenant A. G. Chichester, severely. 2nd Royal Fusiliers (attached to Royal Irish)—Lieutenant H. H. Drummond-Wolff, severely. Royal Marine Light Infantry—Lieutenant E. McCausland, severely. 19th Hussars—Lieutenant D. Barclay, slightly. 2nd Battalion Duke of Cornwall's Light Infantry—Lieut.-Colonel W. S. Richardson, severely. 1st Battalion Royal Highlanders—Captain R. C. Coveney, Captain G. B. Cumberland, severely; Captain G. M. Fox, Lieutenant J. A. Park (since dead), Lieutenant Livingstone, Captain F. L. Speid. 1st Battalion Gordon Highlanders—Lieutenant A. G. Pirie, slightly. 1st Battalion Cameron Highlanders—Lieutenant A. G. Blackburn, severely; Lieutenant H. H. L. Malcolm. 2nd Battalion Sutherland Highlanders (attached to Cameron Highlanders) — Lieutenant S. Macdougall, slightly. 2nd Battalion Highland Light Infantry—Lieutenant R. F. M.

* This should have been nineteen non-commissioned officers and men killed and six missing.

Synge, slightly; Lieutenant A. R. Heneage, slightly; Lieutenant H. Midwood, severely; Lieutenant G. T. J. Carey, severely; Lieutenant W. M. M. Edwards, severely. Staff, Royal Artillery—Lieutenant and Adjutant H. V. Covan, severely. F 1 Royal Artillery—Captain H. S. Dalbaic, severely. Chaplain—Rev. J. Bellord, slightly.

The fulness of Sir Garnet Wolseley's official report renders it unnecessary to add much in the way of details of the battle.

The night march was, of course, the great feature of the attack. It offered many advantages; not only was the attacking force able to avoid (as Sir Garnet says) having 'to advance over a glacis-like slope, in full view of the enemy, and under fire of his well-served artillery for about five miles;' but also it was able to avoid the heat of the day-time in one of the hottest months in the Egyptian year, and further to have a period of fourteen hours light for pursuit of the defeated army.

The action, it must be admitted, was a short one, barely twenty minutes elapsing between the time when the enemy opened fire and his being in full retreat. Into those twenty minutes, however, was crowded a great deal of hard fighting, as the loss on both sides clearly shows.

It is much the fashion to describe Tel-el-Kebir as a surprise. It is so called in Sir Garnet Wolseley's despatch, and to a certain extent it was a surprise, as the Egyptians in all probability never expected a night attack.* At the same time there is no doubt that they knew the British army was in their immediate vicinity, and might come on at any moment, and took precautions accordingly. As a fact they lay down with their arms, and slept behind the earthworks on the night of the

* Arabi subsequently told the late Morice Bey (who conducted him as a prisoner to Ceylon) that at the time of the attack he was in bed, and the English did not leave him time enough to get his boots on.

12th. The best proof of this is the blaze of fire with which both the Second Brigade and the Highland Brigade were received. Prisoners taken afterwards stated that the striking of the tents at sunset was observed, and that pickets were on the watch ever since. Anyhow, the English forces, before they closed with the enemy, were subjected to a perfect hail of bullets.

Sir Edward Hamley, relating the attack of the 2nd Division, writes as follows:—

'Yet a minute or two elapsed after the Egyptian bugle was blown, and then the whole extent of entrenchment in our front hitherto unseen and unknown poured forth a stream of rifle-fire.

'The Egyptian Infantry,' writes one witness, 'clustered thickly in the parapets of the redoubts, and fired down the slopes into the trenches. Hundreds of them, lying down, plied the heads of the advancing brigades with fire.'

An officer of the 46th, Duke of Cornwall's regiment, writing on this part of the attack, says:—

'Suddenly we heard a shot fired; then silence—then a few straggling shots, and it struck us that we were yet some distance from the enemy's works, and that their outposts were only just being driven in (I heard afterwards that some Bedouins had actually run through the 18th Regiment, who were on the right of the works, and that they had given the alarm to the Egyptian Camp). What was our surprise when about 500 yards off, while we were yet marching in quarter column, a long unbroken line of flame issued from the dimly visible works; it was three minutes to five when we saw this, and having quickly extended for attack we lay down. Everybody had orders not to load, and consequently the enemy received no answer to their fire. For three or four minutes this fearful fire continued.'

A curious circumstance occurred with regard to the polygonal redoubt already described as standing 1100 yards in advance of the lines. This was missed by the attacking forces, who must have passed within 200 yards of the work. It is partly accounted for, however, by the prevailing darkness, and partly by the fact, that the gunners in the redoubt, either asleep or unprepared, let the Highland Brigade march past them to the lines without firing a shot. It was only when day broke that the Egyptian artillerymen called attention to the existence of the redoubt by aiming their guns and firing at the spot where Sir Garnet Wolseley and his staff were assembled. This was too much, and the British artillery had to be sent for. After being under case and shrapnel fire for a short time, what were left of the garrison threw down their arms and formed a stream of fugitives which, with ghastly wounds, poured out from the redoubt, and scattered over the country.*

The missing of this redoubt was one of the lucky incidents of the fight. Had the advancing column been aware of its existence they must have paused to take it before storming the lines. In attacking the redoubt the position of the advancing force would have been at once revealed to the enemy, and the fire which was reserved for some minutes later would have at once opened.

The Egyptian guns were 8-centimètre and -centimètre Krupp steel B. L. R. of the old pattern (1868), all mounted on field-carriages. The small-arms were all Remington breech-loaders. The supply of ammunition was practically inexhaustible. At intervals of every three or four yards were found open boxes each containing 1050 cartridges.

The trenches, after the battle, were found to be filled with dead, mostly bayoneted, and the ground in rear as far as the railway station was dotted with the bodies of those shot down in retreat. The British cavalry sweeping around the northern end of the entrenchments, cut down the fugitives by scores, until it became evident that the rout was complete. Most of the bodies were

---

* A Naval Officer who visited the redoubt the following day described it as a perfect 'charnel-house.'

observed to be lying on their backs, as if the men had stopped to have a parting shot at their pursuers.

The Egyptian loss in killed was not far from 2000. There was no return of their wounded, the army organization having disappeared; but 534 were treated at Tel-el-Kebir, during the four days succeeding the battle, twenty-seven capital operations being performed. Of the wounded, 202 were soon able to go to their homes, whilst the remainder were sent to Cairo in charge of Egyptian surgeons. The British medical authorities did all in their power to alleviate the sufferings of these poor creatures, and furnished tins of meat, bottles of brandy, and skins of water to the railway trucks conveying them away. The greater number, who were slightly wounded, managed to get away to the neighbouring villages, and therefore are not counted in the figures above given.* It is stated—and the statement appears credible—that very few superior officers were killed or wounded; and Arabi and his second in command were undoubtedly the first to escape. Arabi himself mounted his horse and rode rapidly towards Belbeis. There appears to be no doubt that proper leaders, in every sense of the word, were wanting in the Egyptian army. It has been both humorously and truthfully remarked that each officer knew that he would run, but hoped his *neighbour* would stay.

The Egyptian soldiers, on the other hand, displayed real courage, as the desperate struggles in the trenches and their heavy loss in killed abundantly prove. The black regiments, composed of Negroes from the Soudan, were especially noticeable for their pluck, fighting bravely

---

* Dr. Shaw, of the Royal Marines, whilst attending one of the Egyptian wounded, happening to turn aside for a moment was shot at by his patient. This ingratitude was too much for the Doctor's Orderly, who, with a bayonet, at once despatched the assailant.

hand to hand with their assailants. It has been well observed that more intelligence and less downright cowardice on the part of their officers might have converted these men into a formidable army.

In the previous encounters between the English and the Egyptians, the artillery and cavalry had borne the brunt of the fighting, and had carried off the honours, but the battle of Tel-el-Kebir was, as Sir Garnet Wolseley states, an infantry action. The tactics employed, a direct assault without flank movements of any kind, were of the simplest description. The object, to get to close quarters with the enemy, and to crush him, was accomplished.

After the attack, Arabi's army ceased to exist. In scattered groups it might be found all over Egypt, but as an organization, it may be said to have been annihilated.

In view of the complete success of Sir Garnet Wolseley's tactics, comment is superfluous. It has been said by competent critics that the mode of attack adopted was rash to the degree of imprudence; that no Commander would dare to employ such tactics against a European foe, and that a night march of nine miles could only be followed by an immediate and successful assault under circumstances so exceptional as to be providential. He has been blamed for having left his camp with his forces so early as seven in the evening on the 12th, and having halted half way from Tel-el-Kebir, and then only after midnight having set out again, a manœuvre which might have endangered the whole result of the movement, and which, perhaps, may account, for the surprise of the enemy's position not being so successful as it might have been.

Again, it has been said that besides a front attack, there should also have been a flank one, in conformity with modern tactics.

In reply to these and other criticisms it may be sufficient to observe that the English Commander-in-Chief formed a just appreciation of his enemy; had a strong conviction as to the proper manner of engaging him; and had unbounded confidence in the officers and men under his own command. What Sir Garnet Wolseley would have done had the enemy been of a different character is another question, the consideration of which does not come within the scope of the present work. The means adopted were exactly adjusted to the end to be attained, and the justification (if any were needed) for the risks run lies in the success which attended them.

CHAPTER XXXIX.

CAPTURE OF CAIRO.

Retreat of the Egyptian Army—Flight of Arabi—His plan for destroying Cairo—The Pursuit—Sir Garnet Wolseley's Despatch—The March to Cairo—The Surrender of Abbassieh—The Surrender of the Citadel—Sir Drury-Lowe and Sir Garnet Wolseley—Arabi's Account of the Battle and his Surrender—Telegrams exchanged between Arabi Mahmoud Sami and Abdel-el-al.

WHEN the Egyptian regiments, mingled together in one wild and disorderly mass, once commenced their retreat no chance of rallying was for a moment given them. The cannon in the redoubts were turned against their former occupants, and the guns of the Royal Artillery rained shrapnel shell on the fugitives. The cavalry sweeping round from the north and charging in amongst them completed the rout. The Egyptians threw down their arms and scattered themselves across the country. Arabi himself with a few of his chief officers caught the train at Belbeis, and got to Cairo the same day, where he quickly began preparations for the destruction of the city.*

No time was lost in reaping the fruits of the morning's work. Advances were at once ordered in two directions, the one along the railway to the important railway centre of Zag-a-zig, whence a double-tracked railway proceeds to Cairo *viâ* Benha, and a single line of

---

* Arabi drew up an elaborate plan for the repetition of the Alexandria outrages. According to this scheme Cairo was divided into a number of districts, and fire was to be applied simultaneously to certain houses indicated. This was to take place after the morning prayer on the 15th, the very day after the city was taken by General Drury-Lowe's force.

rails *viâ* Belbeis ; the other road was along the Ismailieh or Sweet Water Canal to Cairo. Of these movements General Wolseley speaks in his report of September 16th in the following terms :—

'The enemy were pursued to Zag-a-zig, 25 miles from our camp at Kassassin, by the Indian Contingent, the leading detachment of which reached that place, under Major-General Sir H. Macpherson, V. C., a little after 4 p.m., and by the Cavalry Division, under General Lowe, to Belbeis, which was occupied in the evening. Major-General Lowe was ordered to push on with all possible speed to Cairo, as I was most anxious to save that city from the fate which befell Alexandria in July last. These orders were ably carried out, General Lowe reaching the great barracks of Abbassieh, just outside of Cairo, at 4.45 p.m. on the 14th instant. The Cavalry marched sixty-five miles in these two days. The garrison, of about 10,000 men, summoned to surrender by Lieutenant-Colonel H. Stewart, Assistant Adjutant-General to the Cavalry Division, laid down their arms, and our troops took possession of the Citadel. A message was sent to Arabi Pasha through the Prefect of the city, calling upon him to surrender forthwith, which he did unconditionally. He was accompanied by Toulba Pasha, who was also one of the leading rebels in arms against the Khedive. The Guards under H. R. H. the Duke of Connaught reached Cairo early on the 15th instant.

'The result of the battle of Tel-el-Kebir has been the entire collapse of the rebellion. The only place that has not, as yet, surrendered is Damietta, and its capture or surrender can be easily effected at our leisure. The men of the rebel army having laid down or thrown away their arms in their flight, have now dispersed to their homes, and the country is so rapidly returning to its ordinary condition of peace that I am able to report the war to be at an end, and that the object for which this portion of Her Majesty's Army was sent to Egypt has been fully accomplished.'

The seizure of Zag-a-zig was effected in the dashing manner peculiar to all the incidents of the day, and shows what may be done by a few bold men. The squadron of the 6th Bengal Cavalry left with the Indian Contingent, led the way, and when within about five miles of the town broke into a gallop. The horses being somewhat fatigued by the hard work of the preceding twenty hours, were not in a condition to keep

CAPTURE OF CAIRO. 333

together, and, as a consequence, the best got to the front and the others dropped to the rear. The advance of the squadron was therefore composed of Major R. M. Jennings, Lieutenant Burns-Murdoch, R.E., and not above half-a-dozen troopers. These pushed right into the railway station, where were five trains filled with soldiers, and seven locomotives. At the sight of this handful of men, the engine-drivers either surrendered or ran away, except one, who began opening his throttle valve and was shot by Lieutenant Burns-Murdoch, while the Egyptian soldiers, hundreds in number, and too demoralised to think of resistance, threw away their arms, left the cars, and ran off as rapidly as possible. By nine p.m. the entire force under General Macpherson had reached Zag-a-zig, not a man having fallen out by the way.

In the other direction similar energy was displayed. The Cavalry Division crossed the Sweet Water Canal at Tel-el-Kebir, and following the Canal bank proceeded with all practicable speed, keeping up a running fight with Arabi's rear-guard. It reached Belbeis that night and bivouacked. Making an early start the next morning (September 14), and leaving the cultivated ground a few miles south of Khankah, to strike across the desert intervening, it reached Cairo at 4.45 p.m.

The following details of the capture of Cairo, as described by an eye-witness who accompanied the British forces, may be of interest.

The sun was setting as the cavalry reached Abbassieh. The men had been in the saddle since daybreak, at which time they had left Belbeis. The men and horses were thoroughly exhausted after their long march under a blazing sun. But suffering from hunger, parched with thirst, and covered with dust as they were, they yet remained equal to the fulfilment of their task.

The garrison of Cairo was divided into two parts; one from 6000 to 7000 strong at Abbassieh; the other, of from 3000 to 4000 men, at the Citadel of Mehemet Ali, situated on a lofty eminence in the city, and strongly fortified. The former, on being summoned by Colonel Stewart, attached to General Drury-Lowe's force, to surrender unconditionally, at once complied. Captain Watson, R.E., was immediately sent on with two squadrons of the 4th Dragoon Guards, and a detachment of the Mounted Infantry, to demand the surrender of the Citadel. No guides were available, but two Egyptian officers, taken prisoners at Abbassieh, were made to show the way, orderlies being told off to shoot them at once in case of treachery. The route taken was round by the Tombs of the Khalifs, outside the walls of Cairo. The city was entered, without opposition, by the gate at the foot of the hill on which the Citadel stands; by this means only a few hundred yards of the native quarter had to be traversed.

It was now dark, such of the inhabitants as were met were perfectly tranquil, and only looked with curiosity at Captain Watson's party. Arrived at the entrance to the Citadel, the Egyptian officer in command was sent for, and he at once agreed to give up possession of the place. The small British force marched in, and took up position in fours between the outer and inner gates. The Egyptian infantry, nearly 4000 in number, with their arms, paraded by regiments in front of the great mosque of Mehemet Ali, inside the inner gate. They were then ordered to lay down their arms and march down to the Kasr-el-Nil Barracks. This they proceeded to do quite quietly, and as they marched out they passed within a few yards of the English force, whose numbers were concealed by the darkness.

CAPTURE OF CAIRO.

As soon as the Egyptian troops had all left the Citadel, the various gates were handed over to Captain Watson's force. The gates were then closed and guards posted. It was now ten o'clock. The troopers were literally dead-beat. But there yet remained the task of taking possession of the fort on the Mokattan Hill, which was occupied by Egyptian troops, and which commanded the Citadel. Captain Watson, anxious to save his men as much as possible, sent one of the Egyptian officers who had acted as a guide, and told him to order the garrison to march down towards Kasr-el-Nil Barracks, and there pile their arms. The officer returned in a couple of hours with the keys of the fort, and informed Captain Watson that his orders had been carried out.

In the dungeons of the Citadel a large number of unfortunate wretches were found in confinement. Some of them were convicts, but several were British subjects. Many of them had been cruelly tortured by the Egyptian 'Bimbashi,' or Major. They now cried out in piteous terms to be set free. Some actually managed to break loose, and fled with their chains clanking round their ankles. They were, however, retaken and assured that as soon as it was light, all their cases should be inquired into, and such as were not convicts should be set free. A sentry was posted over the gate, with orders to shoot any one attempting to escape. One man did make the attempt, and was promptly shot down.*

It only remains to refer to the combination of courage, energy, and tact displayed by Captain Wat-

---

* This man was not killed, but lived to present himself months after as a witness against the 'Bimbashi' at a court-martial, where, with much pride, he showed his then cured wound to the members of the Court. The Bimbashi was sentenced to eight years' imprisonment with hard labour in chains at Mausourah.

son* in thus with a handful of men taking possession of the strongest fortified work in Cairo, held by a force more than a hundred times that of his own. It should be added that the Egyptian officer who gave up the keys of the Mokattan Fort subsequently put in a claim for the war medal!

The vigour shown by General Drury-Lowe in his march on Cairo, and the inestimable results of that movement, together make it one of the most brilliant achievements of the whole campaign.

By the successful attack on Tel-el-Kebir, Sir Garnet Wolseley at one blow crushed the armed rebellion against the authority of the Khedive.

By General Drury-Lowe's successful march, the most beautiful of Oriental cities was saved from destruction, and its European inhabitants from massacre.

So well had Sir Garnet Wolseley matured his plans before entering on the campaign, that he had predicted his arrival in Cairo on the 16th September. As a fact, he arrived a day earlier, that is to say, on the morning of the 15th, when the railway brought him and the Guards to Cairo at the same time.

Arabi's account of Tel-el-Kebir and the subsequent events is as follows :†—

'Before our trenches, &c., were completed, the British forces attacked us suddenly at sunrise, the firing lasting for some time, when suddenly in our rear appeared a division of cavalry and artillery, which caused the flight of the Egyptian troops on Wednesday, the 29th of Shawal, 1299, which day corresponds with the 13th September, 1882.

'After the flight of the troops I left for Belbeis, the English Artillery following close behind me. When I arrived there I met Ali Pasha El Ruby, with whom I went to Insbuz, and thence by train to Cairo.

'In Cairo we found a Council at the Ministry of War, all the Princes being present. After a long discussion, all being confident that England had no intention of annexing Egypt, it was decided to offer no

---

* Captain Watson is now a Brigadier-General in the Egyptian army.
† *Instructions to my Counsel*, 'Nineteenth Century,' December 1882.

CAPTURE OF CAIRO. 337

more resistance, more especially as England was renowned for dealing always towards others with equity and humanity; and we were confident that if the necessary inquiries were instituted, and the feeling of the people generally understood, England would do her utmost to put a stop to all injustice and give back freedom to them.

' For this purpose I sent a telegram on the 14th September to the Commander of the Abbassieh troops, which numbered about 35,000 men, ordering him to hoist a flag of truce and in person to proceed and meet the Commander of the British troops, informing him at the same time that the war was altogether at an end, it being understood that the intention of the British Government was to preserve the country from ruin.*

' The English troops arrived in Cairo at sunset and were met by Riza Pasha and Ibrahim Bey Fawzi, the Prefect of Police. At 1.30 a.m. Ibrahim Bey Fawzi came and informed me that General Lowe desired to have an interview with me at Abbassieh. The same day the officer in charge at Kafr Dowar (Toulba Pasha) came up to Cairo and was summoned with myself to this interview. We thereupon went to General Lowe at his request, and I sent also for Colonel Ali Bey Yusef, who was then at the Citadel. When Sultan (? Toulba) Pasha met General Lowe he asked us whether we were willing to give ourselves as prisoners to the English Government. We thereupon took off our swords and delivered them to General Lowe, who was acting on behalf of the Commander-in-Chief, telling him at the same time that we only gave ourselves up to the English Government because we were confident England would deal with us justly; it being the prayer of humanity and that of our children that England would see us restored to our rights and privileges; and we appealed to him as the representative of the English Government and of all Englishmen. At the same time we informed the General that we had at Abbassieh 35,000 men (*sic*) and a similar number at Kafr Dowar, Rasheed (Rosetta), Damietta, and other places, but for the safety and peace of our country we had abandoned all idea of resistance, and had surrendered ourselves, being confident that England had no wish to annex the country. The General agreed with this statement, and we remained with him three days, and then were sent to Abdin, where we were under the surveillance of Colonel Thynne up to the 4th October, and were treated kindly and well.'

The defeat at Tel-el-Kebir is thus depicted by Yacoub Pasha Sami, who was the Under-Secretary of

---

* According to *Arabi Pasha*, by Mr. John Ninet, already quoted, the majority of the Council were in favour of defending Cairo. The Citadel, it was pointed out, was in good repair, and it would be easy to act as the French did at the beginning of the century to put an end to any revolt. Arabi however opposed.

VOL. I.   z

State for War in the insurgent camp, to Abdel-el-al at Damietta. The telegram is given textually:—

'At half-past ten à la turque, in the morning, the enemy attacked the line of entrenchments, and firing commenced on both sides. We caused a large number of the enemy to perish beside the line of entrenchments. I found a train about to leave Tel-el-Kebir, and got in with a few wounded. I know nothing after that, except that on leaving Tel-el-Kebir, I saw that a train had been smashed. Please take the necessary precautions.'

The telegrams which passed between Arabi, Mahmoud Sami, Abdel-el-al, and the telegraph-clerk at Kasr-el-Nil, from a short time after the defeat at Tel-el-Kebir until the occupation of the Capital by the British troops, are amusing.* The complete series which follows commences with a telegram from Mahmoud Sami at Talkha to Arabi at Cairo:—

Mahmoud Sami to Arabi: 'Pardon for not having given you an answer from the station of Abou Kebir (Abou Hamid?), for it is by order of Your Excellency that no answer or news was to be despatched until all the soldiers were mobilised (got together?).'

Arabi to Mahmoud Sami: 'Did the train with the horses and cannons arrive with you?'

Mahmoud Sami to Arabi: 'We have two batteries with their horses. The remainder will arrive when the trains return.'

Arabi to Mahmoud Sami: 'Say where the remainder actually is.'

Mahmoud Sami to Arabi: 'It was in accordance with the first telegram of the Under Secretary for War that the two batteries were transported. The train having left with those two batteries previous to the receipt of your telegrams, I have had to have the remainder of the batteries taken on board (*sic*) to the station of Faccous, and I am occupied in getting them into ten waggons. The two batteries which are not ready will arrive by a train from the station of Salahieh.'

Arabi to Mahmoud Sami: 'The enemy are at Zag-a-zig; they will, perhaps, enter Benha to-night. Cut the road.'

Mahmoud Sami to Arabi: 'It is not possible, by my intermediary, to cut the road, but it will be so by your giving the order to Ahmed Bey Nacif. Command the Chief of the railway traffic to immediately make the trains which are at Damietta, Dessook, and Zifta leave for Talkha in order to transport the soldiers.'

* Abdel-el-al commanded the troops at Damietta.

Arabi to Mahmoud Sami: 'Where is the fourth train bringing the horses?'

Mahmoud Sami to Arabi: 'I do not know the spot where the fourth train actually is; I am endeavouring to ascertain.'

Arabi to Mahmoud Sami: 'How many trains have arrived with you at Talkha?'

Mahmoud Sami to Arabi: 'Four trains arrived with me at Mansoorah. I am doing what is necessary to unload them and to send them back to fetch the remainder of the troops. I am awaiting your reply as what you wish done.'

Arabi to Mahmoud Sami: 'Send immediately all the trains to Cairo by the road of Boolak-el-Dacroor.'

Mahmoud Sami to Arabi: 'Ask Ahmed Bey Nachid, engineer, if you think it right, if he can inundate the land round Khalioub and Charkieh by cutting the dykes of Charkieh and the Ismailia Canal, so that the enemy can only follow the Khanka road to Cairo.'

Arabi to Mahmoud Sami: 'I am taking the necessary steps to damage the bridge of Chebin-el-Kanatir. I have written to the traffic-manager and to the Mamoor of Markaz-Meina-el Kam.'

Mahmoud Sami to Arabi: 'It is not prudent to delay cutting the railway. The interruption on the line should be enormous, and should extend beyond Meina-el-Kamp and Belbeis. Cut also the dykes of the Canal-el-Charkieh and the Ismailia Canal, so that el-Khalioubieh and el-Charkieh may be inundated before daybreak. All this ought to be done by Marashli Pasha and Ahmed Bey Nachid, engineer, who I believe are at the present moment at Cairo. Tell me your opinion at once.'

Arabi to Mahmoud Sami: 'I have given the necessary orders to cut the dykes of Charkieh and the Canal of Ismailia so that el-Charkieh and el-Khalioub may be inundated.'

Mahmoud Sami to Arabi: 'Cause the railway to be cut for a long distance, if you think it right, in the direction of Meina-el-Kamp near Zag-a-zig and in the vicinity of Belbeis.'

Arabi to Mahmoud Sami: 'I have given orders to that effect.'

Arabi to Mahmoud Sami: 'After the soldiers reach you, send them immediately by the western line by way of Boolak-el-Dacroor. All the soldiers who arrive are to be sent forward to Cairo as they present themselves by the western line viâ Boolak and el-Dacroor.'

Mahmoud Sami to Arabi: 'Can you cut the railway at Meina-el-Kamp as I told you? Answer quick.'

Arabi to Mahmoud Sami: 'I can do so. I am proceeding to do it.'

Here the conversation between Arabi and Mahmoud Sami comes to an abrupt termination, probably by reason of the arrival of the British troops and the seizure of the telegraph apparatus. The conversation which passed between Arabi and Abdel-el-al and between Abdel-el-al and the telegraph clerk at Kasr-el-Nil at the time Arabi gave himself up to the English, is as follows:—

From Arabi at Cairo to Abdel-el-al at Damietta: 'Send immediately a battalion to Cairo by way of Boolak-el-Dacroor in order to meet the enemy before their arrival.'

Abdel-el-al to Arabi: 'The battalion is ready. It will leave at once viâ Boolak and El-Dacroor.'

Abdel-el-al to Arabi: 'What has happened to the direct line?'

Arabi to Abdel-el-al: 'The enemy are at Zag-a-zig and will, perhaps, interrupt the direct line.'

Abdel-el-al to Arabi: 'At what point is our army now?'

Arabi to Abdel-el-al: 'I do not know where our soldiers went after being dispersed at Tel-el-Kebir. Please enquire at Talkha in regard to that.'

From Abdel-el-al's Mouawin (Police Officer) at Cairo to Abdel-el-al at Damietta: 'I am now at Kasr-el-Nil. To-morrow I shall be with you. Give orders to bring the family to Cairo by way of Boolak-el-Dacroor.'

From Nedin at Cairo to Abdel-el-al at Damietta: 'We are awaiting the arrival of the family at the Boolak-el-Dacroor station.'

Abdel-el-al to Arabi (dated 14th September): 'Where is the enemy now?'

Arabi to Abdel-el-al: 'I do not know what position they occupy, for the Zag-a-zig telegraph line does not answer. It is best to communicate with Mansoorah and obtain information as to the spot where our soldiers are, and send them me viâ Boolak-el-Dacroor.'

It is highly amusing to hear of Arabi inquiring about his soldiers after his flight from the battle-field. The soldiers at that time had had quite enough of Arabi and the military party, and were quietly returning to their villages.

Abdel-el-al answers Arabi in amazement: 'Have you not yet been able to ascertain where our dispersed soldiers are?'

Arabi to Abdel-el-al: 'I have not yet been able to ascertain where they are. Take the necessary steps to find out their position.'

Abdel-el-al to Ibrahim Bey Fauzi, first mouawin at the Ministry of War: 'Be ready in front of the telegraph-instrument so as to speak with us.'

Arabi and Toulba at Kasr-el-Nil to Abdel-el-al at Damietta: 'We

CAPTURE OF CAIRO. 341

happen to be at the Telegraph Office. Let us know what it is you want.'

Abdel-el-al to Arabi and Toulba: 'Tell me what has occurred up to now.'

Telegraph Clerk at Kasr-el-Nil to Abdel-el-al: 'Ibrahim Bey Fauzi has arrived at the office and has gone out in company with the Minister* and Toulba. They are conversing together and will return immediately.'

Abdel-el-al to the Telegraph Clerk: 'Make them come at once for an important question.'

Telegraph Clerk to Abdel-el-al: 'The four (three?) are now deliberating together. No one can call them. They will have finished immediately and will come.'

Abdel-el-al to the Telegraph Clerk: 'Call them at once.'

The Telegraph Clerk to Abdel-el-al: 'The Minister of War and Toulba Pasha have gone to Abbassieh in compliance with the summons of the Commander of the British Cavalry.'

Abdel-el-al to the Telegraph Clerk: 'Where is the Commander of the British Cavalry?'

Telegraph Clerk to Abdel-el-al: 'He is at Abbassieh with his men.'

Abdel-el-al to Telegraph Clerk: 'Did no one oppose his entry to Abbassieh?'

Telegraph Clerk to Abdel-el-al: 'No one opposed his entry. They flew the white flag.'

Abdel-el-al to Telegraph Clerk.—(*Dated September 14th*): 'Call the Minister of War at once to speak with me.'

Telegraph Clerk to Abdel-el-al: 'Up to now he has not returned from the British Commander.'

Abdel-el-al to the Telegraph Clerk: 'Send some one immediately to call him.'

Telegraph Clerk to Abdel-el-al: 'Very good.'

Abdel-el-al to the Telegraph Clerk: 'Have they not yet returned?'

Telegraph Clerk to Abdel-el-al: 'They have not yet returned.'

Abdel-el-al to the Telegraph Clerk: 'Tell us at once the cause of the delay.'

Telegraph Clerk to Abdel-el-al: 'I have sent some one to call them. I do not know the cause of the delay.'

Abdel-el-al to Telegraph Clerk: 'Have they not yet returned?'

Telegraph Clerk to Abdel-el-al: 'They have not returned up to now.'

On September 15th, at 7.25 a.m., Abdel-el-al telegraphs to the Telegraph Clerk at Kasr-el-Nil: 'Send at once for the Minister of War to speak to me.'

Telegraph Clerk to Abdel-el-al: 'Since yesterday the Minister and

* This refers to Arabi, who still styled himself Minister of War.

Toulba Pasha are with the English Commander. I think they have been confined near to him.'

Abdel-el-al to Telegraph Clerk: 'Send a special messenger, at once, to ascertain where they are and inform me immediately.'

Telegraph Clerk to Abdel-el-al: 'He has been assured that they have been locked up near the Commander.'

Abdel-el-al to Telegraph Clerk: 'Send immediately for Yacoub Pasha Sami, Under Minister of War.'

Telegraph Clerk to Abdel-el-al: 'Yacoub Pasha is left for Zag-a-zig.'

Abdel-el-al to Telegraph Clerk: 'Who is actually at the Divan?'

Telegraph Clerk to Abdel-el-al: 'No one is there.'

Abdel-el-al to Telegraph Clerk: 'Why has Yacoub Pasha gone to Zag-a-zig?'

Telegraph Clerk to Abdel-el-al: 'He has gone as a member of the Commission entrusted with negotiating for peace.'

Abdel-el-al to Telegraph Clerk: 'If I send you a telegram for Arabi Pasha can you send it to him?'

Telegraph Clerk to Abdel-el-al: 'I cannot.'

Abdel-el-al to Telegraph Clerk: 'Cannot the Ministry of War speak to him?'

Telegraph Clerk to Abdel-el-al: 'The Minister is in confinement near the English. No one can speak to him?'

Abdel-el-al to Telegraph Clerk: 'Where is Mahmoud Pasha Sami?'

Telegraph Clerk to Abdel-el-al: 'I do not know. The English have ordered the Prefect of Police to fetch him at once.'

Here this amusing conversation was brought to a conclusion by the British authorities taking possession of the Telegraph Office.

CHAPTER XL.

SURRENDER OF KAFR DOWAR.

Events in Alexandria—General Hamley takes Command—Departure of the Highland Brigade—Sir Evelyn Wood takes Command—Attempt to cut the Dyke at Mex—Mahmoud Fehmy brought to Alexandria—The Egyptian Army—Receipt at Alexandria of the news of Tel-el-Kebir—Kafr Dowar given up—The Railway opened—Surrenders at Aboukir and Mex—Disbandment of the Egyptian Army.

THE submission of the Egyptian army in Cairo was speedily followed by surrenders in other places—Kafr Dowar, Aboukir, and Rosetta yielded without a struggle. Fort Ghemil near Port Saïd was occupied on the 21st by the British.

Damietta was the last fortress to hold out. A British force, consisting of the Berkshire, Shropshire, South Staffordshire, and Sussex regiments under Sir Evelyn Wood, was despatched against it on the 22nd September, after negotiations with the Commandant Abdel-el-Al had failed. A portion of the fleet under Admiral Dowell was ordered to co-operate. However, on the 23rd Abdel-el-Al hearing of these preparations capitulated with all his forces.

The surrender of the Egyptian Army at Kafr Dowar was an event of sufficient importance to justify making it the subject of a separate chapter. But to render what follows intelligible, as well as for the sake of completeness, it is necessary to preface the history of that event with an account of occurrences at Alexandria subsequent to the departure of Sir Garnet Wolseley for the Canal.

On the 19th August, the Khedive relieved Ragheb Pasha and his colleagues of their duties, and named Cherif Pasha President of the Council of Ministers. With him was associated Riaz Pasha, who had in the meantime returned from Europe. It was a bitter pill for a man like Riaz who considered himself the one hope of the country to have to serve under Cherif, and it said something for the patriotism of the former that he was able to subordinate to it his conceit.

After the departure of the transports for Port Saïd and Ismailia, General Hamley took the local command, and the fresh transports constantly arriving at Alexandria were very welcome to reinforce the garrison, which had been considerably weakened by the departure of the main body of the army to Ismailia. Only two ships of war were left in harbour, the *Invincible* and *Inconstant*, which latter vessel had lately arrived from England.

The military operations at Alexandria dwindled into insignificance. Both sides confined themselves to strengthening their positions and to making small reconnaissances. Round Mex the Bedouins kept the troops well on the alert, and several minor skirmishes took place. About August the 20th, the defences of Ramleh were strengthened by the mounting of three 7-inch Armstrong M. L. R. guns. Two were taken from the Hospital battery at Ras-el-Tin, and the third was found unmounted near Mex Fort.

On the 31st of August a party of blue-jackets from the *Minotaur* under the command of Commander Hammill, landed at night and demolished, by gun-cotton, a house near the British advanced posts on the Mahmoudieh Canal which afforded cover to the enemy. Some native houses opposite the Villa Antoniades which had been used by the Bedouins as a place whence to take shots at our posts there, had for the same reason to be destroyed.

SURRENDER OF KAFR DOWAR.

On the 1st September Generals Hamley and Alison and the Highland Brigade sailed for Port Saïd and Ismailia, General Sir Evelyn Wood being left in command. Anxious to make the rebel leader believe that the chief attack would be on Kafr Dowar, and to prevent him from sending away his troops to strengthen other positions, the British troops contrived daily to harass the Egyptian lines. Generally the reconnaissances took place at dusk, as the Egyptians seemed to prefer withdrawing their troops under the cover of the darkness. Grown wary by experience, they refused to be drawn out in force, but limited themselves to a brisk artillery fire.

It was at this time that the attempt was made to cut the dyke at Mex, in order to flood Lake Mareotis, the level of which at this season was some feet lower than that of the sea. Although it was reckoned that it would take some weeks, in this way, to raise the water of the lake to its proper level, the stratagem was not devoid of merit. One of its objects was to enable steam-launches with guns to harass the flank of the enemy's position at Kafr Dowar.

Early in September Mahmoud Fehmy, already referred to as having been made prisoner by Sir Garnet Wolseley's force, was brought to Alexandria, and in return for a promise to spare his life, furnished full details of Arabi's plans and position, together with information implicating, it was said, many of the high officials surrounding the Khedive, not excluding even members of his Ministry.

On the 13th September Alexandria received the news of the victory of Tel-el-Kebir with the wildest delight. Early in the morning it was known that the fight had begun, and great excitement was manifested by all classes. About eleven in the forenoon, when the facts were published, this feeling increased perceptibly.

All business was suspended. Processions of Europeans were formed and, preceded by bands of music, paraded amid the ruins of the town. Hats and helmets were thrown into the air, and cheers and cries of 'Viva Inghilterra!' resounded on all sides. The bands played 'God save the Queen' and the Khedivial Hymn by turns. Crowds rushed for the English soldiers on guard at the Tribunals, and embraced them frantically. Sir Edward Malet, the English Consul-General, called to congratulate the Khedive, who also received a congratulatory message from the Queen. Never before had the English been so popular in Alexandria. It took some days before the excitement cooled down and things resumed their ordinary course.

Kafr Dowar was given up to Sir Evelyn Wood on the 16th September. Yacoub Sami, Arabi's sub-Minister of War, represented him on this occasion. Some 6000 men in all laid down their arms. There were 700 captured horses, 50 field-guns with their equipments, and 15,000 Remington rifles. The captured men were allowed to disband, and the officers were lodged as prisoners in the Palace at Ramleh.

General Wood and his staff went out by rail, preceded, as a measure of precaution, by the armour-clad train. The 49th Regiment had been previously sent forward as an escort. Arrived at the bridge crossing the Mahmoudieh Canal, the party proceeded on horseback to Fort Aslam, as the most advanced of the earthworks of Kafr Dowar was called. This formed a part of three long lines of redoubts, flanked on both sides by swampy and impassable ground, and running at right angles across the railway and canal. These defences were supplemented by shelter-trenches and rifle-pits. The position was one of great strength, and if held by good soldiers could only have been taken, if at all, at a great sacrifice of life. Each line of redoubts had a ditch of 15 feet in width in front of it. The distance between the first and second lines was 4000 metres, and between the second and third 5000 metres. Fort Aslam was one of the strongest of the redoubts, and was pierced with embrasures for guns. The passage for the railway trains was blocked by a large mass of masonry, which Sir Evelyn Wood at once caused to be blown up with dynamite. Fort Aslam was capable of being easily defended by 250 good soldiers. The garrison, however, had disappeared, leaving only a dozen or so of officers including Yacoub Sami, who came forward to meet the English Commander. In the fort, which appeared to have suffered but slightly, were found 150 horses, besides quantities of arms and ammunition abandoned by the soldiers. Amongst the cannon were some mounted Krupp guns. Between the first and second lines the remains of a camp for about 2500 men were found, and between the second and third lines, of another camp for the residue of the army. On all sides were found horses and mules, mixed pell-mell with carriages, still loaded with silks, clothes, calico, &c., from the shops and houses pillaged in Alexandria.

The third line of defence, that situated at Kinje Osman, the nearest point to Kafr Dowar, was inferior to the other parts of the defence, being provided only with two insignificant bastions, armed with old cannons and a long line of rifle-pits extending across the railway. Behind it, in the camp of Kafr Dowar, stood 6000 soldiers, armed with Remington rifles, waiting to surrender to the British army. There were also several batteries of artillery and two squadrons of cavalry. The men were anything but warlike in appearance. Many of them had thrown away their uniforms and the greater part wore only the dress of the ordinary fellah.

The natives met with along the line showed not the slightest sign of hostility. On the contrary, they tried to conceal their evident uneasiness at the sight of the British force by assuming a pleased air, and waving white rags as a substitute for flags of truce. At Kafr Dowar itself, crowds of Arabs, mostly refugees from Alexandria, were congregated. Many of these were pillagers and incendiaries of the worst class, and strict orders had to be given to prevent their returning to the scene of their former exploits.

Yacoub Sami, on giving up his sword to General Wood, assured him that no one had been throughout more loyal to the Khedive than he, Yacoub Sami, had been; and as for Arabi, he was a scoundrel and a monster who had refused to listen to his loyal counsels.

One of the first questions put by General Wood was, as to what had become of a Lieutenant named Paolucci, who had deserted some weeks before from the Italian ironclad *Castelfidardo* to join Arabi. This officer in his endeavour to reach the rebels' lines had the misfortune to fall into the hands of Bedouins, who used him in the most brutal manner. Eventually, after five days' wandering, he succeeded in finding his way to the camp at Kafr Dowar, but in a pitiable condition. He was destitute of every rag of clothing, and so exhausted as to be barely able to stand on his legs. Arabi, on hearing him say that his wish was to serve the cause of liberty, allowed him to be removed to the camp ambulance, where he remained till the surrender. In reply to General Wood, M. Paolucci himself was produced. He was now dressed in an Egyptian officer's uniform much too large for him, and was still suffering acutely. The General, without making any observation, handed M. Paolucci over to two marines, with instructions to conduct him to the Italian Consul at Alexandria.* M. Ninet, who had been in the enemy's lines ever since the bombardment and subsequent destruction of Alexandria, had, it was ascertained, left for Cairo on receipt of the news of the taking of Tel-el-Kebir.

General Wood at once gave orders for clearing the railway. Civilians were requisitioned for the work, and so well was this carried out that the following day, which was fixed for the surrender of the arms, the trains were running freely between Kafr Dowar and Alexandria.

Two British battalions were despatched on the 17th, to encamp at Kafr Dowar, and to take delivery of the Egyptian arms. The army which was to surrender had then practically disappeared. The rifles were piled, the officers were in charge, but their men they said 'had gone off to the fields.'

General Wood received the same day the submission of about 1000 men from Aboukir and 4000 from Mex. On the 17th, the Khedive signed a decree disbanding the Egyptian army.

* This officer was subsequently tried by court-martial and sentenced to two years' imprisonment.

CHAPTER XLI.

OBSERVATIONS ON THE CAMPAIGN.

Rapidity of the Campaign—Effect in Europe of Sir Garnet Wolseley's Victory—The French Press—The Victory attributed to English Gold—Professor Palmer's Expedition—M. Ninet's Version of the Events of Tel-el-Kebir—The Question of the Employment of English Gold considered.

ONE of the most remarkable features of the campaign was the rapidity with which it was conducted. The first shot was fired at Alexandria on the 11th July; Sir Garnet Wolseley reached Egypt on the 15th August, and on the 15th September he entered Cairo as a conqueror. It served also to illustrate the power of moving large bodies of troops by sea, with a rapidity and certainty of concentration, impossible on land. The difference between the power of steam and sails may be seen from an apt comparison.

On the 19th May, 1798, Napoleon I. set sail from Toulon with favouring winds. On the 16th June he reached Malta on his way to Egypt, thus occupying twenty-eight days on that short voyage. The head of the column of British transports left England on the 30th July, and reached Alexandria on the 10th August, completing the voyage in eleven days. When in 1800 it was decided to despatch Indian troops to Egypt, they began to assemble at Bombay in the month of December. On the 28th the first detachment sailed, but did not arrive at Suez till the end of April 1801. The remainder of the force under General Baird, followed shortly after, reaching Kosseir, in the Red Sea, on the 8th June, where they disembarked and marched across the Desert to Kench on the Nile. In 1882 the first troops despatched from India left Bombay on the 22nd July, and by the 2nd September the whole of the Contingent, except the 6th Bengal Cavalry, had reached Suez.

Much has been made of the rapidity of the French invasion of Egypt, but Napoleon only entered Cairo on the 23rd July, having left Toulon on the 19th May, whereas Sir Garnet Wolseley left England on the 2nd August, made the long sea-voyage by Gibraltar, and arrived in the capital of Egypt on the 15th September.

With regard to Tel-el-Kebir the shortness of the time occupied in storming the entrenchments has been made use of, more especially by foreign critics, to lessen the credit of the victory. Without pretending that the battle was more than, comparatively speaking, a small affair exceedingly well managed, a few figures will show that there was a real resistance, and that the fighting on both sides was more serious than is generally supposed.

In the descent which England made on Egypt in 1801, with a naval and military force, a series of gallant actions fought between the 8th and 21st of March, when Abercrombie fell at the battle of Alexandria, paved the way for the capture of Alexandria on the 1st of September. This work was done with an average of 12,000 effective troops, at a cost of 3001 men killed, wounded, and missing, and compelled the surrender of 32,180 French soldiers. England of 1801 then did to Napoleon what England of 1882 did to Arabi. But there is this fact to be borne in mind. With 12,000 effectives the English landed and won the battle of Aboukir at a cost in killed, wounded, and missing of 666 men. The enemy was composed of gallant French troops worthy of their opponent's steel. The troops who assailed Arabi's lines at Tel-el-Kebir may be taken roughly at

13,000 men, and the casualties at 460. So that in a struggle of some twenty minutes' duration, the troops of Sir Garnet Wolseley sustained a loss of no less than 460, whilst those of Abercrombie in a long battle in the open with disciplined French troops lost 666. Hence, for six killed or disabled at Aboukir, four were put *hors-de-combat* at Tel-el-Kebir. In the one case the loss was 3·4 per cent of the troops engaged, in the other 5·5.

The news of the victory of Tel-el-Kebir, the capture of Cairo, and the close of the war, produced a profound sensation in Europe. In England the greatest enthusiasm was manifested, and to the events of the campaign was given an importance perhaps in excess of their actual merits.

On the Continent, however, the opposite was the case. The very journals which only a week before had declared that in undertaking to subdue Arabi England had assumed a task the difficulties of which she had scarcely calculated, now went to the other extreme, and described Tel-el-Kebir as a mere military promenade. In the *Debats* M. Gabriel Channes wrote that the fears that an Egyptian Campaign would prove hazardous were groundless. The only difficulties which the English Army had to encounter were due to the vast amount of baggage it had to transport, owing to the men carrying nothing but their arms. According to the same article an army less burdened would have beaten Arabi and reached Cairo in a few days; and if the campaign had lasted some weeks, this was only due to the slowness of the attack. The *Avenir Militaire* maintained that Sir Garnet Wolseley did not shorten the campaign by transferring his base to Ismailia, and that the qualities of the English troops were not exposed to a very severe ordeal. 'The attack on Tel-el-Kebir,' it added, 'against troops ill on the watch, succeeded with a promptitude which

rendered a portion of those qualities useless.' Many of
the Continental journals went further, and unable, in
any other way to explain the dashing fight which in
twenty minutes placed all Egypt at England's feet,
boldly asserted that the victory was bought and paid
for by English gold. They even named the exact sum
—forty thousand Napoleons. It was, perhaps, unfortunate that Professor Palmer's ill-fated expedition into
the Sinaitic Desert, about this time, should have given
an apparent colour to these reports.

One author,[*] whose writings, however, are not always
to be accepted as accurate, states that Sultan Pasha
(already referred to as the President of the Chamber of
Notables) was attached to Sir Garnet Wolseley's force,
with the object of securing by large bribes the fidelity of
the Bedouins in the district between Ismailia and Zag-a-zig. According to the same authority, the Bedouins
received from 3*l.* to 2*l.* a-head, and much of the money
found its way into the pockets of officers of the Egyptian
army from the rank of Lieutenant to that of Colonel.

The events of Tel-el-Kebir are thus referred to by
the same writer:—

'On the 12th September, Arabi learned towards twelve o'clock,
from a Bedouin sheikh, that the English would attack *en masse* the
lines of Tel-el-Kebir towards two o'clock in the morning on the 13th,
throwing themselves on Belbeis to open the road to Cairo. It was
then necessary to guard this point, formerly fortified by the French.
Arabi consequently telegraphed to Toulba Pasha at Kafr Dowar to
send at once one of his best battalions, the last, or nearly the last,
which remained to him, with orders to be in line of battle at Tel-el-Kebir at daybreak on the 13th. At one a.m. the train took away this
detachment, which arrived at Zag-a-zig long after everything was
finished. The battalion then returned on its steps in company with
the fugitives from the battlefield.

'At Tel-el-Kebir, during the night, between two and three a.m., at
the first rifle-shots, the Bedouins, *en masse*, threw themselves on the

[*] Mr. John Ninet.

Egyptian lines, shouting like demons, causing everywhere the wildest confusion. The native troops knew not who was with them or against them. Whole regiments ran like hares without striking a blow (*sic*), and the English, astonished to encounter so little resistance, massacred the fugitives as if at a shooting-party. Three thousand men of trained infantry, all that the army of the East possessed, faced the enemy, and with the last vestiges of the artillery, fired valiantly as long as they were able. More than half of them perished.

'It is confidently asserted that several of the Egyptian officers, hindered in their flight by the gold which they had in their pockets, seeking to lighten themselves, were arrested and pillaged by the soldiers of one of the black regiments. As to the Bedouins, their treason was so well arranged that, by a previous agreement with Sultan Pasha, they, with the speed of the wind, quitted their cantonments without molestation. Not a single sheikh or a single Arab out of the 40,000 or 50,000 who rallied to the side of Arabi, was ever arrested or interrogated. Absolute immunity in their favour. What stronger proof, beyond the facts themselves, could be required of the defection of the Bedouins, thanks to the English gold distributed by Sultan Pasha, and its consequences on the prompt issue of the war?

. . . .

'Sir Garnet Wolseley, with his 35,000 men and his surprising victory, had in reality to fight only 3000 old soldiers, infantry, and artillery all included. The recruits had all quitted their lines before daybreak, at the first cries of the Bedouins at the very outset of the attack.'

In considering M. Ninet's narrative, it must be remembered that he was, from first to last, an avowed ally of the Arabist party, and also that his sentiments towards England have always been of the most unfriendly character. That, under these circumstances, he should seek to explain Sir Garnet Wolseley's success by suggesting treachery and corruption is not altogether unnatural. That Sultan Pasha, as an Egyptian official, may have sought to influence the Bedouins in the way mentioned seems likely enough. But that English gold was employed in the way alleged by M. Ninet, to buy up the officers of the Egyptian army, is too ridiculous for serious consideration. Had it been the desire of the British Government to purchase Tel-el-Kebir, as suggested, it is incredible that by the expenditure of a little additional capital an entirely bloodless victory should not have been obtained.

Further than this, Arabi himself, in all the explanations which he gave of the war, never once hinted at the means alleged by his apologist as having brought about his defeat. The story of the Egyptian officers being so heavily weighted with English sovereigns as to be unable to make good their retreat, reads more like an Oriental fable than anything else.

Notwithstanding arguments like the foregoing, there are many persons in Egypt who, to this day, believe that the battle of Tel-el-Kebir was bought and paid for beforehand. To such it is only necessary to point to the long list of brilliant achievements of the British army in other countries than Egypt, and to ask if these, too, were won by British gold? If not, one would ask why, in a matter which, according to our critics, was of so comparatively insignificant a character as Tel-el-Kebir, English steel required to be supplemented by the more persuasive metal?

CHAPTER XLII.

ENGLAND AND THE PORTE.

Negotiations—Motives of the Porte—Lord Dufferin's Policy—Progress of Negotiations—Signing of the Convention authorised—Battle of Tel-el-Kebir—Turkish Troops no longer required—Negotiations abandoned—Withdrawal of British Troops asked for—Lord Dufferin's Reply—A little good Advice.

As already stated, on the 18th August Sir Garnet Wolseley started from Alexandria with the British force, and on the following day Port Saïd, Ismailia, and Kantara, were occupied.

Notwithstanding this, the negotiations with the Porte for the despatch of the Turkish troops were being, outwardly at least, pressed on by Lord Dufferin. The Turkish Ministers continued to make objections to the terms of the Military Convention.

Meanwhile the export of mules, purchased in Asia Minor for the use of the British force, was stopped, and the drivers were imprisoned. The unfriendly conduct of the Turkish Government in delaying the removal of this prohibition led to remonstrances on the part of Lord Dufferin. It was not until the 23rd August, that the Sultan ordered that the mules and drivers were to be allowed to be embarked.

He, at the same time, sent Lord Dufferin a personal message urging that Alexandria should be the port of disembarkation for the Turkish troops. After an interview with the Turkish Ministers, Lord Dufferin agreed to submit to the British Government the Sultan's request that the troops should land at

Alexandria, and the Sultan's Ministers finally accepted all the other clauses of the Military Convention, with certain amendments. When, however, the issue of the proclamation against Arabi was demanded, the Ministers changed round and proposed to throw aside the Proclamation which had been agreed upon, and by which Arabi was declared to be a rebel, and to issue a mere appeal to his loyalty. Lord Dufferin, assuming an air of surprise at this breach of faith, refused indignantly to listen to any such suggestion, and informed the Ministers that he would not sign the Convention until the Proclamation had been officially communicated.

On the 24th Lord Dufferin was instructed that Her Majesty's Government could not accept the amendments made in the Convention. Again the Turkish Ministers sought out Lord Dufferin with messages from the Sultan, pressing that the landing might be at Alexandria, and assuring the Ambassador that the Proclamation should be communicated the moment that the heads of the Convention were agreed to.

Things began to look as if they were in a way to be arranged, when it was discovered, on the 25th, that the instructions given for the despatch of the mules and the release of the drivers had been cancelled by an order from the Palace. Lord Dufferin was at once instructed that if this information was correct, it was no longer possible for him to continue the negotiations.

On the 27th the Turkish Ministers accepted Aboukir as the place of disembarkation, and promised that before the Convention was signed they would communicate the Proclamation officially, and order its publication in Egypt. Lord Dufferin was instructed that he might sign the Convention on the preliminary condition that the mules and drivers should be released, and a promise given by the Porte to assist in sending them to Egypt, and that the Proclamation should be issued at once.

On the 29th Lord Dufferin reported that he had settled the text of the Convention with the Sultan's Ministers.

The 30th passed without any further communication from the Porte; but in the middle of the night, Saïd Pasha called upon Lord Dufferin at Therapia, with a further message from the Sultan, urging that the troops should go to Aboukir *viâ* Alexandria; and in the morning the Pasha came again with the Sultan's private secretary, and stated that His Majesty was ready to take any step to remove Lord Granville's misgivings if he were allowed to land his troops at Alexandria. He was willing to reduce their number from that originally proposed to 2000 or even 1000. Baker Pasha might go second in command, and take with him as many English officers as he pleased, and the Turkish troops should be as much under English control as they were in the Crimea.

The extraordinary anxiety of the Sultan to show his troops in Egypt at this period is to be accounted for on the supposition that he foresaw the impending collapse of the Arabi revolt, and was desirous that it should not be accomplished without his appearing at all events to have taken part in its suppression. The presence of but a single Turkish battalion in Alexandria would have sufficed to enable him to claim the merit of overthrowing Arabi and his followers. It was however not to be. The Sultan's views were now diametrically at variance with those of the British Cabinet. Sir Garnet Wolseley was, at this time, well to the front, and there was little doubt that he would soon bring the war to a close. Under these circumstances, the presence of a Turkish force in Egypt would only be a source of embarrassment. Accordingly it was necessary to finesse and to play off upon the Porte its own tricks of delay and dissimulation. Accordingly Lord Dufferin was instructed to inform the Porte that Her Majesty's Goverment were willing to meet its proposals, and to receive 2000 or even 3000 troops; but that, in view of the strong objections to Alexandria, it would be preferable that the landing should take place in the Suez Canal.

On the 3rd September the Turkish Ministers were willing that the troops should go to Port Saïd, promising at the same time that the Proclamation should be issued immediately.

On the 24th August Lord Granville had authorised the Ambassador to conclude the Convention as soon as the Proclamation should have been published, the words, 'such point or points on the Canal as may be previously arranged with the British Commander-in-Chief,' being substituted therein for Aboukir, and a Memorandum was to be signed by the Turkish Minister for Foreign Affairs embodying the Sultan's proposals.

On Lord Dufferin proceeding to the Porte on the 6th September to sign the Convention, he found that the Proclamation had that morning appeared in the newspapers in a changed form. Lord Dufferin thereupon declined to sign the Convention. Saïd Pasha said that the publication as it stood was an act of heedlessness, and he undertook that a correction should be published in the official journal. A further discussion ensued as to the form of the stipulation respecting the landing of the Turkish troops in the Canal, Saïd Pasha objecting to the words proposed by Lord Granville, and pressing for the mention of Port Saïd.

Lord Dufferin accepted *ad referendum* an amended paragraph to the effect that the Turkish forces should proceed to Port Saïd, and from thence to whatever point or points might be agreed upon between the two Commanders-in-Chief. The British Government, however, insisted that the clause should state that the Turkish troops would 'enter the Canal at Port Saïd and proceed from thence,' whilst the Sultan wished to substitute the word 'debarqueront,' for 'se rendront à Port Saïd.'

On the 10th September the Ottoman Plenipotentiaries, who seemed unconscious that they were being played with all the time, came to the Embassy with copies of the Conventions and Memorandum for signature. They were authorised to accept the words 'se rendront à Port Saïd.' Lord Dufferin, however, having in the meantime been informed of the views of Her Majesty's Government, stated that he could not accept them. His Lordship would agree to the retention of the words on the understanding that a paragraph should be inserted in the Memorandum, explaining the meaning of the words to be that the troops should 'direct their course to Port Saïd in order to enter the Canal.'

It was now the eve of Tel-el-Kebir, and Lord Dufferin discovered that it was necessary to suspend negotiations on account of the arrest by the Turkish authorities of a number of porters who had been engaged at Sir Garnet Wolseley's request for service in Egypt. The men were released the same day with a promise that such proceedings should not be repeated. The signature of the Convention, as further amended, was authorised by telegram from Lord Granville, on the 13th, on the conditions that the Proclamation should be issued with the amendment required by Her Majesty's Government, and that the Memorandum with the last addition proposed by Lord Dufferin, should be signed simultaneously.

On the 13th the battle of Tel-el-Kebir took place. On the 15th Lord Granville instructed Lord Dufferin, that, in view of the defeat and submission of the Egyptian insurgents, the British Government contemplated shortly commencing the withdrawal of the British troops from Egypt, and presumed that the emergency having passed, the Sultan would not consider it necessary to send troops; and on the 18th his Lordship was authorised to convey to the Sultan, in the most courteous terms, the permission given to his Lordship to drop the negotiation of the Military Convention. He was at the same time to express to his Majesty that the British Government conceived this step to be most consistent with the dignity of the two countries, and that it was not intended or calculated to alter the good and friendly relations between them.

The poor Sultan now began to realise how completely befooled he had been. It was necessary, however, to put a good face on the matter. The Turkish Foreign Minister accordingly answered by expressing the deep satisfaction of the Sultan and his Government at the sentiments expressed on behalf of the British Government. He declared that the wish of Turkey was to maintain unaltered the old friendship between the two countries. Finally, the Minister asked, a little anxiously, what date had been fixed on for the evacuation by the British troops.

This last question was met by Lord Dufferin reminding the Sultan of the sacrifices made by England in order to restore order in Egypt; and stating that whilst those sacrifices had given England power, that power had thrown upon her great responsibility; that the Egyptian Army being disbanded, until the Khedive had organized the means of securely maintaining his authority, it was impossible for England to withdraw her troops, although she had already greatly diminished their number, and had no wish to keep any in Egypt longer than was justified by the circumstances. With regard to the overtures for a closer alliance Lord Dufferin pointed out that the Sultan would remember that the like offer had been made by him on several occasions, without any practical results, owing to the apparent change of His Majesty's views. His Lordship concluded by giving the Porte a little lecture, pointing out that offers of friendship were unsatisfactory without some tangible proof of the willingness of the Ottoman Government to adopt that line of conduct which could alone render their friendship acceptable to English public opinion; and suggested that that proof might be given by inaugurating those internal reforms which were indispensable to the existence of the Empire and to the maintenance of a really good understanding with England.

It would be impossible to conclude the present chapter without some comment on the part played by Lord Dufferin in the events therein related. Perhaps no better way of dealing with the subject can be found than by giving an extract from the concluding portion of his Lordship's despatch of 18th September, 1882, to Lord Granville, which runs as follows :—

'In fact, I can only reiterate that from first to last I have used every means at my disposal to induce the Turkish Government to move quickly and to settle the matter out of hand. I told them at the commencement that I had your Lordship's instructions to press forward the Convention with all despatch; that your private letters, as well as your public despatches, evinced your desire to see that instrument executed; that in asking me to telegraph to your Lordship these repeated references, they were playing into our hands, and that their conduct was so obviously contrary to their interests, that Europe had begun to misjudge the situation. While ruining my reputation as an honest man, they were enhancing it as a diplomatist, for it had begun to be believed that the delay in signing the Convention could not possibly result from their own incomprehensible shortsightedness, but must have been artificially created by the Machiavellian astuteness of the English Ambsssador.'

CHAPTER XLIII.

EVENTS IN CAIRO.

The Khedive's Return to Cairo — Arrangements for the Future — The Expenses of the War — The Cost of the Army of Occupation — Departure of Sir Garnet Wolseley — Sir Archibald Alison takes the Command — Lord Dufferin's Mission — Instructions to Lord Dufferin — The Task before him — Political Arrests — The Egyptian Prisons — Amnesty Decree.

ON the 25th September the Khedive was able to return to Cairo, where a great portion of Sir Garnet Wolseley's forces had assembled. He entered the Capital at 3.30 in the afternoon, and was received with great apparent enthusiasm. His Highness drove from the railway station in an open carriage with the Duke of Connaught, Sir Garnet Wolseley, and Sir Edward Malet. The streets through which he passed were lined the whole way by soldiers of the British Army.

Next followed a series of complimentary banquets and a distribution of honours and rewards to the officers of the British forces. The Order of the First Class of the Osmanieh was conferred by the Sultan upon Sir Beauchamp Seymour and Sir Garnet Wolseley.[*] Other officers also received decorations dealt out with a liberal hand. Later on, an Egyptian medal, in the shape of a bronze star, was struck, and presented by the Khedive to the whole of the British forces which took part in the campaign. By the British Government both Sir

---

[*] About the same period the Sultan bestowed a similar order on his bootmaker at Constantinople. Upon the writer remarking to an Egyptian official on the singularity of the circumstance, the latter replied, 'Yes; but he is a very good bootmaker, you know.'

Garnet Wolseley and Sir Beauchamp Seymour were created Peers of the United Kingdom. An English war medal for Egypt was also issued to the forces engaged.

With the exception of a small force left at Alexandria, Port Saïd, and Ismailîa, the whole of the British forces were concentrated in Cairo, to be reviewed by the Khedive, in the square in front of the Palace of Abdin.

The review took place on the very spot where Arabi and his mutinous troops had defied the Khedive just a twelvemonth before.

The British soldiers, in spite of the hardships of the campaign, presented an imposing appearance, the Indian regiments especially attracting attention.

As soon as the effervescence which followed the restoration had a little subsided, the Egyptian Government and its English advisers began to take thought for the morrow. A decision was arrived at to reduce the British Forces to 12,000 men, which thenceforth constituted the Army of Occupation. The Egyptian army having been disbanded, and there being no other Egyptian force available to maintain order, it became absolutely necessary, apart from any political considerations, to retain this number of Sir Garnet Wolseley's soldiers.

In announcing their intentions, the British Government informed the Egyptian Ministry that England was prepared to defray all expenditure incurred in the suppression of the rebellion, the date of the conclusion of which was fixed at the 30th September. The British Government also intimated that from that date Egypt would be expected to repay all extraordinary expenses which the retention of the Queen's troops in Egypt would entail on the Exchequer of the United Kingdom. The contribution for the 12,000 men to be retained, was fixed at 4*l*. a month per man, making a maximum monthly charge of 48,000*l*. The Egyptian Government was at the same time informed that it was desired to withdraw the troops from Egypt as soon as circumstances would permit, and that such withdrawal would be effected from time to time as the security of the country would allow it.

Pursuant to the intention above indicated, arrangements were at once made for a considerable reduction in the strength of the Army of Occupation. The Indian Contingent embarked, and Sir Garnet Wolseley, as well as a great portion of the army under his command, left for England, Major - General Sir Archibald Alison assuming the command, with the local rank of Lieut.-General.

The importance attached by Her Majesty's Government to Egyptian affairs at this time was shown by the appointment, early in November, of Lord Dufferin to proceed thither on a special mission. His Lordship, who had filled successively the posts of Under-Secretary of State for India, Governor-General of Canada, Ambassador at St. Petersburg, and Ambassador at Constantinople, was probably the most capable man at the disposal of the British Government, and his mission to Egypt was everywhere hailed with satisfaction as preliminary to a satisfactory settlement of the affairs of that country.

Lord Dufferin's instructions were 'to advise the Government of the Khedive in the arrangements which would have to be made for re-establishing His Highness's authority and providing for the future well-being of all classes of the population.'

The principal points to be dealt with were :—1. Reorganization of the army and police force ; 2. The substitution of some better system for the Dual Control;

3. Introduction of improvements in the machinery of those branches of the public service which were now managed by Europeans; 4. The gradual reduction of the foreign element and the increased employment of native Egyptians in all branches of the Administration; 5. The establishment of an improved system of justice for natives; 6. The equal taxation of foreigners and Egyptians; 7. The establishment of institutions favourable to the prudent development of liberty, either by the reassembling of the Chamber of Notables or by such other measures as may be best calculated to secure that end; 8. The prevention of the slave-trade and of slavery; 9. The security of transit across Egypt between Europe and the East, and especially freedom of passage through the Suez Canal.

Lord Dufferin arrived at Alexandria on the 7th November, and was received with all the honours due to his rank. He left for Cairo the same day, the Khedive placing at his disposal the Palace of Kasr-el-Noosa in the Shoobra Road. This, his Lordship shortly after changed for a Palace belonging to Cattaouwi Bey in a more convenient situation.

It is greatly to Lord Dufferin's credit that one of the first matters to which he directed his attention, was a question of humanity, viz., the lot of the many unfortunates whom the late events had relegated to the Egyptian prisons.

It was not to be expected that the Khedivial party should triumph without seeking to wreak vengeance on the heads of their conquered adversaries. Consequently arrests were made wholesale, and the Egyptian prisons were soon overcrowded. The object of the Khedive's advisers seemed to be to make what in sporting language would be called a big 'bag.' Of the leaders of the Rebellion, as already stated,

Mahmoud Fehmy had been captured at Kassassin, and Arabi and Toulba had surrendered to General Drury-Lowe at Abbassieh. In addition to these Mahmoud Sami had been arrested by the police in Cairo. Yacoub Sami had given himself up at Kafr Dowar, and Abdel-el-al at Damietta. But besides, there were about 1200 other political prisoners in the various gaols of Upper and Lower Egypt. The arrests commenced on the 16th September, and according to a Memorandum of Colonel Sir Charles Wilson,* there were in Alexandria 443 so-called political prisoners. In the Cairo prisons and police stations were 199 prisoners charged with political offences; at Tantah, there were in the same category 359 (or according to the Governor's statement, 285); and in the rest of the country 263. These individuals comprised all classes of the population, sheikhs from the mosques, officers and privates of the army, members of the civil service, police officials, merchants and landowners.

The charges against many of these people were of the vaguest character, such as 'stirring up public feeling against the Khedive,' 'assisting the rebels,' &c.; some of them were absolutely ludicrous and comprised such offences as 'dressing up dogs to imitate Sir Garnet Wolseley, and then shooting at them.'

There was reason to believe that a considerable number of the persons arrested were denounced by their neighbours to gratify private malice or revenge. Many of the prisoners were arrested simply as a matter of precaution, or because they were adherents of Halim or Ismail Pasha.

As may be supposed, the prisoners necessarily suffered considerable hardships from overcrowding. But, besides this, instances of ill-usage and, occasionally,

* Late Consul General in Anatolia.

of torture, were brought to the notice of the British authorities. To remedy these evils inspectors were appointed to visit the prisons, and the agents of the British Government made strong representations to the Egyptian authorities to obtain a speedy gaol delivery.

Their remonstrances took effect. A Decree was issued amnestying all Sub-Lieutenants, Lieutenants, and Captains in the army, except those who took part in the demonstrations of the 1st February and the 9th September, 1881, those who were under arms on the 11th July and remained until the submission of the corps to which they belonged, and those who voluntarily enrolled themselves since the 11th July, such persons being, nevertheless, degraded and deprived of their rank and pensions.

Special Commissions were also instituted at Cairo, Alexandria, and Tantah, for the purpose of investigating charges against all political offenders. The most important of these were Arabi and the other rebel leaders.

The proceedings in regard to them will be found related in another chapter.

CHAPTER XLIV.

TRIAL OF THE REBEL LEADERS.

Proceedings for Trial of the Leaders of the Rebellion—The Preliminary Inquiry—Sir Charles Wilson's Opinion on the Evidence—Lord Dufferin's Proposal—Details of the Compromise—The Trial—The Sentence—The Decree commuting the Sentence to Exile—Trials of the other Leaders—Confiscation of the Property of the Rebels—Passages provided to Ceylon—Their Departure—The Minor Offenders—Observations on the Trial.

No sooner was the Khedive's Ministry once more installed in Cairo, than it turned its attention to the trial of the ringleaders of the rebellion. 'This task was peculiarly grateful to Riaz Pasha, for clemency to his opponents is not amongst his virtues. To him Arabi and his party were simply impious, they had dared to question his infallibility—no pope, no king by Divine right, could feel the outrage more deeply; but they were more, they were the curses of the country, for had they not driven away him, the indispensable? Massacre and incendiarism might be forgiven, but not this. There can be no doubt that he pursued them with a deadly zeal, but it is hardly fair to call it hate. He would have crushed them as he would have crushed a scorpion, by any means; it was a holy duty which he owed to his country.

'When the English Government insisted that the prisoners should have a fair trial, and be defended by Counsel, he felt shocked; it was almost like asking him to be accessory to blasphemy. He gravely assured Lord Dufferin that he knew of their guilt, asked him what object there was to be served by further inquiry; and when he found the Ambassador still unconvinced, went away murmuring sadly on the extraordinary growth of theoretical ideas. When Riaz found that the trial was going to be a simple farce, to end in the practical acquittal of all, then his indignation knew no bounds. In one stormy interview with Lord Dufferin, his little form shook with rage; he left the house, wiped the dust from off his shoes, and resigned.' After the foregoing humorous account of the proceedings in regard to Arabi, taken from a work already more than once quoted,* it is desirable to go a little into the details of a trial which excited a good deal of interest both in Egypt and in Europe.

In dealing with the rebels, it must be borne in mind that the Egyptian Government was not altogether a free agent. As far back as the 22nd August, Sir Edward Malet had forwarded to Lord Granville a proposal from Sir Garnet Wolseley that prisoners taken in the course of the military operations in Egypt should be handed over to the Khedive. This was approved by the English Government, subject to the important qualification that 'His Highness should previously engage that none of them should be put to death without the previous consent of the British authorities.' This condition was accepted by the Egyptian Government.

Early in October, the Honourable Mark Napier, Barrister-at-Law, and Mr. Richard Eve, an English solicitor, having arrived in Cairo to conduct the defence of Arabi, Sir Edward Malet telegraphed on the 10th that the Egyptian Government had informed him that, by the Code under which the court-martial was convened, prisoners were not allowed Counsel,

---

* *Khedives and Pashas*, pp. 137-9.

nor would the trial be public, nor foreign officers be allowed to assist. There were no precedents to guide the execution of the conditions made by Her Majesty's Government, and the Egyptian Government considered that if they allowed Arabi to be defended by native Counsel, the condition on that point would be met.

On the 13th Lord Granville instructed Sir Edward Malet to insist that Arabi should be defended by Counsel of his own choice, whether foreign or native, who should have free access to him, that interpreters should be provided, and that the trial should be public; and in answer to further inquiries made, at the request of Cherif Pasha, explained that the view of his Government was that the free choice of their Counsel should be allowed to all the prisoners, but that the Court would be able to control the conduct of the defence, and prevent the trial being unreasonably protracted. Her Majesty's Government assumed that the prisoners would be tried on definite charges, and if time should be requested to procure the attendance of absent witnesses, they considered that Counsel should state what facts they were expected to prove, and that the request should be refused if the object were not to prove any fact material to the charges, but to prove any political reasons or motives.

The necessity of some means being found of speedily proceeding with the trial of Arabi, was more than once pressed by Sir Edward Malet upon the English Government. Public feeling in Egypt among the natives was much excited, and all manner of absurd stories were told about Arabi and his relations with the British Government. These circulated freely in the bazaars, and were readily believed by the more ignorant and fanatical of the population.

Public opinion in Egypt amongst all classes of

Europeans was from the first naturally hostile to Arabi. Those who had suffered by the rebellion were not likely to be over-lenient in their views towards the rebels, and the local European press clamoured loudly for the condign punishment of Arabi and his associates. Opinion in Europe was much divided on the question. In France and Italy, especially, it became the fashion to extol Arabi as a sort of African Garibaldi, whose only fault was his want of success. The same view prevailed to some extent in England also, thanks to the agitation got up by Sir William Gregory, Mr. Wilfred Blunt, and others. Even amongst those who did not believe in either Arabi or the movement of which he was the head, there was a strong suspicion that he was not more guilty than the Sultan and the Khedive, and a feeling that it would be unjust to punish him whilst they were allowed to go free.

This was the state of things when, on the 18th October, Mr. A. M. Broadley, Barrister-at-law, the leading counsel retained by Mr. Blunt to defend Arabi, arrived in Egypt. Mr. Broadley had formerly been a member of the Indian Civil Service, and had since acted as the legal adviser to the Bey of Tunis.

The Egyptian Government showed itself disposed to put every difficulty in the way of Mr. Broadley and his colleague. At first they were refused permission to see their client; next they were told that they could not be permitted to be present at the preliminary investigation, which was to take place immediately. Thanks to the firmness of Sir Edward Malet, who was determined that Arabi should have a fair trial, these troubles were surmounted. An agreement as to the procedure to be adopted was come to by Borelli Bey, a French advocate who acted for the Egyptian Government, and Mr. Broadley, on behalf of the prisoners whom the latter might have to defend.

The *Acte d'Accusation*, or indictment, was to the following effect :—

1. Arabi, Toulba, Mahmoud Sami, Mahmoud Fehmy, and Omar Ráhmi,* were charged with having abused the flag of truce on the 12th July, by withdrawing the troops and pillaging and burning Alexandria, whilst it was flying.

2. Arabi, Toulba, Mahmoud Sami, Mahmoud Fehmy, Omar Ráhmi, and Aly Fehmy, were charged with having incited the Egyptians to arm against the Government of the Khedive.†

3. All six prisoners were charged with having incited the people to civil war, and with having committed acts of destruction, massacre, and pillage on Egyptian territory.

4. Arabi, Mahmoud Fehmy, Toulba, and Mahmoud Sami, were charged with having continued the war after they had heard that peace was concluded.‡

Once arrived in Egypt, Mr. Broadley did not limit his efforts to the defence of the leaders of the rebellion, but soon succeeded in obtaining retainers from others implicated in recent events. In addition to Arabi he undertook the defence of Abdel-al Pasha, Toulba Pasha, Mahmoud Sami, Aly Pasha Fehmy, Sheikh Muhamed Abdu, Yakoub Sami, and Ahmed Bey Rifát. He subsequently accepted retainers from several other and less prominent members of the Nationalist Party.

The Counsel for the accused first appeared before the Commission on the 31st October. In the meantime

---

* Omar Ráhmi was Arabi's Private Secretary.

† This crime comes under Article 55 of the Ottoman Penal Code, which lays down that every one who directly or indirectly incites subjects of the Ottoman Empire to arm against the Imperial Government shall suffer death.

‡ This crime comes under Article 111 of the Ottoman Military Penal Code, viz.:—'Every Commander who, without motive, continues hostilities after he has been officially informed of the conclusion of peace, or of an armistice, shall suffer death.'

the Commission had collected a mass of hearsay evidence, none of it on oath, and consisting mainly of letters and memoranda and of depositions taken, according to the Egyptian procedure, *ex parte* in the absence of the prisoners and their Counsel. It is noteworthy that the President of the Commission, Ismail Pasha Eyoub, had been himself a prominent member of the Council of National Defence, and had actually been with Arabi in the camp at Kafr Dowar.

Amongst the persons examined by the Commission in the presence of his Counsel was Ahmed Bey Rifát, late Secretary to the Council of Ministers and Director of the Press Bureau. Asked by the President Ismail Pasha Eyoub if he the accused had sent off a telegram directing the Governors of Provinces to contradict rumours of massacres in Cairo, and a report that Arabi had received money from Halim Pasha, he replied that he had done so by order of the National Council of which the President himself was a member. The accused went on to give many proofs that the President of the Commission was as great an Arabist as any one. Amongst other statements was one that the President himself accompanied the accused to Kafr Dowar to wish Arabi success.* Asked to explain certain contradictions between statements made on the first and last days of his examination, the accused proceeded to give an account of the ill-usage he had been subjected to in prison just before his first appearance before the Commission, and he asked the Commission if an interrogatory answered under such circumstances had any value. The ill-usage was denied by the Court, but confirmed by Sir Charles Wilson, and the inquiry was adjourned.

* The President admitted the journey to Kafr Dowar, but said he went from curiosity.

On the 1st November news was received that Suleiman Bey Sami, also known as Suleiman Daoud, Lieutenant-Colonel of the 6th Regiment of infantry, and Moussa-el-Akhad, a Cairo merchant and landowner, both implicated in the rebellion, had been arrested in Candia. Shortly after, they were, at the request of the Egyptian Government, sent back to Egypt. Much interest was attached to these prisoners, the first being the person to whom the burning of Alexandria was attributed, and the second being accused of being the principal instigator of the massacre of the 11th June. Both subsequently gave evidence against Arabi.

The examination of Suleiman Sami was taken before the Commission, and directly implicated Arabi in the burning of Alexandria and to some extent in the massacre of the 11th June.*

Moussa-el-Akhad was subsequently examined, but his evidence has not been made public.

According to a work already quoted† both of the two depositions above set forth were taken before the Commission of Inquiry in the absence of Arabi and his Counsel. Consequently the latter addressed a protest to Ismail Pasha Eyoub against the depositions being received in evidence.

Sultan Pasha, late President of the Council of Notables, sent a written statement to the Commission, implicating Arabi in the meeting at Sultan's house in May, at which the deposition of the Khedive was resolved on.‡

The foregoing are believed to be all the documentary evidence of the prosecution which has been made public.

* Suleiman Sami was tried and executed at Alexandria on the 9th June, 1883.
† *How we defended Arabi*, by A. M. Broadley.
‡ Sultan Pasha's statement would appear to be even less receivable in evidence than the depositions of Suleiman Sami and Moussa-el-Akhad above referred to.

The defence laboured under many difficulties. Many of Arabi's papers were said to have been lost from his tent at Tel-el-Kebir, and others were stated to have been taken from his house in Cairo. Some, however, remained in possession of his family, and amongst them was a complete correspondence between himself and the Chief Imaum of the Sultan, and also with the latter's chief secretary.

The correspondence showed unmistakably that Arabi had for a considerable period been acting under direct instructions from Constantinople.

The Sultan's Firmans in which Arabi's merits are fully dwelt on all served to corroborate this view.

Amongst other papers which came into the possession of Arabi's Counsel, were several petitions, bearing thousands of signatures, from many of the leading men in the country, testifying the public approval of the National Party, and the wish of the people to follow the lead of Arabi and his colleagues. Also copies of petitions in the same strain addressed to the Turkish Commissioner to be laid before the Sultan.

The contention of Mr. Broadley was that, from first to last, the Sublime Porte approved the action of his clients, also that the Khedive for a long period prior to the commencement of hostilities wavered systematically between the two parties, and that after the arrival of Dervish Pasha he acquiesced at three Cabinet Councils in the early phases of resistance to the English (an assertion in great measure borne out by the ambiguous terms of the subsequent Proclamations). In addition to the foregoing, Mr. Broadley relied on the fact that Arabi, rightly or wrongly, really headed a great National movement, that he received the moral and material support of nearly the whole of Egypt, and that he was only deserted when he failed to secure success. It must be admitted that the documents in the possession of the accused went a long way to bear out these contentions.

It soon became evident that the charge against Arabi of complicity in the pillaging and burning of Alexandria could not be sustained. Sir Charles Wilson wrote on the 30th October to Sir Edward Malet, as follows :—' I must express my belief that on the existing evidence no English court-martial would convict the prisoners, except perhaps Toulba and Saïd Kandeel,* of any greater crime than that of taking part in a successful military revolt against the Khedive.'

Later on, Sir Charles Wilson made a report to Lord Dufferin, who had arrived on 7th November. The following are extracts :—

'A great number of written statements were accepted as evidence by the Commission without question. The writers, in many cases, never appeared before the Commission, and no steps were taken to elicit further information, or to clear up doubtful points. The prisoners, whilst under interrogation, were at first treated with consideration; but gradually, as it became evident that they would not commit themselves, they were pressed in a way quite contrary to all English ideas of justice or fairness. Men were on more than one occasion told by the prosecutor, in a forcible manner, that they were not speaking the truth; that they must go back to their cells, think over the matter, and come before the Commission next day.

'The only direct evidence incriminating Arabi was that of Suleiman Sami, who stated that Arabi had not only ordered him to burn Alexandria, but to kill the Khedive. The evidence of this man was open to grave suspicion. He was arrested at Crete and brought to Alexandria, where he was received by the Governor and the Préfet de Police, one of whom accompanied him some distance in the train. Immediately on his arrival at Cairo he was brought before an extraordinary sitting of the Commission, which lasted till between eight and nine p.m. No notice was sent to me of the prisoner's arrival, or of the intention of the Commission to examine him, though I live close to the building in which the Commission sits. The next morning, when Suleiman Sami's examination was continued, he was confronted with two other prisoners,

* Saïd Kandeel was the Prefect of Police at the time of the massacre at Alexandria on the 11th June. He was subsequently tried and exiled.

who at once contradicted his statements on important points. His bearing before the Commission produced an unfavourable impression, as he was the only prisoner who showed want of dignity and weakness when questioned. He was also so deeply implicated himself in the burning and looting of Alexandria, that it was only natural he should try to incriminate others. As regards the specific charges against Arabi Pasha it appeared to me,—

'1. That if there were any abuse of the white flag on the 12th July, a fact in itself not easy to prove, it was through ignorance and not through design. I may mention that white flags were flying on the Aboukir forts throughout the whole of the military operations.

'2. That there was no evidence to connect Arabi with the massacre at Alexandria on the 11th June, and that it is doubtful whether a deliberate massacre of Europeans was ever intended. That the massacres at Tantah and other places after the bombardment were caused by the low-class refugees from Alexandria, and that they ceased as soon as the troops were sent down. That, after the first excitement had passed, order was preserved, and that there are instances of orders having been sent by Arabi to the Governors of towns, &c., to preserve order and protect Europeans.

'3. That the evidence which connects Arabi Pasha with the burning of Alexandria is conflicting, and that there is no sufficient proof that he ordered the town to be destroyed. The portion of the town actually burned by the troops seems to have been small. The fire appears to have broken out about four p.m. on the 12th, and the troops evacuated the town on the same evening. It then became the duty of the Civil Governor to preserve order, as far as he could, until the English occupation of the 14th. It is difficult to say where Arabi's responsibility ended and that of the Civil Governor commenced. It is also probable that some of the fires were lighted by the Bedouins, who had assembled contrary to the wish of Arabi, and had entered the town on the 12th, and possibly also by British shells.

'It is certain, however, that the houses in the Place Mehemet Ali were burned by Suleiman Sami and his regiment. Suleiman Sami asserted that he acted under orders from Arabi. On this point he was contradicted by Arabi and others, and some prisoners stated that Arabi sent messengers to prevent the burning of the houses. It must be remembered that no evidence was taken for the defence, and that no witnesses were cross-examined.'

Under these circumstances it became necessary to consider what was best to be done. On the 18th November Lord Dufferin wrote to Lord Granville as follows :—

'I have the honour to inform your Lordship that I saw the Khedive to-day, and gave his Highness to understand that I thought it very unlikely that sufficient proof would be forthcoming to authorise the execution of Arabi and the political prisoners, and I suggested the alternative of deportation. I was glad to find that his Highness was prepared, if required, to accept this result, provided Arabi and his family were removed from the country *en bloc*, and his property forfeited; in which event the Egyptian Government would allow a maintenance for his women and children, who, the Khedive observed, ought not to be punished for their father's fault. At the same time His Highness begged that no decision should be come to before the few days demanded by his Government to consider the question had elapsed.'

Towards the latter part of November all parties interested became more or less disposed to accept a reasonable compromise, somewhat on the lines indicated in Lord Dufferin's letter.

The English Government was aware of the block caused in Egyptian affairs and in the projected reforms by the trial, the proceedings of which Mr. Broadley spoke of extending over some months.

The Egyptian Government, after being informed of the inconclusive character of the evidence, and being given to understand that no capital punishment would be allowed, had lost all heart in the business, and now only longed to get the rebels out of the country. Mr. Broadley, on behalf of the accused, was equally willing to accept a compromise. With a tribunal such as that before which he was to plead, he felt that his chances of success were small. He might, indeed, drag on the proceedings for an indefinite period, but in the end the solution would probably be less satisfactory to his clients than would result from a well-considered arrangement 'out of court.'

The details of the compromise arrived at, and the credit of initiating which must be given to Lord Dufferin, were as follows:—1. All charges against Arabi, Mahmoud Sami, Toulba, Aly Fehmy, Abdel-el-al,

Yacoub Sami, and Mahmoud Fehmy Pasha, except that of simple rebellion were to be withdrawn. 2. All the prisoners were to be arraigned on a charge of simple rebellion, to which they should plead guilty. 3. A sentence of death was to be recorded on this plea, but a Decree commuting the sentence to exile from Egypt was to be immediately read. 4. The prisoners were to lose their rank and property, but the possessions of their wives should not be forfeited. 5. The prisoners were to give their *parole* to proceed to any British possession indicated, and remain there till permitted to depart.

Only a very few persons were informed on the evening of Saturday, 3rd December, 1882, that Arabi would be brought before the Court-martial the following morning.

The following correspondence had passed during the day between the President of the Commission of Inquiry and the prisoner's Counsel :—

Letter from the Commission of Inquiry to Messrs. Broadley & Napier.

' The Commission of Inquiry is of opinion that Arabi Pasha should be sent before the Court-martial, charged with rebellion, a crime provided for by Article 92 of the Ottoman Military Code, and Article 59 of the Ottoman Penal Code. Unless, therefore, there be any objection on your part, the Commission will send the accused immediately before the Court-martial.

'(Sealed) ISMAIL EYOUB.

' *Cairo, 2nd December*, 1882.'

Letter from Messrs. Broadley & Napier to the President of the Commission of Inquiry.

' We have no objection to Arabi Pasha being sent before the Courtmartial on the conditions stated in your Excellency's letter of this day's date.

'(Signed) A. M. BROADLEY.
M. F. NAPIER.'

The proceedings were exceedingly simple, everything having been arranged beforehand. A room had been fitted up as a Court House in the prison, the old Daïra Sanieh, and the proceedings were public. At nine o'clock on the 4th, H. E. Raouf Pasha, the President, and the other members of the Court-martial, took their seats. Sir Archibald Alison sat at a desk to the right of the President, and Sir Charles Wilson on the left. The prisoner was on Sir Charles Wilson's left, his Counsel sitting just beneath him. He wore a dark greatcoat with a white cachemire scarf round his neck. He looked somewhat thinner than he was previous to the bombardment of the forts of Alexandria. He had grown a short beard which was partly grey.

The report of the Commission of Inquiry to the Court-martial was then handed in, the following is a translation of this document :—

Report of the Commission of Inquiry to the Court Martial.

'We have the honour to inform you that, having terminated the inquiry concerning Arabi, the Commission considers that there are grounds for sending him before the Court-martial charged with the crime of rebellion as provided for by Article 92 of the Ottoman Military Code, and Article 59 of the Ottoman Penal Code. It therefore sends the said Ahmed Arabi before the Court for trial charged with the said crime. We send you at the same time the complete *dossier* containing the results of our inquiry into this affair.'

The President of the Court asked the prisoner if he acknowledged himself guilty of rebellion against His Highness the Khedive in the following terms :—
' Arabi Pasha, you are charged before this Court, after due inquiry by the Commission of Inquiry, with the crime of rebellion against His Highness the Khedive, a crime provided for by Article 92 of the Ottoman Military Code and Article 59 of the Ottoman Penal Code. Are you guilty, or are you not guilty, of the crime with which you stand charged ?' Mr. Broadley

then handed in a paper to the effect that acting under the advice of his Counsel, Arabi pleaded guilty to the charge. The following is a translation of the written plea:—'Of my own freewill, and in accordance with the advice of my Counsel, I acknowledge that I am guilty of the crime with which I am charged.'

The Court then rose, the President remarking that judgment would be delivered that afternoon at three p.m. H. E. Borelli Bey, Counsel for the Government, was not present either at the morning or afternoon sitting.

At the time named the Court was densely crowded, several ladies being present, and there was a gathering of Arabs outside the prison. The President, first of all, handed an official document condemning Arabi to death, which was read, and of which the following is a translation :—

The Sentence.

Considering that Ahmed Arabi Pasha has pleaded guilty to the crime of rebellion, a crime provided for by Article 92 of the Ottoman Military Code and Article 59 of the Ottoman Penal Code. Considering that in consequence of this plea of guilty, no other course is open to the Court but to apply Article 92 of the Ottoman Military Code and Article 59 of the Ottoman Penal Code, already quoted, which punish with death the crime of rebellion. For these reasons, the Court unanimously condemns Ahmed Arabi to death for the crime of rebellion against His Highness the Khedive, in accordance with the terms of Articles 92 of the Ottoman Military Code and 59 of the Ottoman Penal Code. This sentence is to be submitted for the sanction of His Highness the Khedive.

(Sealed)   Raouf Pasha.

Immediately afterwards the Decree commuting the sentence to exile for life was read.

Arabi saluted the Court and sat down, and the Members of the Court prepared to retire, the sitting having lasted only six minutes. At this moment an incident occurred. Mrs. Napier, wife of the junior Counsel for Arabi, had brought into Court a bouquet of white roses for the accused, which, immediately after the reading of the Decree, was presented to Arabi in open Court. This was a little too much for the audience, who had restrained their feelings during the reading of the Decree, and loud hisses arose. After this manifestation the crowd gradually dispersed.

On the 7th December Mahmoud Sami, Abdel-el-al, Toulba, and Aly Fehmy, were arraigned before the Court-martial on the charge of rebellion, and on being called on to plead, they all pleaded guilty. The prisoners were again brought up in the afternoon for sentence to be passed on them. They were all sentenced to death, and immediately after the Khedive's Decree commuting their sentence to banishment for life was read.*

On the 10th December the same formality was gone through with regard to Yacoub Sami and Mahmoud Fehmy.

The following is a translation of the undertaking signed by the accused:—

'We, the undersigned, swear by God who gave the Koran, and engage by our personal word of honour, that we accept to go to the place which the Government designates for us, and to stay there.

'(Signed)   Mahmoud Sami.   Yacoub Sami,
                  Ahmed Arabi.   Toulba Ismet.
                  Ali Fehmi.   Abdel-el-al Hilmi.'
                  Mahmoud Fehmi.

* It was on this day that Riaz Pasha sent in his resignation.

By a Khedivial Decree, dated 3rd Seffer, all the property of the seven rebels was declared to be confiscated to the State, and a Commission was appointed for the purpose of taking possession and administering the same.

A day or two later, Ceylon was fixed upon as the prisoners' place of exile, and the steam-ship *Mareotis*, belonging to the 'Moss Steam Ship Company, Limited,' was chartered for the purpose of transport; Morice Bey, an English officer in the Egyptian service, was told off to accompany the prisoners.

On the 25th December the Decree of degradation was read in public, at the Kasr-el-Nil Barracks, to the seven rebels—Arabi, Toulba, Ismet, Abdel-el-al, Mahmoud Sami, Aly Fehmy, Mahmoud Fehmy, and Yacoub Sami.

On the 26th December the seven principal rebels left Kasr-el-Nil by special train at eleven o'clock at night for Suez, *en route* for Ceylon, accompanied by a suite of sixty persons, male and female, and by a guard of thirty men of the 60th Rifles, under the command of Major Fraser, who occupied the same carriage as Arabi.

After the disposal of the leading rebels the Egyptian authorities were induced by Lord Dufferin to turn their attention to the lesser offenders.

It was of course impossible, after the lenient sentences passed on Arabi and the other leaders of the National Party, to attempt to inflict capital punishment on any of those who simply followed his lead.

On the 29th December a Decree was issued exiling a large number of the chief remaining prisoners for various periods to Massowah, Souakim, and other places. Others were released either with or without bail on their undertaking to live quietly on their country estates.

TRIAL OF THE REBEL LEADERS. 385

The result of the trial of the rebel leaders produced, at first, a feeling of stupefaction on the European colony in Egypt. When the nature of the judicial farce which had been enacted began to be understood, the sentiment above mentioned gave place to one of profound indignation against the Egyptian Government and its English advisers. In passing upon Arabi and his associates a sentence which was regarded as merely nominal, it was said a premium was put upon rebellion, massacre, and pillage.

Such was the view universally entertained. Amongst the foreign population, England lost in one day all the popularity she had gained at Tel-el-Kebir. 'On ne plaisante pas avec la justice,' remarked an eminent foreign advocate to the writer. With the natives the worst impression was created. The idea of a compact having been made by England with Arabi was strengthened and confirmed. With many the belief in Arabi's Divine Mission was raised to a certainty. The action of England was by a great class of the population attributed to fear. It was given out that Arabi was never really going to Ceylon, and that if he did he would return to raise an overwhelming army and expel the unbelievers. The most moderate charged England with having bribed Arabi, or, at the very least, with having held out, as a reward for his surrender, the promise of immunity for his past misdeeds. The general opinion amongst the most intelligent, both of Europeans and natives, was that the political revelations to be made at the trial would be of so grave and compromising a nature as to render it imperative to quash all proceedings in hot haste, unless England wished to find herself in a quandary.

VOL. I.   C C

Probably the real motives which led to the sudden collapse of the trial were somewhat as follows.

Substantially Arabi was charged : 1. with rebellion ; 2. with a treacherous abuse of the white flag ; 3. with complicity in the massacre, incendiarism, and pillage at Alexandria and elsewhere.

So far as the treacherous abuse of the white flag was concerned it would have been extremely difficult to have inflicted any punishment for it. At the time when the white flag was hoisted Arabi was by order of the Khedive and his Government defending the Alexandria forts to the best of his ability against the English ships of war. It is hard to see how an Egyptian Court-martial could under these circumstances convict the accused of using the white flag to the detriment of the English forces. Again, the extent of the privileges enjoyed by a military commander who has hoisted the white flag is a moot point and one of great delicacy. Lord Wolseley has laid it down in *The Soldier's Pocket Book*, that almost any act, not being one of direct hostility, is permissible under the protection of a flag of truce. It would be a very nice point, for military legists to decide whether troops could be moved or withdrawn while negotiations were proceeding with an enemy. The point raised in this count of the indictment was of so difficult and delicate a nature that the prosecution would, under any circumstances, probably have abandoned it in the event of the trial having come on in the regular course.

Till a very few days before Arabi was actually brought up for trial it was the firm intention of Her Majesty's Government and of the Egyptian Government to have him tried for complicity in the massacres, pillage and incendiarism, in addition to the charge of rebellion.

TRIAL OF THE REBEL LEADERS.

It must be remembered, however, that Arabi was an English prisoner of war, and that the honour of the British nation was involved in his being ensured a fair and impartial trial. Had the Khedive's troops or Egyptians captured Arabi the Egyptian Government would have been free to deal with him as they thought proper. However, as the Egyptian Government had not the means of capturing the rebel chief, it is useless to discuss what might have been the result. One has to deal with facts as they stand.

An important question, and one which could have been raised by the defence, was as to the competence of the so-called Court-martial. As has already been related, the Egyptian Army had been disbanded by Khedivial Decree in the previous month of September. How far under these circumstances the means existed of assembling any Court-martial at all was open to doubt. In the event of this being decided in favour of the accused, the question would arise as to what other Court (if any) was competent. However, up to the time, no such question having been raised, the British Government contented itself by appointing Colonel Sir Charles Wilson to watch the case. Sir Charles was a man of sound judgment, great experience, and not likely to be swayed by the clamour of humanitarians. His instructions were clear and precise.

After fifty-two days had been spent in examining witnesses for the prosecution, and their case had been practically closed, he went through the case most carefully, having been instructed simply to confine himself to stating whether, in his opinion, a *primâ facie* case had been made out against Arabi of complicity in the massacre of June 11th, of complicity in the incendiarism of Alexandria, and of complicity in the massacres that took place in other parts of the country after the bombardment of the forts of Alexandria.

After a painstaking examination Sir Charles Wilson came to the conclusion that there was no evidence forthcoming on which Arabi could be convicted of complicity with the massacre of June 11th, neither was the evidence adduced as to Arabi's complicity with regard to the incendiarism of Alexandria of a satisfactory nature, and it did not appear possible to connect him with the other massacres. The only evidence against Arabi appeared to be of a negative character; that Arabi could have prevented the massacres and other atrocities appears to be freely admitted by his best friends, but this was not sufficient ground for hanging him.

Such being the state of the case it became necessary to consider what steps should be taken to rid the country of Arabi and his accomplices. The preliminary proceedings had already occupied upwards of two months; the defence would probably have required as much time; thus it would have been at least three months before a verdict could have been arrived at. This delay was intolerable, the current business of the Ministries and Administrations was seriously interfered with in consequence of the great attention being paid to these rebels. Even the consideration of the Indemnity Question was in abeyance.

It was determined that if Arabi could be induced to plead guilty of rebellion, an easy way out of the difficulty could be found. As has been stated, Arabi was accordingly arraigned on the charge of rebellion and pleaded guilty. The trial, it is true, was looked upon as a farce, and it appeared to be so, but according to the Ottoman Code, the Court-martial could only sentence the prisoner to death, and further, this sentence could not be passed until it had been approved by the Sovereign. The sentence was accordingly submitted to the Khedive, by whom it was sanctioned, and he at once commuted it to banishment for life.

Every one who has the interests of Egypt at heart must regret the result of the trial. At the same time, it is not easy in the face of so many complications to see how it could have been otherwise.

END OF THE FIRST VOLUME.

www.ingramcontent.com/pod-product-compliance
Lightning Source LLC
Chambersburg PA
CBHW071656170426
43195CB00039B/2210